The Psychology of Written Language

WILEY SERIES IN DEVELOPMENTAL PSYCHOLOGY

Series Editor
Professor Kevin Connolly

The Development of Movement Control and Co-ordination
J. A. Scott Kelso and Jane E. Clark

Psychobiology of the Human Newborn
edited by Peter Stratton

Morality in the Making: Thought, Action and the Social Context
edited by Helen Weinreich-Haste and Don Locke

The Psychology of Written Language: Developmental and Educational Perspectives
edited by Margaret Martlew

Further titles in preparation

The Psychology of Written Language
Developmental and Educational Perspectives

Edited by

Margaret Martlew
Department of Psychology, University of Sheffield

JOHN WILEY & SONS
Chichester . New York . Brisbane . Toronto . Singapore

British Library Cataloguing in Publication Data

Martlew, Margaret
The Psychology of written language.—(Wiley series in developmental psychology)
1. Written communication—Psychological aspects
I. Title
153.6 P211

ISBN 0-471-10291-1

Library of Congress Cataloging in Publication Data

Main entry under title:

The Psychology of written language.

(Wiley series in developmental psychology)
Includes indexes.
1. Written communication—Psychological aspects.
2. Developmental psychology. I. Martlew, Margaret.
II. Series
P211.P79 1983 001.54′3′019 82-21933

ISBN 0-471-10291-1

Typeset by Activity, Salisbury, Wilts, and Printed by the Pitman Press, Bath

For James Egan Bedell; with deep affection and gratitude, though sadly, he can never read it.

Acknowledgements

I wish to thank Professor K. J. Connolly, the series editor, for his generous support and advice. I am indebted to him for the time and consideration he has given, particularly when problems have arisen. I should also like to thank my two sons for their impatient cynicism which developed as meals became more erratic. It provided a powerful incentive. I also wish to thank the editors, especially Michael Cole for his helpful suggestions, and the publishers for kindly granting permission to reproduce the following chapters:

A. R. Luria; The development of writing in the child, In M. Cole (ed.) *The Selected Writings of A. R. Luria*. New York: © M. E. Sharp Inc., 1978. L. S. Vygotsky; The prehistory of written language, Reprinted by permission of the publishers from *Mind in Society: The Development of Higher Psychological Processes* by L. S. Vygotsky, edited by Michael Cole, *et al.*, Cambridge, Mass.: Harvard University Press, Copyright © 1979 by the President and Fellows of Harvard College.

List of Contributors

CARL BEREITER, *Department of Applied Psychology, Ontario Institute for Studies in Education, Toronto, Ontario M5S 1V6, Canada.*

LYNETTE BRADLEY, *Department of Experimental Psychology, University of Oxford, Oxford OX1 3UD, England.*

PETER BRYANT, *Department of Experimental Psychology, University of Oxford, Oxford OX1 3UD, England.*

CHARLES R. COOPER, *Department of Literature, C-005, University of California San Diego, La Jolla, California 92093, USA.*

CECILIA DE GÓES, *Departmento de Technologia Educacional, Centro de Eduçăcao & Ciencias Humanas, Universidade Federale de São Carlos, São Carlos 13560, Brazil.*

ANGELA HILDYARD, *The Ontario Institute for Studies in Education, Toronto, Ontario M5S 1V6, Canada.*

KELLOGG W. HUNT, *The Florida State University, Tallahasee, Florida 32306, USA.*

ALEXANDRIA R. LURIA, *1902–1977.*

PIERRE MARCIE, *Unité de Recherches Neuropsychologiques et Neurolinguistiques (U.iii), INSERM, Laboratoire de Pathologie du Langage. ERA No. 274 au CNRS, Paris, France.*

MARGARET MARTLEW, *Department of Psychology, University of Sheffield, Sheffield S10 2TN, England.*

ANN MATSUHASHI, *Department of English, University of Illinois at Chicago Circle, Chicago, Illinois 60680, USA.*

DAVID OLSON, *The Ontario Institute for Studies in Education, Toronto, Ontario M5S 1V6, Canada.*

MILLICENT POOLE, *Department of Education, Macquarie University, North Ryde, New South Wales, Australia.*

CHARLES READ, *Wisconsin Research and Development Center for Individualized Schooling, University of Wisconsin–Madison, School of Education, Madison, Wisconsin 53706, USA.*

MARLENE SCARDAMALIA, *Department of Psychology, York University, Downsview, Ontario M3J 1P3, Canada.*

HANS-LEO H. M. TEULINGS, *Department of Experimental Psychology, University of Nijmegen, 6500 HE, Nijmegen, The Netherlands.*

ARNOLD J. W. M. THOMASSEN, *Department of Experimental Psychology, University of Nijmegen, 6500 HE, Nijmegen, The Netherlands.*

LEV, S. VYGOTSKY, *1896–1934.*

CYNTHIA WATSON, *Department of English, Louisiana State University, Baton Rouge, Louisiana 70803, USA.*

Contents

Foreword

"I am convinced more and more day by day that fine writing is next to fine doing, the top thing in the world." So wrote John Keats. Arguably writing is man's greatest invention. Whilst it is possible to develop culture without a written language, the transmission of knowledge and ideas is immensely facilitated and extended by some means of recording which loosens the immediate space and time bounds. Important human activities such as law, science, trade, poetry, history and technology would be rudimentary indeed were it not for some means of recording ideas, feelings and facts. Graphic inscriptions have their roots in the need to communicate efficiently. From rock paintings and engravings there developed pictograms, ideograms and eventually phonetic writing, culminating in the notion of an alphabet. A good deal of scholarly effort has been devoted to investigating the evolution of writing from the first systematic script invented something over 5000 years ago by the Sumerians. Surprisingly rather less attention appears to have been devoted to the systematic analysis of the ontogeny of writing.

In any complex technological society the inability to read and write imposes very severe restrictions on the individual. In an important document published a few years ago Lord Bullock and his colleagues wrote, "... we underline our conviction that standards of writing, speaking and reading can and should be raised. The first thing that is required is a redefinition of what is involved." (*Language for life*, HMSO, 1975, p.7). Education is inextricably linked with the capacity to produce visible language. How then do children acquire this intellectual tool, this cultural amplifier? Dr Martlew has collected together a set of essays which examine a number of important and varied issues associated with learning to write; theoretical questions about the precursors of written language, conceptual and syntactic aspects of composing text, orthography, the relationship between reading and writing, social, psychological and neurological problems associated with the acquisition of writing, and the motor skills involved in handwriting are all treated. The authors have each made significant contributions to our knowledge about how the capacity to write develops in children; they come from several disciplines and several countries. Two important, and in the English speaking world little-known, essays by the great Russian psychologists L. S. Vygotsky and R. A. Luria are also reproduced. This is one of the first books devoted to the development of written language and as such it admirably fulfils the aims of this series. It begins the redefinition that the Bullock Committee wrote about and in so doing it opens up fundamental scientific problems, the importance of which is matched by their practical significance.

Kevin Connolly

Preface

We take literacy so much for granted that it is difficult to imagine what life would be like without it, civil records, legal documents, personal memoranda, books, letters to friends; these illustrate just a few ways in which we rely, both immediately and indirectly, on written language. As Gelb (1952) says: 'Writing exists only in a civilisation and a civilisation cannot exist without written language.' Writing is a visible, verbal communication system in which an interactive discourse is conducted across space and time through the medium of highly conventionalized symbols. It exercises a powerful influence in our lives, important in itself and as a tool for learning. In practical terms, academic progress in school depends on an adequate degree of fluency, and most jobs require a basic competence in written language.

Writing involves a range of psychological processes and educational practices. It is obviously an integrative activity involving many complex procedures working in parallel, the age and experience of the writer affecting the degree to which these integrative processes operate. Investigating these processes has both theoretical and applied implications. A fuller and deeper understanding of writing is important for teachers in assisting children to develop their writing abilities. Such investigations also extend not only our understanding of written language, but our theoretical insight into the development of language and cognition.

The knowledge and skills which writing demands, and how individuals develop and utilize these, formed the basis for selecting the topics and authors for this book. The book is designed to give a review of our current theoretical and empirical knowledge of the development of written language. The contributors, drawn from psychology and education, focus on those topics which provide the context for our present knowledge of writing. These topics are related to their own particular research interests but they are also set in the prevailing theoretical framework; for example, compositional processes and motor skill development. As well as reporting current research, therefore, the book provides a broad basis for our understanding of written language, showing what progress has been made, how it has been achieved, and how the various aspects of writing relate to other areas of psychological theory.

The development of writing embraces a wide range of research interests: motor skills, neuropsychology, language, cognition and communication together with applied research in education. These also cover the component features which constitute the writing process. In order to examine in detail what these component processes involve, each chapter deals with different aspects of written language production. The book is divided into five sections which focus on the conceptual and linguistic aspects of composition (Parts I and II), orthography and handwriting (Part III), preliteracy and early acquisition of writing (Part IV) and differences and disorders in written language (Part V). The original material reported, together with the critical reviews of the various topics, means the book offers a broad analysis of written language. The inclusion of the essays by Luria and Vygotsky on the early stages of written language is more than a semantic connection. These offer an important and stimulating approach, despite being written in the first half of the century, and are of contemporary interest both for their ideas and the way these ideas are expressed. Many of the chapters are of immediate practical significance, particularly in showing what constraints affect the acquisition of written language and how these can be overcome.

MARGARET MARTLEW

Reference

Gelb, I. J. (1952). *A Study of Writing*. University of Chicago Press, Chicago.

Part I

Composing Text: Conceptual Aspects

John Sheffield, Duke of Buckingham: *Essay on Poetry*.	Of all the arts in which the wise excel Nature's chief masterpiece is writing well.
Samuel Johnson: *The Adventurer*.	Composition is, for the most part, an effort of slow diligence and steady perseverance, to which the mind is dragged by necessity or resolution.
Francis Bacon: *Essays, of studies*.	Reading maketh a full man, conference a ready man and writing an exact man.
Horace: *Satires*.	Often you must turn your stylus to erase if you would hope to write something worth a second reading.
Quintillian: *De Institutione Oratoria*.	Let our literary compositions be laid aside for sometime, that we may, after a reasonable period return to their perusal, and find them, as it were, altogether new to us.

The Psychology of Written Language
Edited by M. Martlew

CHAPTER 1

A Theory of the Writing Process

CHARLES R. COOPER and ANN MATSUHASHI

This chapter outlines a theory of composing in writing. Our approach has been to take a common-sense view of writing as a matter of planning, decision-making, and problem-solving and then to attempt to answer this question: What plans and decisions must a writer make in order to produce a written text? Our method has been to read widely on a great many topics which promised to inform us about the writing process. In addition, we have relied on our own intuitions as writers and writing teachers, and on a great deal of anecdotal information from writers at work. Though our reading has ranged widely across a number of sources, topics, and academic fields, our theory relies primarily on current work in psycholinguistics (especially work in speech production) and in discourse theory. The work in psycholinguistics has been particularly fruitful for our conjectures about written sentence production. The work in discourse theory has been especially helpful in our considerations of the differential constraints of various discourse types on global discourse planning.

While we feel quite modest about our theory and uncertain about particular parts of it, we present it here in an assertive, unqualified manner so that we and others may draw firm hypotheses from it for testing in experimental studies and in observations of writers at work. Whether it is a good theory time will tell. For us a good theory is a useful theory: intriguing to practicing writers as an account of their work, stimulating to teachers of writing as a rich source of implications for the improvement of writing instruction, and compelling to researchers as a basic for generating testable hypotheses about the complex psycholinguistic processes by which written discourses are achieved.

Even if our theory is a good theory, it will be only one of several productive bases for studying the writing process; and it might be seen as useful to researchers using quite different modes of research. Since academic research into the writing process is such a recent endeavor, we believe it is important to stress the importance of flexibility and open-mindedness. We are certain that new insights and findings will come from a number of differing perspectives, and we are quite settled in our conviction that no single methodology will come to dominate research in this area. Such common-sense conclusions as these should be obvious to anyone who has followed recent research on language development in young children.

Since we wish readers to consider our theory in the context of a wide range of compelling perspectives on the writing process and of productivemethodologies for its study, we want to discuss briefly some of theseperspectives and methodologies before we outline our own theory.

Rhetorical Theory and Discourse Theory

There is an implied composing process in Aristotle's rhetoric, a process of producing the persuasive spoken monologue on a public policy issue. Aristotle's handbook on how to do this successfuly, *The Rhetoric*, ranges widely across major composing issues still of current concern: pre-composing heuristics (the topoi), audience awareness, and organizing the discourse, with special attention to getting started and winding down. The composer's task of meeting (or adapting to) the rhetorical situation is central to *The Rhetoric*.

Current discourse theory is also rich in implications for the writing process. Kinneavy (1971), for example, goes well beyond creating discourse categories (referential, persuasive, expressive, literary) to conjecturing about the unique cognitive requirements of each discourse type. Using James Moffett's discourse sequences (1968, 1981) as the basis for a writing program in Third College at the University of California at San Diego, Rise Axelrod and Charles Cooper have been attempting to devise discourse-specific pre-writing sequences and peer-critique guides. Though we assumed there would be rhetorical and hence composing differences among our types and modes, we were startled to discover the magnitude of the differences. For example, the writer's task is hugely different when writing about a single incident in his past and a phase of several weeks in his past; and yet both are in the personal experience narrative mode. Still in the same mode, and sharply different from these first two, as well as from each other, are first-hand biography which narrates an important development over several months in the life of an acquaintance and first-hand biography which characterizes an acquaintance in terms of a striking quality or life theme and then selects anecdotes to support the characterization. This latter type of first-hand biography is actually organized like persuasion, a series of arguments (the anecdotes) supporting a position on a controversial issue or policy question (the characterization). We want to claim that the writing process differs among these four types of personal experience writing in the way that ideas, scenes, and events are recalled and reformulated and then patterned into discourse. We believe that a good many of those differences are directly inferrable from the writing products in that mode. Of course, in our work these inferences are supported by masses of introspective and anecdotal data from our students and from our own attempts at these writings.

Now that rhetoricians and discourse theorists have begun reading psycholinguistics, so must psycholinguists and cognitive psychologists begin reading rhetorical theory and discourse theory (see Brewer, 1980, for a careful though incomplete survey of current discourse theory by a psychologist). We believe that until they do, the implications of schema theory for writing process research, to take just one example, will go unrealized; and we believe that cognitive psychologists will be able to keep the attention of an important group of readers – informed school and college writing instructors – only if psychologists demonstrate how their writing process theories complement and refine current discourse theory.

Text linguistics and Text Structure Studies

We view text linguistics (Van Dijk, 1980; Grimes, 1975; Halliday and Hasan, 1976) as a refinement of current discourse theory; as a special form of discourse analysis. Work in this area has already given us new precision in identifying the cohesive structure (Halliday and Hasan, 1976; Rochester and Martin, 1979; Cherry and Cooper, 1981, for a practical application in a study of writing development) and the information system (Jones, 1977; Clements, 1979; Cooper and Gray, 1981) in texts. Important specialized studies of text features and text structure have been completed on the decriptive writing of children and adolescents (Stahl, 1977) and the unrehearsed oral narratives of adolescents and adults (Chafe, 1980; Labov, 1972). All of these new studies move us closer to identifying the essential features and abstract structures of written texts. Because these studies identify and, most important, predict composing problems writers must solve and decisions they must make at the macrostructure level, they must necessarily inform writing process studies. Only certain current enthusiasms prevent researchers from recognizing how much may still be learned about writing process from writing products. A comprehensive, multi-level, discourse-specific analysis of writing products will be rich in insights about the writing process (Kinneavy, 1971) and about writing development (Stahl, 1977; Kroll, 1978; Cooper and Gray, 1981; Cherry and Cooper, 1981). Even at the clause level, descriptions of given–new, topic–comment, and case roles lead to useful conjectures about writers' decisions in producing clauses. At the least, the neglect of discourse studies will severely limit what can be learned in process studies. The best process studies move back and forth between observations of writing process and examination of the writing produced by the process. The writing is one form of 'objective evidence' (Hayes and Flower, 1980, p. 21) by which insights about process are corroborated. (See Cooper (forthcoming) for a comprehensive review of procedures for describing written texts.)

Anecdotal Reports from Professional Writers

We have in mind the interviews in *Writers at Work* the *Paris Review* interview series; but interviews with writers appear in many places, and occasionally writers will write about their own work. Of course, there is no theory of the writing process in any of these interviews or reports. However, reading a large number of them provides a surprisingly comprehensive view of the writing process. One of us once read carefully one volume of the *Writers at Work* series, classifying statements about the various conventional stages in the writing process. Though the statements were few, scattered, and quite unsystematic in individual essays, in the whole volume a rich, detailed picture of the writing process emerged. There is clearly much to be learned about writing processes from the lore of writers at work. Perhaps writers would be willing to be interviewed more closely about their writing rituals, procedures, and processes. At the least it seems careless to ignore the practitioners of an art we wish to study.

Case Studies of Writers at Work

A more systematic study of writers at work, novices of all ages as well as professionals, may be carried out as case studies of individuals (Bissex, 1980). Such studies are observational and descriptive, concerned primarily with gathering information unobtrusively in the writer's own habitat or in a special setting, even a classroom, where writers may proceed as they usually do. When such research does go on in classrooms, it becomes much like ethnographic research (Graves, 1975, 1981). Usually, case studies involve repeated interviews with writers as well as close examination of their work, but the researcher may also just sit by and look on, without intervening or presenting special tasks. His main concern may be with the full social context in which the writing occurs. Such studies seem especially promising for the study of very young writers in school classrooms.

Intervention Studies with Writers

Closely related to ethnographic case studies are intervention studies in which writers (novices or professionals) may be studied one at a time, but in which the researcher gives the writers specific tasks to accomplish or requests that they verbalize as much as possible about their writing decisions (Emig, 1971) in order to produce a 'verbal protocol' of their writing activities (Hayes and Flower, 1980). In this mode of research tasks are assigned not to test specific research hypotheses, as in experimental studies, but only to permit further exploratory probes into writers' decisions, choices, and processes (Della-Piana, 1978; Cooper and Odell, 1976).

Temporal Studies of Speech and Writing

There is a full and interesting literature on temporal studies of speech production, or pause studies, as they are usually called (Goldman-Eisler, 1968; Siegman and Feldstein, 1979; Chafe, 1980; see Matsuhashi, 1982, for a review; also see Fromkin, 1980, for studies of error during the production of speech and writing). In these studies inferences are made about the psycholinguistics of speech production from the patterns of pauses in speech. We are just beginning to see the first temporal studies of the writing process (Matsuhashi, 1981), and we believe these will be an important new direction for research in our field. These studies seem to us to have promise for informing us about quite small-scale microlevel production decisions at the clause level.

Studies of the Differences between Talk and Writing

As we learn more about the differences between conversational interchange (talk) and sustained written monologues, we will be able to devise stronger theories about constraints unique to writing and reading (Chafe, 1982; Kroll and Vann, 1982; Rubin, 1980; Vygotsky, 1962, pp. 98, 144). We believe such studies will be particularly useful for theories of learning to write for very young children. We know enough to say writing is not talk written down. Written monological discourse has patterns, hierarchies of abstraction levels, and cohesive ties which are quite different from those in conversational interchange. The transition from talk to writing seems now to be a good deal more complicated and demanding than we had imagined (Rubin, 1980).

Experimental Studies

So far all of the topics and methodologies we have mentioned in this brief listing seem to us useful ways to produce better theories. All seem valuable.

All require the close attention of theorists and researchers in our field. None has any special claims to priority over the others. In concert, these varied approaches will produce more and more interesting theories of the writing process; and as these theories emerge, we will need to test them as well as we can in experimental studies and focused case studies. Actually, some of the methodologies we have mentioned above can be used in experimental studies. For example, timed videotape results from studies of writing production would be appropriate to test certain hypotheses, and in our view both ethnographic studies and case studies can be as compelling in testing theory as conventional experimental studies. The Scardamalia and Bereiter chapter in this book illustrates very well one productive direction that experimental work can take.

MEMORY AND CONSCIOUSNESS

Lying behind any theory of the production process of composing in writing must be a set of assumptions about memory and consciousness. There are several theories of how the brain stores information and experience and retrieves it. We will not attempt to review them here, but we do want to make a few comments about memory and consciousness that seem particularly important to a theory of composing in writing.

We know that retrieval from memory is not an automatic, machine-like process. The brain is not an autonomous organ where storage and retrieval operate predictably and efficiently (Rapaport, 1951). Ongoing thought cannot be directed moment by moment in the way that one directs a car down a freeway. Thought is notoriously distractable. During ongoing thought, even when we are very much concerned with completing a task like reading a book or with observing an ongoing event like a football game, we daydream or fantasize. We are aware of bodily sensations or feelings. We may unexpectedly find ourselves engaged in an interior monologue with someone. We may dwell on unfinished business or on personal obligations, sometimes obsessively.

There is nothing pathological in these distractions from directed thinking. Ongoing normal thought includes imagery and daydreams (Singer, 1977). Several states of consciousness – sensations, images, daydreams, monologues, fantasies, sudden anxieties, directed thought – alternate in the flow of awareness. Writers at work are especially susceptible to alternating states of consciousness. Sitting immobile, their information-processing capacities more available to internal than external stimuli, writers are continually surprised by what memory or the preconscious makes available to consciousness. As often as not what appears is not at all useful, or does not seem to be at the time, especially when the writing is going badly. And yet all of the non-directed states of consciousness, especially creative thinking and expression, are crucial to ordered thinking, (Rapaport, 1951). What appears automatically, unwilled, from the preconscious can be just the solution to an intractable problem in writing which has resisted a solution from directed thought. Very competent writers are unusually successful at going along with this varied flow, of using it to discover and shape what they want to say (Kubie, 1958).

What is available in a writer's consciousness at any given moment, what can be held and rehearsed in short-term memory while other relationships are sought or arise spontaneously, is simply unpredictable. We truly do learn what we think as we see what we have to say; and, of course, the developing graphic record of what we have already said contributes, like memory and consciousness, to what we say next.

PLANNING

With this brief reminder that thought is not always a tidy, directed process, particularly for a writer at work, we can now consider the notion of planning in human problem-solving. With Miller *et al.* (1960) we believe that the concept of planning is seminal for understanding human thought and problem-solving. From them we can borrow a definition of 'plan' for our theory of the writing process: 'A plan is any hierarchical process in the organism that can control the order in which a sequence of operations is to be performed' (Miller *et al.*, 1960). By this definition a plan can be a rough guide to some activity as well as a detailed specification of every operation to be performed in that activity. The same plan can be either general or specific, molar or molecular, depending on the context: a writer's plan for producing a short narrative embedded in a long explanatory discourse is molecular in relation to the plan for the whole discourse, but molar in relation to the plan for generating one of the sentences within the short narrative.

While some plans are co-ordinate to each other and are executed as sequential chains, the crucial plans are *superordinate* to other plans, are further up in a hierarchy. The small-scale sequential plans are useless unless they are under the control of a higher plan: a series of grammatically correct sentences can be entirely inappropriate, unless constructed under the guidance of a higher plan (or metaplan) to select meaningful content or to produce a discourse segment appropriate for a particular audience. What is crucial in the execution of complex human behaviors – even a behavior like cleaning one's fingernails – is the intricate co-ordination of a hierarchically related set of plans, some in focal, some in subsidiary, awareness; some in parallel with others; some occurring alone; each one capable of being repeated or relinquished; each one capable of being refined, extended, or eliminated on the basis of continuous feedback from one's own nervous system.

How exactly is a plan executed? During purposeful behavior we choose to put certain plans in control of our thinking and actions. *Purpose* and *choice* are the key terms here. When we choose to execute a large plan, we bring it into the focus of our attention, monitoring the plan and subplans carefully so that we know how far we have progressed with each of them at any given instant. As a plan moves along we hold the immediate phase of the plan in short-term memory store, where we may also co-ordinate strategies or tactics of several plans running simultaneously. One way of freeing short-term store for other planning activities is to make written specifications for larger plans, as in making a tentative outline of a written discourse. Adults ordinarily learn a great many ways to make use of external memory devices to record plans and thereby 'forget' them temporarily. Finally, we should point out that we can launch some plans even though we are not aware of the specific strategies we will need to complete them.

In addition to plans for carrying out actions we also have plans for operating on ongoing private experience; daydreams, associations, images (Singer, 1977). There are very noticeable individual differences in the way people use their private thoughts and associations, judgments, impressions, images, and daydreams. Some simply let them pass. Others, however, make a special note of them, rehearsing them in short-term memory long enough for them to be stored effectively. Such attention and rehearsal require specific plans. People who have such plans have distinct advantages as thinkers and writers. Larger amounts of symbolic material and more novel combinations of the material are available to them; retrieval is more likely since imagery increases the likelihood of retrieval; and rehearsed and re-rehearsed private associations from long-term memory increase the chance of forming more complex connections with other associations and with different categories of response, auditory rather than verbal, imagaic rather than algebraic. Such people are 'practiced daydreamers'. They have an 'entirely different internal environment' (Singer, 1977). They give high priority to processing internal stimuli, which, again, can be either private associations and daydreams or judgments and impressions of things observed, a face, an object or a landscape, an overheard bit of conversation. They have well-practiced plans for processing these associations and observations. Writers know about plans for operating on ongoing private experience. Here is Pablo Neruda on such plans: 'There is also the reserve of feelings. How can those be preserved? By being conscious of them when they come up. Then, when we face the paper, this consciousness will come back to us more vividly than the emotion itself' (Neruda, 1978).

Miller, Galanter, and Pribram distinguish among three types of plans: algorithmic systematic, heuristic strategy, and random search. Pursuing these distinctions for a moment will provide further helpful context for our theory. Though a desperate writer, blocked for hours or days from a solution to a writing problem, may feel he is using an unproductive random plan as he struggles helplessly, and although the solution may surprise him when it does come, he is almost certainly not searching randomly for a solution. Humans are probably incapable of truly random thinking. The global plans (or metaplans) we have for guiding sub-plans preclude it. The schematic organization of all our knowledge precludes it. There is some pattern to every problem-solving search.

Humans do use algorithmic systematic planning, though. Where a problem is well defined and the area of search circumscribed, a systematic plan will be appropriate. If a writer takes a break to pull weeds in the garden and one contact lens falls out while he is tugging at a well-rooted clump of crabgras, he will search systematically for the lens, should his first quick random scannings fail to disclose the lens. He will identify the limits of the area to be searched, beginning in one corner or along one side and then systematically covering the whole area. He can be confident he will find the lens; as confident as he would be that an algorithmic algebraic equation would correctly solve a simple problem of an appropriate type. But when he finds the lens and returns to his desk, he will not get very far with the piece he is working on if he limits himself to algorithmic planning. We cannot think of any problem at any level of abstraction in writing which can be solved algorithmically, by a systematic search of some limited domain. One might argue that sentences are produced by a limited set of algorithmic transformations but only, we think, if one ignores the influence of discourse context on sentence production. The only algorithms for writing we can think of are ones not for composing but for editing: using a dictionary or spelling list to check the spelling of a word, or a thesaurus to substitute a synonym or near-synonym for a word a writer believes he has used too often. A writer might very well use some systematic plan of research to gather information on a topic (readings in pomology and visits to Florida orange groves and frozen concentrate plants for a book on oranges) but that, we would argue, is not part of the writing process itself. After the research the writer still must organize the material and compose it; and that sort of planning requires heuristic strategies.

Finding a lost contact lens is a good example of a well-defined problem for which an algorithmic solution is available: systematic search of a limited area. The thinker's task is not so much searching for a solution to the problem as it is defining the problem. Once the problem is defined or recognized, then the solution is apparent, or at least not too difficult to find.

The problems to be solved at all levels in writing, from discourse design to sentence production, are good examples of ill-defined problems. In writing, the problem is not predicting the possibility of success with a chosen solution to a well-defined problem but rather continuously, relentlessly forming plans and subplans to search for solutions to innumerable ill-defined problems. In writing, the problem is not to identify the one solution which will solve the whole discourse problem, as in algorithmic problem-solving, but rather to generate many proposed solutions which may be tested for appropriateness at each point in the unfolding text, as in heuristic problem-solving. This continuous, relentless testing requires discernment and selection among a vast number of possibilities or alternatives.

PLANNING WRITTEN DISCOURSE: GLOBAL DISCOURSE PLANS

With this general background information on memory, consciousness, and planning we can now move a step closer to theorizing about a particular act of composing in writing. Before specifying how a writer plans at the sentence or constituent level we will need to talk about global discourse planning. This will require a discussion of the way that a particular purpose, audience, and occasion for writing lead to a certain discourse type with its characteristic structure.

Purpose and Audience

Any discourse of more than a sentence or two requires a global plan: the writer will have problems to solve or decisions to make that are more global and abstract than sentence or constituent plans. Crucial global decisions must be made about the purpose for the writing and about the readers (or audience) for the writing. It is very easy to underestimate the importance of a conception of purpose and audience for writing. Any piece of written discourse, like any communication act, can only occur in a full communication context. Certain critical context features are always present and always bear forcefully on the communicator's plans, indeed determine everything about the shape, direction, and details of content and language of a written communication. These global context features, dominated by purpose and audience, may not be in the writer's awareness but they are powerfully present, nevertheless. Concepts of purpose and audience effect the composing process in significant ways. For writers of all ages, and especially for older writers and practiced professionals, the structure, tone, style, register, syntax, and lexical choices (diction) of their writing will change when their dominant purpose for writing shifts or when their audience changes.

Professional writers of all kinds – novelists who are also essayists or critics, reporters, technical writers, academics – usually write for a great many different audiences. They are the first to say that in a persuasive piece their intended audience will have everything to do with the kinds of arguments they choose and the sequencing of the arguments. They know well that in explanatory writing audience is the main consideration in how much information to include; in how detailed, or exhaustive, or technical one might be. Indeed, the importance of information level in explanatory writing is the easiest way to see the difference audience will make in a writer's strategies and tactics: it overwhelmingly determines everything about explanatory writing at every level.

The range of audiences is very wide in written discourse. One can write for oneself, for an intimate friend, for an individual stranger, for known groups, for distant, unfamiliar groups. In school the writer can conceive of a teacher-as-audience in very different ways: trusted adult, teacher in a teacher–learner dialogue, or examiner. In class the writer can write to a particular peer, to peers as a group, to younger students in the school, to members of a peer working group or committee which may include a teacher or administrator (Britton *et al.*, 1975).

Taking account of the needs of various audiences is difficult for young writers (Kroll, 1978); but as writers mature and become less egocentered, they are able to vary their discourse in noticeable ways for different audiences (Crowhurst and Piché, 1979).

Writers' plans are influenced by their conception of audience, but they are also influenced even more powerfully by their conception of the purpose or function of the piece of writing. As a result of important work in discourse theory (Moffett, 1968; Britton *et al.*, 1975; Kinneavy, 1971), we have come to understand many of the ways in which purpose affects the written product. This research has produced several ways of classifying writing into discourse types which correspond to the major purposes in the full range of purposes writers can have.

Discourse Types

In our view the best organized and most comprehensive of the new discourse classification schemes is that of Britton and his colleagues (1975). We will use it to illustrate the striking differences in the major discourse types and sub-types. The point to keep in mind is that each of these types and sub-types requires different plans of a writer. Like awareness of audience, awareness of purpose pervades all decisions the writer makes at the global discourse level, and also has an impact on propositional and lexical planning at the sentence level.

(All definitions in the following outline are from Britton *et al.*, 1975.)

I. Expressive. Language close to the self, revealing the speaker, verbalizing his consciousness, displaying his close relationship with the reader. Possibly not highly explicit. Relatively unstructured. Examples are tentative notes for a writing project, diaries, personal letters to close friends, gossip columns, some editorials.

II. Poetic. A verbal construct, a patterned verbalization of the writer's feelings and ideas. This category is not restricted to poems but would include such writings as a short story, a play, a shaped autobiographical episode.

III. Transactional. Language to get things done, i.e. it is concerned with an end outside itself. It informs, persuades, and instructs.

A. Conative: transactional writing for instruction or persuasion.
  (1) Regulative: language which lays down a course of action to be followed, makes demands, issues instructions where compliance is assumed, and makes recommendations which carry the weight of authority or the force of the speaker's wishes.
  (2) Persuasive: since compliance cannot be assumed, an attempt is made to influence action, behavior, and attitude by reason and argument or other strategy.

B. Informative: transactional writing to make information available.
  (1) Record: eye-witness account or running commentary.
  (2) Report: the writer gives an account of a particular series of events or the appearance of a particular place (i.e. narrative and/or descriptive).
  (3) Generalized narrative or descriptive information: the writer is tied to particular events and places but he is detecting a pattern of repetition in them; and he expresses this in generalized form.
  (4) Analogic, low level of generalization: genuine generalizations but loosely related; i.e. the relationships are not perceived and/or not made explicit.
  (5) Analogic: generalizations related hierarchically or logically by means of coherently presented classificatory utterances.
  (7) Analogic–tautologic (speculative): speculation about generalizations; the open-ended consideration of analogic possibilities.
  (7) Tautologic: hypotheses and deductions from them. Theory backed by logical argumentation.

Logic, conception, planning, and execution all differ as a writer shifts from one of these types to the other. Though the full range of differences among these types has not been decribed exhaustively as yet, in fact, the work has barely begun, we know that they differ in substantial ways (Crowhurst and Piché, 1979; Watson, 1979; Cooper and Watson, 1981). The major difference, of course, is not at the sentence level, though it is there as well, but at the discourse level; at the level of the global structure or plan of the piece.

Structure

Every type of discourse has its characteristic structure, a structure that can only be learned through extensive experience with each discourse type as a reader and writer. Through this experience writers gradually come to internalize the structures of a great many different types of discourse. We can speak of these internalized structures as schemas (Chafe, 1977) or as scripts (Schank and Abelson, 1977). As hypothesized, they are tremendously useful to a writer. Their absence or their lack of refinement explains why certain discourse types are unattainable or very difficult for young writers. The notion of scripts also helps to explain why the development of writing ability is such a long, slow process and why it must necessarily be related to reading development.

One way to examine the structure or patterning in written discourse is to ask what role each sentence (or T-unit – Hunt's (1965) designation for an independent clause) plays in the discourse. This question needs to be asked two ways:

(a) what is the *functional* (propositional or semantic) role the sentence plays, what does it add to the information in the discourse, and just how does it achieve that addition; and

(2) what is the *structural* role the sentence plays, what is its contribution in the hierarchy of superordinate, subordinate, and co-ordinate relationships sentences have with one another in extended discourse?

Functional Sentence Roles

Each sentence makes a unique and identifiable contribution to the meaning of the discourse. These contributions occur in a pattern predictable from the stereotypical structure for the particular discourse type the writer is working in. Each major discourse type, then, will have a different pattern of sentence semantic roles.

Very little research has been done on sentence semantic roles (Christensen, 1967; Winterowd, 1970; Larson, 1967; Pitkin, 1977). With Larson's work as a starting point, we have devised our own system for classifying sentence semantic roles. The fifteen roles in our system are grouped into five categories: generalizing, rhetorical, sequencing, relationship, and development. Since it is a new system, we present it here in its entirety so that we may illustrate fully the range of functional sentence roles available to a writer as written discourse unfolds sentence by sentence.

Generalizing roles

(1) State: the State role is the role of generalization or theme or thesis. It asserts the controlling and central idea of the discourse. The State role will usually appear in the first few sentences of explanatory or persuasive discourse, and then may appear again in the various subsections of such discourse, where secondary generalizations or themes will be asserted. In expressive or personal-narrative writing the State role may be used to cover what Labov (1972) calls the Abstraction role. State nearly always occurs at a high level of abstraction in the discourse.

(2) Restate: the Restate role is simply a restatement in other words of the previous statement. Restate usually has the purpose of clarification or emphasis, but in the first draft writing of novices it may reflect uncertainty about how to shift the abstraction level down in order to begin developing a State assertion. It may occur at a high level of abstraction in the discourse, as when it follows State, or at a low level, following, say, Qualify. In our scheme Restate always follows immediately after the T-unit it restates, without intervening T-units.

Rhetorical roles

(3) Summarize: the Summarize role usually appears at the conclusion of a discourse, though it may also appear at several internal points. It serves simply to summarize what has gone before. It will usually be at a high level of abstraction, and it will not introduce new information.

(4) Conclude: the Conclude role serves two important functions in discourse: (a) to draw a specific conclusion from facts or opinions just presented; a role which can occur at several points in a discourse, at the end of a paragraph or section, or even as a separate brief transition paragraph between sections, and (b) to 'exit' from the discourse, to announce that one is finished. Conclude differs from Summarize in that Conclude either draws new conclusions or explicitly announces an exit, while Summarize simply collates or synthesizes what has gone before. In narrative writing Conclude covers the Coda role noted by Labov (1972).

Sequencing roles

(5) Add: the Add role serves to add one assertion to the next at the same level of generality.

(6) Replace: the Replace role is the role of reformulation or alternatives. While Replace always occurs at the same level of abstraction as the T-unit preceding it, it is different from Restate, which is reserved for the rewording of a State T-unit and must follow directly after that T-unit. Replace is the role of 'or' in discourse: one thing or the other thing.

(7) Narrate: the Narrate role has the function in discourse of naming an event or a series of events in a time sequence. Certain forms of discourse – expressive, personal-experience narrative, biography, history, journal, reportage – may have T-units exclusively or largely in the Narrate role. In such discourse Narrate may be interrupted occasionally by only one other role – Evaluate.

Even though Narrate is placed here with Sequence roles, it often plays an important part in persuasive and explanatory writing along with other Development roles. Like these latter roles – Exemplify, Define, Describe – Narrate can produce a short narrative incident which is being presented as an example in an argument or an illustration in an explanation.

Relationship roles

(8) Contrast/Compare: the Contrast/Compare role serves explicitly to contrast or compare the assertion in the preceding T-unit. Contrast/Compare is the role of 'but' in discourse.

(9) Infer: the Infer role serves to identify an explicit inference drawn from the preceding T-unit or sequence of T-units. Infer suggests that something new is to be learned from the previous assertions.

(10) Evaluate: the Evaluate role serves to make a judgment or to reflect on assertions in preceding T-units. It does not so much reflect a new insight to be drawn from what has been said, as with Infer, as it reflects a judgment about it. Evaluate plays an important role in narrative, where it may occur at any point that the writer steps aside to comment or reflect on, or evaluate, the action. In narrative it is recognized as a definite break in the narrative line, usually with a shift in verb tenses.

(11) Cause/Result: the Cause/Result role expresses the consequence or result of what has just been said. It may point to what produced an event just identified or what effects the event produced.

(12) Qualify: the Qualify role functions generally to restrict the meaning of an earlier assertion. In narrative writing Qualify functions to narrow and focus an opening State role establishing the occasion for the narrative. In this way Qualify may be used to cover what Labov (1972) calls the Orientation role in narrative. Some explanatory or persuasive pieces may open with orienting sentences prior to a State

T-unit identifying the thesis of the piece, but this is the only instance in which Qualify will precede the T-Unit to which it relates logically.

Development roles

(13) Exemplify: the Exemplify role functions to provide examples, facts, and illustrations for an assertion.

(14) Define: the Define role functions simply to provide a definition of a word or concept in a previous assertion. T-units beginning 'this means' will usually be Exemplify rather than Define. Unless there is an explicit, focused definition in the T-unit it cannot be classified as Define.

(15) Decribe: the Describe role seems to provide one or more details of an *object* or *person* in order to assist the reader in seeing the object precisely or understanding it fully.

Using this sytem of identifying sentence semantic roles, we can suggest paradigmatic patterns for short pieces of reporting and generalizing to illustrate how different sentence-to-sentence planning would be in each case.

Reporting a personal experience might begin with Qualify (in the sense of the orientation role Labov (1972) identifies in narrative), move directly to Narrate, digress now and then to Evaluate the experience being narrated, and conclude with a more general Evaluate (see Table 1).

TABLE 1

Sentence	Role in reporting
1	Qualify
2	Qualify
3	Narrate
4	Narrate
5	Narrate
6	Narrate
7	Evaluate
8	Narrate
9	Narrate
10	Narrate
11	Narrate
12	Evaluate

By contrast, generalizing might begin with State (the main generalization), perhaps move to Restate (repeating the generalization in a slightly different way), then Define a crucial term, give two examples (Exemplify) related by

TABLE 2

Sentence	Role in generalizing
1	State
2	Restate
3	Define
4	Exemplify
5	Exemplify
6	Contrast
7	Exemplify
8	Exemplify
9	Infer
10	Summarize
11	Conclude
12	Conclude

Contrast, draw an inference from the examples (Infer), and, finally, Summarize and Conclude (Table 2).

The important thing to note is that the discourse type and the writer's corresponding schema will constrain, if not fully determine, the writer's choice of the appropriate semantic role for the next sentence. This decision is made before the writer makes any of the propositional or lexical decisions for the sentence, and for this reason planning for functional semantic roles in written discourse is made within the context of discourse type and schema rather than as part of sentence production itself.

Structural Sentence Roles

Each sentence also plays its part in the abstraction hierarchy of the discourse. These structural roles have been identified in previous research as superordination, subordination, and co-ordination (Christensen, 1967; Grimes, 1975, pp. 103, 104; Nold and Davis, 1980). Written discourse is hierarchical in structure in that some sentences (or T-units) are at a higher level of abstraction than others and serve to organize the discourse. These high-level superordinate sentences can state the main argument in a persuasive piece, the thesis in generalization, or the orientation in narrative. There will usually be an immediate downshift in abstraction, a subordinating of the next sentence. The down shifts may go to deeper and deeper levels as the discourse progresses, with sections of co-ordinate sentences at the same level of abstraction to develop a point or narrate an event, but quite regularly there are superordinating upshifts, usually at the beginning of paragraphs or at the conclusion.

These structural patterns look very different for the various major discourse types, as we can illustrate with paradigmatic patterns for reporting and generalizing.

Superordination SUPER (1)
Subordination SUBORD (2)
Co-ordination CO-ORD (3)

Reporting a personal experience might begin with SUPER (1) to orient the reader, shift down immediately to SUBORD (2) for narration sustained for long periods at CO-ORD (3), upshifting occasionally to SUPER (1) at the end of paragraphs to evaluate the experience.

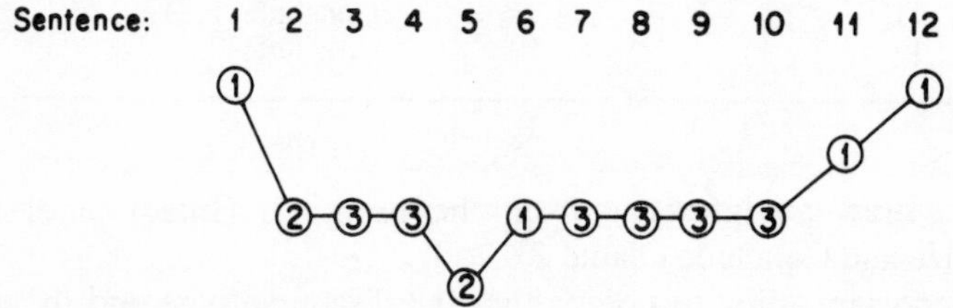

Levels in the diagram indicate levels of abstractions. Sentences 1 and 12 are at the highest level, Sentence 5 at the lowest level.

By contrast, generalizing might begin with SUPER to state the thesis, shift down with SUBORD to give an example, shift down still further to offer details, change to SUPER to offer mid-level generalizations occasionally, and then go to SUBORD to present further examples, using CO-ORD to develop examples at the same level of abstraction.

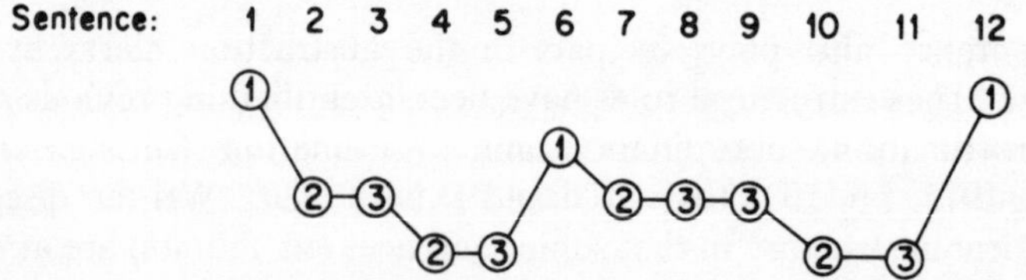

In extended pieces of reporting and generalizing the structural differences are much more pronounced than in these abbreviated paradigmatic diagrams.

In written discourse these two major types of sentence roles – functional semantic roles and structural abstraction-level roles – are not independent. SUPER often occurs with State or Evaluate, SUBORD with Exemplify or Define, CO-ORD with Add or Narrate; but only the structural roles analysis will reveal the hierarchical organization of the discourse in its several abstraction levels.

As with functional roles, the writer's planning decision about which structural role to apply next is guided by his internalized schema for the discourse type he is writing. It is a decision reflecting global discourse planning, rather than sentence production planning, the topic for the next section.

We can summarize this section on global discourse plans by saying that the plan a writer shapes and the strategies he chooses to achieve the plan will be pervaded and dominated by his choice of purpose and audience. He may want primarily to express his feelings, persuade someone, or merely transmit information. He may write for a single intimate confidant or a mass of faceless strangers. Usually his choice of purpose and audience will require him to produce a kind of discourse whose structure he has internalized (learned) as a schema or script. Guided by this schema, he will plan sentences which play appropriate functional (semantic) and structural (hierarchical) roles in the discourse.

We must emphasize that a writer's decisions about purpose and audience may not be made once and for all before beginning to compose a particular piece. They may be remade, readjusted, refocused many times as composing proceeds; and during revision and editing many changes or additions may reflect a better awareness of who the readers will be, and what the writer hopes to accomplish with them.

All that remains in this theory of the composing process is to describe the process of sentence production itself, but this will involve more complexities than the reader might think.

PLANNING WRITTEN DISCOURSE: SENTENCE PLANS

We want to outline in this section the plans a writer must make in order to achieve a written sentence. Since we are conjecturing about a most ill-defined problem, we risk offering a stage-by-stage account in order to look at all of the decisions a writer must make. Because our interest is in describing these decisions fully we have presented them in an idealized order. This list might be considered the bank of tacit knowledge from which a writer deliberately constructs a text. We have, in this chapter, knowingly ignored the real-time pressures and the recursive nature of decision-making during composing. While all the decisions we specify may be required to produce any sentence in a multi-sentence discourse, certain decisions might be prominently foregrounded and consume larger amounts of planning time and effort than others. These variations would result from different writing situations (arguing versus explaining, drafting versus revising) and from the age and writing experience of the writer.

Even though the global discourse constraints outlined in the previous section most definitely have an effect on sentence planning, this present section on sentence plans is concerned only with theorizing about the writer's plans beyond the point where purpose, audience, occasion, and typical discourse structure have made their contribution to the decision about what sentence to construct next.

The reader must assume, then, that the account that follows is an idealized explanation of how a competent writer produces one sentence well into a discourse for which the writer has essentially solved – or is in control of – the global discourse decisions discussed in the previous section. How does this writer produce that sentence? What plans and decisions must be involved in that cognitive, scribal action?

Formulating a Proposition

The first step is to formulate a proposition; to plan the message. Searching long-term memory, attending to various states of consciousness, the writer identifies the next unit of meaning or the next chunk of information or experience. Guided by a stereotypical schema for the discourse type, the writer chooses a chunk of information or experience on the basis of its salience in memory and pertinence in the discourse.

It is important to realize that propositions are formed well before language has been attached to them. In fact, we will be pretty far down this list of stages in producing a sentence before we arrive at language. Propositions are formed and sorted among probably below the level of conscious awareness. Once we are aware of them we have moved several stages into the production process. It is an intriguing possibility that the criterion of acceptability for a proposition – the decision to include it in the discourse – is success in processing it through the stages to be described below.

At any rate, a crucial strategy in planning a written discourse is choosing the propositions which will extend the discourse. This is the first of a series of decisions which will turn a holistic purpose into a linear series of propositions expressed in conventional grammatico-graphic patterns.

Framing the Proposition

The next stage involves choosing a predicate for the proposition and singling out the people or objects to be included in the expression of that proposition. Unless an action or state (the predicate, or verb) can be matched with particular objects or people, and unless the relationships or roles among these particulars can be specified, the proposition cannot be 'framed' and eventually expressed. This stage involves 'choosing a frame on which the sentence can be hung' (Chafe, 1977).

We have still not yet arrived at language: we do not know which verb will appear in the predicate or just which nouns will identify the objects or people.

This stage has been talked about by others (Chafe, 1977) in the terminology of case grammar (Fillmore, 1968). The 'roles' are grammatical relationships represented by noun cases and have been identified as agentive, affected, recipient, attribute, instrumental, locative, temporal, and effected (Quirk *et al.*, 1972). The 'frames' are case frames which explicitly show the role that each noun in subject or object/nominative positions will play in the sentence.

The frame for the proposition provides the basis for a grammatically complete assertion, with at least a subject and predicate and often also an object or nominative complement. It specifies the basic sentence parts and their relationships. It permits one clause to be formed. Again, it does not specify the lexical items for the frame, much less any modifiers that might go with them.

This is mainly a *test stage* where writers discover whether they can verbalize a 'thought'; whether they can frame a proposition pushing up toward consciousness.

According to Fillmore's grammar certain grammatical slots, such as subject or object, can host a variety of these semantic roles. For example, subjects can be agentive, instrumental, affected, temporal, or locative. Objects can be effective, recipient, locative, and affected. Yet there are certain clear constraints. For example, an indirect object can be only affected or recipient. Because semantic roles can be slotted into varied grammatical slots, we can speak about roles being chosen *prior* to the decision about the specific grammatical ordering of elements, as well as prior to the decision about which particular lexical items will appear in the slots.

Agentive: animate being instigating or causing the happening denoted by the verb (brief definitions are from Quirk *et al.*, 1972).

Joan Didion autographed copies of her new book.

Affected: a participant (animate or inanimate) which does not cause the happening denoted by the verb, but is directly involved in some other way.

Several critics attacked the *Poet Laureate*.
My Number 2 *pencils* were lying on the table.
I've ruined this *draft*.

Recipient: animate being passively implicated by the happening or state.

I've bought *you* a new thesaurus.
John unwillingly heard the criticisms from his writing workshop.

Attribute: a subject or object complement which has the role of attribute of the subject or object.

That man at the bar is my *literary agent*
They elected Jix *chairman* of the Conference on College Composition and Communication.

Instrumental: expresses the unwitting (generally inanimate) material cause of an event.

The *copying machine* smudged my copies.

Locative: the subject or object of the clause designates the place of the state or action.

My *study* has two small library tables.
We haunted the Mexican food *restaurants*.

Temporal: the subject of the clause designates the time of the state or action.

Friday was the day that manuscript was due.

Effected: an object that refers to something which exists only by virtue of the activity indicated by the verb.

Styron has written a new *novel.*

Placing the Proposition

Next, the writer must decide on the speech act for the proposition, 'placing' it in the context of 'What I want to achieve with this audience'. This decision makes greater demands on cognition and requires more careful planning in conversational discourse than in written discourse, but is it an important consideration in writing nevertheless. Though the range of speech acts is very wide in conversation, they make a describable and limited set which can be organized into five categories (Searle, 1975):

Representatives (asserting, suggesting, swearing, stating, hinting)

Composing in writing is a complex psycholinguistic process.

Directives (requesting, questioning)

> Why don't you put a semi-colon between these two clauses?

Commissives (promising, vowing, pledging, contracting, guaranteeing)

> You can be sure that I will come home early from the beach to try to finish this section of the theory.

Expressives (apologizing, thanking, congratulating, welcoming, deploring)

> I'm grateful to you for giving this draft such a close, critical reading.

Declarations (dismissing, sentencing, naming)

> I'll call this stage in the process 'placing'.

In terms of speech act theory the main thing to note about non-fictional written discourse is that virtually all of it is simply strings of assertions (representatives, in the outline above). In explanatory and persuasive written monological discourse, even in expressive written discourse, as James Britton or James Kinneavy define it, the propositions will take the form of assertions or statements.

In placing the proposition, in deciding on the speech act, the writer is still planning below the level of language. This decision involves deciding, among all the wide range of intentions a writer can have in making an utterance, on just the particular intention for this next proposition. Again, this decision in writing is relatively simple: the writer usually maintains the same speech act from proposition to proposition throughout the discourse. By contrast, in a brief conversation of a few minutes, the two speakers may range across all the categories of speech acts in the outline above.

Even in written language, though, there may be an issue of whether to make the proposition direct or indirect. For example, we might say 'Speech act theorists have yet to work out carefully the implications of their theory for written monologues', or we might say 'As a way of extending their impressive current work on speakers' intentions in conversations, speech act theorists may wish to turn their attention in the near future to writers' intentions in extended written monologues.' The first assertion is 'direct', the second 'indirect', in that it is more tactful, more obliging or accommodating. Both are assertions, both contain essentially the same information, but each has a slightly different intent: the direct one is tough, the indirect one is sweet. That sort of decision may come up again and again in a single written discourse which consistently attempts to maintain the same purpose and the same audience relation.

Another form of indirectness a writer may choose from time to time is satire or irony, using an occasional proposition in these modes just for variety. We might write 'A reader coming new to discourse theory may have some initial difficulty with the chapter on abstraction in Moffett's *Teaching the Universe of Discourse*', or we might write 'A reader coming new to discourse theory is hereby forewarned: in his chapter on abstraction in *Teaching the Universe of Discourse* Moffett occasionally places his own abstraction ladder so unsteadily against his discourse tree that he is in danger on nearly every page of falling through the branches with his shoulder bag of apples'.

To summarize: with a proposition formed, a proposition for which a sentence-frame can be identified, the writer decides how to place the proposition in the context of his discourse intent. It is just here in this rapid series of pre-lexical stages in producing a proposition that writers must be guided by a clear sense of purpose and audience. They choose the speech act they will make with this next proposition, the persona they wish to present to these particular imagined readers.

Directing the Proposition

The next decision establishes the direction the writer expects to go in the discourse. This choice identifies what the writer intends to talk about next. It is essentially a decision about which people or objects to place in the subject position in the clause. Recall that in the framing stage the predicate and then the people or objects are chosen for the proposition and their roles or relationships identified. Only now, however, does the writer decide which one of the roles will become the subject of the clause.

Actually, for our purposes here, it is more accurate to talk about the writer's deciding on the *theme* of the clause, rather than its subject. As we will see, the two, theme and subject, are usually the same, but not always. In addition, in certain inverted clauses or in passives, the subject will not be the first element. Consequently, it is better to talk about the *theme* of the sentence as its first major element (Quirk *et al.*, 1972; Halliday, 1967). These two sentences will provide illustrations:

THEME AND SUBJECT
Some professional writers revise their work extensively.

THEME SUBJECT
This part of the text the writer developed by a series of overlapping free-writes.

In the first sentence the theme is also the grammatical subject, but in the second sentence it is not.

Here is a more striking example of the lack of congruity between theme and subject.

THEME
This box of newly-sharpened Number 2 Dixon Ticonderoga pencils

SUBJECT
the writer received as a gift from his anxious publisher.

Connecting the Proposition

At this stage the writer decides which information in the sentence may be treated as *new* and which as *given* (Quirk *et al.*, 1972; Chafe, 1974). Unlike the just-previous decision about directing the proposition, a decision based solely on where the writer wants to go next in the discourse, this next decision is determined altogether by the writer's assessment of what the *reader* either already knows from some other source or will remember from previous propositions in the developing discourse. Directing the proposition, deciding on its theme, is a decision made only within the context of each clause or sentence. By contrast, connecting the proposition, deciding on what is given and what is new, takes account of what has preceded in the discourse.

Given information usually goes in the subject position and new information goes in the predicate. Although we might think that the grammatical subject always contains the most important information in extended written discourse, this is clearly not the case. The new information the writer presents is usually not in the subject position. New information is sometimes called the 'information focus' (Quirk *et al.*, 1972) and though it is usually the predicate of the sentence, it may be a whole clause, a single word, or even a syllable. The easiest way to locate it is to read the sentence aloud with previous sentences and see where the intonational emphasis lies within the sentence. That location will be the new information or the information focus.

Since given and new information in written discourse cannot be illustrated with single sentences, we will present longer sections from both fiction and non-fiction.

> The bulk of writing in our society is of a professional or quasi-professional nature. *The practitioners* are, in part, aided by the conventions, practices and 'house-style' of the agency for which they write, and by their experience of public communication in general. *This* would also hold true for internal documents which circulate in large organizations like industrial enterprises, the civil service, etc.

> *Writers in this situation* need never have pondered the problem of audience: *they* have merely, so to speak, to serve their apprenticeship. *They* adjust themselves to the ground rules.
>
> (Britton, *et al.* 1975, p. 59)

The given information which is always in the subject slot here, is italicized. We can see at a glance how much of this sort of explanatory discourse is new information, and the same holds true for a more personal sort of explanatory writing:

> When it became generally known a year or so ago that California was suffering severe drought, many people in water-rich parts of the country seemed obscurely gratified, and made frequent reference to Californians having to brick up their swimming pools. *In fact a swimming pool* requires, once it has been filled and the filter has begun its process of cleaning and recirculating the water, virtually no water, but the symbolic content of swimming pools has always been interesting: *a pool* is misapprehended as a trapping of affluence, real or pretended, and of a kind of hedonistic attention to the body. *Actually a pool* is, for many of us in the West, a symbol not of affluence but of order, of control over the uncontrollable. *A pool* is water, made available and useful, and is, as such, infinitely soothing to the western eye.
>
> (Didion, 1979, pp. 63 and 64)

For contrast, we present next a descriptive section from a recent novel. Though new information predominates still, and though given information is usually in the subject slot – especially with the personal pronouns towards the end of the passage – there are some sentences which contain only new information and some in which the given information is not in the subject slot. (For a discussion to follow about differences between theme and given/new information, the themes in these sentences are in brackets.)

> [In the old days of ice wagons and coal wagons] householders used to cut busted boilers in half, set them out on the grass plots, and fill them with flowers. [Big Polish women in ribboned caps] went out in the spring with cans of Sapolio and painted *these boiler-planters* so that they shone silver against the blaring red of the brick. [The double rows of rivets] stood out like the raised skin patterns of African tribes. *Here (the women)* grew geraniums, Sweet William, and other low-grade dusty flowers. (*I*] showed *all of this* to Humboldt Fleisher years ago. ... (*I*] took Humboldt on the El to the stockyards. [*He*] saw the Loop. [*We*] went to the lakeshore and listened to the foghorns. [*They*] bawled melancholy over the limp silk fresh lilac drowning water. But [*Humboldt*] responded mostly to the old neighborhood. [*The silvered boiler rivets and the blazing Polish geraniums*] got him. [*He*] listened pale and moved to the buzzing of roller-skate wheels on the brittle cement. [*I*] too am sentimental about urban ugliness. In the modern spirit of ransoming the

> commonplace, all this junk and wretchedness, through art and poetry, by the superior power of the soul.
>
> (Bellow, 1973, pp. 71, 72)

We should remind the reader that these in-print examples of written discourse illustrate only certain prominent features of written language from which we infer what must be involved in the various stages of producing a written sentence. The decisions to direct and to connect a proposition are made *before* the lexical items are selected for the proposition. In that sense these polished, professional selections are a bit misleading. They are products whose temporal, psycholinguistic process of achievement we are trying to describe.

Notice that the theme in each sentence is not always the same as the given information, though both are ordinarily the first major elements. Recall that deciding on the theme (directing the proposition) is a prior and different decision from choosing what is to be given (connecting the proposition). Directing points the discourse in the direction the writer wants to go. Connecting brings the reader along accommodatingly.

In addition to the placement of given and new information in the nearly-formed proposition the writer must still make one other crucial decision required to accommodate the reader and to create coherent text: a decision to insure cohesion with the previous proposition and with the entire preceding text. Cohesion is achieved in English by reference, substitution, ellipsis, conjunction, and lexical cohesion (Halliday and Hasan, 1976). In non-fictional written discourse, reference and lexical cohesion are by far the most comon types. The main types of reference are the following:

R1 Pronominals (he, him, his, she, her, hers, it, its, they, them, their, theirs)
R2 Demonstratives and definite articles (this, these, here, that, those, there, then, the)

and the main types of lexical cohesion the following:

L1 Same item
L2 Synonym or near synonym
L3 Superordinate
L4 General item
L5 Collocation

In addition to the codes above, we might use in the analysis of the non-fiction piece below C for conjunction, E for ellipsis, and S for substitution. As it turns out, none of these latter types of cohesion appear.

When it became generally known a year or so ago that California was suffering
severe drought, many people in water-rich parts of the country seemed obscurely
gratified, and made frequent reference to Californians having to brick up their
L1 R1
swimming pools. In fact a swimming pool requires, once it has been filled and the
L5 (swimming pool) L1
filter has begun its process of cleaning and recirculating the water, virtually no
water, but the symbolic content of swimming pools has always been interesting; a
L1
pool is misapprehended as a trapping of affluence, real or pretended, and of a kind
L1
of hedonistic attention to the body. Actually a pool is, for many of us in the West, a
L1 L1 L5 (hedonistic) L5 (hedonistic) L1
symbol not of affluence but of order, of control over the uncontrollable. A pool is
L1 L5 (California)
water, made available and useful, and is, as such, infinitely soothing to the western
eye.

(Didion, 1979, pp. 63 and 64)

Since cohesion is specifically a system for creating text by linking sentences, the analysis of the above passage begins only with the second sentence and does not include any instances of cohesive ties within sentences.

Even with all of the complexities we have already illustrated, this theory of written sentence production is not yet complete. So far, still below the level of exact lexical choice, we have seen how a thought is formulated as a proposition, which is then framed as a test of its verbalizability, and then placed as a speech act, directed to keep the discourse headed where the writer wants to go, and, finally, connected to the accumulated written discourse. Involving a rapid-fire series of conjectures about the role and arrangement of the major sentence elements, all of these decisions must be made for every proposition that finally makes its way to the page. The real time required to move through this series of stages which bring a proposition just to the verge of expression with the lexicon will probably be only milli-seconds, if it can ever be measured at all. What fills time in relatively long pauses before some sentences or clauses is the writer trying out and rejecting many propositions before 'finding' one which is appropriate and expressible.

This new proposition must emerge before a writer can choose lexical items, present them in the appropriate grammatical forms, store this graphic image in short-term memory, and begin transcribing the new sentence.

Wording the Proposition

Only now do we arrive at language, at specific lexical choices, at the words which will express the proposition. With all of the crucial decisions that have been made to prepare for this stage we might think the words and phrases for the propositional structure would simply click into place at this point, but such is not the case. We can illustrate what is involved at this stage by returning to a sentence we used earlier:

Joan Didion autographed copies of her new book ...

Arriving at the wording stage of this sentence – but before we have chosen the words – we have decided to make an assertion without irony or indirectness; to use a sentence frame which involves a personal voluntary action which includes two individuals/objects, one to be agentive, the other to be effected; to use the agentive as the theme; and, let us say, to place the new information in the predicate and to insure cohesion by choosing nouns which will reiterate with previous nouns or collocate with them. Now we still have more decisions to make than we can be comfortable with. For the agentive theme shall it be

Joan
Ms. Didion
That well-known woman essayist and fiction-writer
A woman writer who used to go to McClatchy High School in Sacramento
Joan Didion
Slight, serious Joan Didion
A woman?

And for the main verb shall it be

autographed
signed
is putting her signature on
is writing in?

And for the affected object shall we say

copies of her new book
copies of a new book
copies of the new book
her new book
her latest book, *The White Album*
her newest book, a collection of articles published previously in various magazines
some book?

The choices seem infinite, especially when we begin considering all the possibilities for modifying or qualifying the main verb and the agentive and affected nouns, but in fact they are considerably constrained by all the pre-lexical decisions made at earlier stages. Certainly they are constrained also by the whole context of the discourse in which the proposition appears.

The difficulty writers may have at this stage has been discussed in terms of codability (Chafe, 1977). Some objects (common machines like the automobile) are easy to code, and some objects (exotic machines used for highly specialized manufacturing processes) are difficult to code if we are writing about observations we have made. In addition, young or sophisticated writers will encounter many difficult-to-code experiences. For example, a *Los Angeles Times* reporter would probably write

> Joan Didion autographed copies of her new book.

or

> Slight, serious Joan Didion signed copies of her latest book, *The White Album*.

But a 10-year-old on a reportage assignment to a bookstore from his Grade 4 class would be likely to write

> A woman was writing in some books.

He would probably not know about autographing sessions, and would certainly not know about Joan Didion or have any idea why Californians would line up to have her write in their books. Hence, he would face a situation of low-codability.

The decisions about wording the proposition may not be complete before transcription begins, though usually they will be. We do occasionally observe a writer pausing for a long time to choose a word or phrase well into the proposition.

Presenting the Proposition

At this stage, having filled in the propositional frame with a complete array of lexical items, the writer is ready to make the grammatical decisions which will enable him to present the proposition in standard edited written English. Here the issues of usage come into play, mainly those of agreement and verb tense.

Storing the Proposition

Except for decisions about punctuation and spelling, the writer has now made all the decisions involved in producing a written proposition and can place the complete plan temporarily in short-term memory store while he proceeds to transcribe or type it. For propositions of more than just a few words the complete plan will have to be rehearsed and re-rehearsed in short-term store so that portions of it are not lost before the transcription is complete. The limitations of short-term memory, it can hold only a few items for only a few seconds without careful rehearsal, create serious disadvantages for young or unpracticed writers. Until they gain some confidence and fluency with spelling, their short-term memories may have to be loaded up with letter sequences of single words or with only two or three words (Hotopf, 1980). This not only makes for a slow writing process, but it also means that all other planning processes must be shut down during the transcriptions of short letter or word sequences.

Transcribing the Proposition

And now, for the first time, physical activity enters the process of producing a written proposition. This seems simple enough, even automatic, and yet when we view it developmentally it turns out to be quite complicated. In fact, in the early stages of learning to write, transcribing a proposition is a considerable physical struggle, quite tiring after just a few minutes, and requiring focal awareness letter by letter.

Transcription, inscription might be the better word, always involved the hand, either with a writing instrument or at a keyboard. It is a complex, distal, highly refined psychomotor act, which develops very gradually over a number of years (Thomassen and Teulings, Chapter 8, this volume; deAdjuriaguerra and Auzias, 1975), from the erratic lines and figures of the pre-schooler, to the discontinuous, shaky letters of the first-grader, and finally to the continuous cursive writing of the fifth- or sixth-grader.

The main thing to be understood is that hand transcription of propositions gradually becomes refined and practiced so that planning for it does not dominate the writer's consciousnes, does not occupy focal awareness during the task of writing. A major goal of the development of writing ability is for transcription increasingly to occupy subsidiary awareness, enabling the writer to use focal awareness for other plans and decisions. In practiced writers, transcription of certain words and sequences can be so automatic as to permit planning the next proposition while transcription of the previous one is still under way. These automatic sequences have been referred to as 'integrated movement sequences' (Smith, 1975). Fluent, practiced writers have thousands of these for individual words and for short word sequences, like common phrases. With these integrated movement sequences the writer is programmed 'to run off a complex motor act as a unit – as an integrated sequence' (Smith, 1973, p. 125) that does not need to be broken down into its component parts, the letters or the ductus of each letter or the ligature between letters. Once the proposition has been transcribed it becomes part of the unfolding graphic record of the discourse. It can now be pondered and changed or even stricken from the record.

As a postscript to this outline of our theory we would like to argue that only at the graphomotor stage is planning to produce written discourse automatic. To us the issue of automaticity is a central problem in theories of composing in writing. It is central both to descriptions of skilled performance and to descriptions of the changes that may come about as writers age and gain more experience with composing. The issue is essentially that of the constraints on short-term or working memory. At least one current theorist argues that fluent writers devote 'very little conscious attention' to 'producing grammatical sentences' (Flower and Hayes, 1980). Quite clearly, our theory of sentence production challenges that assumption.

In our view planning to produce written discourse can be guided by underlying syntactic and discourse competence – by a great many interconnected schemata acquired from years of experience with text as a reader and writer, but it is nearly totally a consciouss, non-automatic planning process. Everything is always new. Each new proposition, each new clause, requires focal, effortful planning. Furthermore, nearly all major levels in a complex hierarchy of planning levels must be reviewed or checked before a new clause can be produced. Even the most experienced writer must give focal attention to each new step in the process. Certain phrase and sentence schema may provide local constraints, and a discourse schema may guide the process from a lofty abstraction level; but each clause is still new. It must be planned. Only the most formulaic, ritualistic expressions, for instance; 'Dear sir', 'Sincerely yours', may be simply remembered and recorded. Even often-used phrases; 'In reference to your letter of July 4', must be reconsidered at least briefly in each instance for appropriateness of register along a formal–informal continuum which reflects the writer's assessment of his relationship with this particular correspondent. Did the writer have lunch in Auckland with the correspondent two months ago on a selling trip to New Zealand? Then perhaps the writer would want to begin much more informally: 'It was really good to hear from you. I remember our lunch together very well. I've thought about it several times just recently and have been hoping you would write.

In your July 4 letter ...'.

As we have noted above, the only automatic actions in the writing process are certain much-practiced letter or word transcription sequences which are produced by graphomotor plans. But even these actions are not automatic for beginning writers. Just here is where writing and reading processes differ in practiced literates: reading is largely automatic, while text creating remains almost entirely non-automatic in even the most skillful writers. Fluent reading is not possible without a high degree of automatic, parallel processing. The goal is to become unaware of the text as text and to focus on the developing representation of the text in memory. By contrast, even the most effortless writing requires close attention to planning every clause and sentence. As well as we presently understand the problem, we would want to argue that there is nothing automatic about planning a sentence.

CONCLUSION

Our approach to theorizing about composing in writing has been to account for a wide range of plans and decisions written language would seem to require of writers. We acknowledge readily that we offer less a comprehensive theory than a list of necessary decisions which any adequate theory will eventually have to include. Our list of plans and decisions can be summarized simply as follows:

Global discourse plans: decisions which pervade discourse production
- Purpose
- Audience
- Structure (schema)
  - Specific discourse pattern (type, mode, genre)
  - Sentence semantic role
  - Sentence abstraction level

Sentence plans: decisions required to produce any sentence
- Propositional decisions
  - Formulating
  - Framing
  - Placing
  - Directing
  - Connecting
- Lexical decisions
  - Wording
  - Presenting
- Storing in short-term memory
- Executing the graphomotor plan

What seems to us novel in our theory is our discussion of the place of sentence semantic roles and abstraction levels in text production and our account of stages of sentence production. With the latter there are five immediate problems: we are conjecturing about production processes from descriptions of already-produced sentences; we ignore subtle but important decisions about style; we imply a linear, almost mechanical, process of sentence production; we say far too little about developmental differences in sentence production; and we ignore the possible influences of writing situation and discourse type on sentence production. All we can do here is acknowledge these problems and hope that others will be able to overcome them. Eventually, what we would like to be able to explain, of course, is the process of producing the kinds of sentences William Gass (1979, pp. 56–8) attributes to Wallace Stevens, James Joyce, and Henry James:

> the word in each case finds its place within a system so supremely organized it cannot be improved upon – what we would not replace and cannot change … sentences which follow their own turnings inward out of sight like the whorls of a shell, and which we follow warily … sentences which make an imaginary speaker speak the imagination loudly to the reading eye … we subside through sentences like these … to float like leaves on the restful surface of that world of words to come.

But we do not claim to explain fully such sentences in this chapter. It may be that no theory of writing can ever account for them.

REFERENCES

Bellow, S. (1973). *Humboldt's Gift*. Viking Press, New York.

Bissex, G. (1980). *GYNS AT WRK: A Child Learns to Read and Write*. Harvard University Press, Cambridge, Mass.

Brewer, W. F. (1980). Literary theory, rhetoric, and stylistics: implications for psychology. In *Theoretical Issues in Reading Comprehension* (eds. R. J. Spiro, B. C. Bruce, and W. F. Brewer), pp. 221–39. Lawrence Erlbaum, Hillsdale, New Jersey.

Britton, J., Burgess, T., Martin, N., McLeod, A., and Rosen, H. (1975). *The Development of Writing Abilities (11–18)*. Macmillan, London.

Chafe, W. (1974). Givenness, contrastiveness, definiteness, subjects, topics, and point of view. In *Subject and Topic* (ed. C. N. Li), pp. 27–55. Academic Press, New York.

Chafe, W. (1977). The recall and verbalization of past experience. In *Current Issues in Linguistic Theory* (ed. R. W. Cole), pp. 215–46. Indiana University Press, Bloomington, Indiana.

Chafe, W. L. (ed.) (1980). *The Pear Stories: Cognitive, Cultural, and Linguistic Aspects of Narrative Production*. Ablex, Norwood, New Jersey.

Chafe, W. L. (1982). Integration and involvement in speaking, writing, and oral literature. In *Spoken and Written Language* (ed. D. Tannen). Ablex, Norwood, New Jersey.

Cherry, R., and Cooper, C. R. (1981). Cohesive ties and discourse structure: a study of writers at ages 9, 13, 17, and 21. Unpublished typescript, University of California at San Diego.

Christensen, F. (1967). *Notes Toward a New Rhetoric*. Harper & Row, New York.

Clements, P. (1979). The effects of staging on recall from prose. In *New Directions in Discourse Processing* (ed. R. O. Freedle), pp. 287–330. Ablex, Norwood, N.J.

Cooper, C. R., and Gray, A. (1981). Sequencing and staging information in explanatory discourse: a developmental study. Unpublished typescript, University of California at San Diego.

Cooper, C. R., and Odell, L. (1976). Considerations of sound in the composing process of published writers. *Research in the Teaching of English,* **10**, 103–15.

Cooper, C. R., and Watson, C. (1981). The sentences of nine-year-old writers: influences of ability and discourse type. Unpublished typescript, University of California at San Diego.

Crowhurst, M., and Piché, G. L. (1979). Audience and mode of discourse effects on syntactic complexity in writing at two grade levels. *Research in the Teaching of English,* **13**, 101–9.

deAjuriaguerra, J., and Auzias, M. (1975). Preconditions for the development of writing in the child. In *Foundations of Language Development*, vol. 2 (ed. E. H. Lenneberg and E. Lenneberg), pp. 311–328. Academic Press, New York.

Della-Piana, G. M. (1978). Research strategies for the study of revision processes in writing poetry. In *Research on Composing: Points of Departure* (eds. C. R. Cooper and L. Odell), pp. 105–134. National Council of Teachers of English, Urbana, Illinois.

Didion, J. (1979). *The White Album*. Simon & Schuster, New York.

Emig, J. (1971). *The Composing Process of Twelfth Graders*. National Council of Teachers of English, Urbana, Illinois.

Fillmore, C. (1968). The case for case. In *Universals in Linguistic Theory* (eds. E. Bach and R. T. Harms), Holt, Rinehart & Winston, New York, pp. 1–88.

Flower, L. S., and Hayes J. R. (1980). The dynamics of composing: making plans and juggling constraints. In *Cognitive Processes in Writing* (eds. L. W. Gregg and E. R. Steinberg), pp. 31–50. Lawrence Erlbaum, Hillsdale, New Jersey.

Fromkin, V. A. (ed.) (1980). *Errors in Linguistic Performance: Slips of the Tongue, Ear, Pen, and Hand.* Academic Press, New York.

Gass, W. (1979). *On Being Blue: A Philosophical Inquiry*. David R. Godine, Boston.

Goldman-Eisler, F. (1968). *Psycholinguistics: Experiments in Spontaneous Speech.* Academic Press, London.

Graves, D. L. (1975). 'An examination of the writing processes of seven year old children. *Research in the Teaching of English*, **9**, 227–41.

Graves, D. L. (1981). Writing research for the eighties: what is needed. *Language Arts,* **58**, 197–206.

Grimes, J. (1975). *The Thread of Discourse*. Mouton, The Hague.

Halliday, M. A. K. (19678). Notes on transivity and theme, Part 2, *Journal of Linguistics,* **3**, 199–244.

Halliday, M. A. K., and Hasan, R. (1976). *Cohesion in English*. Longman, London.

Hayes, J. R., and Flower, L. S. (1980). Identifying the organization of writing processes. In *Cognitive Processes in Writing* (eds. L. W. Gregg and E. R. Steinberg), pp. 3–30. Lawrence Erlbaum, Hillsdale, New Jersey.

Hotopf, N. (1980). Slips of the pen. In *Cognitive Processes in Spelling* (ed. Uta Frith), pp. 287–307. Academic Press, New York.

Hunt, K. (1965). *Grammatical Structures Written at Three Grade Levels*. National Council of Teachers of English, Urbana, Illinois.

Jones, L. K. (1977). *Theme in English Expository Discourse*. Jupiter Press, Lake Bluff, Illinois.

Kinneavy, J. L. (1971). *A Theory of Discourse*. Prentice-Hall, Englewood Cliffs, New Jersey.

Kroll, B. M. (1978). Cognitive egocentrism and the problem of audience awareness in written discourse. *Research in the Teaching of English,* **12**, 269–81.

Kroll, B. M., and Vann, R. J. (1981). *Exploring Speaking – Writing Relationships: Connections and Contrasts*. National Council of Teachers of English, Urbana, Illinois.

Kubie, L. S. (1958). *Neurotic Distortion of the Creative Process*. Noonday Press, New York.

Labov, W. (1972). *Language in the Inner City: Studies in the Black English Vernacular*. University of Pennsylvania Press, Philadelphia.

Larson, R. L. (1967). Sentences in action: a technique for analyzing paragraphs. *College Composition and Communication,* **18**, 16–22.

Matsuhashi, A. (1981). Pausing and planning: the tempo of written discourse production. *Research in the Teaching of English,* **15**, 113–34.

Matsuhashi, A. (1982). Explorations in the real-time production of written discourse. In *What Writers Know: The Language and Structure of Written Discourse* (ed. M. Nystrand). Academic Press, New York.

Miller, G. A., Galanter, E., and Pribram, K. H. (1960). *Plans and the Structure of Behavior*. Holt, Rinehart, & Winston, New York.

Moffett, J. (1968). *Teaching the Universe of Discourse*. Houghton Mifflin, Boston.

Moffett, J. (1981). *Active Voice*. Boynton/Cook, Montclair, New Jersey.

Neruda, P. (1978). *Memoirs*. Penguin, London.

Nold, E. W., and Davis, B. E. (1980). The discourse matrix. *College Composition and Communication,* **31**, 141–52.

Pitkin, Jr. W. (1977). X/Y: Some basic strategies of discourse. *College English,* **38**, 660–7.

Quirk, R., Greenbaum, S., Leech, G., and Svartvik, J. (1972). *A Grammar of Contemporary English*. Longman, London.

Rapaport, D. (1951). Toward a theory of thinking. In *Organization and Pathology of Thought* (ed. D. Rappaport), pp. 689–730. Columbia University Press, New York.

Rochester, S., and Martin, J. R. (1979). *Crazy Talk: A Study of the Discourse of Schizophrenic Speakers*. Plenum, New York.

Rubin, A. D. (1980). A theoretical taxonomy of the differences between oral and written language. In *Theoretical Issues in Reading Comprehension* (eds. R. J. Spiro, B. C. Bruce, and W. F. Brewer), pp. 411–38. Lawrence Erlbaum, Hillsdale, New Jersey.

Schank, R., and Abelson, R. (1977). *Scripts, Plans, Goals, and Understanding: An Inquiry into Human Knowledge Structures*. Lawrence Erlbaum, Hillsdale, New Jersey.

Searle, J. R. (1975). A taxonomy of illocutionary acts. In *Minnesota Studies in the Philosophy of Language* (ed. K. Gunderson), pp. 344–69. University of Minne sota Press, Minneapolis.

Siegman, A. W., and Feldstein, S. (eds.) (1979). *Of Speech and Time: Temporal Speech Patterns in Interpersonal Contexts*. Wiley, New York.

Singer, J. L. (1977). Ongoing thought: the normative baseline for alternate states of consciousness. In *Alternate States of Consciousness* (ed. N. E. Zinberg), pp. 89–120. Free Press, New York.

Smith, F. (1973). *Psycholinguistics and Reading*. Holt, Rinehart, & Winston, New York.

Smith, F. (1975). The relation between spoken and written language. In *Foundations of Language Development*, vol. II (eds. E. H. Lenneberg and E. Lenneberg), pp. 347–60. Academic Press, New York.

Stahl, A. (1977). The structure of children's compositions: developmental and ethnic differences. *Research in the Teaching of English*, **11**, 156–63.

Van Dijk, T. (1980). *Macrostructures: An Interdisciplinary Study of Global Structures in Discourse, Interaction, and Cognition*. Lawrence Erlbaum, Hillsdale, New Jersey.

Vygotsky, L. S. (1962). *Thought and Language*. Massachusetts Institute of Technology, Cambridge, Massachusetts.

Watson, C. (1979). The Effects of Maturity and Discourse Type on the Written Syntax of Superior High School Seniors and Upper Level College English Majors. Unpublished Doctoral Dissertation, State University of New York at Buffalo.

Winterowd, W. R. (1970). The grammar of coherence. *College English*, **21**, 828–35.

The Psychology of Written Language
Edited by M. Martlew

CHAPTER 2

Writing and Literal Meaning

DAVID OLSON AND ANGELA HILDYARD

The central problem in all uses of language, whether in speech or in writing, is the expression and recovery of meaning. Yet in spite of the obvious centrality of meaning to language, theoretical developments in the concepts of meaning in linguistics and philosophy have not been well integrated into a psychological theory, nor has the theory of meaning been sufficiently rich to account for the important differences in the management of meanings in oral and written language. The purpose of this chapter is to sketch out, and to support with some evidence, some of the distinctive properties of meaning in oral and written language, particularly the oral language of ordinary conversations and the written language of prose texts that are so fundamental to schooling.

Some of the differences in the structure of meanings of oral utterances and written texts are simple consequences of their occasions of use and the purposes to which they are put. Thus, oral conversational utterances tend to be hastily planned, casually employed, and express informal content. Written texts, on the other hand, tend to be planned carefully, used selectively, and to express formal bodies of knowledge.

These functions are not randomly assigned to these forms; it is reasonable to suppose that oral and written forms are differentially employed because they optimally serve a somewhat restricted set of functions. Vachek (1976) differentiated these functions:

> Written language is a system of signs which can be manifested graphically and whose function is to respond to a given stimulus (which as a rule is not urgent) in a static way, i.e. the response should be permanent (i.e. preservable), affording full comprehension as well as a clear survey of the facts conveyed, and stressing

> the intellectual side of the facts. On the other hand, spoken language is a system of signs that can be manifested acoustically and whose function is to respond to a given stimulus (which, as a rule, is urgent) in a dynamic way, i.e. the response should be quick, ready, and stressing the emotional as well as the intellectual side of the facts concerned (p. 121).

Furthermore, there are a series of mental activities that we apply almost exclusively to written texts rather than oral utterances; we study them, memorize them, learn from them, analyze, summarize, paraphrase, and evaluate them. These specialized activities are encouraged by the fact that writing provides a means for the preservation of language and that these preserved records serve as the primary archival form in a literate society.

The development of a written form not only preserves the language but, in so doing, it divorces the speaker from his utterance, thereby giving the language a life and a meaning of its own. We get some indication of the autonomy of written texts if we notice that we frequently talk as if texts had written themselves. Thus, while we ordinarily ask 'What did he/she mean?' we also apply the same predicates to written texts and ask 'What does it say?' or 'What does it mean?' In an earlier paper, Olson (1980) argued that the divorce of the speaker from his speech was the source of the authority of the written word. In this chapter we shall argue that the divorce is important to the development and use of a particular form of meaning, namely literal meaning. As we shall see, literal meaning has to do in part with what a text means rather than with what a speaker means by his text. But a full theory of literal meaning and its relation to written language requires that we examine more carefully what sentences mean, what speakers mean, and the nature of the context relating the two.

According to Webster, 'literal' means 'according to the letter or verbal expression; not figurative or metaphorical; following the letter or exact words; not free (a literal translation)'. Four aspects of this definition are noteworthy. Firstly, literal meanings have a special relation to the wording, the surface structure of language 'according to the letter or verbal expression'. That is, literal meanings imply or presuppose a device for the preservation of the very words, or as we shall say, for the preservation of what was said.

Secondly, literal meanings suggest a particularly close tie between the form of the expression and the intention expressed by that form, between what is 'said' and what is 'meant'. This relationship between what is said and what is meant is sometimes taken to be so direct that it bypasses the need for context in computing the speaker's meaning. Hence, such language has been referred to as decontextualized speech (Greenfield, 1972; Greenfield and Bruner, 1969), disembodied speech (Donaldson, 1978), or as language in which 'the meaning is in the text' (Olson, 1977). However, all of these descriptions are misleading in that if context is irrelevant, such meanings become equivalent to linguistic meaning. As we shall see, this assumption is not warranted. Hence although we wish to preserve the spirit of that distinction, we shall make it by specifying the various roles that context plays in determining *any* meaning, whether casual, literal, indirect, or metaphorical.

Thirdly, literal meanings have an obvious etymological relation to literacy. We may expect that literal meanings have some particular or favored relation to written language.

Finally, the definition of literal suggests that all three of these aspects are interdependent; that if one preserves the very words, one also preserves the literal meaning of those words and that the primary instrument for this preservation is written language. All of these assumptions deserve more careful scrutiny and their consideration forms the basis of this chapter.

THE PRESERVATION OF 'THE VERY WORDS'

Since literal meaning is presumed to depend upon the preservation of the very words, let us first consider what means are available for preserving the very words. The most fundamental means is to preserve the sentence surface structure in working memory during the course of understanding speech. Sachs (1967) and Jarvella (1971) have shown that the surface structure of an utterance is preserved in working memory until a meaning is assigned. Once meaning is assigned to a constituent, the exact words are dropped from memory, and a new constituent is assembled. Jarvella, for example, had people listen to a prose passage, interrupted them every so often, and asked them to write down as much of the immediately preceding passage as possible. The subjects tended to recall verbatim only the constituent on which they had been operating; the sentence preceding that constituent was recalled only as gist. The 'very words' were lost after processing and only the meanings were stored in long-term memory. Such meanings could, of course, be given expression but often in new words, that is, as gist. Bransford *et al*. (1972) also showed that in the recall of semantically related sentences, subjects are frequently unable to differentiate the sentences which were actually presented from those which expressed semantic relations implicit in those sentences. This same point is nicely illustrated in Seleskovitch's (1978) discussion of the processes involved in interpreting from one language to another at international conferences. She argues that it is impossible to translate directly from one language into another:

> Interpreting could never consist of a mere word-for-word translation from one language to another ... between the time the interpreter hears a message and the

> time he re-expresses it in another language, he must have carried out the essential process of analyzing its meaning (p. 84).

The verbatim surface structure of an utterance, then, is briefly stored in working memory during which time an analysis of the constituents must be completed. Secondary analysis or reanalysis of the sentence is difficult if not impossible. Hence problems of assigning alternative 'readings' for an oral utterance rarely arise. On the other hand, it is quite possible to re-examine the meanings which have been extracted long after the original sentence has been lost from working memory. Nonetheless, short-term memory is one means of preserving 'the very words', even if only for a brief period.

Is it ever possible to retain the surface structure for longer than this brief period? It would appear that there may indeed be some means, such as direct quotation and various oral mnemonic devices, including verse, song, and rehearsal. Let us examine these possibilities in more detail.

By the use of direct quotation the speaker purports to have preserved not only a set of meanings but also the surface structure of their expression. Moreover, speakers generally know when they are paraphrasing and when they are directly quoting, although there are frequent arguments both as to whether or not, in fact, *A* said '*x*' and if s/he did, whether or not s/he meant '*y*' and so on. Whether one preserves the very words or simply the gist may depend in part on the context. A politician will usually be very careful to preserve the very words because those words will determine both the implications and loopholes. Hence the secretary to presidential candidate Ronald Reagan had to offer the disclaimer: 'The Governor's words do not always reflect his total meaning' (*The Globe and Mail*, 27 February, 1980). In other social situations it may be more to the raconteur's advantage to preserve just some of the words. In most cases, however, memory for form appears to be tied to memory for meaning, and substantial parts of the surface structure may be lost, as this example shows:

> 'Get away from here, you dirty swine', she said.
> 'There's a dirty swine in every man', he said.
> 'Showing your face round here again', she said.
> 'Now, Mavis, now, Mavis', he said.
> She was seen to slam the door in his face, and he to press the bell, and she to open the door again.
> 'I want a word with Dixie', he said. 'Now, Mavis, be reasonable.'
> 'My daughter', Mavis said, 'is not in.' She slammed the door in his face.
>
> (Muriel Spark, 1963, p. 7)

[Later, Mavis retells the incident].

> 'You could have knocked me over', [Mavis] said. 'I was just giving Dixie her tea; it was, I should say, twenty past five and there was a ring at the bell. I said to Dixie, "Whoever can that be?" So I went to the door, and lo and behold there he was on the doorstep. He said, "Hallo," he said. I said, "You just hop it, you." He said, "Can I see Dixie?" I said, "You certainly can't," I said. I said, "You're a dirty swine. You remove yourself," I said, "and don't show your face again," I said. He said, "Come on Mavis." I said, "Mrs. Crewe to you," and I shut the door in his face.
>
> (Muriel Spark, 1963, p. 11)

We may note that the gist of the conversation is preserved and also many of the forms of expression, particularly the colorful ones, 'dirty swine', and so on. Yet, overall, the wording is altered somewhat, perhaps in order to enhance the status or role of the speaker, or perhaps because of limitations in memory. 'Get away from here, you dirty swine' becomes 'You're a dirty swine, remove yourself'. And 'Now, Mavis, now Mavis' becomes 'Come Mavis' and so on.

There are forms of language, though, where the surface structure and specific words form an indispensable component of the meaning – for example, the punch line of a joke, a well-timed retort, a command and the like. Several studies (e.g. Kintsch and Bates, 1977; Keenan *et al.* (1977); Bates, *et al.*, 1977) have shown that the delayed recall of these language forms may be quite robust. Kintsch and Bates (1977), for example, found that even after 5 days, subjects recalled the surface forms for jokes and asides even if they could not for topics and details. Kennan *et al.* (1977) found subjects were able to distinguish target sentences from true paraphrases for such forms as figures of speech, mock insults, and jokes. Bates *et al.* (1977) found that memory for surface form was particularly good for 'marked' forms; that is, those forms which are more informative or more novel. In addition, they suggested that surface form reflects pragmatic aspects of meaning rather than the more semantic or propositional aspects of meaning. Hence, surface form is more likely to be remembered in ordinary conversational language than in laboratory text. If meaning is construed broadly to include both pragmatic and logical components, then it is impossible to determine if the surface form is being generated from that underlying meaning or whether the surface form has in fact been stored. More sensitive recognition measures (Jacoby, 1979, personal communication) suggest that form is indeed preserved over substantial intervals. But again it is unlikely that such forms can be mentally scanned, or 're-read' as they would be if they were currently available in working memory or could be retrieved from a written document or long-term memory.

This memorability of certain forms of language has, of course, been picked up and exploited in sayings, aphorisms, proverbs, slogans, verse, song, and so on; yet another indication of the preservation of 'the very words'. As Havelock (1976) and others have shown, this memorability is at the basis of the oral tradition; an archival form which is particularly important in non-literate societies.

In oral societies, and to a lesser extent in our own, important cultural information is 'stored' for re-use in formalized speech including poetry and ritualized speech. These devices permit the recall of discourse structures much longer than a single expression, indeed sometimes of immense length. At first sight, such memory appears to preserve language verbatim, that is, on a word-by-word basis. More careful analysis has shown, however, that this is not the case. Lord (1960), Goody (1977), and Finnigan (1979) all found that the recall is not verbatim recall but reconstruction from a scheme or formula on each occasion of performance. Thus, if a transcription of the poem was made on two occasions, the two performances would not be identical although, to be sure, they might be extremely similar and thematically identical. Finnigan (1979) in her studies of oral poetry of the Limba of Sierra Leone, wrote:

> I discovered that when I was told that two stories were 'the same', this statement meant something other than that the exact words were the same. When I asked a Limba assistant to elucidate the words I could not catch fully while trying to transcribe taped stories, he could not be made to understand that I wanted the *exact* words on the tape. As far as he was concerned any comparable phrase with roughly the same meaning would do (p. 9).

Goody (1977) adds:

> ... exact repetition, as both Parry and Lord were well aware, seems more characteristic of the written transmission of written literature than the reproduction of oral verse. .... But even the most standardized segments of oral sequences never become so standardized, so formulaic, as the products of written man. Reproduction is rarely if ever verbatim (p. 118).

Long-term oral memory for language, then, is rarely word-for-word, verbatim memory; indeed, both Lord (1960) in his study of the oral poets of Yugoslavia and Goody (1977) in his study of the LoDagga and the Gonja noted that there was no word for *word*, but only for a 'bit of speech' which could apply equally to a sound, a morpheme, a sentence, or a theme. Further, Francis (1975) found that when children in our society first learn the word 'word' they use it to refer to a bit of print not a bit of speech.

As with direct quotation so, too, with other oral language devices. It seems that primarily the meaning is preserved along with some aspects of the surface structure of the expression. The extent of the preservation of the expression, whether key words or the entire utterance, depends upon the importance of those words to the particular meanings expressed. Rarely, if ever, do these oral devices preserve the words in a verbatim fashion. Indeed,

Goody (1977) has suggested that recall in an oral culture is better construed as reconstruction from a set of meanings by means of a set of formulas for generating expressions. Verbatim recall, on the other hand, is based upon the notion of an 'original', of which each reproduction is a 'copy', that original being stored somewhere in written form. Writing is an instrument *par excellence* for preserving 'the very words' and for making possible the re-reading and re-analysis of those words. Writing's somewhat unique power in preserving 'the very words' would explain, in part, writing's association with literal meaning. The other source of the association can be traced to written language's somewhat unique relation to context, the second assumption of literal meaning.

THE ROLE OF CONTEXT IN LITERAL MEANING

Let us turn now to the issue of the role played by context in literal meaning. Basic to traditional analyses of the role of context in literal meaning is Grice's (1957) theory of meaning intention. Following the linguistic convention of distinguishing sentences as linguistic objects from utterances of those sentences in particular contexts by particular speakers, Grice first differentiated the sentence meaning, the meaning that a sentence may have in any context, from the speaker's meaning, the meaning that the speaker intends to express by means of that sentence. Ordinarily, the sentence meaning is the conventional way of expressing a speaker's meaning. But, as Grice has shown, what the sentence means is often somewhat different from what a speaker intends by that sentence. This is particularly apparent in the case of indirect meaning or implicatures of which Grice (1975) has identified two forms, conversational implicatures and conventional implicatures.

To account for conversational implicatures, Grice introduced a set of Conversational Maxims which are used as guides by a listener and a speaker for the interpretation of any particular sentence in any particular context. The general principle, which Grice called the Co-operative Principle, stated: 'Make your conversational contribution such as is required, at the stage at which it occurs, by the accepted purpose of direction of the talk exchange in which you are engaged'. In being co-operative, speakers observe the following maxims:

Quantity:	Make your contribution as informative as required.
Quality:	Do not say what you believe to be false.
Relation:	Be relevant.
Manner:	Be perspicuous, that is, avoid obscurity, ambiguity, prolixity and incoherence.

These maxims, as suggested, inform a listener how to construct a speaker's meaning on the basis of sentence meaning and context. By means of the maxims, the listener may derive additional inferences which are determined neither by knowledge of context alone nor on the basis of the relation of that sentence to that context. These additional features are conversational implicatures. Thus, if the speaker says 'He's a fine friend' in the context of having been deserted, the sentence violates the Quality maxim, from which the listener may infer that the sentence is being used sarcastically. The speaker's meaning is in fact the opposite of the sentence meaning.

Karttunen and Peters (1975) have attempted to integrate the second type of implicature, conventional implicature, within the logical framework of model theoretic semantics. According to Grice, an implicatum is an implicature which is derived from what was said but is not logically entailed by that expression. Conventional implicatures are those implications which are derived from the choice of the specific words themselves. They are, Karttunen and Peters have suggested, equivalent to the pragmatic presuppositions which are induced by such words as *fail, manage, again, even*, and the like. To use one of Karttunen and Peters' examples, if a speaker says

(1) John managed to find a job.

he '... commits himself to the view that it isn't easy to find a job, or at least not easy for John'. In saying that sentence the speaker warrants the implicature that the job was difficult to find, although this is not what the speaker actually or literally said. Hence, even if the implicature is false, the speaker would not have said anything false. 'The truth of (1) depends solely on whether John actually found a job, the rest is a conventional implicatum to which the speaker commits himself by using the word *manage*' (p. 2). The boundary, however, may not be as strict as this. If, in fact, it was easy for John to find the job, then by uttering sentence (1), the speaker has uttered a sentence which is false. The speaker and the listener are aware that the word *manage* carried certain meanings and that these are implicated each time the word is used. Nonetheless, truth/falsity rests primarily on the truth of the complement.

Ordinarily these pragmatic presuppositions or conventional implicatures define the 'common ground' of discourse, 'the set of propositions that any participant is rationally justified in taking for granted' (p. 3). That is, conventional implicatures are not introduced by the sentence alone, but ordinarily are previously established as part of the common ground of the discourse; they are part of the *context* of the utterance.

Although the differentiation of what was meant (i.e., conventionally and/or conversationally implied) from what was said is critical to an analysis of literal meaning, it may lead to two tempting but incorrect theories of literal meaning. The first is that literal meaning is synonymous with sentence meaning (what was said) and so is its timeless, context-free linguistic meaning, the Fregean 'sense' of the sentence. But the literal meaning of a sentence cannot be the 'sense', for literal meaning is meaning in a particular context. Consider an argument between two children *A* and *B*:

(2) *A*: I'm bigger than you.
(3) *B*: I'm bigger than you.

These two sentences have the same linguistic meaning, or sentence meaning, or as we shall say later, they have the same semantic structure, but they have opposite literal meanings which we could express as:

A: bigger (*A*, *B*)
B: bigger (*B*, *A*)

The two sentences map into their contexts differently, they determine different truth-conditions and therefore they have different literal meanings.

The second possible, but incorrect, theory concerns the conflation of the verbatim memory of 'the very words' with the literal meaning of what was said. As we have seen, even literal meaning depends upon context, hence recall of the surface form of the language is not equivalent to the literal meaning. Yet the preservation of the very words, however briefly, is a necessary condition for the computation of literal meaning. Moreover, improving the preservation of the wording, as in the case of writing, may be critical to the computation of the literal meaning.

Two fairly recent approaches, one from speech act theory (Searle, 1975, 1979) and the other from model–theoretic semantics (Bierwisch, 1979), help to clarify the relationship between sentence meaning and speaker's meaning and the role of context in deriving one from the other. Searle (1975, 1979) calls upon the Gricean distinction of what is said from what is meant, to help account for two non-literal uses of language, metaphor, and indirect speech acts. In neither of these cases, Searle argues, does the literal meaning of the sentence correspond to what the speaker meant by the sentence. In the case of a metaphoric utterance, such as 'John is a chicken', a listener may know that John is not literally a chicken but rather has some of the secondary properties we associate with chickens, such as cowardice. And in the case of an indirect speech act, such as the teacher's comment 'Someone is talking', a child may know that the teacher is not merely describing a situation but requesting silence (Sinclair and Coulthard, 1975). However, in order to understand these indirect devices in which what was 'said' and what was 'meant' diverge, it is necessary to consider the case in which the relationship is more direct – that is, literal meaning.

Literal meaning, as we pointed out above, does not correspond to linguistic/sentence meaning, but rather to an utterance spoken by a particular individual in a particular context on a particular occasion in such a way as to determine a set of truth conditions. Searle, too, points out that some contextually dependent elements, which call attention to particular features of the context, are explicitly marked in the sentence in the form of indexical elements, definite descriptions, and the like. Background assumptions or knowledge of the world which is not marked in the semantic structure of the sentence may also form the basis for the determination of the set of truth conditions.

> Thus even in literal utterances, where speaker's meaning coincides with sentence meaning, the speaker must contribute more to the literal utterance than just the semantic content of the sentence, because that semantic content only determines a set of truth conditions relative to a set of assumptions made by the speaker, and if communication is to be successful, his assumptions must be shared by the hearer. (Searle, 1979, pp. 95–6).

That is, sentences have meanings *in contexts* and that interdependence of sentences and contexts in the determination of truth conditions is central to a theory of literal meaning. It is a relationship which has been spelled out in more detail in Bierwisch's (1979) model theoretic analysis of meaning.

Bierwisch is more explicit in his handling of sentence meanings, contexts or possible words, and speaker's meanings. He too begins his analysis by adopting the linguistic assumption that the semantic structure of a sentence is not to be identified with the meaning of the utterance of that sentence in a particular context. According to Bierwisch's view, an utterance meaning (including the reference of an expression) depends jointly on semantic structure (the sense of an expression) *and* the context. Furthermore, Bierwisch points out that the semantic structure generally fixes a set of semantic presuppositions, a set of conditions that a possible context must meet in order to yield an utterance meaning. We may note that this corresponds to Searle's (1979) point that the literal meaning of an utterance depends upon unexpressed knowledge of the world and to Karttunen and Peters' (1975) analysis of the common ground of a particular conversation or discourse. In the utterance (2) above, for example, the context must contain an addressee internally represented as the extension of the term 'You', a speaker internally represented as the extension of the term 'I', and *A* and *B* must actually possess some sizes which can be compared. These contexts or 'possible worlds', together with the sentence meaning, make up the utterance meaning (or speaker's meanings or speaker's intentions). If a possible world does not satisfy the semantic presuppositions of the sentence – that is, if the sentence does not have an appropriate context – no utterance meaning can be derived from it (p. 14). Bierwisch (1979) adds a final concept. Not only does he claim that an utterance meaning is a certain state of affairs belonging to a possible world, he suggests that 'an utterance is, in a sense, an instruction to modify a given context *W* [possible world] ... thus the thought expressed by an utterance is a change in the structure of a mental state' (p. 15).

We have therefore, three components in our analysis of meaning:

$$\text{(semantic structure)} + \text{(possible world)} \rightarrow \text{(meaning)}$$

Formally, a semantic structure is a function from a context into a set of truth conditions. For our purposes we may say that a sentence meaning is a function from a possible world into a speaker's meaning or intention, a state of affairs asserted as true by the speaker or requested by the speaker, and so on. These three components are all we will need for our consideration of literal meanings. The semantic structure (or linguistic form) is what is preserved in 'the very words'; the speaker's meaning (or intention or utterance meaning), is what the speaker attempts to express or communicate by means of that expression; and the route from the sentence to the speaker's meaning is the context or possible world.

Let us enlarge briefly on this last point. A context, in a traditional sense, is only roughly equivalent to a possible world. A context implies an actually occurring spatial and temporal state of affairs. A possible world, on the other hand, implies a set of presuppositions in terms of which a sentence is related to a meaning whether that set is physically given or only stipulatively assumed. A possible world, then, may in the normal case be the spatial and temporal context, but in other cases it may be an imagined, hypothetical or even counter-factual world. Kripke (1972) states: 'A possible world is given by the descriptive conditions we associate with it. ... Possible worlds are *stipulated*, not discovered by powerful telescopes' (p. 267). This is a somewhat stronger sense of possible world than that employed by Bierwisch (1979) and others, but it adds an important consideration. In the ordinary case the possible world is the known world based on assumed and shared perceptions, beliefs, feelings, and expectancies, and that possible world makes up the context which serves as the presuppositional basis of the sentences expressed. We will call this ordinary possible world *PW* (or sometimes simply the real or assumed world). In the extraordinary case, we are talking about possible worlds in the Kripke sense, that world specified by a set of stipulative descriptive conditions such as those represented by conditionals, counterfactuals, and so on. Kripke continues:

What do we mean when we say 'In some other possible world I might not have given this lecture today'? We just imagine the situation where I didn't decide to give this lecture or decided to give it on some other day. Of course, we don't imagine everything that is true or false, but only those things relevant to my giving the lecture; but, in theory, everything needs to be decided to make a total description of the world (p. 267).

As mentioned, such possible worlds are stipulated, and the semantic structure of the sentence is the principal, if not the only, means available for stipulating a possible world. That is, the context or possible world, *PW*, is created on hearing or reading the sentence rather than being simply given and being presupposed by the sentence. Such *stipulated* possible worlds are a special case of the nature of context *PW* in the construction of literal meaning.

What then is literal meaning? We have identified literal meaning with a speaker's meaning, not with a sentence meaning. Miller and Johnson-Laird (1976) make the same point: 'Perhaps we should say that there is no such thing as the literal meaning of a sentence, only the literal meaning that a given listener places on a given utterance of it' (p. 704). All understood meanings, literal or otherwise, are speaker's meanings. What then is special about literal meaning and why is it so closely related to written language?

Within the family of speaker's meanings, it is worth contrasting literal meaning with casual meaning as well as with such indirect meanings as indirect speech acts and metaphor. For casual meaning, as in ordinary conversational language, a sentence *S* is fitted into its context, *PW*, such that the properties of *PW* are taken as the presuppositions of *S* in computing the meaning *M*. The important property of casual meaning is that *PW* is taken as invariant and if the presuppositions of *S* happen not to correspond to the structure of *PW*, it is *S* which is transformed into *S′*, a gloss of *S* which does fit the structure of *PW*. In casual speech, then, the weight of interpretation falls on *PW* in determining the meaning *M*, thereby making allowance for some degree of vagueness and impression in *S*; any wording will do, a wink is as good as a nod, if *PW* is well established.

Literal meaning occurs only when *S* is taken as invariant in the computation of *M*. The clearest examples of literal meaning occur when the presuppositions of *S* do not correspond to *PW* and the listener/reader is required to construct a stipulated *PW* in which *S* could mean *M*. Literal meaning requires the preservation of *S* while *PW* is transformed into *PW′* in computing *M*.

Indirect speech acts and metaphorical speech result when both *S*, the semantic structure, and *PW* are incompatible but rather than transforming *S* or *PW*, they are both taken as invariant and *M* is altered or transformed into a marked form *M′*. To revisit Searle's example, if someone says:

(4) John is a chicken

S cannot be applied to *PW* to yield *M* because *S* violates *PW* the shared knowledge that John really (in *PW*) is a person. That is, *M* violates the Gricean maxim of quality, hence one must compute a new speaker's meaning *M*′, the metaphorical meaning that John is a coward.

Similarly if someone says:

(5) Your hand is on my knee

and *S* in fact corresponds to *PW*, the resulting *M* is true but redundant. Hence, it fails to respect the Gricean maxim of quantity. Again then one may derive a new meaning *M*′, the indirect meaning that the listener should remove her hand, and so on.

An additional comment on literal meaning is required. As Bierwisch (1979) pointed out, an utterance is an instruction to modify a possible world. In the simplest case the sentence applied to the given context *PW* adds to that context to produce *PW*′. And all sentences which are genuinely informative have just that effect; they add to our knowledge of the world or at least to the topic of conversation. But to transform *PW* into *PW*′ when *PW*′ is merely an increment of information in *PW* is vastly different from transformation of *PW* into *PW*′, when *PW*′ is a stipulated possible world determined by *S*, rather than presupposed by *S*. This latter occurs, for example, in dealing with counterfactual utterances, logical entailment, and the like which are the clearest cases of literal meaning and, as we have argued elsewhere, are the most closely associated with literate competence (Olson and Hildyard, 1980).

To summarize, we have examined the ways in which context is utilized in understanding sentences, or as we have put it, how sentences map contexts onto intentions. These alternative relations between sentences and contexts are summarized in Table 1. All meaning, *M*, assumes a context or possible world and a semantic structure; the important theoretical point in whether *S* or *PW* or both are taken as invariant in determining that meaning. In casual meaning the context *PW* is taken as invariant, and one glosses the semantic structure from *S* to *S*′ in order to compute a meaning *M*. A well-known example is Piaget's young subjects who, when faced with a collection of three ducks and two rabbits and asked: 'Are there more ducks or animals?' apparently gloss the question to the more regular form 'Are there more ducks or rabbits?' and answer 'More ducks.' Another example comes from Donaldson (1978) who discovered that when children were shown a

TABLE 1 Some relations of sentences and contexts in the determination of meaning

S	+	PW	→		M
Semantic structure or linguistic meaning or sentence meaning or sense		Knowledge of the world or knowledge of context or possible world			Intended meaning or speaker's meaning or utterance meaning or reference
Varieties of M					
Casual meaning.					
(*PW* is invariant)					
$S + PW \rightarrow M^*$					
$S \rightarrow S'$		Piaget:		S :	Are there more ducks or animals?
$S' + PW \rightarrow M$				$\rightarrow S'$:	Are there more ducks or rabbits?
		Donaldson:		S :	Are all the cars in the garages?
				$\rightarrow S'$:	Are all the garages full?
		Hildyard and Olson:			Red dots
					Does the picture show that the dots are not red?
		Adult:			No it doesn't.
		Children:			Yes they are.

Literal meaning. (S is invariant) $S + PW \rightarrow M^*$ $PW \rightarrow PW'$ $S + PW' \rightarrow M$	Are there more rabbits or animals? John is a chicken (Really).
Indirect speech act and metaphor. (S and PW are invariant) $S + PW \rightarrow M^*$ $M \rightarrow M'$ $S + PW \rightarrow M'$	John is a chicken. You have more than me. I hear talking.

collection of four cars, only three of which were in the garages, they apparently glossed the question 'Are all the cars in the garages?' into the simpler question 'Are all the garages full?' and answered 'Yes'.

We have frequently found the same transformation from S to S' in our own research. Hildyard and Hidi (in preparation) found that if pre-school children are told 'John forced Mary to eat the worm' and then asked 'Did Mary eat the worm?' they reply 'No.' When further questioned they justify their answer by saying 'Nobody eats worms.' That is, they gloss the semantic structure represented by the factive verb *forced* into some more neutral verb like *tried to get her to* in computing a meaning. They gloss S to S' and hence compute a casual meaning.

In another experiment (Hildyard and Olson, in preparation) pre-school children were shown a collection of red dots and asked: 'Does the picture show that the dots are red?' They correctly answered 'Yes' but when further questioned, they added 'Yes, *they* are' (i.e., Yes, the dots are red). Adults, on the other hand, when further questioned said 'Yes, *it* does' (i.e., Yes. The picture shows that). Children, apparently have transformed the question to S': 'Are the dots red?' The differences become more apparent when they are asked 'Does the picture show that the dots are not red?' Adults answer 'No'; children 'Yes'; when further questioned, adults say: 'No, *it* doesn't', children 'Yes, *they* are'. Clearly, children have disregarded the embedding construction, 'Does the picture show ...'. Both of these studies indicate they alter S to S' in the process of comprehension; they compute a casual meaning not a literal meaning.

In literal meaning, then, it is the semantic structure S which is taken as invariant and the context which is altered, either by adding some information to PW to produce PW', or by constructing a possible world having the properties stipulated by S, a stipulated PW. Piaget's questions, we suggest, require the construction of a stipulated PW in that the child must imagine a world other than that perceptually available, one in which there really are two disjoint collections, one of ducks and one of animals, which can then be compared. Or again, to understand the sentence 'John is a chicken' literally, one must imagine a world in which John really is a chicken (He appears to be a human being).

Finally, indirect speech acts and metaphor require that both the semantic structure S and PW are taken as invariant but some part of the co-operative principle is violated. In such cases the listener would preserve S and PW but compute a marked or indirect form of meaning. These indirect forms have been more carefully distinguished by Searle (1979) and will not be examined any more fully in this chapter.

The progressive development from casual to strictly literal meaning may help to clarify the stages children pass through in their comprehension and production of utterances. In the earliest stages the child may know *PW*, and know what a speaker intends, that is *M*, and on the basis of these two s/he may work out the semantic structure of *S*. Several writers have suggested that this is the means whereby a child learns the language (Olson, 1970; Macnamara, 1972; Nelson, 1974) although the point is often abbreviated to saying that the child knows the meaning intention and uses that meaning to crack the linguistic code or, even more elliptically, to say that the child uses the context to learn the language. From our perspective all three parts are relevant: a semantic structure, a possible world, and a meaning intention; and an adequate theory of language development will have to include, as aspects, a theory of the acquisition of linguistic structure *S*, a theory of knowledge of the world *PW*, and, most importantly, a theory of meaning intentions *M*. Meaning intentions are critical in that they are the only means for linking *S* to *PW*; that is for relating language and thought. Moreover, intentions are what are shared in the course of talk exchanges and the acquisition of linguistic structure is in the service of the expression and recovery of those intentions (Schlesinger, 1977). Finally, intentions regulate action as well as language, and so provide a common ground for cognitive processes.

At the earliest stages of language acquisition, then, the meaning intention, *M*, may be identified with the semantic structure. As the child becomes more sophisticated linguistically, which is to say that s/he has control over the various semantic (and pragmatic) structures of *S*, s/he can see that, in certain contexts, certain meanings can be expressed by, and only by, certain semantic structures. Neither of these cases, however, provide clear evidence for literal meaning that is the use of *S* to alter *PW* to *PW'*. That is, earliest utterances appear to be redundant with their contexts rather than informative.

Later, we find increasingly clear indications of the comprehension and expression of literal meanings as children come to regard *PW* as no longer simply invariant, and begin to use utterances to add information to *PW* if that information is compatible with *PW* or can be anticipated on the basis of their knowledge of *PW*. Finally, children not only revise *PW* on the basis of *S* but can imagine a possible world stipulated by *S* and in which *S* could literally mean *M*. That is, when the child can hold the semantic structure *S* and operate upon *PW* to produce a possible world *PW'* in order to recover the meaning *M* literally intended by the speaker, we have clear evidence of the child's comprehension of literal meaning *M* of *S*.

But note that such operations require the preservation of *S*, the semantic structure expressed by 'the very words' and writing is the primary means for the preservation of *S*. This brings us to the third aspect of our definition of literal meaning.

LITERAL MEANINGS AND LITERACY

We noted at the outset that literal meaning was a meaning directly associated with the very words and that it therefore involved a particular relation to context. That relation was not, as we may have expected, a decontextualized meaning, a meaning independent of context; rather it was the intended meaning *M* of *S* in either a pre-established *PW* or in a stipulated *PW*. But it was a meaning that preserved the linguistic form of *S* without adding to, subtracting from, or otherwise altering *S* in the process of constructing that meaning. The only guarantee of the constructions of a literal meaning of *S* therefore is a device for preserving *S*. At the outset we noted that short-term memory was one, if temporary, device. Writing is an ideal device for the preservation of *S*, hence we have the conceptual basis for the putative relationship between writing and literal meaning.

Writing not only preserves *S* temporarily, for as long as it takes to construct a literal meaning *M*. It preserves *S* even after *M* is constructed. With written text, *S* is no longer simply a means to *M*. It is a structure in its own right. It thereby becomes a subject of study for linguists who are primarily interested in the study of the structure of *S*. But does its preservation in writing alter the comprehension and production processes of ordinary, now literate, language users.

We have already mentioned one way; writing preserves *S* long enough for the revision of *PW* or the stipulation of *PW* to occur. *S* is not so conveniently transformed to *S′* if *S* is preserved in writing; and with development and with increased linguistic sophistication children become increasingly adapt in constructing such possible worlds. Indeed, it may be the case that an elaborate linguistic system, that is a more elaborate and systematic knowledge of the linguistic structures *S*, is more important to the construction of literal meaning than the presence of a written record. Reading, more so than listening, does seem to have a systematic tendency to lead comprehenders to differentiate what a text means from what it in fact said (Hildyard and Olson, 1982). But even more important is the comprehender's knowledge of the syntactic and lexical options available in *S*. Clearly, a primary determinant of the construction of a literal meaning *M* is the listener's knowledge of linguistic form.

But there is a second way. As *S* is preserved even beyond the construction of *M*, it becomes possible to differentiate what was *said, S,* from what is *meant, M*. Moreover, as we noted at the outset it becomes possible to ask not only what a person *meant* but also what the sentence *meant*; to differentiate sentence meaning from speaker's meaning. That is, not only does it become possible to compute an appropriate literal meaning *M* of *S* on certain occasions, it becomes possible to compare what the sentence literally means with what a person means by *S* on that particular occasion. These two things are rarely identical, and never consistently identical in ordinary discourse. Ordinary speakers, like Reagan, seldom say precisely what they mean: they hint, insinuate, say the opposite of what they mean, more than they mean, less than they mean, in ordinary oral discourse. Speakers depend upon context and shared intentionality to get their meanings across. But as a consequence, oral discourse is a mixture of casual, literal and indirect meanings. The power and challenge of writing is that it permits one to systematically work out a consistent set of relations between sentence meaning *S* and speaker's meaning *M*.

The consistent relations between semantic structures and intended meaning we may call a *style*. Once a speaker or writer can compute both what a sentence means and what he or she means by a sentence on any particular occasion, these two sets of meanings may be consistently related to manage some particular style such as that distinctive style we associate largely with literacy and schooling, the written logical prose of the textbooks and encyclopedias. Its distinctive property is that the intended meaning *is* the literal meaning of *S*.

The power of literal meaning, as we have seen, is its ability to stipulate a possible world which serves as its context for comprehension. Unlike ordinary oral discussion, which simply appeals to a previously established possible world for its presuppositional base, the context may be constructed through the text. Such text is therefore an ideal device for the acquisition and expression of new knowledge and new points of view, and that, in fact, is the primary role that it plays in schooling. But as such text depends less upon a previously established and shared *PW*, the weight of the meaning *M* falls upon the semantic structure *S*. Hence, such texts assume a greater knowledge of linguistic structure even while they assume less prior knowledge of *PW*. Indeed the emphasis on *S*, in literal meaning, not only assumes an elaborated knowledge of *S*; the attempt at management of literal meanings is also the occasion for the learning of, and elaboration of, *S*. As the burden of meaning *M* falls upon *S* in written prose text, more specialized structures are required in *S*. Historically, we see just such an elaboration of *S* through the widespread borrowing from French and Latin that occured in seventeenth-century English. Obviously, reading and writing such text is decisive in the radical elaboration of children's semantic structures that occur during the school years.

THE MANAGEMENT OF MEANING IN ORAL AND WRITTEN LANGUAGE

We have seen that literal meanings, meaning in which the structure of *S* is treated as invariant and *PW* is revised or created by stipulation in the construction of the speaker's intended meaning, may occur in either oral or written discourse as long as some device for the preservation of linguistic form is preserved long enough to construct that meaning. short-term memory is ordinarily adequate for that purpose, but if *S* is complex or if *M* is unusual or if *PW* must be constructed rather than retrieved, short-term memory may be inadequate and writing, a device for preserving *S*, may be required. Hence, written language is particularly suitable for the management of literal meaning.

More importantly, writing preserves *S* even after *M* is constructed, and both what the sentence means and what a speaker meant by it become subject to scrutiny and comparison. In this way one can come to argue with him or her self over text. Incidentally, this awareness is one that develops about the time children learn to read (Robinson *et al.* in preparation). Sentence meanings and speaker's meanings are not merely different but, as we have seen, may be related in a distinctive way to yield a particular style of discourse. One such style is that of literal prose text in which the attempt is made to make the meaning of the sentences equivalent to the authors' intended meaning. It is with the comprehension and production of such text, in which the burden of the meaning falls upon the semantic structure, that children become skilled during the school years. It is in learning to write effectively that these requirements are most critical. Hence, we shall conclude with some discussion of the difficulties in writing literal prose text.

LEARNING TO SAY AND WRITE WHAT YOU MEAN IN LITERAL PROSE

There are several problems that arise in the expression and recovery of meaning in writing that warrant some comments. First, the common ground of discourse, *PW*, which is shared by interlocutors in speech, is not so readily shared in writing. In oral conversational language, interlocutors usually have some shared personal knowledge both of situations and of each other, minimally the knowledge based upon personal appearance and on the common spatial and temporal context. Even before schooling, children show some sensitivity to the need for this common ground of discourse, both in their ability to talk to different listeners in somewhat different ways (Shatz and Gelman, 1973) and in describing events differently depending upon whether or not their listener has had some prior knowledge of the event (Menig-Peterson, 1975). It is not clear if children talk differently to an individual than to a group or audience, a skill certainly relevant to writing. Yet the problem of constructing a common ground is much more serious in writing in that the author may have no personal knowledge of the reader(s) and the written word may be read in a different spatial–temporal context than that in which it was written.

Linguistically, this altered context is marked by the decrease in deictic expressions, expression which take their meanings from the immediate context: this, that, there, here, there and the like (Tannen, 1982). As a consequence, written text requires a special procedure for establishing a common ground of discourse, and that procedure, as we pointed out earlier, is largely through the semantic structure of the sentence.

The unusual burden which, in writing, falls upon the semantic structure in the formation of utterance meaning entails a second requirement for effective writing. Because of the more limited assumptions that may be made about context, the meanings or intentions expressed and/or recovered depend more critically upon the sentences involved. Whereas in casual speech the weight may fall upon *PW* in the construction of meaning, in written text it falls upon *S*. The text becomes, in a sense, its own context. Rather than simply presuppose a shared common world of discourse, that world has to be established stipulatively through sentences. To put this point another way, since the writer cannot assume that mere mention will serve to retrieve the relevant known people and events which will then serve as the ground for the discourse, those utterances will have to be used to *construct* a common presuppositional ground for the subsequent discourse. Conventionalized means for establishing such a ground include the provision of a setting, a topic sentence, a title or the like. In writing, then, the ground is often constructed rather than presupposed.

The third demand imposed in writing effectively follows from the second. Since the sentences in a written text must both provide an adequate recipe for the construction of a given and shared presuppositional base and since the primary, if not the exclusive, means of constructing the meaning of discourse comes from the sentences, those sentences have to be chosen and edited sufficiently to provide an unambiguous and adequate ground for the construction of that intended meaning. To meet such requirements sentences must be sufficiently precise and unambiguous to permit almost any reader to construct essentially the same meaning.

Admittedly some forms of writing rely more heavily upon the semantic structures of the sentences in the specification of their meanings than do others. Personal letters about prearranged topics may be almost as elliptical in writing as speech, because the shared presuppositional base *PW* contributes substantially to the meaning; but as writing assumes the more educational and intellectual functions that weight falls primarily upon the semantic structures. For semantic structures to serve this primary role in the construction of meaning, two further demands must be met. First, written utterances must 'mean what they say'; that is the sentence meaning in the shared world *PW* must be an adequate representation of the speaker's meaning. As we have pointed out repeatedly, the semantic structure is never in and of itself an adequate ground for the expression or recovery of intended meaning. Sentences have meaning only in a possible world. But for written texts that possible world is not known or shared *a priori*, it is constructed on the basis of the semantic structures. Hence, assumed knowledge of the world cannot be taken as an adequate ground for the disambiguation of ambiguous sentences. The writer has to judge whether or not it would be possible to 'read' the sentence any other way. In our terms the writer's additional test is whether there is another plausible possible world in which *S* could mean something other than what the writer intends; the writer must compare what the sentence means with what he as a writer means by it. If they are discrepant the utterance must be reformulated to exclude that alternative. Although one can never exclude all possible grounds for misinterpretation, failure to exclude the most probable ones leads to the humorous ambiguities found, for example, in one insurance company's accident report form; 'The guy was all over the road. I had to swerve a number of times before I hit him'.' (Tannen, 1982). Knowing the situation, and knowing that people usually attempt to avoid accidents, most readers could compute the speaker's intended meaning. Yet one could, without violating the semantic structure, construct another possible world in which the writer attempted to hit the other car and hence derive an alternative, literal, meaning for the sentence. In writing, then, it is not enough to find a semantic structure which in a presupposed but unstipulated context could yield the intended meaning. Rather, the semantic structure must be chosen, edited, and revised such that in conjunction with the shared world of discourse, constructed at least in part stipulatively, it yields the speaker's intended meaning. Writing, therefore, both allows and requires more care in planning and in revision than does speaking.

A further implication of the burden that falls upon the semantic structures relative to the context in written language is that it becomes critical that the rules of syntax and the meanings of words are shared between the speaker and writer. Unlike spoken language, these conventions cannot be negotiated on a direct interpersonal basis because, in school-like prose at least, it is uncertain who the readers are and what meanings they will attribute to the words involved. In such cases, therefore, it is necessary to establish some standard, or court of appeal, such as teachers and dictionaries, to adjudicate the meanings of expressions. Hence, in learning to write, a child is being inducted into the norms and standards of the larger society and its institutions.

Finally, not only is the writer working out a particular relation between a sentence meaning and an intended meaning in a particular case; he or she must adopt and maintain a consistent relation between sentence and intention throughout the text. That is, the text must have a consistent style.

We have perhaps overemphasized the discontinuity between speaking and writing. Although written text provides a primary case of meaning in which the weight falls primarily upon conversationalized semantic structures, it is by no means the only case. Story telling and story understanding, reporting unusual experiences to strangers, and the like would call upon many of the same processes that are required in writing. But the deployment of linguistic means for the construction of a presuppositional base which will permit the appropriate interpretation of a sentence, the appropriate formulation of a semantic structure which in conjunction with that stipulated presuppositional base specifies the intended meaning, the detection and revision of that semantic structure such that there is no plausible alternative possible world in which that semantic structure could have a meaning substantially different from the intended one, and the mastery of conventional forms for the representation of various intentions, these are all skills which are extensively recruited in writing and which, as a consequence, make written language one of our highest cultural achievements.

ACKNOWLEDGMENT

We are indebted to the Spencer Foundation for their financial support.

REFERENCES

Bates, E., Masling, M., and Kintsch, W. (1977). Recognition memory for aspects of dialogue. *Program on Cognitive Factors in Human Learning and Memory Report No. 69*. University of Colorado, Institute for the Study of Intellectual Behavior, Boulder, Colorado.

Bierwisch, M. (1979). Utterance, meaning and mental states. Mimeo.

Bransford, J. D., Barclay, J. R., and Franks, J. J. (1972). Sentence memory: a constructivist versus interpretive approach. *Cognitive Psychology,* **3**, 193–209.

Donaldson, M. (1978). *Children's Minds*. Fontana/Collins Co. Ltd., Glasgow.

Finnigan, R. (1979). Literacy and literature. Mimeo.

Francis, H. (1975). *Language and Childhood: Form and Function in Language Learning*. Paul Elek, London.

Goody, J. (1977). *The Domestication of the Savage Mind*. Cambridge University Press, Cambridge.

Greenfield, P. (1972). Oral and written language: the consequences for cognitive development in Africa, the United States, and England. *Language and Speech*, 169–78.

Greenfield, P., and Bruner, J. S. (1969). Culture and cognitive growth. In D. A. Goslin (ed.), *Handbook of Socialization: Theory and Research*. Rand-McNally, Chicago.

Grice, H. P. (1957). Meaning. *Philosophical Review,* **66**, 377–88.

Grice, H. P. (1975). Logic and conversation. In P. Cole and J. L. Morgan (eds.), *Syntax and Semantics*. Vol. 3: *Speech Acts*. Academic Press, New York.

Havelock, E. (1976). *Prologue to Greek Literacy*, Ontario Institute for Studies in Education Press, Toronto.

Hildyard, A. and Hidi, S. *Children's Comprehension of Factive Verbs*. In preparation.

Hildyard, A., and Olson, D. Forms of comprehension of written text. In W. Otto (ed.) *Reading Expository Materials*. In preparation.

Hildyard, A. and Olson, D. (1982). On the comprehension and memory of oral versus written discourse. In D. Tannen (ed.), *Spoken and Written Discourse*. Ablex, Hillsdale, New Jersey.

Jarvella, R. J. (1971). Syntactic processing of connected speech. *Journal of Verbal Learning and Verbal Behavior,* **10**, 409–16.

Karttunen, L., and Peters, S. (1975). *Conventional Implicature in Montague Grammar*. Presented at the First Annual Meeting of the Berkeley Linguistic Society, 15 February. Berkeley, California.

Keenan, J., MacWhinney, B., and Mayhew, D. (1977). Pragmatics in memory: a study of natural conversation. *Journal of Verbal Learning and Verbal Behavior*, **16**, 549–60.

Kintsch, W., and Bates, E. (1977). Recognition memory for statements from a classroom lecture. *Journal of Experimental Psychology: Human Learning and Memory*, **3**, 150–68.

Kripke, S. A. (1972). Naming and necessity. In D. Davidson and G. Harman (eds.), *The Semantics of Natural Language*. D. Reidel, Dordrecht, The Netherlands.

Lord, A. B. (1960) *The Singer of Tales*. (Harvard Studies in Comparative Literature, 24). Harvard University Press, Cambridge, Mass.

Macnamara, J. (1972). The cognitive basis of language learning in infants. *Psychological Review,* **79**, 1–13.

Menig-Peterson, C. L. (1975). The modification of communicative behavior in pre-school aged children as a function of the listener's perspective. *Child Development,* **46**, 1015–1018.

Miller, G. A., and Johnson-Laird, P. N. (1976). *Language and Perception*. Cambridge University Press.

Nelson, K. (1974). Concept, word and sentence. Interrelations in acquisition and development. *Psychological Review,* **81**, 267–85.

Olson, D. (1980). On the language and authority of textbooks. *Journal of Communication,* **30**, 186–98.

Olson, D. R. (1970). Language and thought: aspects of a cognitive theory of semantics. *Psychological Review,* **71** (4), 257–73.

Olson, D. R. (1977). From utterance to text: the bias of language in speech and writing. *Harvard Educational Review,* **47**, 257–81.

Olson, D. R., and Hildyard, A. (1980). Literacy and the comprehension of literal meaning. Paper presented at the conference on The development and use of writing systems. Bielefeld, Germany, 19–22 June.

Robinson, E., Goelman, H., and Olson, D. Some cognitive consequences of differentiating said from meant. In preparation.

Sachs, J. S. (1967). Recognition memory for syntactic and semantic aspects of connected discourse. *Perception and Psychophysics,* **2**, 437–42.

Schlesinger, I. M. (1977). *Production and Comprehension of Utterances*. Erlbaum Associates, Hillsdale, New Jersey.

Searle, J. (1975). Indirect speech acts. In P. Cole and J. Morgan (eds.), *Syntax and Semantics, vol. 3: Speech Acts*. Academic Press, New York.

Searle, J. (1979). *Expressions and Meaning: Studies in the Theory of Speech Acts*. Cambridge University Press.

Seleskovitch, D. (1978). *Interpreting for International Conferences: Problems of Language and Communication*. Pen and Booth, Washington.

Shatz, M., and Gelman, R. (1973). The development of communication skills: modifications in the speech of young children as a function of listener. *Monographs of the Society for Research in Child Development,* **38** (152).

Sinclair, J. M., and Coulthard, R. M. (1975). *Towards an Analysis of Discourse: The English used by Teachers and Pupils*. Oxford University Press, London.

Spark, M. (1963). *The Ballad of Peckham Rye*. Penguin Books, New York.

Tannen, D. (1982). Spoken and written language and the oral/literate continuum. In D. Tannen (ed.), *Spoken and Written Discourse.* Ablex, New Jersey.

Vachek, J. (1976). *Selected Writings in English and General Linguistics*. Mouton, The Hague.

Note: The first part of this paper is adapted from 'Literacy and the comprehension of literal meanings' to be published in F. Coulmas and K. Ehlich (eds.), *Writing in Focus,* Mouton, The Hague, in press.

The Psychology of Written Language
Edited by M. Martlew

CHAPTER 3

The Development of Evaluative, Diagnostic, and Remedial Capabilities in Children's Composing

MARLENE SCARDAMALIA AND CARL BEREITER

In this chapter we discuss the results of a novel experimental procedure for investigating children's composing processes. The study to be reported examines how various cognitive processes interact during evaluation and revision. These processes include (1) language production, (2) evaluation, (3) tactical decisions (such as whether to delete or rewrite), and (4) executive control of the overall process (allocating resources to the various subprocesses and switching from one to another). Although the study deals only with what we shall call the CDO (COMPARE, DIAGNOSE, OPERATE), part of the composing process, it has general implications for understanding children's competencies and limitations in composition.

The procedure used in this study was designed to illuminate parts of the composing process that generally do not emerge from darkness under the searchlight of thinking-aloud protocol analysis. Applying the latter technique to adults, Flower and Hayes (1979) find, for instance, that novice writers do not 'pop up' from text generation to higher levels of evaluation or planning as frequently as expert writers do. Why not? There are several possibilities. Novices may not know that 'popping up' is a good thing to do. This would indicate a deficient, or at least a different, composing strategy. Another possibility is that higher-level considerations are avoided because novices lack the rhetorical knowledge that would make them fruitful. Still another possibility is that some people may know that 'popping up' is a good thing, and possess the necessary rhetorical knowledge, yet fail to do it when their attention is absorbed with lower-level text generation problems. This would indicate a difficulty in executive control. Thinking-aloud protocols generally do not allow for deciding among these possibilities because revealing the necessary information would involve subjects in 'thinking about their thinking', something which is (for good reason) discouraged in protocol analysis. Furthermore, such clues as may come out of the protocols of adults are rarely to be found in the protocols of children, which tend to be sparse in anything other than content generation.

When we set out on the present line of investigation it seemed to us that the key requirement for studying what children could and could not do in composition was to find ways of regulating or circumventing problems in executive control. We saw writing as a very complex activity in which the child could not possibly attend to all its requirements simultaneously (Scardamalia, 1981). Attention to one thing means neglect of another, and so one can never be sure that the child's failure to do something in writing indicates a lack of competence. It may merely reflect an inability to direct cognitive resources to that aspect of writing when it is needed. This is particularly true of the higher-level concerns of writing such as the formulation of plans and goals, attention to audience, and evaluation. The lower-level concerns involved in generating text and getting it down on paper are necessarily pre-emptive. If they are ignored, nothing gets written. If they take up all the child's resources, then the higher-level concerns will not be dealt with, even though the child might have the competence to handle them if he were not burdened by the other concerns also.

Problems of executive control might be thought of as a kind of hobble, analogous to that placed on a horse so that movement of one limb interferes with movement of another. If one wished to study the horse's ability to jump, gallop, canter, etc., one would first wish to remove the hobble. Inferences based on how well the horse could perform these feats while hobbled would be risky. In children, the hobble of executive control is part of their psychological system and cannot simply be removed. Furthermore, it is not irrelevant to their other abilities. Limited attentional capacity is an outstanding characteristic of the human information-processing system and all our skills and strategies, if they are to be effective, must be adapted to this central capacity limitation. In other words, we must learn our jumping, galloping, and cantering in such a way that we can do them while hobbled. But in order to understand the development of writing abilities, and even to understand the constraints that may be placed on them by limitations in executive control, we need to have ways of manipulating that factor.

We tried to do this by using the technique of 'procedural facilitation' (Bereiter and Scardamalia, 1981; Scardamalia and Bereiter, 1980). This consists of designing and teaching children a simplified executive routine that requires fewer attentional resources while nevertheless allowing the child's system of production to remain essentially intact. By reducing the resource demands of the executive, the procedure may permit under-lying competencies to appear. The procedure is seen as useful for assessing such competencies and for inferring the effect of executive limitations on normal 'hobbled' performance.

In this study, the technique was applied to facilitating an important sub-process of composition which we call the CDO process (COMPARE, DIAGNOSE, OPERATE). Figure 1 is a diagrammatic representation of this process as we currently conceive of it. The CDO process is, of course, a theoretical, not an observed, entity. While the whole experiment to be reported is based on the model shown in Figure 1, it does not presuppose the validity of this model. Rather, the experiment, among other things, serves as a check on the model's fit to reality.

During the course of composition, two kinds of mental representations are built up and stored in long-term memory. These are a representation of the text as written so far, and a representation of the text as intended, which includes the whole text, not just parts already written. The CDO process is initiated by a perceived mismatch between these two representations.

We conceive of the CDO process as an interruption to other composing processes, so that it ends with a return to the interrupted process, whatever that might be (reading, planning, generating, etc.). Figure 1 does not show how the process starts, how the initial comparison between written and intended text is instigated. That is a matter of considerable uncertainty, and one that is by-passed in the present investigation by using a facilitating procedure that routinely starts the process.

The model in Figure 1 is a simple feedback loop, similar to a TOTE unit (Miller *et al.*, 1960). When COMPARE detects a mismatch, attention shifts to DIAGNOSE, which may involve search of the text and a search of rhetorical knowledge stored in long-term memory for a possible cause of the detected mismatch. One possible outcome of diagnosis is a decision to alter intentions rather than to alter the text. In terms of the present model, this means exiting from the CDO process. A more elaborate model could incorporate not only this route to resolving the mismatch but also the more complex possibility of a 'negotiated settlement' in which both the actual and the intended text are altered. Figure 1 traces the more common and simple route by which the text alone is altered in order to remove a perceived mismatch with intentions. The OPERATE phase has two components. In CHOOSE TACTIC, a general kind of text change is elected, such as changing wording, deleting, or adding on. The writer may also elect to leave things as they are and exit here, but if the tactic chosen involves revision, the writer will move on to the GENERATE CHANGE phase, where a specific enactment of

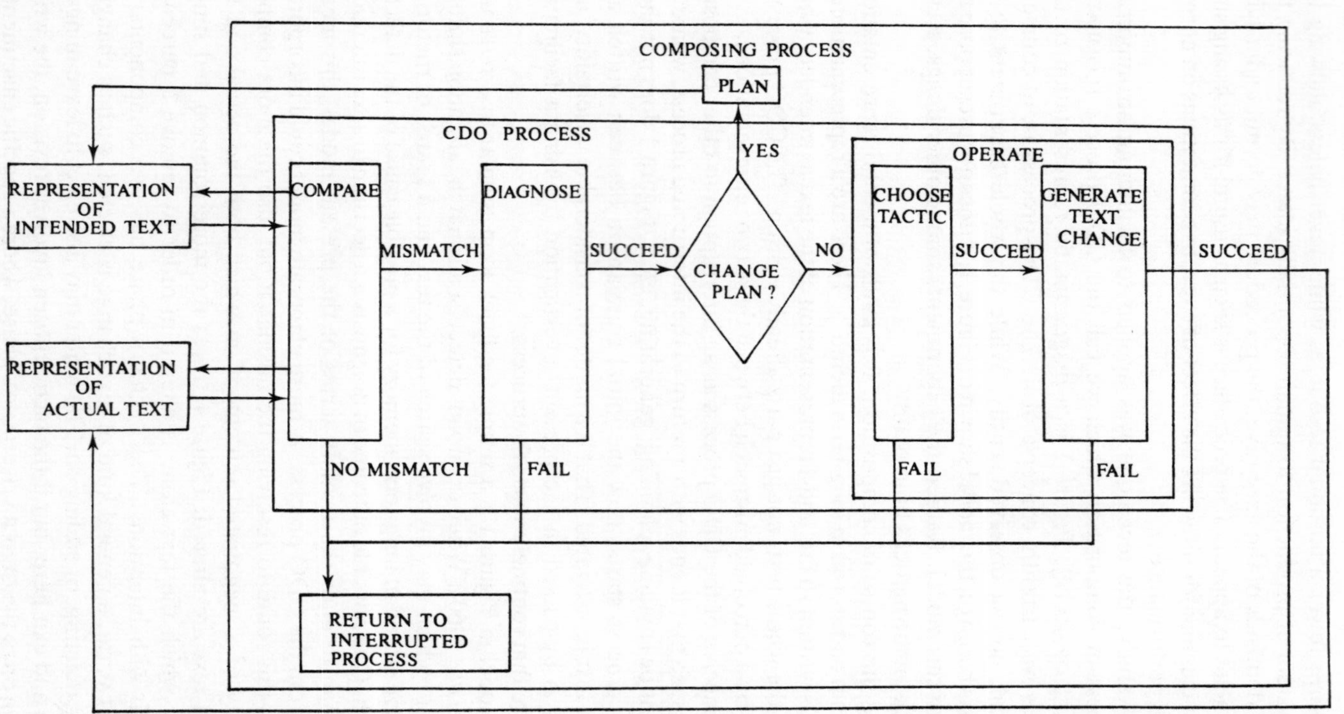

FIGURE 1 Model of the CDO (COMPARE, DIAGNOSE, OPERATE) process in composition

the chosen tactic is made. This leads to a modified text representation, and a new COMPARE, which leads to a new CDO cycle. The process keeps cycling until either removal of the mismatch or a failure at some point causes control to return to the interrupted process.

The model obviously purports to show what goes on in revision, but we do not refer to it as a model of the revision process for several reasons. A major reason is that 'revision' refers to something that happens to a text, and we want to keep it clear that what we are studying here is a cognitive process, and that when we examine texts it is because of what they may show about cognitive processes. Also, it is important to keep in mind that the CDO process may go on even though revision does not occur. The process may fail to result in the text being changed for a number of reasons. It may also result in text changes that we would not normally call revisions. The latter occurs if a CDO process is initiated during original composition and the chosen tactic for removing the mismatch is to take care of the problem through what is written next, rather than alter existing text.

Children notably do very little revision, and what they do usually consists of minor changes to conform to conventional usage (Nold, 1981). It therefore seemed that the CDO process might be a fertile object of inquiry in trying to understand the development of writing competence, and particularly the interaction of competence and performance factors. Children's weaknesses in revision have often been attributed to an inability to see their texts from the reader's or an objective point of view (Kroll, 1978). This would imply a defect in the COMPARE stage of the CDO process, such that other parts of the process never get activated. But the problem could as well lie elsewhere; in the inability to diagnose, in poor choice of tactics, or in a failure to generate adequate remedies. On the other hand, it could be that the problem is not with elements of the process at all, but in organizing those elements and in incorporating the CDO sub-process as a whole into the larger composition process. The problem, in other words, could be a problem of executive control. Children might have the necessary competence to carry out the CDO process but they cannot, in a sense, *afford* to do so, because the executive burden might be too great and would threaten to disrupt the whole composing process.

Research into these intriguing possibilities is normally hampered by the invisibility of the CDO process. In this study the procedural facilitation used had the dual function of lessening the executive burden of implementing the CDO process while producing an observable trace of its main stages. When used during original composition the procedure went like this: after writing a sentence, the child selected one of eleven possible evaluations that best characterized the preceding unit of text. This task corresponded to COMPARE in the process model. The child then had to explain orally how the evaluation applied (DIAGNOSE). Following this, the child chose one of six directives indicating possible tactics to employ (CHOOSE TACTIC). These tactics ranged from leaving things as they were, to adding more information, to scrapping a sentence and writing a new one. Unless the child elected to leave things, this step was followed by some alteration of the written text (GENERATE REVISION). This procedure was repeated as each additional sentence of text was produced.

For simplicity, we shall call this the Alternating Procedure. The name highlights its main facilitating feature. Instead of leaving the CDO process to occur spontaneously, sporadically, or perhaps not at all, it occurred in a regular way, alternating with text generation, and keyed to sentence endings. Movement from step to step within the process was also part of the routine, and the executive burden was further reduced by limiting COMPARE and CHOOSE TACTIC to finite choices rather than leaving them as open-ended tasks that might entail heavy processing loads in their own right.

There are two ways in which the experimental procedure falls short of fully representing the process depicted in Figure 1. First, the CDO process as represented there is an iterative process that may go through several cycles before a particular mismatch is removed. In the present study, in order to keep children's working time within a reasonable limit, the children went through only one cycle at each step. At the end of the chapter, however, we shall mention interesting preliminary findings about what happens when children try successive CDO cycles.

The second limitation has to do with the level of mismatches dealt with. The CDO process is conceived of as a very general one that may respond to any kind of perceived mismatch from a doubtful spelling to a general feeling that an essay is not turning out right. There is no assurance, of course, that a person will have equal competence in handling mismatches at all levels. That will depend, among other things, on the availability of relevant rhetorical knowledge. To keep the scope of the present study within reasonable limits we focused on a range of mismatch possibilities that was above the level children were known to attend to and yet not at such a high level that it might be altogether baffling to them. Therefore, we excluded evaluation cues at the level of mechanics (spelling, punctuation, etc.) and concentrated on relatively simple considerations of appropriateness, coherence, and audience response.

The Alternating Procedure may be thought of as a reduced and somewhat simplified *working* model of the CDO process. It is simpler than the conceptual model shown in Figure 1, which in turn, as we have noted, is simpler than we believe the actual process to be. Simplifications of this kind are inevitable in theoretical research and they are most pronounced in the early stages of theory development, where first approximations are being sought. The trick, always, is to introduce simplifications that will highlight main principles and to avoid simplifications that nullify them. In a field as little developed as writing research, it is hard to judge in advance which effect experimental simplifications will have. We believe, however, that the results of this first experiment show the Alternating Procedure to be quite promising in this regard. It appears to set into motion a cognitive process that is new for most children, to bring into view some surprising competencies, and also to render certain handicaps of young writers more understandable than they were before.

DESCRIPTION OF THE EXPERIMENT

An experiment was conducted in which elementary-school children at three grade levels composed and revised short opinion essays, using variations of the Alternating Procedure that has already been described briefly. We wanted to see what children's composing behavior looked like (and how it felt to them) under procedures that brought evaluation out into the open and made it a matter of routine. Ninety children were involved, thirty in each of grades 4, 6, and 8 (ages approximately, 10, 12, and 14 years). They came from schools in a predominantly middle-class area of Metropolitan Toronto.

Half the children in each grade used the Alternating Procedure in the way that has already been mentioned, and that will be described in more detail below, a way which called for them to go through a CDO (COMPARE, DIAGNOSE, OPERATE) cycle after each sentence was composed. The other half of the students wrote their compositions first and applied the Alternating Procedure afterwards, sentence by sentence. We shall call the first group the 'on-line' group and the second group the 'evaluation after' group.

In order to teach children the on-line procedure, the experimenter demonstrated it by composing a short paragraph herself, using the Alternating Procedure. Writing on the topic, 'Is it better to be an only child or to have brothers or sisters?', she wrote the following first sentence:

> Yes, it's better to have both.

Then she stopped and turned to the list of evaluations at her side, each of which was written on a separate slip of white paper. After reading her first sentence over, she started thinking aloud, demonstrating how to use the evaluations as an aid to thinking. For instance, pointing to evaluation number 9 (shown in Table 1), she remarked, 'It says I'm getting away from the main point. ... No, that's not a problem I have to think of yet. I'm just trying to get to my main point. So this won't help me.' Moving evaluation

TABLE 1 Evaluations used to facilitate COMPARE operations

Evaluative Phrases
1. People won't see why this is important
2. People may not believe this
3. People won't be very interested in this part
4. People may not understand what I mean here
5. People will be interested in this part
6. This is good
7. This is a useful sentence
8. I think this could be said more clearly
9. I'm getting away from the main point
10. Even I am confused about what I am trying to say
11. This doesn't sound quite right

number 9 aside, she turned to number 8, saying, 'Now here's one that says I could have said what I said more clearly. That's for sure! I'd better keep this one here and think more about it.' In this way the experimenter considered each evaluation, moving it aside if it was judged irrelevant, and keeping it if it was judged relevant. Then she looked for the most appropriate among the relevant evaluations, asking herself, 'Now, what's the main problem?'

Having selected an evaluation, she turned to the directives (listed in Table 2), which were printed on separate blue slips of paper. She went through the same thinking-aloud process as with the evaluations, considering each directive as to its relevance and chose the most promising of the relevant ones. In considering the relevance of directive 5, for instance, she would say something like: 'Let's see, this says I'd better say more. I don't really think saying more would help. I've got to get this part right before I say more.' Finally, depending on the directive chosen, she revised her sentence in accordance with her evaluation or left it alone.

TABLE 2 Directives used to facilitate TACTICAL CHOICE

Directive Phrases
1. I think I'll leave it this way
2. I'd better give an example
3. I'd better leave this part out
4. I'd better cross this sentence out and say it a different way
5. I'd better say more
6. I'd better change the wording

After this activity was completed she wrote her next sentence and went through the entire cycle again. For each new sentence the evaluation and directive cards were shuffled and run through, to stress the point that there was no special order in which they were to be used. (Evaluations and directives were not numbered on the experimental materials, and children were explicitly urged not to treat them in a fixed order but to arrange them in any way that helped them think.)

Proceeding as described, the experimenter produced a nine-sentence paragraph in approximately 15 minutes. Although the experimenter's thinking aloud was not fully scripted, it covered essentially the same ideas when performed in individual sessions with each of forty-five subjects. Care was taken to model the use of each evaluation and directive with approximately equal frequency. The amount and kind of thinking modeled varied, however, according to the evaluation being considered, from a quick, impressionistic judgment in the case of 'People will be interested in this part', to a high-level review of the whole text in the case of 'I'm getting away from the main point.'

After the procedure was demonstrated, the children were put through a short check-out phase. Given the topic 'Is winter the best season?', the experimenter wrote the first sentence and the children applied the Alternating Procedure to it. The sentence given was 'Winter is it.', a sentence chosen for its susceptibility to a variety of evaluations and directives. (It could be judged satisfactory and left as it was; it could be judged unclear and reworded, expanded, or replaced.) After executing the Alternating Procedure on this sentence the children were asked to compose the next sentence on the topic themselves and apply the procedure to it. The purpose of this check-out phase was to eliminate any children who could not handle the mechanics of the procedure (the quality of their choices was not a consideration). No children had difficulty with the procedure, however, and so all proceeded to the next, independent composition phase.

In the next phase children wrote original compositions on the topic 'Should children choose the subjects they study in school?', applying the Alternating Procedure after writing each sentence. The experimenter recorded each selection and placement of the evaluations and directives. She also asked children to justify their choices, recording their responses on audiotape. The experimental session was concluded with an interview in which children were questioned on their experience and how it compared with their usual writing experience. The entire session lasted about 90 minutes.

Procedures for children in the 'evaluation after' group involved a simple modification of those just described. The day before the experiment, these children wrote in class on the prescribed topic. In the experimental sessions, which were again conducted individually, they revised these previously written compositions. The experimenter's demonstration was modified to suit the 'evaluation after' procedure. She presented an already-written composition and went through it sentence by sentence, thinking aloud as she applied the evaluation/revision procedure. The content of the demonstration, however, was identical to that used in demonstrating the 'on-line' procedure, so that children in both conditions were exposed to the same original text, the same revisions, and the same verbalized thought leading up to the revisions. Children went through the same two-sentence check-out procedure as in the 'on-line' group (and again all children succeeded in handling the procedure). They then applied the procedure to their own compositions and finally went through the same interview as children in the other group.

These two variations in procedure, the 'on-line' and the 'evaluation after', were chosen for their naturalistic and theoretical interest. They represent two of the ways that evaluation and revision actually go on in writing; as part of the composing of an original draft and as a separate process applied to a completed draft. The two approaches differ in their cognitive demands. On-line revision poses the problem of keeping plans for future text in mind while pausing to reconsider text already written. It has, however, a potential compensating advantage for text generation, in that on-line evaluation may have forward-acting effects such as suggesting additional things to write. Revision afterwards presents less threat of losing hold of plans and intentions, but it makes the task of revision more constrained, since revisions must be fitted to following, as well as to preceding, text. Thus, if one procedure were found to be more facilitating than the other for children of a certain age, this might give us clues as to what parts of the writing task were commanding their attention. We could consider, for instance, to what extent they were concerned with hanging on to plans as compared to thinking of new material to include in their compositions.

FINDINGS

The key assumption underlying this experiment was that providing children with a simplified executive routine for sentence-by-sentence evaluation and revision would reduce executive control problems and thereby give latent evaluative, tactical, and language production abilities of children an opportunity to reveal themselves. Let us therefore look first at evidence bearing on this assumption. First, it is relevant to note that none of the ninety children from grade 4 to grade 8 were unable or unwilling to use the Alternating Procedure, in spite of its apparently cumbersome nature. Children in grades 4 and 6 in the 'on-line' condition, who had to go through the procedure on each sentence before composing the next, nevertheless produced compositions of the same average length as the 'evaluation after' group, who wrote their compositions under normal classroom test conditions. Grade 8 children did produce significantly less in the 'on-line' than in the 'evaluation after' condition. Since this effect did not appear with younger children, however, it cannot reasonably be attributed to inability to handle the procedure. A behavioral indicator of difficulty with, or reluctance to go through, the procedure, is the choice of evaluative and directive statements that allow one to 'by-pass' the revision task. By choosing favorable evaluations and/or by choosing the directive, 'I think I'll leave it this way', a student could largely circumvent the procedure and proceed through the composition with little extra effort. Only six of the ninety children consistently chose a 'by-pass' strategy; four of these were in the youngest group.

In follow-up interviews, children were unanimous in declaring that the procedure helped them do something they did not normally do and had found difficult, namely, evaluating their writing in detail. Seventy-four percent, in fact, declared that the procedure made the whole process of writing easier. They usually explained this on the basis of mental activity stimulated by use of the 'cards' (evaluative and directive statements):

> 'Easier, because I don't usually ask myself those questions. It made me able to correct sentences; it was a good guide.'
>
> 'Easier. You're kind of answering the kinds of questions a teacher would ask when she is marking your paper, so it helps you correct mistakes before she marks.'
>
> 'Yeah, made it easier. If there were cards like that in class everyone would get it done fast.'
>
> 'They gave me a little bit more thinking. They made me think more about what I wrote.'
>
> 'Much easier, because they helped me look over the sentence, which I don't usually do.'
>
> 'I guess it's a little easier. You can use the cards to realize what you're saying. After a little while ... you wouldn't have to use the cards but could get it in your head and it would be faster. Right now I'd need to use the cards because I don't think of those questions.'

The 12 percent who thought the procedure made writing on the whole more difficult referred either to the need to think more carefully or to the time it required:

> 'I never thought closely about what I wrote. I thought about it and if it was good I wrote it down, but I never went sentence by sentence.'
>
> 'Takes more time when you're using the cards, so it's probably harder; but it makes your writing better.'

The remaining children judged the procedure to make writing harder in some ways, easier in others, citing factors similar to those noted by the other children. In summary, it appeared that the procedure was working as intended. It provided children with an executive routine that they generally experienced as facilitating. It also made it possible for them to incorporate activities into their writing that they already knew something about but that they usually omitted. According to the children's reports, the Alternating Procedure had a marked effect on their composing processes. Before probing more deeply into the nature of this effect, we must see what, if any, effect carried through into the written products.

Effects of the Procedure on Written Products

Judging from norms of the National Assessment of Educational Progress (1977), children in this study revised more than normal. In the National Asessment study, children were asked to look over compositions they had just written to see if they wanted to change anything, ample time being allowed to make changes. At grade 4, 40 percent of the children made no changes; in the present study the corresponding number was 20 percent. At grade 8, 22 percent of the National Assessment sample made no changes, compared to less than 7 percent in the present study.

In this section we consider the effects of this revision activity on children's texts. Before pursuing such effects, however, it is helpful to consider how successful children in this age range are in revising esays on this same topic when left to their own devices. Data are available on this from an earlier study we conducted (Bracewell *et al.*, 1978). Here we found that among grade 4 children there was no discernible tendency for them to make compositions better or worse by revision (and little agreement between raters as to whether changes were for better or worse). Raters did begin to agree on the revisions made by Grade 8 students, but they agreed that the tendency was for compositions to be made worse by revision! Thus, any tendency for children to make changes for the better in this study could be taken as a showing beneficial effects from the experimental procedure, since baseline performance is to produce changes that are neutral or negative. It is also informative to note that, whereas children were nearly unanimous in believing that the Alternating Procedure had a positive effect on their composing processes, they were far from unanimous in believing that the resulting compositions were better than what they usually produced. Children expressed concern about offsetting factors such as newness of the procedure and difficulty with the topic.

Against this background of acknowledged difficulties, we will consider first how well children coped with individual revisions, then see how successful they were in improving the overall quality of their compositions.

Ratings were made of each individual change that children elected to make. Raters were given original and revised versions of texts with all the differences underlined but were not informed which was the original and which the revised. Instead, one composition in each pair was randomly designated to be treated *as if* it were the original; the raters then judged whether each discrepancy noted on the other version constituted a change for the better, a change for the worse, or a change that made no difference in quality.

Two raters, one an editor and one a former junior high school English teacher, judged each separate change. The score finally assigned to a composition was the number of changes judged to be for the better minus the number judged to be for the worse. Although the two raters did not agree at all closely in their judgements (r for scores assigned to compositions = 0.24), they agreed in assigning scores of a positive tendency to all grades and conditions. The grand means of +0.83 based on one rater and +1.16 based on the other rater are both significantly different from zero at beyond the 0.001 level ($t(87) = 3.71$ and 4.19). An analysis of variance showed no significant difference between grades or conditions. Thus there was a pervasive tendency for changes for the better to outnumber changes for the worse.

We now turn to the question of whether these changes added up to revised texts of significantly higher quality than the original. The answer is no, at least in so far as we can tell from the following analysis. The final thirty compositions written in either condition by subjects at each age level were rank-ordered on the basis of overall impression of quality. On the basis of these rankings the top-ranked child in the 'on-line' condition was matched with the top ranked child in the 'evaluation after' condition, the second-ranked with the second-ranked, and so on. Thus fifteen pairs of essays roughly matched for quality were formed. The original essay of the child in the 'evaluation after' condition was then added to the set containing that child's revised essay. The final compositions produced in both the 'on-line' and 'evaluation after' conditions were compared to this 'original'. This procedure was used to get around the problem that there were no intact original essays for the on-line condition against which final compositions could be compared. Original and revised compositions were presented in pairs to raters, with the order varied randomly so that raters did not know which was which. At no age level, for either condition, was the final composition judged to be significantly different from the original.

There is a seeming paradox in children's ability to make individual changes for the better but not to have these amount to any overall improvement. The paradox is removed, however, if two additional factors are considered. The first is the level of evaluation and revision carried out.

There were two evaluative phrases children could select that would suggest they were directing their attention to overall text concerns when they made the revision. These two phrases were 'I'm getting away from the main point' and 'Even I'm confused about what I'm trying to say.' These two phrases were seldom used at any age level. Generally, children were concerned with small units of language, as we will discuss in greater detail later, and they evaluated these only in relation to local context. A second fact accounting for the seeming paradox is that while positive changes outnumbered negative changes, they did not outnumber them by very much. The average revised text contained one more change for the better than changes for the worse. This was a statistically significant advantage, but not one that could be expected to influence overall impressions of text quality.

To summarize the results so far, we find that, when children use the Alternating Procedure, they experience it as helping them to incorporate evaluation and revision phases into their composing and that they do make changes that are mostly judged to be in a positive direction. Many negative changes are also made, however, and the overall result is that compositions are not improved. These results, taken at face value, are not incongruous. If, in fact, children had seldom previously evaluated and revised what they wrote, then it stands to reason that they might lack some of the competencies necessary to do so effectively. Among the possibilities to be considered is that they are unable to judge the effect of what they write, that they are unable to diagnose the sources of trouble, that they make unwise decisions about the general kind of change to undertake, or that they lack the sentencing skills needed to bring off the changes they intend. We shall turn now to examining each of these possibilities in turn.

Quality of the Evaluations

A semi-professional writer went through each text and after each sentence chose the evaluative statement from Table 1 that corresponded best to her own evaluation. The phrase actually chosen by the child was then judged according to whether it was the same one chosen by the rater, different but also appropriate, somewhat appropriate, or not fitting at all. The percentages of subjects falling into the different categories are shown in Table 3. The scores of three subjects in two different cells are missing due to audiotape difficulties. It can be seen from Table 3 that in grades 6 and 8 the children's choices of evaluations corresponded very closely indeed to the choices of the semi-professional writer. Even at grade 4, most of the choices are either exactly the same or ones that the rater judged to be appropriate. Only 10 per cent of the grade 4 children *ever* made a choice judged altogether inappropriate; 5 percent of grade 6 children did so, and no grade

TABLE 3 Appropriateness of evaluations: percentage of subjects in categories based on mean appropriateness ratings

	Grade					
	4		6		8	
Rating category	On-line	After	On-line	After	On-line	After
Same as expert picked	23	47	60	93	71	67
Not same, but appropriate	62	47	33	7	29	33
Somewhat appropriate	15	6	7	0	0	0
Not appropriate	0	0	0	0	0	0

8 children did. Children at all grades would thus appear to be surprisingly capable when it comes to making evaluations of their writing.

The first four evaluations shown in Table 1 are criticisms expressed in terms of reader reaction ('People may not believe this', etc.). The last four are criticisms expressed either as unqualified assertions or as personal opinions ('I think ...'). This distinction was built into the list with the thought that it might reveal a developmental trend toward more reader-related criticisms. Such tendency as did appear, however, was in the opposite direction. Excluding instances in which positive evaluations were chosen, the proportion of reader-related criticisms went from 47 percent in grade 4 to 35 percent in grade 6 and 30 percent in grade 8. Thus, older students were attributing more problems with their writing to personal dissatisfaction than to anticipated dissatisfaction of the reader.

Quality of Diagnoses

The same semi-professional writer who judged the evaluations also judged the children's explanations of their evaluations. Again, the standard was how closely the child's judgment corresponded to that of the expert. Some responses could not be classified according to this standard. Either the subject (a) gave a justification, the intent of which was not clear; (b) repeated the evaluation phrase instead of constructing a justification; or (c) could not elaborate on the evaluation. Percentages of subjects giving such unclassifiable responses, responses that generally can be taken to indicate difficulty with the task, are shown in the unclassified category at the foot of Table 4. This table also shows how the remaining responses were classified against the expert standard. Evidently, children showed much less accord with expert judgments when it came to justifying their evaluations. Mean ratings on the 4-point scale (unclassified responses were not included) go from 2.00 at grade 4 to 2.56 at grade 6 to 2.98 at grade 8. Thus, it is only at grade 8 that the explanations are judged, on the average, to be appropriate.

A reading of the transcripts of children's explanation shows why they end up with ratings that do not correspond closely to those an expert would make. For the most part, children focus on overly specific details. Thus, while the expert is dealing with issues at the text level, tracking meaning and finding the intent of a sentence confusing, the child is concerned about the effect of a certain word or phrase in that sentence. Another way in which they fail to construct an expert diagnosis is to give up on a perceived problem too soon. They manage to criticize a sentence, often astutely pointing out some critical reader response that it is likely to provoke. Then they ignore this insight and proceed with a justification of the sentence based on why it was written in the first place.

TABLE 4 Appropriateness of diagnosis: percentage of subjects in categories based on mean appropriateness ratings

Rating category	Grade 4 On-line	Grade 4 After	Grade 6 On-line	Grade 6 After	Grade 8 On-line	Grade 8 After
Same as expert picked	0	0	0	27	21	20
Not same, but appropriate	23	27	47	20	43	60
Somewhat appropriate	31	20	13	20	0	13
Not appropriate	8	13	13	7	0	7
Unclassified	38	40	27	26	36	0

It would thus appear that, although children show an ability to form accurate impressions of the effectiveness of their writing, they do not identify accurately the source of the difficuties they perceive.

Choice of Remedial Tactics

The tactical choices represented by the directives in Table 2 are of a very general sort and one can seldom assert with confidence that, in a particular instance, a particular choice is good or bad. Such choices as altering the wording or saying more are often difficult to evaluate without knowing what sort of change of wording or addition the writer has in mind. On the other hand, when a sentence has been evaluated as unclear and the sentence itself is garbled, adding more information is not the most promising way of trying to clear matters up. We asked the same rater who had judged the choices of evaluations to judge the choices of directives. In this case, however, the judgement was simply whether the chosen tactic was a high-probability choice or a low-probability choice for dealing with the problem that the child had identified. The percentage of tactics judged to be of high probability increased from 50 percent at grade 4 to 74 percent at grade 8. (Chance level cannot be computed, although it is necessarily at least 17 percent and is unlikely to be as high as 50 percent.) There is thus evidence of a developmental trend toward the choice of more promising ways of responding to evaluations.

Table 5 shows the distribution of choices of directives for the several grade levels and the two treatment conditions. There is little indication of any difference between grade levels. This implies that the improvement with age in the quality of tactical choices is due to a better fit between tactic and problem, not to a change in the popularity of the various choices. It is especially noteworthy that the choice to leave the text the way it is shows no dramatic change with age, although the fourth-graders in both conditions choose it more frequently than the older children.

There is an interesting difference between treatment groups. Decisions to say more or to give an example account for only 6–8 percent of the choices at each grade level in the 'evaluation after' condition but account for 18–20 percent of the choices at each grade level in the 'on-line' condition. It seems that in the on-line condition, children frequently used the evaluation to suggest additional material to include in their compositions. For children who have already completed a draft, evaluation seldom results in material being interpolated.

The data do not permit us to draw firm conclusions about the competence of children to select promising general tactics for revision. The data suggest, however, that such choices may not be very well attuned to perceived

TABLE 5 Percentage of times each directive was chosen

Condition	Grade	Directive					
		I think I'll leave it this way	I'd better give an example	I'd better leave this part out	I'd better cross this sentence out and say it a different way	I'd better say more	I'd better change the wording
On-line	4	68.3	12.2	0	0	7.3	12.2
	6	54.5	12.7	1.8	10.9	5.5	14.6
	8	63.5	9.5	3.2	0	9.5	14.3
Evaluation After	4	60.6	3.0	3.0	9.1	4.6	19.7
	6	50.0	2.1	0	20.8	6.3	20.8
	8	49.5	1.9	3.7	6.5	3.7	34.7

problems at grade 4 and that substantial progress is made in the following 4 years.

Effectiveness of Execution

The most pertinent evidence we have of children's ability to carry out intended changes in their compositions is the high frequency of changes that raters judged to be for the worse. Since the children demonstrated ability to evaluate their texts in ways that conformed to expert judgments, the frequency with which their changes made things worse would seem to reflect serious difficulties in managing written language. The flavor of these difficulties can be gained from examining those instances in which children elected to strike out and replace an entire sentence.

There were thirty instances of children choosing this tactic. In eleven of these thirty instances the child was unable to come up with a recast sentence and instead rewrote the original sentence with some minor word or phrase change. For example, an eighth-grader elected to cross out and rewrite the following sentence:

> The reason they wouldn't do well is because if the subject chosen by the teacher is one the student hates, the student won't try, and will do badly.

The student eventually rewrote the sentence exactly as before, except for changing the last word to 'poorly'!

At the other extreme, we have five instances in which children replaced a sentence with one that said something entirely different. In changing their minds about what they wanted to say, these children may have been demonstrating an important effect of the Alternating Procedure, but in changing the content they by-pass the problem of finding alternative means of expressing an idea.

In the remaining fourteen sentences some more or less major overhaul was attempted, while preserving the idea of the original version. The most successful of these attempts was the following:

> *Original version*
> I think we shouldn't because when we have math or any subject we might pick something that would be too easy and also teachers teach us math or any subject.
>
> *Revised version*
> I think students shouldn't get to pick out any subject because we might pick out some work that's too easy for us.

This is an example of cleaning up a sentence that badly needed it. Note, however, that the basic plan of the sentence remains intact. All the successful examples were of this kind. They preserved the original sentence plan in the revised version, altering it by the addition or deletion of material, or by splitting it into shorter sentences. The four instances of children trying to make a fresh start at expressing an idea are all clear failures. In the following attempt, for instance, the child appears to hold on to the original idea, but one version is as elliptical as the other:

Original version
The school gives him maths and sciences how is he going to be a carpenter.

Revised version
There are some jobs that you don't need some classes like history.

In the next example the child, apparently trying to expand on the point made in the original, loses hold of the original point altogether, and produces an incoherent statement.

Original version
Teachers are very important because a child has to learn something before they could go on to something else.

Revised Version
A child shouldn't choose his or her subject because the teacher might not know if the child knows how to do it or not.

The task of reformulating a sentence in order to accomplish some objective more successfully would appear to be a very complex task. It presents executive problems and competence demands of its own, quite apart from those involved in getting up to the point of attempting such a reformulation. Most children in the sample avoided the task altogether. When they attempted it they seemed to be successful only if they preserved the plan of the original sentence.

INTERPRETATION

Let us now reconsider the CDO model sketched at the beginning of this chapter in the light of experimental findings. Judging from self-report and textual evidence, we must conclude that under ordinary circumstances the CDO process is not run through by children at all. With support from the Alternating Procedure, however, children were able to carry out the steps of the process as depicted in Figure 1, and to do it with some measure of effect even on their first attempt. Although they recognized the process as different from their usual procedures, they accepted it as reasonable and helpful. There is nothing to suggest any fundamental incongruity between cognitive behavior fostered by the Alternting Procedure and the normal workings of their cognitive systems.

This constitutes significant support for the model of the CDO process depicted in Figure 1. An experiment such as the present one may quite properly be considered a simulation experiment (Brown and Campione, 1980). In computer simulation, the test of a model's completeness and validity is that the model can actually be run on a computer and that it yields traces compatible with those that are obtained from human subjects. Here the test is that the model was shown to 'run' on human subjects who are not already 'programmed' to run that way, and that it yielded traces compatible with those of an expert writer whose performance is taken as criterial. Beyond that, our human subjects can do something the computer cannot, which is tell us about the experience. This provides an important kind of evidence on psychological validity in addition to the purely formal evidence of fit between 'simulated' and natural traces.

Two previously noted limitations on the scope of the experiment are relevant at this point, however. First, the CDO process as depicted is an iterative process that keeps cycling until a mismatch has been removed or until failure occurs at some point. This iterative aspect of the model was not tested. We have done some preliminary research with an iterative revision procedure (Scardamalia *et al.*, 1980). Although only two iterations were used, it was clear that for some children the process was divergent; instead of progressively changing the text toward some desired goal, they shifted focus from one cycle to the next and sometimes undid what they had accomplished on the previous cycle. Iterative refinement of text would seem to call for a top-down control not represented in the model (and not provided for in the Alternating Procedure), a control which ensures that successive changes are related to the same goal. The second limitation is that the present experiment dealt with a kind of middle level of mismatches between text and intention. The model assumes that the process remains the same for mismatches at all levels from proofreading to detecting major structural problems. This assumption remains to be tested, and we can only say of the present study that it gives us no reason to doubt it.

A third limitation of the Alternating Procedure is that it depends on routinely triggering the CDO process instead of leaving it to be triggered spontaneously by perceived problems. What difference this might make in the functioning of the COD process is not obvious, however. Some adults, on learning of the Alternating Procedure, have proclaimed that they could not tolerate using such a procedure themselves. While we suspect that these people underestimate their adaptability, they no doubt have a point. In mature writers the Alternating Procedure would be running in parallel with a well-developed natural CDO process, so the routine triggering would be redundant and occur too frequently, especially since adults likely plan text in much larger units than young children do. Adults might also be reacting to the limited range of evaluations available. This does not mean, however, that the applicability of the CDO model for adults is being called into question, only the simplifications that were introduced in order to activate the process in children. None of the chidlren interviewed gave even a hint about such interference, either from the routine triggering or from the limited set of evaluations available. The only evidence that might suggest interference is the reduction in amount of text produced by grade 8 children in the 'on-line' condition. For the younger children all indications are that he Alternating Procedure filled a void, initiating cognitive operations that were not otherwise occurring.

If we accept the Alternating Procedure as at least a rough working model of the CDO process, then we can use children's performance in the experiment as a source of information about their competencies with respect to various aspects of the CDO process.

As a start on pulling findings together, we shall go through one complete protocol. This is from a grade 8 student who produced one of the lower-rated compositions for that grade. (Numbers are added for reference.)

Original version
(1) I think students should choose their own subject because only they know what they want to be or do. (2) this way student will choose a subject so that is more fun and he or she will enjoy school. (3) This way student could not say that he doesn't like the subject. (4) And he will be forced to do a better job. (5) This way student learns just the things he needs to learn.

Revised version
(1) I think students should choose their own subject because only they know what they want to be or do. (2) This way student will choose a subject so he or she will enjoy school. (3) This way student could not say that he doesn't like the subject. (4) And not do good job. (5) This way student learn just the things he need to learn.

Of two raters who compared these versions, not knowing which was which, one rated them as equal in overall quality and the other rated the original as slightly better. The changes are, in fact, slight and they seem unrelated to major problems with the text. Thus, on the surface, we have what is typical at this grade level (cf. Bracewell *et al.*, 1978), little revision activity and what there is tending to make things worse. When we follow the writer through the steps in the CDO process, however, we see quite a bit of relevant mental activity going on.

First sentence: I think students should choose their own subject because only they know what they want to be or do.

COMPARE: This is a useful sentence. (MATCH: GO TO NEXT SENTENCE.)

(*Comment*: Child added that it was a useful sentence 'because it says what I think is right'.)

Second sentence: This way student will choose a subject so that is more fun and he or she will enjoy school.

COMPARE: This doesn't sound quite right.

DIAGNOSE: It doesn't sound clear.

CHOOSE TACTIC: I'd better change the wording.

GENERATE CHANGE: Deletes 'that is more fun and'.

(*Comment*: DIAGNOSE does not proceed to the point of identifying what sounds wrong. Instead it restates but actually shifts the identification of the mismatch. The change generated does not follow the chosen tactic. Nevertheless deletion, a fairly uncommon practice in students of this age, was successfully accomplished and resulted in a more grammatical sentence. Possibly deleting the indicated clause was the only substantial change the child could find that did not conspicuously worsen the sentence. This would suggest that the child may have covertly gone through several CDO iterations before coming up with the overt change.)

Third sentence: This way student could not say that he doesn't like the subject.

COMPARE: This is good. (MATCH: GO TO NEXT SENTENCE)

(*Comment:* Given the child's overall language skills, an accurate evaluation.)

Fourth sentence: And he will be forced to do a better job.

COMPARE: Even I am confused about what I am trying to say.

DIAGNOSE: I was confused. I couldn't write what I meant.

I should'nt put 'force' here. If you're responsible you shouldn't have to be forced.

CHOOSE TACTIC: I'd better leave this part out.

GENERATE CHANGE: Replaces sentence with 'And not do good job'.

(*Comment:* The child claims that the sentence does not convey the meaning he is after. The effort to diagnose the problem goes awry, however, when the child's attention is captured by a single word, 'force', that to him seems incongruous with the general idea he is trying to develop. Remediation then focuses on the troublesome word rather than on developing the idea more fully. Removing the word 'force' results in removing the one main clue to the writer's idea, that students must develop self-defined constraints on their behavior.

Fifth sentence: This way student learns just the things he need to learn.
COMPARE: This is a useful sentence. (MATCH: EXIT)

This protocol is typical in showing initial reactions, at the COMPARE stage, that are reasonable and that, if appropriately followed up, would lead to an improved text. Serious troubles arise at the DIAGNOSE stage, however. This protocol illustrates one of the most prevalent troubles. Children may sense a difficulty at an abstract level, as in the case of the fourth sentence cited above. As soon as they start searching for the cause, however, their attention is captured by some salient concrete element and they lose hold of the higher-level goal that was motivating the search. We have discussed elsewhere this stimulus saliency problem as it affects control of attention in composing (Bereiter and Scardamalia, 1981) and in logical problem-solving (Scardamalia, 1973, 1975). An elaborated CDO model would show a complex search process within the DIAGNOSE box. The executive demands of this sub-process are probably high and, without procedural support, children will tend to lose hold and fall back upon simple diagnostic procedures that have minimal information-processing demands. Identifying a concrete element as the source of the problem would be one of these.

Another problem which appears at the diagnostic stage is simply faulty knowledge. This appears most commonly when children replace a perfectly good informal expression with a stilted or even unidiomatic formal-sounding one. The problem starts at the diagnostic stage with identifying the informal expression as not sounding right. The same problem appears at the semantic rather than stylistic level in the current protocol, with the child's concern about the word 'force'. The child's original use of the term was quite appropriate, if we accept the following gloss on sentences 2 to 4 of his text:

> If students can choose their own subjects, then a student can no longer excuse poor work by saying that he doesn't like the subject. This will force him to do better work.

Here 'force' refers to an internal compulsion resulting from circumstance. In judging the word to be inappropriate, however, the child seems to be using a more restricted sense of the word that means a direct external compulsion.

These phenomena can be accounted for by the 'Monitor Theory' proposed by Krashen (1977). According to Krashen's theory, language is generated out of an unconsciously acquired rule system, but conscious rules may be brought to bear on it via a Monitor that modifies the output of the unconscious system. The system of unconscious rules is far richer than the set of rules available to the Monitor. In the cases before us, we are seeing instances of the unconscious system's rules being more 'correct' than the conscious rules. (This is not always so, as with people whose conscious rule systems contain the standard pronoun case forms but whose unconscious rule systems continue to crank out 'for he and I'). Thus the child's unconscious or intuitive definition of 'force' is more fully in tune with standard usage than is the more simplistic concept he brings forth consciously. Similarly, the children who edit out an acceptable informal expression may be assumed to have generated that expression out of their unconscious rule systems and then applied inadequate conscious rules which wrongly classify the expression as inappropriate in writing. Such inadequate rules are to be expected in children relatively new to written language, of course. Our only point is that it is in the DIAGNOSE phase that these rules are brought into confrontation with text generated according to a different rule system. In a skilled writer the consciously available rules will normally serve as an aid in discovering the source of intuitively sensed inadequacies. Thus they serve as powerful tools in diagnosis. For children, however, consciously available knowledge seems as likely to be an obstacle as an aid to accurate diagnosis.

While there is much that we do not yet understand about children's difficulties in the DIAGNOSE and OPERATE phases of the CDO process, we can in a very broad way attribute them all to lack of practice; to lack of practice, that is, in the CDO process itself. Further writing experience may or may not include practice of this sub-process. It seems possible therefore that a person might grow up to be a fluent and prolific writer without ever developing much skill in diagnosing text problems and remedying them.

This brings us to the question, untouched by the present experiment, of what it takes to activate the CDO process spontaneously, and of why it is that the process does not seem to be activated in children. Many conjectural explanations are possible, but the present experiment contributes one finding which limits a free range of conjecture. This is the finding that children are quite apt at detecting mismatches between intended and actual text, when prompted to look for them. This ability must surely have arisen from experience and practice of some kind.

Our own conjecture on these points, based on a variety of empirical observations but certainly not firmly grounded on evidence, is that children frequently execute the COMPARE phase of the CDO process but go no farther. They detect mismatches between actuality and intention just as they detect mismatches between the general quality of their texts and the lists they read. Instead of proceeding to diagnosis and operation, however, they return to the interrupted procedure. They retain, though, some trace of such mismatches in long-term memory where they contribute to a growing data file on their shortcomings as writers. Hence the widespread belief of children that they are incompetent in writing. This belief is commonly blamed on teacher criticisms, but, in our view, it is much more deeply rooted in children's writing and reading experience than that (see also Bracewell, 1980).

This short-circuiting of the CDO process may have several contributing causes. One likely cause is incompletely developed mental representations of actual and intended texts. These representations may be developed to the point where the child can detect that something is amiss, but not far enough for the child to discover what it is. This is analogous to the experience one may have in traveling somewhere over an indistinctly remembered route. One senses that things do not look right and therefore begins to suspect that one has taken a wrong turn, but the mental representation of how things should look is not sufficiently clear to indicate where the wrong turn might have been made, or even to establish definitely that one is off course. A common response in the travel situation is just to keep going and hope things will become clearer. This is what children seem to do in writing.

Another possible contributing cause could be a prior history of failed attempts at remediation. As we have observed, children's attempts at remediation are frequently not successful and they often amount to little overt change at all. If children's occasional ventures into the CDO process have yielded only negative results, then it makes sense that they should learn to by-pass it.

There is another kind of short-circuiting observable in children's protocols which seems to occur in mature writers as well. This is a direct jump from COMPARE to GENERATE CHANGE. In these cases the mismatch first comes to consciousness in the form of a perception that some other word would be better, that a comma is missing, etc. This very rapid procedure, which seems to be mainly of value in catching slip-ups, may be enough to keep a COMPARE process going during composition. However, it would not develop the knowledge and skills necessary to deal with mis-matches that require diagnosis and deliberate search for alternatives.

Finally, we must consider the possibility that children avoid the CDO process normally because it threatens loss of hold on the composing process as a whole. We know from questionnaire evidence (Keeney, 1975) that school-age writers are concerned about external distractions that may cause them to forget what they intended to write. The CDO process represents an internal diversion of attention which they might wish to avoid for the same reason.

The Alternating Procedure offers promise as an instructional device because its routine alleviates some of the danger of losing hold of the composing process. It also leads children into the DIAGNOSE and OPERATE phases of the CDO process, which they normally miss. Thus it has the potential of boosting the amount of experience through which skills in diagnosis and remediation may be developed. Finally, however, the CDO process must come to be triggered spontaneously, not through routine cueing. We cannot expect that practice with the Alternating Procedure would lead to a greater tendency for the system to respond spontaneously in an appropriate way. If we are correct, however, in our conjecture that spontaneous activation of the CDO process depends on refined development of mental representations of text, then it is clear that whole other dimensions of writing development are involved. The ability to plan, the ability to apprehend and elaborate rhetorical problems, the ability to encode large linguistic units in mentally manipulable form, these are some of the other aspects of writing development that impinge on the starting point of the CDO process. They also suggest the larger context of composing operations in which the CDO process plays its significant and revealing part.

ACKNOWLEDGMENTS

The study on which this chapter is based was supported by the Social Sciences and Humanities Research Council of Canada. We are also grateful to the Alfred P. Sloan Foundation for funding research that has served as background for the current work. Special thanks go to Clare Cattani, Sondra Gartshore, and Roz Klaiman for their assistance in the conduct and analysis of this study, and to Carol Broome, Edith Acker, and Charlene Reader for their preparation of this manuscript.

REFERENCES

Bereiter, C., and Scardamalia, M. (1981). From conversation to composition: the role of instruction in a developmental process. To appear in R. Glaser (ed.), *Advances in Instructional Psychology*, Vol. 2. Lawrence Erlbaum Associates, Hillsdale, New Jersey.

Bracewell, R. J. (1980) Writing as a cognitive activity. *Visible Language, 14*, 400–422.

Bracewell, R. J., Scardamalia, M., and Bereiter, C. (1978). The development of audience awareness in writing. *Resources in Education* (October. ERIC Document Reproduction Service No. ED 154 433.

Brown, A. L., and Campione, J. C. (1980). *Inducing Flexible Thinking: The Problem of Access* (Technical Report No. 156). Center for the Study of Reading, University of Illinois at Urbana-Champaign, Champaign, Illinois.

Flower, L., and Hayes, J. R. (1979). Writing as a Cognitive Process: A Model of the Writer in Action. Unpublished manuscript, Carnegie-Mellon University.

Keeney, M. L. (1975) An investigation of what intermediate-grade children say about the writing of stories. Unpublished doctoral dissertation, Lehigh University, Bethlehem, Pennsylvania (Order No. 76–5091).

Krashen, S. D. (1977). The monitor model for adult second language performance. In M. Burt, H. Dulay and F. Finacchiaro (eds.), *Viewpoints on English as a Second Language*, pp. 153–61. Regents, New York.

Kroll, B. M. (1978). Cognitive egocentrism and the problem of audience awareness in written discourse. *Research in the Teaching of English,* **12**, 269–81.

Miller, G., Galanter, E., and Pribram, K. (1960). *Plans in the Structure of Behavior*. Holt, Rinehart, & Winston, Inc., New York.

National Assessment of Educational Progress (1977). *Write/Rewrite: An Assessment of Revision Skills; Selected Results from the Second National Assessment of Writing*. U.S. Government Printing Office, Washington, D.C. (ERIC Document Reproduction Service No. ED 141 826).

Nold, E. W. (1981) Revising. In E. H. Frederiksen, M. F. Whiteman, and J. F. Dominic (eds.), *Writing: The Nature, Development and Teaching of Written Communication.* Lawrence Erlbaum Associates, Hillsdale, New Jersey.

Scardamalia, M. (1973). Mental processing aspects of two formal operational tasks: A development investigation of a quantitative neo-Piagetian model. Unpublished doctoral dissertation, The Ontario Institute for Studies in Education.

Scardamalia, M. (1975). Two formal operational tasks: a quantitative neo-Piagetian and task analysis model for investigating sources of task difficulty. In G. I. Lubin, J. F. Magary, and M. K. Poulsen (eds.), *Piagetian Theory and the Helping Professions*. University of Southern California Publications Dept., Los Angeles.

Scardamalia, M. (1981). How children cope with the cognitive demands of writing. In C. H. Frederiksen, M. F. Whiteman, and J. F. Dominic (eds.), *Writing: The Nature, Development and Teaching of Written Communication*. Lawrence Erlbaum Associates, Hillsdale, New Jersey.

Scardamalia, M., and Bereiter, C. (1980). *Procedural facilitation as a way of helping children attain more complex levels of thinking.* Paper to be presented at NIE-LRDC Conference on Thinking and Learning Skills.

Scardamalia, M., Cattani, C., Turkish, L., and Bereiter, C. (1980). Part–Whole Relationships in Text Planning. Unpublished manuscript, The Ontario Institute for Studies in Education.

PART II

Composing Text: Syntactic Development

Erasmus: *Adagia*.	The desire for writing grows with writing.
Horace: *Ars Poetica.*	With a nice taste and care in weaving words together, you will express yourself most happily, if a skillful setting makes a familiar word new.
Jonson: *Explorato: Consuetudo*.	A strict and succinct style is that where you can take away nothing without loss, and that loss be manifest.

The Psychology of Written Language
Edited by M. Martlew

CHAPTER 4

Sentence Combining and the Teaching of Writing

KELLOGG W. HUNT

It was over 20 years ago, in 1961, that the National Council of Teachers of English appointed an *ad hoc* committee 'to review what is known and what is not known about the teaching and learning of composition ... for the purpose of preparing ... a special scientifically based report on what is known in this area' (Braddock *et al.*, 1963, p. 1).

Months later, after sorting through hundreds of studies, the committee voiced this judgment:

> Today's research in composition, taken as a whole may be compared to chemical research as it emerged from the period of alchemy: some terms are being defined usefully, a number of procedures are being refined, but the field as a whole is laced with dreams, prejudices, and makeshift operations. Not enough investigators are really informing themselves about the procedures and results of previous research before embarking on their own. Too few of them conduct pilot experiments and validate their measuring instruments before undertaking an investigation. ... And far too few of those who have conducted an initial piece of research follow it with further exploration or replicate the investigation of others. (Braddock *et al.*, 1963, p. 5)

Today a similar committee with a similar assignment would be able to report some very real progress at precisely the points the earlier committee cited. A whole new way of teaching composition has been developed, and its success has been tested with a scientific fairness, thoroughness, and precision that methods of teaching have not often been subjected to before. And in the field of syntactic development which helped inspire this composition research, some new terms have been defined usefully, some new procedures have been refined, some new measuring instruments have been validated, and experiments have frequently been replicated.

This chapter will first review the syntactic development research which provided some of the background and the impetus for this new way of teaching composition, and will then review a recent and remarkably convincing appraisal of the effectiveness of this way of teaching.

SYNTACTIC DEVELOPMENT IN 1960

If the NCTE's *ad hoc* committee in the early 1960s had been reporting on purely objective measures of the language development of school children, they might naturally have turned first to the 1960 edition of *The Encyclopedia of Educational Research*. Under the article entitled 'Language Development' they would have found that

> These studies have been well summarized by McCarthy ... who concludes that mean sentence length is the most reliable, easily determined, objective, quantitative, and easily understood measure of linguistic maturity.

But before the decade was over mean sentence length would no longer be the most reliable, easily determined, objective, quantitative, and easily understood measure of linguistic maturity.

If the NCTE committee had looked further into McCarthy's (1954) summary, they would have read:

> It is interesting to note ... that length of clause remains fairly constant in Grades 4 to 12. ... Apparently length of clause is somewhat controlled or restricted by the nature of language and whatever increase in sentence length occurs at higher age levels is brought about largely through the addition of more subordinate clauses (p. 523).

Before the 1960s were over it would be shown that the summary above was mainly wrong: the increase in sentence length at higher age levels – beyond high school, for instance – is due only slightly to an increase in subordinate clauses, and due mainly to an increase in length of clauses; clause length does not remain constant from grades 4 to 12.

In the decade of the 1960s, these three statements about average sentence length, average clause length, and the frequency of subordinate clauses were all challenged and supplanted by studies that examined the writings of schoolchildren across a wide span of time from 4th grade to 12th, from the beginning of writing in the public school grades to the end of public school years. Later, skilled adults were added to the developmental continuum;

and children of average IQ have been compared with those of superior IQ. Most recently, the performance of children with widely different languages has been studied in the same way.

THE INADEQUACY OF SENTENCE LENGTH

Analysis of samples of writing from grade 4 to skilled adults (Hunt, 1965), confirm McCarthy's observation that average sentence length does increase with age. Here are the means for grades 4, 8, 12, and skilled adults in order of age: 13, 16, 17, and 25 words. The numbers do increase, even when we count as a sentence whatever stretch of intelligible language a person writes between a capital letter and a period, a full stop. However, a closer look at what young children write between a capital letter and a stop shows that sentence length is a far from satisfactory index of maturity. For instance, here is a sentence written by a 4th grader of average IQ that is more than twice as long as the average for the skilled adult sample and more than three times as long as the average for high-school seniors. Is he some kind of child prodigy? Some kind of genius? Here is the sentence.

> I like the movie we saw about Moby Dick the white whale the captain said if you can kill the white whale Moby Dick I will give this gold to the one that can do it and it is worth sixteen dollars they tried and tried but while they were trying they killed a whale and used the oil for the lamps they almost caught the white whale.

Obviously the sentence is prodigiously long not because its author is prodigiously advanced for his age, but rather because he has not yet learned how to punctuate. If he had learned that, as he will in a year or two, he would have cut this up into several sentences – perhaps as many as six.

It would be grammatically allowable to cut the passage into six sentences, beginning one of the sentences with *and*, and another with *but*. Here is the passage so punctuated.

(1) I like the movie we saw about Moby Dick, the white whale.
(2) The captain said if you can kill the white whale, Moby Dick, I will give this gold to the one that can do it.
(3) And it is worth sixteen dollars.
(4) They tried and tried.
(5) But while they were trying they killed a whale and used the oil for the lamps.
(6) They almost caught the white whale.

The passage cannot be cut up into more than six chunks without creating at least one sentence fragment. Here is such a fragment.

I like the movie. We saw about Moby Dick.

Each of the six above contains exactly one main clause with or without some subordinate clauses attached to it.

A BETTER INDEX THAN SENTENCE LENGTH

Such units were given the name of 'minimal terminable unit' or, for short, 'T-unit'.

An investigation into the number of T-units per sentence turned out to be interesting and revealing. In our fourth-grade passage there are six T-units per sentence. That is an unusually high number even for a fourth-grader. Most 4th graders punctuate better than he did, but not all of them punctuate very well, and they average 1.6. By punctuating better, 8th graders cut that number down to 1.4; 12th-graders cut down to 1.2; and skilled adults are about the same, 1.2. Every compound or compound-complex sentence contains more than one main clause, and so has two or more T-units. Here is a sentence with two T-units:

They tried and tried, but while they were trying they killed a whale and used the oil for the lamps.

The number of T-units per sentence is a measure of T-unit co-ordination.

At the same time, the average number of words per T-unit turns out to be revealing too. For our 4th-grade passage it is sixty-eight divided by six, giving eleven. For a 4th grader that is very high. The average score for them is about 8.6. For 8th-graders the score is 11.5; for 12th-graders, 14.4; for skilled adults, 20.3. Average number of words per T-unit (T-unit length) turns out to be a much better index of age than is sentence length. And if we see the arithmetical relation between the three measures discussed so far – words per sentence, T-units per sentence, and words per T-unit – we come to a new understanding. We now see that sentence length *increases* with age because T-unit length *increases* with age, and in spite of the fact that the number of T-units per sentence *decreases* with age. Understanding this relation also explains why sentence length is as good an index of age as it is, and also why it is no better, why it is not as good an index as T-unit length.

Readers with an inclination for mathematics will quickly see that for any passage, of whatever length, the following formula will hold true:

$$\frac{\text{No. words}}{\text{No. T-units}} \times \frac{\text{No. T-units}}{\text{No. sentences}} = \frac{\text{No. words}}{\text{No. sentences}}$$

SUBORDINATE CLAUSES AS INDEXES OF MATURITY

Looking back now to the article already cited from the 1960 *Encyclopedia of Educational Research* we see that our investigation has refined the assertion that sentence length is an index of maturity. We would now add that T-unit length is a better index. We have not yet examined McCarthy's assertion about number of subordinate clauses and length of subordinate clauses, but we will turn to those next.

In school grammars a clause is usually defined as 'a group of words with a subject (or co-ordinate subjects) and a finite verb (or co-ordinate finite verbs)'. Sometimes a 'finite' verb is decribed as one with a 'tense and number marker'. Infinitives and participles are not 'finite' forms. The definition of clause given above is the one to be understood in this chapter. How many clauses appear in the following sentence?

> The captain said 'If you can kill the white whale, I will give this gold to the one that can do it'.

There are four clauses here, and their skeleton subjects and verbs are these: 'captain said', 'you can kill', 'I will give', 'that can do'. The first is the main clause, the other three are subordinate clauses. Four clauses per T-unit is unusually high. In the 4th grade passage we have been working with, we have six T-units containing eleven clauses, an average of almost two clauses per T-unit. That is extremely high for a 4th-grader. The average for them is 1.3; for 8th-graders, 1.4; 12th-graders, 1.7; skilled adults, 1.8.

Those figures will become more meaningful if we talk about sets of ten T-units so as not to talk about tenths of a subordinate clause. If 4th-graders average 1.3 clauses per T-unit, that means that for ten T-units (with exactly ten main clauses) 4th-graders will average three subordinate clauses. Eighth-graders, with about 1.4 clauses per T-unit, will have, in ten T-units with exactly ten main clauses, four subordinate clauses; one more than 4th-graders. twelfth-graders appear to make a big jump to 1.7 clauses per T-unit, that is, with ten T-units (and ten main clauses) they will have seven subordinate clauses. Skilled adults average only a shade more, 1.8: in ten T-units with ten main clauses they will average eight subordinate clauses, only one more than 12th-graders. In number of sub-ordinate clauses there appears to be a big jump between grades 8 and 12, but no big jump before or after.

CLAUSE LENGTH AS AN INDEX OF MATURITY

What is the mean length of these clauses, measured in numbers of words? To get that score we simply divide the number of words by the number of clauses. For our 4th-grade passage,. with 68 words and 12 clauses, the score is 68 divided by 12, or 5.7. That score is low for a 4th-grader. The average for them is 6.6. The older groups go up steadily: next 8.1, 8.6, 11.5. Notice the big jump from 8.6 for 12th-graders to 11.5 for skilled adults. That is a gain of 2.9 words, almost 3.0. The average 12th-grader has gained only 2.0 words since he was a 4th-grader. So if he is ever to write like a skilled adult he has farther to go than he has come since he was back in the 4th grade.

We are now in a position to re-evaluate McCarthy's (1954) statement about what it is that makes the length of sentences increase with the age of the writers. Already we have seen that the sentence length increases because T-unit length increases. But what makes T-unit length increase? Is it because more subordinate clauses are added, keeping the length of the clauses about the same, or because the clauses are lengthened, keeping the number of clauses about the same? We now have some data on which to base an opinion. McCarthy's statement was that:

> Apparently length of clause is somewhat controlled or restricted by the nature of language, and whatever increase in sentence length occurs at higher grade levels is brought about largely through the addition of more subordinate clauses. (p. 522)

Our data indicate that if either of these indexes is controlled or restricted at higher grade levels by the nature of language, it is the number of subordinate clauses, not the length of clauses. In number of subordinate clauses 12th-graders are close to skilled adults, but in length of clauses they have a very long way to go. Whatever increase in sentence length occurs at higher age levels is brought about largely through the lengthening of clauses, not the addition of more subordinate clauses.

The reader with an interest in mathematics will see that we can now make an addition to our earlier formula:

$$\frac{\text{No. words}}{\text{No. clauses}} \times \frac{\text{No. clauses}}{\text{No. T-units}} = \frac{\text{No. words}}{\text{No. T-units}}$$

SYNOPSIS OF CLAUSE LENGTH TO SENTENCE LENGTH

We can combine this formula with the previous one to provide ourselves with a synopsis of factors that show the relation between clause length (words per clause), subordinate clause ratio (clauses per T-unit), T-unit length (words per T-unit), T-unit co-ordination index (T-units per sentence) and, finally, sentence length (words per sentence). Written as fractions, the synopsis looks like this:

$$\frac{\text{No. words}}{\text{No. clauses}} \times \frac{\text{No. clauses}}{\text{No. T-units}} = \frac{\text{No. words}}{\text{No. T-units}} \times \frac{\text{No. T-units}}{\text{No. sentences}}$$

$$= \frac{\text{No. words}}{\text{No. sentences}}$$

A TEST OF THE THEORY

Finally let us apply what we have learned. Let us suppose that we do not know who wrote the Moby Dick passage and we want to establish the approximate age of the writer. Judged by his sentence length he is a very superior adult. But he co-ordinates T-units excessively and that is immature, so we know he is not really a superior adult; such adults know how to punctuate. Judged by his T-unit length he is a very superior 4th-grader – almost an 8th-grader. But his T-unit length is so high because he wrote so many subordinate clauses in one of his T-units: three. At the same time his clause length is quite low, 5.7, whereas the average for 4th-graders is 6.6. That low score is due to that one sentence with so many subordinate clauses. Our data are good enough to tell us what is confusing the picture.

Suppose we ignore that one sentence with three subordinate clauses, and get the synopsis figures on the rest of the passage. On the five remaining T-units the average length is 8.8, very close to our 4th-grade average of 8.5. His subordinate clause index is now 1.4, very close to our 4th-grade average of 1.3. His words per clause, his clause length, is 6.3, within 5 percent of the 4th-grade average of 6.6. So when we omit the one exceptional sentence, he comes to look like a very average 4th-grader, which is exactly what a larger sample, 1000 words instead of fifty or sixty, showed him to be.

SHORT T-UNITS MOVE TO LONG ONES

So far the increase in T-unit length has been described by giving the shift in mean that occurs with age. That figure does not give the full picture of the change over time. We can describe that change better if we talk about 'short' T-units (by which we will mean all those less than 10 words long); 'middle length' (from 10 to 20); 'long' (above 20). At all ages investigated, from a third to a half of the T-units are of 'middle length'. The real action is at the extremes. Over time, short ones are consolidated into long ones. The youngest students write a great number of shorts and almost no longs. Skilled adults write twice as many longs as shorts.

Here are the figures for the four age groups: 4th-graders write forty-two times as many shorts as longs (and their longs are not very long); 8th-graders write five short ones for every long one; 12th-graders write one and a half shorts for every long; skilled adults write only half a short for every long, and many of their longs are very long. The action is at the extremities, and that is what affects the means.

WHOSE AVERAGES ARE THEY?

The averages that have been given for each grade are those for 1000 words of writing by each of eighteen students with average IQ scores, 90–110. The subject-matter of their writings was not controlled by the researcher; he simply asked the teachers to 'have every student in this class write more than a thousand words on whatever topics you and he would ordinarily choose. Just make sure that all writing is done under your close supervision so that it will be his work alone.'

The writers, who are here called 'skilled adults', are simply those who happened to write non-fiction articles in *Harpers* and *Atlantic* magazines for January, February, and March of 1964. No attempt was made to select the 'better' writers from those issues, the rationale being that a subjective choice might bias the results in a personal way, and that all whose articles were accepted must be skilled writers even if not professional writers.

In comparing these people with average IQ schoolchildren, one of the continuums is obviously broken: the age continuum is kept intact, but the IQ continuum is broken. What their IQ's were in grade school was not asked.

HOW ABOUT MENTAL AGE?

Shortly after the analysis of writing by schoolchildren of average IQ scores was completed, a comparison of children with superior IQ scores (above 130) was made (Hunt, 1967). At the 4th-grade level there was no significant difference between the two in clause length, but the difference in the subordinate clause index was significant at the 0.005 level, with the superior students ahead, of course.

At the top end of the public school system the direction of growth is different; it is in clause length, as was noted earlier in referring to the McCarthy (1954) statement. For this index, at the 12th-grade level, the difference between the high IQ students and the average is significant at the 0.005 level. For the average students we said earlier that, to equal skilled adults in clause length, they had farther to go than they had gone since they were in the 4th grade. For the superior students the situation is quite different. They are already closer to the skilled adults in clause length than they are to their average IQ classmates.

The high IQ 12th-graders write even fewer subordinate clauses per T-unit than their average classmates; but in T-unit length, the product of the other two indexes, the superior students are significantly ahead of the average ones. This situation supports the earlier evidence that in the early grades both clause length and number of clauses increase but for full maturity it is clause length that will grow, not the other index. In fact, it may well be that, among high-school and college students, clause length is a better index of maturity than is T-unit length, even though T-unit length is the better measure to cover the full age span. The superior performance of high IQ 4th-graders and 12th-graders suggests that syntactic maturity scores may be correlated more highly with mental age than chronological age scores.

WHAT DID THEY WRITE ABOUT?

Researchers have investigated writing development over less than the whole span of developmental years up to 4 or 5 at the most, and have been content with a relatively brief corpus to represent each student. They have often controlled the subject-matter of their writing sample, perhaps by having students write in response to a movie, or pictures, or perhaps by assigning a carefully limited topic. The study I have just reviewed has been criticized for not controlling the subject-matter of the writings in some such way, or for not at least specifying more exactly what topics were written on at different grade levels.

My choice not to control the subject-matter may have been unwise, but I still do not think so, particularly after making one small effort to get one theme from all grade levels in response to a movie.

There were several aims which influenced my decision. One aim was to get a substantial body of writing from each student, 1000 words each, so that I could look for what might be called 'within-student' variations. Another aim was to cover the whole span of maturation, at least 10 years, and many more if I included adults. Those two aims would make problems. I knew that 4th-graders write so few words on a given topic that it would take a dozen or more sittings to produce 1000 words. Twelfth-graders, on the other hand, would produce so large a corpus on a dozen or more topics that I would have to select from their writings and I was reluctant to do that. If I wanted to include skilled adults I knew I could not make them write on the same twelve or more topics as the 4th-graders.

Furthermore, I was not sure that it fitted my purpose to limit the subject matter to movie-watching or any assigned expository or descriptive topics. I wanted to study the syntax schoolchildren use in whatever writing they do in their daily lives at their various ages. Since they do virtually all their writing in school for their teachers, if they do any at all, it seemed most natural simply to take a fair-sized sample of that writing, whatever topics the various ages wrote on.

I was looking for longitudinal coverage, not lateral. If I could find any new significant measures over a long time-span, then it would be entirely possible for anyone to go back and check for lateral variations at any age due to different topics, different situations, different audiences, or anything else. I have no doubt that there are such lateral variations, and that they are worth investigating. In the final chapter of *Grammatical Structures* (Hunt, 1965) is a section called 'The Influence of Subject Matter'. It ends this way:

> We need to know whether subject matter, or mode of discourse, or treatment of subject matter tends to change characteristically as a child matures. This study merely assumes as much. We need also to isolate and describe more clearly the effect of subject matter on grammatical structures.

WHY DO CLAUSES GET LONGER?

The analyses which produced the five indexes reported on so far, also produced thirty-one others that were found by an analysis of variance to be significantly different for age between the three grades 4, 8, and 12. There is no space here to discuss those thirty-one, except to say that what school grammarians call modifiers of nouns were found to increase significantly among older writers, and that nominalizations of whole sentences or parts of them also increased among older writers.

The fact that successively older writers produce successively longer T-units and clauses can be pictured in either of two ways: as a process of adding or of consolidating. The addition theory would say that older writers have more to say (as of course they do) so they add those thoughts to the shorter clauses and T-units they would otherwise be writing. The teaching implication might be that students need to live more, read more, think more in order to write more maturely, which is no doubt true.

THE CONSOLIDATION PICTURE

The consolidation picture emphasizes something much less obvious to the general population; the generative–transformational picture of what Chomsky (1968) called in the early 1960s 'kernel' sentences and 'sentence-combining transformations'. The model for Hunt's analysis in *Grammatical Structures* (1965) was Robert B. Lees' *The Grammar of English Nominalizations* (1960).

The consolidation picture says that, given certain things to say, the older writer has the syntactic ability to transform a larger number of kernel sentences into a single T-unit and a single clause. That is what makes his clauses and T-units longer. He gets greater length because he gets greater depth.

The implication for teaching might be to increase this ability by direct methods, if possible. If that could be done, then one of the consequences might be improved writing quality.

However, such a desirable outcome was by no means assured. It might be that direct methods could no more improve this ability to consolidate than direct methods can appreciably affect IQ scores, except in so far as students can improve their ability to take tests. It might also be that the direct methods would improve the ability to consolidate but not improve writing quality, just as improving IQ scores by teaching students how to take tests will not make them more intelligent persons – except when taking tests.

In the course of *Grammatical Structures* Hunt (1965) pointed out many occasions where the youngest writers failed to reduce and consolidate sentences as an older one would, and how such reduction and consolidation would increase clause length and T-unit length: 'Moby Dick was a whale. The whale was very strong.' Two sentences, two clauses, two T-units; average T-unit length five words, average clause length five words. 'Moby Dick was a very strong whale.' One sentence, one clause, one T-unit; average T-unit length and clause length increased to seven words (p. 105).

A RECOMMENDATION FOR TEACHING

The study closed with a recommendation.

> This study suggests a kind of sentence-building program that probably has never been produced, or at least not systematically and fully. The aim would be to widen the student's span of grammatical attention and concern. The method would be for him to reduce independent clauses to subordinate clauses and nonclauses, consolidating them with adjoining clauses and T-units. He could work up to structures of considerable depth and complexity comparable to those exhibited by twelfth graders and superior adults. (p. 157)

A CONTROLLED SUBJECT EXPERIMENT

In order to settle the question of whether in fact older students do have superior ability to reduce sentences and consolidate them with others, Hunt (1970) designed an experiment giving students of various ages an opportunity to perform the desired operation on a passage written in extremely short, simple, kernel-like sentences. What the students would say was controlled; how they said it was up to them.

The passage chosen was designed by a colleague, Dr Roy O'Donnell, who had already used it as an evaluatory instrument for a 6th-grade curriculum. It provides numerous opportunities to produce complex nominals by the addition of modifiers. Here is the passage with its directions.

ALUMINIUM

> *Directions:* Read the passage all the way through. You will notice that the sentences are short and choppy. Study the passage, and then re-write it in a better way. You may combine sentences, change the order of words, and omit words that are repeated too many times. But try not to leave out any of the information.

Aluminum is a metal. It is abundant. It has many uses. It comes from bauxite. Bauxite is an ore. Bauxite looks like clay. Bauxite contains aluminium. It contains several other substances. Workmen extract these other substances from the bauxite. They grind the bauxite. They put it in tanks. Pressure is in the tanks. The other substances form a mass. They remove the mass. They use filters. A liquid remains. They put it through several other processes. It finally yields a chemical. The chemical is powdery. It is white. The chemical is alumina. It is a mixture. It contains aluminum. It contains oxygen. Workmen separate the aluminum from the oxygen. The use electricity. They finally produce a metal. The metal is light. It has a luster. The luster is bright. The luster is silvery. This metal comes in many forms.

The passage was rewritten by fifty students from each of grades 4, 6, 8, 10 and 12. Within each grade students were chosen on the basis of their IQ or, for some grades, standardized achievement scores, so as to represent a very close to normal distribution of scores. Twenty-five skilled adults, persons who had published recently in *Harpers* or *Atlantic* magazines, also participated.

Their performance provides an exemplary display of the ability which was hypothesized. That ability is manifested whenever a student 'reduces' an input kernel sentence to a subordinate clause (in this particular passage it is almost always an adjective-relative clause) and consolidates it into a more inclusive sentence: 'Aluminum is abundant' is reduced to 'which is abundant' and is consolidated into another T-unit

Aluminium, which is abundant, is a metal.

Or the input may be converted to 'less than a clause' by deleting the subject or deleting the finite verb, or deleting both as when 'It is abundant' loses both subject and verb so that only the adjective 'abundant' survives to be consolidated with an adjoining T-unit to produce

Aluminum is an abundant metal.

By this process some of the most senior writers consolidated all six first inputs into a single clause twelve words long like this:

> Aluminum, an abundant and useful metal, comes from bauxite, a clay-like ore.

Successively older students do more and more of this. I will not report on the results in detail, but will only report the number of inputs, out of thirty-two, that were reduced and consolidated with the adjoining expressions. Grade 4 reduced and consolidated an average of 4.1 inputs; grade 6, 10.9; grade 8, 16.0; grade 10, 18.6; grade 12, 19.1; skilled adults, 22.5. Across intervals of 2 years the score go up every time. There can be no doubt that this ability is related to age.

Of course the average clause length goes up at every interval. Here are those lengths in order: 5.19, 5.76, 6.79, 7.35, and 7.85. For what I here call average adults to distinguish them from 'skilled adults', the score was 8.40, and for skilled adults the score was 9.95.

The correlation between the clause length scores and the number of inputs reduced to 'less than a clause' is 0.87, a very high correlation considering that a correlation of no higher than 0.15 would still be significant at the 0.01 level. This explains how clauses are lengthened.

The relations between length and number of consolidations such as was hypothesized on the evidence given in the study of normal free writing gets extremely strong support from this experiment.

DOES THIS HAPPEN IN OTHER LANGUAGES?

The study just described has been replicated in the Netherlands by Reesink and others (1971), who, reporting their findings in *Psychological Abstracts*, conclude: The similarity between Dutch and American children in syntactic development is outstanding'.

To see whether this kind of syntactic development occurs in languages completely unrelated to English, a simplified version of the *Aluminum* experiment was performed in Fijian, Indonesian, Korean, Laotian, Marshallese, and Japanese. An instrument was devised which was expected to be understandable in any culture, and it was translated into each of the languages named above. Here is the English version:

THE CHICKEN

> *Directions:* Read the story all the way through. You will see that it is not very well written. Study the story, and then write it over again in a better way. You will want to change many of the sentences, but try not to leave out any important parts of the story.

> A man lived in a farmhouse. He was old. He lived alone. The house was small. The house was on a mountain. The mountain was high. The house was on the top. He grew vegetables. He grew grain. He ate the vegetables. He ate the grain. One day he was pulling weeds. He saw something. A chicken was eating his grain. The grain was new. He caught the chicken. He put her in a pen. The pen was under his window. He planned something. He would eat the chicken for breakfast. The next morning came. It was early. A sound woke the man. He looked out the window. He saw the chicken. He saw an egg. The chicken cackled. The man thought something. He would eat the egg for breakfast. He fed the chicken a cup of his grain. The chicken talked to him. He talked to the chicken. Time passed. He thought something. He could feed the chicken more. He could feed her two cups of grain. He could feed her in the morning. He could feed her at night. Maybe she would lay two eggs every morning. He fed the chicken more grain. She got fat. She got lazy. She slept all the time. She laid no eggs. The man got angry. He blamed the chicken. He killed her. He ate her for breakfast. He had no chicken. He had no eggs. He talked to no one. No one talked to him.

Those translated versions were then rewritten by children aged about 9, 13, and 17 who were native speakers of one of the languages named. The papers for each of the languages except Japanese were scored for words per T-unit by a native speaker of that language who also was a teacher. For each language the mean of the scores for the oldest students was above the mean of scores for the middle age group, and that was above the mean for the youngest group. The papers in Japanese were scored differently, for number of S-constituents per T-unit, and in Japanese too the three groups fell into order. The chance of the three groups falling into this order for one language is 1 in 6. The chance of it occurring in six languages is something like 1 in 46,000.

This evidence suggests that this kind of syntactic development is a charcteristic of all languages, and so corresponds to a biological characteristic of all people; one which develops naturally with maturity.

THE FIRST SENTENCE-COMBINING CURRICULUMS

The first major sentence-combining curriculum was begun by John Mellon for 7th-graders in 1966; the results were published the next year (Mellon, 1967). For half the school year his students studied a transformational grammar which he had written and which ended with rules for combining sentences in specific ways, each way having its own symbol. During the second half of the year they began the exercises. These consisted of a series of short sentences to be combined in a certain way that was signaled both by indentation and by the symbols for specific transformations. Mellon's sentences were neither self-consciously bizarre nor banal; instead they seem to have come live out of adult, hard-working prose. Finishing one would be gratifying. Here is a sample of moderate difficulty.

> *Problem*
> The children clearly must have wondered SOMETHING.
> The bombings had orphaned the children.
> SOMETHING was humanly possible somehow.
> (T:wh – T:exp)
> Their conquerors pretended SOMETHING (T:infin)
> Chewing gum and smiles might compensate for the losses (T:fact)
> The losses were heartbreaking.
> They had so recently sustained the losses.

By following the signals, the students would produce this sentence:

> The children whom the bombing had orphaned clearly must have wondered how it was humanly possible for their conquerors to pretend that chewing gum and smiles might compensate for the heartbreaking losses which they had so recently sustained.

At the end of the year the control students and the experimentals wrote papers that were then analyzed for T-unit length and a number of other measures. The control students had gained almost nothing, but the experimental students had gained what looked to be 2 years' syntactic growth.

Grading a small fraction of the papers written as the post-test showed, to quote Mellon, 'no undesirable effects stemming from the sentence combining practice'. This was hardly a rousing endorsement for the curriculum.

In this way the first 'signaled' exercises were born. Each problem had just one right answer. By following the specified directions the students produced a sentence that was mature and, it seems to me, well-shaped, as a sentence can be by itself. On can easily suppose that the difficult exercises, combining as many as a dozen sentences, stretched the abilities of the 7th-graders so that they wrote longer T-units on the post-tests. But such exercises would teach nothing about the relation of a sentence to its context, and sentences live only in that society, as parts of whole discourse. At least this study showed that syntactic maturity could be increased by direct methods.

In 1969 Hunt (Hunt and O'Donnell, 1970) began to devise a different kind of exercise for 4th-graders to see whether they too could profit from sentence-combining. They could not possibly be taught a grammar, nor could they learn symbols for combining kernels; but their performance on the *Aluminum* passage indicated that they could combine sentences in a stylistically satisfactory way without any instruction on how to do so. Why not make a curriculum out of a series of short discourses like *Aluminum*, except more interesting to this age level? So about 100 such discourses were created, ranging from two sentences to more than twenty. Here is a sample.

(1) I made a present.
(2) The present was for my mother.
(3) I wrapped the present.
(4) I wrapped it in gold paper.
(5) The gold paper had stars on it.

Exercises like this have come to be called non-signaled or 'open' exercises Here there is no instruction to delete all of the second sentence except the prepositional phrase of purpose. There is no instruction to delete the third sentence and co-ordinate the predicate of the fourth sentence with the predicate produced from sentences (1) and (2), etc. Even without such instructions or, more accurately, only without such instructions, many 4th-graders will, intuitively, do just what the instructions would have called for, that is, produce:

I made a present for my mother and wrapped it in gold paper with stars on it.

THE INCREASE IN SENTENCE-COMBINING

Since those early days the sentence-combining movement has grown substantially. A half-dozen texts are on the market, and are used in hundreds if not thousands of schoolrooms. In 1978, more than 350 people representing over 100 institutions in thirty-eight states and Canada came to Oxford, Ohio, to attend the Miami University Conference on Sentence Combining and the Teaching of Writing.

Every few years a survey of the printed studies appears, and dozens of doctoral candidates have written their own. One of the most recent and perspicacious is by Kerek *et al*. (1980a) who list thirty-five major studies, at least one for every grade from first up through all levels of college. The list even includes one study for adults. Every one of these studies has tested the success of the curriculum in some way that the experimenter considers objective. Almost always there is a pre-test and a post-test for a control and an experimental group, and almost always the evaluation of the pre-and post-tests includes an analysis of T-unit length, clause length, and subordinate clause ratio. Almost always the experimental group is significantly ahead in T-unit length even if not clause length. The usual gain seems to be about 2 years in 1.

A CHALLENGE TO SENTENCE COMBINING

At this point it is important to ask, of syntactic maturity gains, 'So what? What good comes of increasing syntactic maturity, if nothing else comes from it?'

A recent experiment by Smith and Combs (1980) threatens to take the wind out of sentence-combining researchers who get significant gains in syntactic maturity but can show no gains in writing quality. With college freshmen, Smith and Combs report that they can get a significant increase in syntactic maturity scores in 2 hours of class time in either of two ways. These are by telling students that the reader will be a highly intelligent person who is influenced by long, complex sentences; or by presenting them with a two-class-hour programmed text in sentence-combining exercises. They measure the effect of these two brief treatments by behavior on the *Aluminum* passage and on an ordinary writing task.

If in 2 hours or less Smith and Combs can bring about the changes that other researchers have taken 100 hours, a whole term, to accomplish, then what to do sentence-combining researchers have to be proud of?

AN ANSWER TO THAT CHALLENGE

There is an answer to that question, I think, and the rest of this chapter will be devoted to it. The answer is, in brief, that the sentence-combining program tested in 1976 at Miami University in Oxford, Ohio (Kerek, *et al.*, 1980a) did in fact improve the writing quality of experimental students to an unusual extent. I will summarize the study in some detail because the treatment is unique, and because the thoroughness of the testing for writing quality is state-of-the-art. The treatment is unique in that sentence-combining constituted the whole course. It is almost unique in that the syntactic problem of how best to combine the given sentences became a syntactic–semantic–rhetorical problem of 'What is the difference in meaning between these various combinations of the same underlying sentences, and which of those meanings best enhances the rhetorical purpose of the discourse as a whole.'

MATCHING THE STUDENTS AND THE TEACHERS

The students involved were 290 freshmen drawn from the lower 80 percent of the entering class who happened to be assigned randomly by computer to the six sections which were to become the experimental group and to another six which were to become the control group. The sections were equal in size and met at comparable times of the day on the same days of the week. The students in the two groups were not significantly different in ability as measured by their SAT and ACT scores.

The teachers for the two groups were carefully matched. They were paired according to age, academic rank, years of experience, and assessed teaching effectiveness. Control sections were taught by teachers who accepted the traditional method, and experimental sections by teachers who welcomed a new approach. With the help of the English Department Chairman and the Director of Freshman Composition, teachers were also matched on the basis of student evaluation.

PRE-TESTS AND POST-TESTS

Both groups of students wrote eight compositions, and wrote them at the same time. The first of these served as the pre-test and the last served as the post-test. Students wrote both test papers in 2-hour periods under equivalent and rigorously controlled conditions.

Of the many procedures to maintain comparable testing conditions, and to eliminate the possibility of bias in the evaluations yet to come, the handling of writing topics was the most important. The pre-tests and post-tests for both groups were going to be used as the basis for a four-way comparison. To find out whether the two groups started off writing equally well at the outset the two sets of pre-test scores would be compared. How much a group improved under instruction could be ascertained by comparing its pre-test scores with its post-test scores and computing the difference, the amount of gain. Once the gain scores for each group were ascertained, it would be clear which group had improved more.

If the scores for this four-way comparison were to be as unbiased as possible, it was essential that, as the scorers read each paper, they be blind as to whether it was experimental or control, and whether pre-test or post-test.

To provide such blindness, two equal topics were needed, A and B. For the pre-test, half of each group was assigned topic A, and half topic B. For the post-test, each student was assigned the topic he had not written on before. Both topics were an exposition that invited descriptive and narrative supporting details.

CONTROL AND EXPERIMENTAL CURRICULUMS

The program followed by the six control sections was traditional in many colleges. Its texts were a book of readings (*The Harbrace Reader*), a rhetoric (McCrimmon's *Writing with a Purpose*), and a syllabus. The syllabus prescibed the essays to be read and analyzed, the modes of development to be explained and practiced (description, definition, comparison and contrast, classification, cause and effect, argument, persuasion, and rhetorical analysis) and the elements of writing to be discussed (thesis development, paragraph construction, sentence structure, levels of usage, diction, and tone). It also allotted time for introducing writing assignments and for evaluating student compositions.

The six experimental sections wrote the same eight themes, but otherwise their curriculum was completely different. They spent all their time, inside class and out, on sentence combining. The only text was William Strong's *Sentence Combining: A Composing book*; this consists of ninety passages written in extremely simple kernel-like sentences. The student is to rewrite each passage in the best way he can. The early passages are short descriptive paragraphs but the later passages are complex narrative and expository blocks of paragraphs. To supplement that text, additional model exercises on appositives, infinitives, complex prepositional phrases, and parallel constructions were recreated. Some of Strong's exercises were adapted in order to emphasize such writing elements as organization and tone.

Here is part of an early exercise from Strong's text.

(1) The ashtray squats.
(2) The ashtray is fat.
(3) The ashtray is ugly.
(4) The ashtray is in the middle of the table.
(5) It is a monstrosity.
(6) The monstrosity is porcelain.

The experimenters report that early in the term students typically combined those into sentences like 'The fat and ugly ashtray squats in the middle of the table. It is a monstrosity of porcelain.' A few weeks later they often produced sentences that were less ordinary: 'In the middle of the table squats the fat and ugly ashtray, a monstrosity of porcelain'; 'Fat and ugly, a porcelain monstrosity, the ashtray squats in the middle of the table.' There are scores of ways in which Strong's input sentences can be rewritten.

AN EXPERIMENTAL CLASS

A typical assignment in the experimental section would be for all students to rewrite one of Strong's exercises. Two or three students would be given ditto masters on which to write their versions or perhaps someone would type mimeo stencils. The instructor would make sure that, for the next class, two or more versions would be presented so that all students could see them and discuss them as solutions to the rewriting assignment. Any student who liked something he had done could present it for class appraisal by using the overhead projector. Students were constantly aware of the wide variety of options available for combining the various sentences, and were constantly looking for reasons to prefer one option rather than another. In the continual search for reasons for such preference, the instructor would advance any principle of rhetoric he knew that was pertinent to the problem at hand.

The focus of the course was never on how to write long T-units. It was always on how to write good ones. A sentence in context needs to be judged as part of a rhetorical whole.

This course used the sentence-combining format even for teaching organization of the whole discourse. For several of Strong's discourses the kernel sentences were rearranged so as to violate the original sequence, thus leaving the student to decide how to reorder them into paragraphs and into the whole essay.

The kernel sentence format was also used in teaching tone. Strong presents sixty kernels on Cesar Chavez, which the students used in order to produce an essay whose tone was distinctly favorable to Chavez. For the next assignment they were told to make whatever syntactic and lexical changes were necessary to produce an essay clearly hostile to Chavez. Such an assignment involves sentence combining, but it also involves much more.

GRADING THE TESTS

At the completion of the 15-week semester the process of evaluation began. With the help of substantial grant funds it was possible to carry out what I suppose was the most thorough and most rigorously controlled evaluation of an experimental English program ever undertaken in the United States.

Twenty-eight college English teachers were employed for a 4-day period during Christmas vacation. Most of them held Ph.D.s in English and the rest held MA.s except for one B.A. who was well qualified by virtue of his extensive experience with Educational Testing Service. In college English teaching experience they averaged more than 12 years each, and none had fewer than 3 years.

Meticulous care was taken to preserve the double-blind anonymity of the test papers, and the same care was taken to provide optimal conditions for the training and work of the graders, and to assure that no grader knew what grade had been given to a test by any of his team-mates. Each of the 190 pre-tests and the same number of post-tests were scored on a scale from 1 to 6 for overall quality. Four graders scored each paper that way, and the average of those scores was the mark recorded for that paper. This kind of rating was called holistic.

Each paper was also scored for six separate attributes: ideas, supporting details, organization and coherence, sentence structure, diction and usage, voice. The last, voice, was defined as 'the extent to which the essay speaks with individuality and distinctiveness of tone'. Each of the six attributes was scored separately on a scale from 1 to 6. This kind of rating was called analytic.

Each paper was scored analytically by four graders who had not graded it holistically. Their gradings would confirm or disconfirm the grading of the holistic graders and would go into more detail and tell in which attributes each group was superior.

In addition to the holistic and analytic ratings the papers were scored a third way; by forced choice. The idea is to choose papers by one experimental and one control student who started out equal on their pre-test and then require a rater to decide which of the two was better at post-test – preserving anonymity, of course. There turned out to be 134 pairs of students such that each of the two got a pre-test score within a quarter point of the other. The post-tests by each of these pairs was then judged by ten scorers.

By all three modes of judging the experimental students came out ahead, and since the holistic score is the one most usually employed in grading English compositions, and most likely to be reliable, it is that scoring which will be interpreted first.

At the outset of the grading the graders were told to try to assign about equal numbers of papers to each of the six scores and not to aim for a bell curve distribution with just a few getting the bottom score of 1 and a few the top score of 6. In a 6-point scale there is no middle score: the close-to-average paper wil get either a 3, 'slightly below average', or a 4, 'slightly above average'.

INTERPRETING THE HOLISTIC RESULTS

On the pre-tests the scores for the controls and experimental students were not significantly different from each other; but on the post-tests, with the scores covaried to offset the slight difference on pre-tests, the experimental students were superior, and the difference was significant ($p < 0.001$).

The superiority of the experimental group can be made meaningful by other interpretations. The control students improved during the semester one-fifth of a point; the experimental students moved up half a point, that is two and a half times as far. In other words, the controls moved 7.4 percent of the remaining distance to the top score of 6; the experimentals moved 18.9 percent of the distance.

Another way to interpret the results of the holistic grading is to ask how many individuals of each group showed losses and how many showed gains during the semester, and how many stayed the same. The number of students who stayed the same was eleven for the controls and eleven for the experimental students also. The number whose grades went down was fifty-one for the controls, and, for the more fortunate experimental group, only thirty-three. The number whose grades went up was seventy-seven for the controls and 107 for the experimental group. In summary, the experimental group had more students go up and fewer go down.

Yet another way to interpret the results of the holistic grading would be to ask: 'If you were below average at the outset, what was your chance of being above average at the end, if you were a control student? What if you were an experimental student?' A student who got a score of 4 had to be considered above average by all four of his judges, or had to get as many points above 4 as he got below 4.

Here is the answer to that question. On the pre-test, 103 controls and 120 experimental students scored less than 4; at the end of the semester only nineteen of those controls came up to 4 or above, whereas fifty of the experimental group did so. That is, if you were below average to start with, you had two and a half times as good a chance of coming up to a 4 if you were put into one of the experimental sections, as if you were put into a control section.

If you were 4 or above on the pre-test, what was your chance of falling down below a 4 on the post-test if you were a control or an experimental student? Among the controls, thirteen who began above 4 ended up below 4; among the experimental students only eight suffered that dismal fate. Again, your chances were better with the experimental group.

Did the experimental program help one set of students, perhaps the good students, the poor students, or perhaps the average students, at the expense of the others? The answer was no. If you put all students together and divide up that whole entity into four equal quartiles on the basis of pre-test scores, you find that the gain shown between pre-test scores and post-test scores was greater for experimental students than for controls within every one of the quartiles. At all levels you were better off with the experimental group.

INTERPRETING THE ANALYTIC RESULTS

The analytic rating in which six attributes were each scored separately confirmed the outcome of the holistic rating: the experimental students did write better. In fact, they were superior in each of the six attributes, and in five of them the difference was statistically significant. The only attribute in which their superiority was not significant was 'organization and coherence'.

It is not surprising that a course in sentence combining would substantially improve sentence structure, but that it should improve 'ideas', 'supporting details', 'diction and usage', and even 'voice' is, at least at the superficial level, hardly to be expected. But this course was not limited to sentence combining in any narrow sense; it was focused instead on how to rewrite the given kernels in the most fully effective way.

INTERPRETING THE FORCED CHOICE RESULTS

By now it will be no surprise when I report that on the third way of comparing the two groups of papers, that is by forced choice, the experimental group came out ahead again. They had seventy-nine wins, forty-two losses, and thirteen ties. To interpret the data another way, the ten judges made a total of 1340 individual judgments; 785 of them favored the experimental group, 555 favored the controls. That is 59 percent versus 41 percent, just one percentage point away from 60–40. These differences are statistically significant by a chi-square test.

If we look at each section separately to see how each instructor made out, we find that each experimental instructor had more wins than losses, whereas only one of the control instructors had that much success. Since three of the six instructors in each group were graduate assistants, we must acknowledge that even the three inexperienced teachers with the experimental curriculum had better success than even the three experienced teachers did with the traditional curriculum.

THE STUDENTS' OPINIONS

On the last day of the semester, sentence-combining students expressed their opinions about the course by responding to four questions. Their overall response was clearly positive. Two out of three students said they liked sentence combining as an approach to writing. The same proportion said they would recommend such a course to a friend. Nearly three out of four felt that the course had helped them increase their writing skills.

THE FOLLOW-UP

Twenty-eight months later, when those students who had stayed in school were juniors, a follow-up testing was done under conditions as close as possible to conditions at the time of the post-test. About half the original students from the two groups participated, writing in a 2-hour period on the same topic they had used for their post-test.

This time the grading was handled at Educational Testing Service of Princeton, New Jersey, and the graders knew only that the papers before them had been written by college students somewhere. They regraded, double-blind, the original post-tests and the delayed post-tests for both experimental and control students. Again four graders used the holistic method; a different four used the analytic method. The forced choice grading was dispensed with as unnecessary.

These ETS graders found that, for this half of the original sample, the experimental students were significantly superior on the post-test, just as the Miami graders had found the whole sample to be. The ETS graders found this superiority to be manifest on the holistic rating, and all six categories of the analytic rating.

But the papers written twenty-eight months later told a different story. The experimental students received slightly higher grades than they did on the post-tests, but the control students had improved so much that they virtually had caught up with the others. The experimental students still got slightly higher grades on the delayed post-test, both with the holistic and the analytic gradings, but none of these differences was significant at the 0.05 level.

The researchers concluded that the sentence-combining instruction had accelerated the process of qualitative improvement which students without such instruction also achieve, much more slowly, through normal maturation and experience.

SYNTACTIC MATURITY OF THE TWO GROUPS

In addition to comparing the two groups as to the quality of their writing, they were also compared as to syntactic maturity, that is, T-unit length, clause length, and subordinte clause ratios. At the outset of the experiment there was no statistically significant difference between the syntactic maturity scores of the two groups, just as there was no difference in writing quality. By the end of the semester the sentence combiners, whose writing quality had gained so much, had gained correspondingly in syntactic maturity, and they were superior to the control group at the 0.001 level in clause length and T-unit length. Toward the end of the junior year the control group who had, by then, improved significantly in writing quality, had also increased significantly in syntactic maturity, specifically in clause length and T-unit length at the 0.01 level. Meanwhile, the sentence combiners, who had improved little in writing quality, had not improved much in syntactic maturity either. Now, toward the end of the junior year, there was no significant difference between the two groups in syntactic maturity, just as there was none in writing quality.

A few paragraphs back, in describing the changes in writing quality, it seemed appropriate to say that in one semester the sentence combiners had improved as much as the other students would in 28 months of normal academic experience. The same can be said for their changes in syntactic maturity.

THE STUDENTS' OPINION

At the end of their junior year there remained for the experimental students only one statistically significant residual superiority: their self-confidence. On a questionnaire administered last of all to both groups, there was only one statement on which the responses of the two groups differed with statistical significance. The statement was 'I consider myself a competent writer'. Of the sentence combiners, two-thirds (67.1 percent) responded positively, and less than 10 percent (9.6 percent) negatively. Among those traditionally taught only a little more than half (54.2 percent) responded positively, and 27.1 percent negatively, that is almost three times as many as among sentence combiners.

Responses differed also on a related statement: 'I like to write.' Among sentence combiners, nearly two-thirds (63.0 percent) again agreed with the statement, and 17.8 percent disagreed. Among the control students only half (45.8 percent) agreed with the statement and 32.2 percent, almost twice the percentage for sentence combiners, said they did not like to write.

THE RESEARCHERS' OPINION

Looking back upon the course, the researchers evaluate their curriculum in this way:

> The sentence-combining curriculum followed by the experimental students is but one of many possible sentence-combining curriculums. This is an especially important point because sentence-combining material has become increasingly varied and sophisticated since we designed our curriculum in the summer of 1976. Even though we used sentence-combining exercises as effectively as we knew how, it has become clear in retrospect that we might have done better. ... We are convinced, in other words, that sentence combining can be an even more effective way of teaching writing than this study reveals (Kerek, *et al.*, 1980b, p. 186).

THE RELATION OF SYNTACTIC MATURITY TO WRITING QUALITY

There is no doubt in my mind that syntactic maturity is related to writing quality; but I do not know how close the relation is. If we could get a great body of writing from students of all ages under comparable conditions, and have them all rated holistically as the Miami students were rated, then I would expect us to get a fairly high correlation between syntactic maturity scores and writing quality scores. But it does not surprise me that we get virtually no correlation when we consider students all of the same age, or within a year or two of each other.

An analogy might be drawn betwen height and weight among schoolchildren. Almost always a child gets taller with age. Almost always he gets heavier with age. In fact, if you get heights and weights for all students from kindergarten to graduation you will find a high correlation between one and the other. But if you get the correlation between the two for kindergarten alone or 12th grade alone, the correlation will be low. Step into a classroom and you will see that the heaviest are not always tall.

Having tried to establish in *Syntactic Structures* that T-unit length was significantly correlated with age, I also tried to show that variation could nonetheless be large. I showed that two prose writers, both excellent, could have widely various T-unit length scores, one 9.4, between 4th grade and 8th grade, and the other 22.6, well above the skilled adult mean. One writer was Hemingway in *The Killers*, the other was Faulkner in *Barn-Burning*. There is also wide variance between Hemingway's *The Killers*, with a T-unit length between grades 4 and 6 and the same author's *Francis Macomber*, where the T-unit length is right at the 12th-grade mean. All three writings are superb.

An attempt to decribe this variance in meaningful terms is the aim of 'The stability of T-unit length: a preliminary investigation', by Stephen Witte and Anne Davis, in *Research in the Teaching of English* for February 1980.

For the next decade the aim of sentence combining will not be to see how to get the greatest syntactic maturity gain, but how to get the greatest writing quality gain.

It is certainly interesting in the Miami study to see how, with both control and experimental groups, syntactic maturity scores go up over a period when writing quality is going up, and how they remain the same over a period when writing quality is remaining the same. But the time has probably come when sentence-combining curricula have outgrown syntactic maturity scores, or have reduced them to only an interesting sidelight to the main action.

BRADDOCK TWENTY YEARS AFTER

Twenty years ago Braddock's committee suggested that 'Research in this area [teaching written composition] ... has not frequently been conducted with the knowledge and care that one associates with the physical sciences.' But surely the Miami study is an example to the contrary. In the area of language development 'some terms are being defined usefully, a number of procedures are being refined'. In sentence-combining curricular research it is no longer true that investigators fail to 'inform themselves about the procedures and results of previous research before embarking on their own', or that 'too few of them conduct pilot experiments and validate their measuring instruments before undertaking an investigation'. Nor is it true that 'far too few of those who have conducted an initial piece of research follow it with further exploration or replicate the investigations of others'.

Incidentally, if there is today more research in written composition that is conducted with the care that one associates with the physical sciences, then much of the credit should go to the book which asked for such work and helped show how to get it.

REFERENCES

Braddock, R., Lloyd-Jones, R., and Schoer, L. (1963). *Research in Written Composition*. National Council of Teachers of English, Urbana, Illinois.

Chomsky, N. (1968). Remarks on nominalization. In R. A. Jacobs and P. S. Rosenbaum (eds), *Readings in English transformational Grammar*. Ginn, Waltham, Mass.

Hunt, K. W. (1965). *Grammatical Structures Written at Three Grade Levels*. NCTE Research Report No. 3. National Council of Teachers of English, Urbana, Ill.

Hunt, K. W. (1967). *Sentence structures used by superior students in grades four and twelve and by superior adults*. Co-operative Research Project No. 5–0313. USOE, Washington, D.C.

Hunt, K. W. (1970). *Syntactic Maturity in Schoolchildren and Adults*. Society for Research in Child Development Monographs, No. 134. University of Chicago Press.

Hunt, K. W., and O'Donnell, R. C. (1970). *An Elementary School Curriculum to Develop Better Writing Skills*. Co-operative Research Project No. 8–0903. Florida State University, Tallahassee, Fl. (ERIC Document Reproduction Service No. ED 050 108)

Kerek, A., Dalker, D., and Morenberg, M. (1980a). *Sentence Combining and College Composition*. Miami University, Oxford, Ohio.

Kerek, A., Dalker, D., and Morenberg, M. (1980b). Sentence combining and college composition. *Journal of Perceptual and Motor Skills Monograph*, 1980.

Lees, Robert, B. (1960). *The Grammar of English Nominalizations*. Mouton, The Hague.

McCarthy, D. (1954). Language development in children. In L. Carmichael (ed.), *Manual of Child Psychology*. Wiley, New York.

Mellon, J. C. (1967). *Transformational Sentence-combining: A Method for Enhancing the Development of Syntactic Fluency in English Composition*. Co-operative Research Project, No. 5-8418. Harvard University, Cambridge, Mass. (ERIC Document Reproduction Service No. ED 018 405)

Reesink, G. P., Holleman-van der Sleen, S. B., Stevens, K., and Kohnstumm, G. A. (1971). Development of syntax among school children and adults: a replication-investigation. *Psychological Abstracts,* **47**, No. 10536.

Smith, W. L., and Combs, W. E. (1980). The effects of overt and covert cues on written syntax. *Research in the Teaching of English*, **14**, 19–38.

Witte, S., and Davis, A. (1980). The stability of T-unit length: a preliminary investigation. *Research in the Teaching of English,* **14**, 5–17.

The Psychology of Written Language
Edited by M. Martlew

CHAPTER 5

Syntactic Change: Writing Development and the Rhetorical Context

CYNTHIA WATSON

Empirical research in composition is experiencing a renaissance. The field is in the midst of an exciting and unprecedented proliferation of new ideas, new methods, and new interdisciplinary synthesis. Over the past 15 years writing investigators have moved well beyond the taxonomic recording of surface characteristics. Their work now consistently addresses more abstract and superordinant planes. Researchers who study the visible structures of written language are giving equal time to such invisible structures as the interlocking dependencies between language and context, between cognition and composing, and between theory and empirical observations. Instead of giving only parenthetical attention to coherent linguistic and psychological theory, investigators presently seek inferential strands which could lead them from the observable product or behavior to the unobservable and, perhaps, universal psycholinguistic construct.

The development in one well-established branch of composition research, the study of written syntax, aptly represent the field's more general empirical movement away from an exclusive focus on readily observable surface structures. Syntactic research has evolved through two stages since 1965. In the beginning, investigators recorded primarily age-correlated changes in syntax for the chief purpose of guiding the teaching of composition. There was comparatively little discussion of rhetorical and cognitive theory; implications focused almost exclusively on the classroom.

In the second stage, which is at its height today, researchers are now devising studies whose primary purpose is to use measures such as syntactic density and types of embedding to test rhetorical theories on texts written under varying communication conditions. While researchers still examine pedagogical implications, they also draw tentative inferences about cognition.

The present direction in composition research (illustrated here by the developments in syntactic work) reflects our growing efforts to plumb the covert activities both concealed and signaled by the mantle of written language. These efforts have resulted in a substantial change in the way we view composition: we have had to abandon what Britton *et al.* (1975) has called the 'insidious global view' of writing. As researchers and teachers we have, until very recently, assumed that writing, as act and as product, is an indivisible and relatively impenetrable phenomenon which does not vary appreciably from occasion to occasion. Now, however, we begin to see that writing admits of fluid, shifting constituents. In order to study it we must predict and look for the discrete, meaningful systems which support, indeed which are, written discourse.

If we dare not view writing as a global, inflexible whole, then when we study writing development we are obliged to control not just for age or sophistication but for an ever-growing list of powerful independent variables such as topic, audience, purpose, and psychological distance. The recent history of syntactic research demonstrates how we are beginning to pay careful attention to these rhetorical and cognitive forces which may be quite distinct from the influences of maturity.

The following discussion centers around nine studies completed within the last 15 years. These works not only represent the two stages of development in syntax research, but they also, through their interrelationships, form a synthetic whole out of which grow certain fascinating inferences about thinking and writing.

Representing early studies of maturity-linked syntactic change in the writer's language are Hunt's *Grammatical Structures Written at Three Grade Levels* (1965) and Loban's *Language Development* (1976). The second stage of development is embodied in seven reports: Rosen (1969), Pope (1974) Jensen (:1973), Watson (1979), Cooper and Watson (1980), Crowhurst and Piché (1979), and Miller (1980). These studies have proven the importance of linguistic changes not motivated by increasing maturity. Their findings have considerably complicated the study of writing development. From them there has issued a new methodological imperative: do not collect developmental data too casually, for the subject's age is only one among many variables which may affect the shape of a written product. A whole range of writer–topic–audience relationships, which have little to do with age, may be responsible for measurable and informative linguistic variations in writing.

To summarize, our movement from global to more elaborated assumptions about writing, our acknowledgment that measurable change in written language can be attributed to something other than chronological maturity, and our increasing concern for guiding theory all share a single unifying direction: in general, our research aim is shifting from recording only directly observable writing phenomena to devising studies which may allow us to make inferences about psycholinguistic causes and processes which can be viewed only indirectly.

SYNTACTIC MATURITY AND THE GLOBAL VIEW

Syntactic research can be considered a kind of empirical barometer of conditions in all sectors of composition research. The shifting currents in syntax are part of the *leit motif* also present in non-syntactic studies. Likewise the oft-documented history of syntax depicts issues and evolutions which are not peculiar to that field alone but which generalize to all of composition research. This is particularly true of the recent movement from the global to the elaborated perspective on writing.

In order to locate a representative and widely acknowledged point of origin for significant trends in the study of written syntax, we need only look to Hunt's (1965) landmark study, *Grammatical Structures Written at Three Grade Levels*. This pivotal work has contributed to basic composition research in three very significant ways. It gave us our first set of broad-based normative findings on syntactic maturity; Hunt's work, perhaps more than any other syntactic study, still functions as a ground-zero source of comparative figures for other researchers.

Like his maturity norms, Hunt's T-unit (see Hunt, Chapter 4, this volume), a syntactically defined minimal unit of discourse, has also found its way into many studies, where it has proven stable and sensitive enough to withstand 15 years of use and criticism. Witte and Davis (1980) have criticized mean T-unit length because it is not stable when used to measure the syntactic complexity of a single writer's work on different occasions. While mean T-unit length certainly seems best used to make estimates on large data bases, we should remember that it was its very 'instability' that led researchers like Rosen to conclude that non-maturity variables influenced syntax.

Finally, *Grammatical Structures* helped form a natural cross-disciplinary bridge into the field of transformational generative linguistics. Though his own report did not itself rely upon transformational grammar, the T-unit was so compatible to transformational grammar analysis that many who read his report immediately saw the connection: mean T-unit length (Hunt,

Chapter 4, this volume) facilitates discussion of frequency, type, and theoretical depth of embedding within an objectively defined unit of discourse.

While *Grammatical Structures* remains a touchstone in syntax research, much has happened since the mid-1960s. What we are learning from tests of theories about variety in written discourse (Kinneavy, 1971; Britton *et al.*, 1975; Moffett, 1968) forces us to re-evaluate the syntactic maturity norms in Hunt's 1965 report and in reports similar to it (see, for example, Loban, 1976).

Our growing discontent with the global view of writing motivates our current skepticism about earlier findings on syntactic maturity. Because we no longer believe that chronological development is solely responsible for linguistic change, we are currently very actively questioning findings gathered without regard for variables within the communication context.

The global view has fostered in both composition instruction and research a kind of rhetorical tunnel vision. In the classroom this restrictive view still powerfuly directs teaching methods (Britton *et al.* 1975). It leads to such practices as either teaching a single type of discourse (for example, explanatory) or teaching several types of discourse without acknowledging that they are indeed very different. It leads also to an artificial and frozen writer–audience relationship; generally, classroom writing is directed at a one-person adult audience: the teacher.

This same innocence about the role that rhetorical factors play in shaping written discourse has also had, until about 10 years ago, a strong effect on research. Analogous to the globalist classroom practices are the 'shotgun techniques' (O'Donnell *et al.*, 1967) which prevailed in Hunt's and Loban's work. Neither researcher controlled for topic, purpose, or audience variables.

One of the most serious results of this inattention can be seen in the fairly unsystematic ways they collected their writing samples. Both researchers, focused on measuring syntactic maturity, assumed they were dealing with only one major independent variable: the age or ability of the writer.

Examining their methods from the privileged perspective of hindsight, we can see how their research techniques failed to acknowledge such theoretically crucial factors as purpose or focus of discourse (Kinneavy, 1971; Britton *et al.*, 1975; Lloyd-Jones, 1977) and psychological and temporal distances between the writer and his/her topic and audience (Moffett, 1968).

Hunt, for example, seems to have had only one overriding criterion guiding the collection of his writing sample which was quantity. He collected 1000 words worth of unassisted school writing from each of his subjects.

Like Hunt, Loban collected his writing sample without regard for extralinguistic variables. Ironically, he did exercise great care with his parellel oral sample by controlling topic and speaker–hearer dynamics. This discrepancy bespeaks the belief that, though spoken language subsumes a rich variety of context-sensitive styles and structures, written language does not. Writing is just writing.

If context does indeed influence written syntax as much as the writer's age does, then we face some unkowns when we refer to normative figures from global studies of syntactic growth. We do not know, for instance, what type of writing produced Hunt's developmental profiles. Self-expressive? Explanatory? Persuasive? A random mixture? Current theory and research tells us that such differences can be vitally important.

If we compare a group of 12th-grade writers to Hunt's norm of 14.4 words per T-unit, and if our groups falls short of that norm, what are we to deduce? Is our group syntactically less fluent than his? Has writing ability indeed declined since the 1960s? Or was our group of students taught and tested upon a type of writing that Hunt did not collect? We cannot answer these questions satisfactorily until our present efforts to sort among maturational and rhetorical factors in writing produce and replicate consistent findings. We have certainly begun this work of refining our notion of syntactic maturity; but since such work has opened a multitude of other questions bearing on the relationship between thinking and writing, we have a considerable distance to go before we understand the multifaceted nature of the interaction between maturity, context, and cognition.

SYNTACTIC MATURITY, CONTEXT AND COGNITION

As we have seen, *Grammatical Structures* has had a dual function in the evolution of composition research. Functioning as the *new*, it has engendered literally hundreds of studies which have employed Hunt's methods and measures. As long as researchers continue to study syntactic complexity, Hunt's work will have a perpetual newness.

Functioning as the *old, Grammatical Structures* has served as a sturdy *status quo* against which we have reacted in our growing awareness of rhetorical variables and cognitive inferences which can be drawn from systematic syntactic patterns that accompany rhetorical shifts. One of the fruits of this reaction is the fact that the term 'syntactic maturity' is gradually being redefined to encompass consistent non-developmental syntactic variations arising from alterations in the communication context.

Seven syntactically focused studies between 1969 and 1980 have endeavored to cull non-developmental linguistic changes from among age-related changes. For the most part these experiments focus mainly on identifying exceptions to the global syntactic maturity rule. They only breifly extrapolate to implications about cognitive differences between different types of writing. Their strikingly similar findings, however, do make the drawing of some tentative inferences irresistible.

Among those recent studies which have helped redefine syntactic maturity, Rosen's (1969) investigation of syntax and the varied functions of writing subjected Hunt's maturity norms to close scrutiny. Rosen believed that mean T-unit length, as Hunt used it, was much too gross a measure of syntactic fluency, that it masked a potentially powerful set of non-developmental rhetorical forces. Like O'Donnell *et al.*, he criticizes Hunt's disregard for topic and type of discourse. His findings, based on writing done by fifty superior 15- and 16-year-olds, confirmed his hypothesis that the nature of the writing task influences mean T-unit length at least as much as the writer's maturity does.

Noting that the mean T-unit length differences between expressive and referential (roughly, explanatory) writing were greater than the maturity difference Hunt found between 8th- and 12th-graders, Rosen concludes that the term syntactic maturity is misleading. Mean T-unit length is sensitive to linguistic differences that have nothing to do with the writer's age. He warns composition researchers and writing evaluators not to fall prey to the global conception of syntactic maturity, 'for individuals do not on the whole write long or short T-units but seem to vary the length of their T-units according to the task facing them' (p. 189).

Jensen's (1973) findings on oral language complement Rosen's written-language results. She investigated linguistic change in the conversations of 5th-graders speaking in both casual and careful styles. The contexts for eliciting casual and careful language differed in both the purpose of discourse (problem-solving conferences vs. reportage, or explanation) and in the speaker–audience relationships (child-to-child vs. child-to-adult).

Her results on grammatical control and lexical fluency underscore the powerful influence that purpose and audience exert on spoken discourse. She found, for instance, that mean T-unit length, clause length, and subordination frequency were greater in careful speech (report to adult) than in casual (conference with peer). Conversely, she discovered that there was greater lexical and syntactic pattern variety in casual speech than in careful.

Discussing the implications of her findings, she advises that 'attempting to alter the characteristics of a variety of language styles so as to resemble a single (i.e., global) arbitrarily selected norm is not only unsound but unrealistic. Language is modified by the context in which it occurs' (p. 349).

In another study of oral language Pope (1974) reports that there are numerous statistically significant differences between the narrative and explanatory syntax of 4th-graders. Their explanatory language is characterized by longer T-units, more clauses per T-unit, and more sentence embeddings than is their narrative language.

The research on rhetorical variables thus far presented has all focused on a single age group, so that no comparison to the maturity variable is possible save through juxtaposition with developmental findings in other studies like Hunt's. A recent experiment (Watson, 1979) was designed to remedy this: it isolated not only three different types of student-written discourse, but two different age groups.

In her examination of syntactic variety, Watson described and compared the syntactic differenes among expressive, explanatory, and persuasive writing produced by superior high-school seniors and upper-level college English majors. Within the parameters of a single study she was able to confirm and extend previous findings on rhetorically motivated and age-motivated syntactic fluctuations.

Though she analyzed a total of seventeen syntactic features, a sub-set of four features adequately represents the dramatic contrasts she found between global syntactic maturity and syntactic growth within the three separate discourse categories. These were mean T-unit length, non-clause adjective modifiers, free modifiers, and final free modifiers. Mean T-unit length is the average length of T-units, counted in words per T-unit and traditionally used to measure syntactic maturity. Non-clause adjective modifiers are constructions which are assumed to be the result of relative clause reduction. They include single-word prenominal adjectives and participials, infinitivals, and prepositional phrases which modify nouns. Free modifiers are all non-restrictive modifiers – both clausal and non-clausal. They are set off by commas, dashes, or parentheses. Constructions which may function as free modifiers are:

(1) non-restrictive subordinate clauses used as sentence modifiers;
(2) non-restrictive relative clauses;
(3) noun, verb, or adjective clusters;
(4) adjective series;
(5) absolutes (verb clusters with subjects);
(6) prepositional phrases (Christensen, 1967).

Final free modifiers are those free (non-restrictive) elements that occur at the end of a sentence.

Of all the features she studied only two, free modifiers and final free modifiers, were stable measures of maturity only, both globally (regardless of discourse type) and within each separate type of discourse. The frequency of these modifiers clearly distinguished high-school writing from college writing, with college writers using them significantly more often.

No other syntactic feature was free of interaction effects between maturity differences and discourse type differences. Global mean T-unit length, for example, was significantly greater in college writing (14.63 words) than in high-school writing (13.25). But an analytic breakdown by discourse type revealed no significant maturity difference in persuasive mean T-unit length. Maturity difference in expressive discourse, however, was quite impressive (college: 14.18 words, high school: 12.05 words).

Students' use of non-clause adjective modifiers created similarly revealing interactions. Globally measured frequencies of these structures show a significant maturity difference: college juniors and seniors use them significantly more frequently across all three discourse types (college; 111.24 per 60 T-units, high school: 80.30 per 60 T-units). Upon closer inspection, however, these non-clause adjectives are seen to behave very differently within the separate types of discourse. Again, as with mean T-unit length, persuasive discourse shows no maturity-motivated gain in adjective frequency while explanatory and expressive do.

What all this means is that globally measured syntactic growth does not necessarily reflect growth patterns within a single discourse type. In Watson's study neither mean T-unit length nor non-clause adjective frequency showed significant increase in persuasive writing over the span between 12th grade and the junior/senior year in college. Conversely, the dramatic growth in syntactic complexity reflected in increased expressive T-unit lengths accounts for most of the overall global increase in complexity. Precious little of the significant global increase in the use of non-clause adjective modifiers can be attributed to increases in persuasive writing. Instead, the dramatic differences between high school and college frequencies in expressive and explanatory discourse are responsible for the globally measured rise in adjective frequency over the 4-year span.

It seems we cannot apply globally derived syntactic maturity norms to persuasive writing in these two instances. Increase in syntactic complexity does not proceed evenly across all types of writing.

Comparing Watson's findings to Hunt's, we note some telling discrepancies. Her superior 12th-grade writers' globally measured mean T-unit lengths (13.25 words) indicate that they lag about 1 year behind Hunt's average 12th-graders (14.4 words). Her upper-level college English majors (14.63) are just about on par with Hunt's 12th-graders. A breakdown by discourse type reveals that her 12th-graders' persuasive T-units (14.32 words) match Hunt's global figure while their expressive T-units dip dramatically to a mere 12.05 words per T-unit.

A number of conclusions might be drawn from this crazy-quilt of conflicting figures. First, basing our judgment only on the global findings, we could assume that Watson's subjects were perhaps not as syntactically fluent as Hunt's, even though they were selected for their superior writing ability. Secondly, looking at the analytic breakdown, we could say that her

12th-graders wrote more maturely when they wrote persuasively and less maturely when they wrote expressively. Third, we might conclude that her subjects' discourse type-specific deviations from both her own and Hunt's globally measured mean T-unit lengths have nothing to do with maturity, but rather with the varying rhetorical demands of writing for different purposes. Finally, we might conclude that, for extralinguistic reasons, growth in each discourse type must be measured by a different standard.

The last two conclusions seem the most sensible. Watson's subjects certainly did not revert to some earlier stage of psycholinguistic development when they wrote expressively. Neither could they have suddenly matured 3 years' worth each time they produced their syntactically more complex persuasive discourse.

THE SPECIAL CASE OF PERSUASION

The syntactic uniqueness of persuasive discourse (highest complexity, lowest growth) in the Watson study is made all the more interesting by other research findings. San Jose (1973), Perron (1977) and Cooper and Watson (1980) all found persuasive discourse to be syntactically more complex than other types. The fact that their 3rd, 4th, and 5th-grade subjects duplicate the syntactic patterns of much older high-school and college writers is rife with implications about the presence of a psycholinguistic universal. When high syntactic density is consistently linked with one discourse type, and when that linkage spans 13 years of growth, we must begin to speculate about the reasons for these patterns. We must ask questions like: What underlying force causes written persuasion to be so syntactically dense? Does the persuader's increased attention to audience somehow motivate more complex syntax? Are the cognitive activities demanded by persuasion more complex or mature than those peculiar to other types of writing? If so, do these more complex schema naturally find expression in measurably more complex structures?

The recent work of three investigators has results in the formulation of initial answers to two of these questions. Crowhurst and Piché (1979) address the question of audience in persuasive discourse. Miller (1980) theorizes about rhetorical and cognitive maturity – also in persuasive writing.

The 6th- and 10th-graders whose syntax Crowhurst and Piché analyzed wrote persuasive, descriptive, and narrative discourse. They not only wrote different types of discourse, but they wrote for two audiences – best friend and teacher. While the investigators once again found persuasive writing to be syntactically more complex, they made two other important discoveries. First, as writers mature between 6th and 10th grade, they begin to respond to different audiences with varying syntactic complexity; the more distant the audience, the longer the T-units. Secondly, it is persuasive syntax upon which audience has its most profound impact.

Crowhurst and Piché have, through a syntactic measure, isolated a possible psychological variable, the relationship between writer and audience – which may account for the oft-replicated findings on syntactic density in persuasive writing. The increased attention to audience demanded by persuasive tasks clearly seems to affect the writer's syntactic choices. While the audience variable creates significant syntactic differences in all discourse types, the greater gap in persuasion contributes to its much-documented high complexity.

Crowhurst and Piché may have taken us one step closer to understanding persuasive discourse and its long T-units, but we have much yet to learn. How, for example, can we account for the marked lack of syntactic growth in persuasion between 12th grade and the junior/senior year in college? In Watson's study the discourse type showed the *highest* syntactic complexity coupled with the *lowest* growth rate.

Miller (1980) reports a classroom experience which parallels the no-growth situation Watson found in persuasive syntax. She discovered a common problem occurring in thirty sections of freshman composition: students, having developed a certain level of rhetorical fluency in descriptive and explanatory writing, suddenly lost it when asked to write persuasively to a distant audience on an abstract topic. The greater psychological distance between writer and audience, and writer and topic, seemed to be the culprits, for when Miller subsequently assigned persuasive writing on a familiar, concrete topic addressed to a close audience, their fluency returned.

Miller conjectures that 18- and 19-year-old basic writers stand at a developmental threshold which prevents them from writing effective persuasive pieces. Using Kohlberg's (see Duska and Whelan, 1975) developmental stages of moral maturity to guide a persuasive assignment, she found that her novice writers all grouped into Kohlberg's 'conventional' stage. The conventional thinker is not de-centered enough, nor free enough from the expectations of family, peer group, or country, to make spontaneous, objective and relativistic judgments. Being 'nice' and maintaining order for its own sake are two values which motivate this person to respond to problems with received knowledge or conventional wisdom.

For Miller, Kohlberg's work outlines the progress of valuing which parallels and interacts with rhetorical maturity: 'the development of the Aristotelian *ethos* toward trustworthy, creditable, and authoritative content' (p. 11). She believes that expecting family-centered freshmen to possess the rhetorical virtuosity that enables relativistic judgments in persuasive writing is not reasonable.

Drawing upon Miller's inferences we might conclude that the relative stasis in persuasive T-unit length between late high school and late college is related to the developmental impasse she witnessed. Perhaps de-centration and the growing ability to make objective, relativistic value-judgments motivate syntactic complexity in persuasion. Lack of increase in this complexity may indicate a plateau in cognitive development, and/or it may be a symptom of the writer's pre-occupation with the struggles of persuasive rhetoric, which in turn deflects the writer's attention away from sentence-level concerns for syntactic elegance and complexity.

CONCLUSION

We have seen how purpose or type of discourse consistently correlates with syntactic complexity. We have also seen evidence of uneven growth rates across the writing spectrum. Finally, we have seen that writers respond to a distant audience by producing longer T-units, the longest being in persuasive discourse. These findings form but a small core of evidence, but they are enough to put the lie to the global notion of writing. The fluctuating syntactic rhythms which they reveal imply two courses of action – one which leads to the classroom and one which leads to further study of the relationship between thought and writing.

Because experimental results find their ways into classrooms in the forms of evaluative norms and teaching methods, it is important that findings be as clear a reflection of reality as possible. Global syntactic norms such as Hunt's and Loban's must give way to norms that are sensitive to (at least) audience and purpose. Judging a student's less complex expressive syntax against a global norm does not give a fair estimate of that student's syntactic maturity.

In addition to refining measurement and evaluation we must, for the purpose of instruction, add much more detail to our current knowledge of syntactic growth patterns within discourse types. If we are, for example, to use sentence-combining methods to greatest advantage, we need to know at what age students experience bursts of syntactic growth in a discourse type and at what age they reach plateaus. With this information we will be able to develop exercises which support different types of writing at the most appropriate developmental stages.

The T-unit and other syntactic measures will continue to be very useful in basic research. As long as we study the relationship between the mind and the written work, and as long as we assume that systematic linguistic patterns imply systematic cognitive patterns, we can continue to rely on large syntactic profiles derived from many pieces of writing to give us useful information. The pairing of syntactic measures with various independent variables, such as audience and purpose, has already proved productive. Further pairings are needed to sort among other subtle forces in the rhetorical context. Correlations of syntactic variables with level of abstraction, with ability level, and with teachers' estimates of writing quality, have all been done, but the focus has been on general writing. What we now need are careful explorations of constructs like these within the different types of discourse whose empirical realities are currently being established. We must observe whether or not general writing ability is stable across all kinds of writing. Do good writers excel at all types of writing tasks? We must discover how development proceeds in different kinds of writing. Does expressive writing fluency peak at the same time as explanatory and persuasive? How does expressive (or persuasive or explanatory) writing change as the writer matures?

There is much for us to learn yet from syntactic research. Our heightened awareness of predictable variety in writing gives us a more adequate framework within which to study composition than we had 15 years ago. We no longer stop with global taxonomies, but we use our mapping of surface structure as a test of theoretical constructs. And until we are able to gather independent evidence about cognition, syntax will serve as one fruitful source of inferences about the relationships between thought and written language.

REFERENCES

Britton, J., Burgess, T., Martin, N., McLeod, A., and Rosen, H. (1975). *The Development of Writing Abilities*, pp. 11–18. Macmillan Education Ltd., London.

Christensen, F. (1967). *Notes Toward a New Rhetoric*. Harper and Row, New York.

Cooper, C. R., and Watson, C. (1980). *The Effects of Discourse Type and Writing Quality on the Written Syntax of Fourth Grade Students* (Research in progress). University of California at San Diego and Louisiana State University.

Crowhurst, M. and Piché, G. L. (1979). Audience and mode of discourse effects on syntactic complexity in writing at two grade levels. *Research in the Teaching of English,* **13**, 101–109.

Duska, R., and Whelan, M. (1975). *Moral Development: A Guide to Piaget and Kohlberg*. Paulist Press, New York.

Hunt, K. W. (1965). *Grammatical Structure Written at Three Grade Levels*. National Council of Teachers of English, Urbana, Illinois.

Jensen, J. M. (1973). A comparative investigation of careful and casual language styles of average and superior fifth grade boys and girls. *Research in the Teaching of English*, **7**, 338–50.

Kinneavy, J. L.·(1971). *A Theory of Discourse*. Prentice-Hall, Englewood Cliffs, New Jersey.

Lloyds-Jones, R. (1977). Primary-trait scoring of writing. In C. R. Cooper and C. L. Odell (eds.), *Evaluating Writing: Describing, Measuring, Judging*. National Council of Teachers of English Urbana, Illinois.

Loban, W. (1976). *Language Development: Kindergarten Through Grade Twelve*. National Council of Teachers of English, Urbana, Illinois.

Miller, S. (1980). Rhetorical maturity: definition and development. (Unpublished manuscript, University of Wisconsin at Milwaukee.)

Moffett, J. (1968). *Teaching the Universe of Discourse*. Houghton Mifflin, Boston.

O'Donnell, R. C., Griffin, W. J., and Norris, R. C. (1967). *Syntax of Kindergarten and Elementary School Children: A Transformational Analysis*. National Council of Teachers of English, Urbana, Illinois.

Perron, J. D. (1977). Written syntactic complexity and the modes of discourse. Paper read at the annual meeting of the American Educational Research Association.

Pope, M. (1974). The syntax of fourth graders' narrative and explanatory speech. *Research in the Teaching of English,* **8**. 219–27.

Rosen, H. (1969). An investigation of the effects of differentiated writing assignments on the performance in English composition of a selected group of 15/16 year old pupils. Doctoral dissertation, University of London.

San José, C. P. M. (1972). Grammatical structures in four modes of writing at fourth grade level. Doctoral dissertation, Syracuse University.

Watson, C. (1979). The effects of maturity and discourse type on the written syntax of superior high school seniors and upper level college English majors. Doctoral dissertation, State University of New York at Buffalo.

Witte, S. P., and Davis, A. S. (1980). The stability of T-unit length: a preliminary investigation. *Research in the Teaching of English,* **14**, 5–17.

PART III

Writing: Creating Visible Language

Richard Mulcaster, 1582: *The First Part of the Elementarie.*	The English tung hath in it self sufficient matter to work on her own artificiall direction, for the right writing thereof.
Charles Dickens: *Pickwick Papers*.	'Do you spell it with a "V" or a "W"?, inquired the judge. 'That depends on the taste and fancy of the speller, my Lord', replied Sam.
Quintillian: *De Institutione Oratoria*.	Men of quality are in the wrong to undervalue, as they often do, the practise of a fair and quick hand in writing, for it is no immaterial accomplishment.

The Psychology of Written Language
Edited by M. Martlew

CHAPTER 6

Orthography

CHARLES READ

Writing is the representation of specific linguistic forms. For this reason, photographs and paintings are not writing, even though they may communicate a message. For this reason, too, writing requires a writing system, a shared way of pairing representations with linguistic forms. This chapter will survey some of the major variables among writing systems, with emphasis on variables in alphabetic systems that are likely to affect learning and performance. At first, one is likely to suppose that the most important property of a writing system is its regularity, or lack thereof. This chapter will suggest that regularity is a rather perplexing variable which can be understood only in relation to a number of others. In the process the chapter will raise a few issues which seem especially open to research now, and it will refer to the major literature on writing systems for those who wish to go further.

We will look at writing systems primarily as they may affect the process of writing rather than reading. Research on reading has been more extensive in every respect than research on writing; studies of the properties of writing systems are no exception. In the last decade there have been several extended discussions of orthography and reading (Kavanagh and Mattingly, 1972, section one; Gleitman and Rozin, 1977; Kavanagh and Venezky, 1980) but few if any comparable discussions of orthography and writing. It might be supposed that one could infer the relationships between orthography and writing from those between orthography and reading, but in fact these processes are neither identical nor complementary in the ways in which they employ orthography. An orthography which represented intricate phonetic detail would make life harder for both the writer and reader it seems; but one in which phrase boundaries were indicated explicitly might ease the reader's task at the expense of the writer (Frase, 1982). Conversely, an orthography which represents units of language which are relatively accessible to awareness may benefit both the writer and the reader, at least at the beginning stages, while one which varies from dialect to dialect may ease the writer' s burden (again, at least in learning) at the expense of the reader. So whether the orthographic needs of the writer and the reader are similar, different, or even unrelated, depends on the orthographic property in question, the task, and the user's stage of development. As a result, it is appropriate to distinguish the writer's orthographic requirements from those of the reader.

A word about terminology. Because there is no general agreement on the matter, it may be appropriate to state at the outset how I propose to use certain key terms dealing with writing systems. *Alphabet* and *orthography* I reserve for writing systems which represent the speech sounds of a language (to one level of detail or another): *alphabet* will refer to the character set employed, while *orthography* will refer to the principles by which the alphabet is set into correspondence with the speech sounds. By contrast, the expressions *character set* and *writing system* will refer to the symbols and the assignment conventions, respectively, in systems of written representation in general, not limited to those in which alphabetic characters represent (roughly) speech sounds. Since most actual writing systems are mixed cases, representing language in more than one way, the distinction between alphabetic and non-alphabetic cannot be made without some degree of arbitrariness, but it is indispensable. *Level of language* refers here to a series of linguistic units ordered according to relative inclusion: words are made up of syllables, and syllables are made up of segments or phones, for instance. An overlapping concept is that of the *abstractness* of linguistic units, which for me is a measure of analysis such that more abstract units are analyzed out of less abstract ones, starting with the physical speech event, the variations in sound pressure which strike our ears. In this sense, the phonetic segment, or phone, is an abstraction from the acoustic event, being a segmentation and categorization of it. Similarly, the phoneme is more abstract than the segment, since phonemes are further categorizations of segments on the basis of their physical similarity and distribution.

From these remarks, and from other discussions of writing systems, it may appear that abstractness and level of language are identical; both being measures of the 'distance' of a given unit from the physical event. In my sense, these two are not identical: one refers to an analytic relationship, while the other refers to an inclusion relation. It is clear that the word is a larger, more inclusive, unit than the syllable, but it is not at all clear that the word is more abstract than the syllable; the word is not defined in terms of sequences of syllables in the sense that the phoneme is defined as a class of phones. Another respect in which the level of a linguistic unit differs from its abstractness is that a unit at any level may be analyzed and described more or less abstractly. An utterance, for instance, is a relatively large linguistic unit which may include several words, but it is often described in terms of its acoustic form, that is, non-abstractly. This same distinction holds for every linguistic unit: the syllable is larger than the phoneme and it is usually defined as a particular sequence of phonemes (or phoneme-types, such as consonants and vowels), but it may be described more concretely in terms of its acoustic shape.

Finally, a term which cuts across the last two is *accessibility*, meaning the availability of some unit to awareness and manipulation. In this sense it is clear that both the word and the syllable are relatively accessible, compared with the phone. For various reasons, speakers of a language generally find it considerably easier to identify, count, and rearrange the words and syllables of an utterance than the phones or phonemes. Evidently, this is especially true for young children at the age at which they begin to write (Liberman *et al.*, 1977). Since writing, even in the limited sense of representing speech with marks is a manipulation of the spoken language, the accessibility of units turns out to be an important property, even if one that is difficult to measure.

Ironically, in the succession of linguistic units from utterances to phones by way of words, morphemes, syllables, and phonemes, the most familiar and perhaps most accessible – namely words and syllables – are among the most difficult to define formally. This problem becomes obvious even in introductory textbooks; see, for example, the discussion of the word in Hockett (1958, pp. 166–168) or the discussion of attempts to define the syllable in Ladefoged (1975, pp. 218–222). The difficulty of identifying these units in a particular language, as opposed to defining them in general, however, varies with the language. As we shall see below, syllables are easier to identify in Japanese than they are in English. Thus the accessibility of units depends upon the language in question and is somewhat independent of the difficulty of stating a cross-linguistic definition.

LEVELS OF REPRESENTATION

Clearly, writing systems may represent linguistic units at various levels, particularly those of morphemes, syllables, or phonemes. We can readily conceive of writing systems which represent more or less inclusive units, such as phrases or phones, and indeed there are such systems, but the representation of entire phrases is not used for natural languages, and the representation of phonetic segments (as in phonetic transcription) is used only for special purposes, not for the communication of meaning. Let us consider first the possibility of a writing system which consistently represents words or (more likely in languages with complex words) morphemes, the meaningful constituents of words. *Canoes* would then be represented by a symbol for *canoe* together with (not necessarily followed by) one for plural. There would not normally be any salient similarity between the symbol for *canoe* and the one for *canal* or for *shoe*, that is, no indication of similarity in syllabic or phonemic form. Neither would there necessarily be any similarity between the characters for *canoe* and for *boat*; a logographic writing system need not directly reflect semantic or conceptual structure. Given that every natural language has a substantial inventory of morphemes, let alone words, this writing system would require a set of characters numbering tens of thousands.

The writing system of modern Chinese is, of course, roughly of this logographic sort; most of the 50,000 or so characters represent words of the language. However, most writing systems are mixed cases, and that of Chinese is no exception. It is not even unambiguously logographic, since most 'words' are single morphemes and single syllables. For that reason the characters can be used as a syllabary in writing foreign names. Moreover, most of the characters include both a logographic/morphemic and a phonetic component, the latter indicating some part of the pronunciation of the word (see Chao, 1968; Martin, 1972; Wang, 1973; and Gleitman and Rozin, 1977). Still, the compound sign as a whole is a unique representation of a word and may be considered a logogram. This basic system has been in use since at least 1300 BC, with an early development away from rather pictorial signs and, more recently, a gradual fusion of phonetic complements with semantic components within characters, and in the People's Republic, a simplification of characters. In the last 5 years, the People's Republic of China has considered moving toward Romanization, but the present system has advantages (explained below), and any change will certainly not come quickly.

SYLLABIC WRITING SYSTEMS

A syllabary typically provides at least one character for each possible syllable of a language, with no internal structure corresponding to individual phonemes, in general. Though syllabaries were the forerunners of alphabetic writing, they are not now widely used, Japanese being the only major language written syllabically. The number of symbols required varies greatly according to the nature of the language; Japanese, with its relatively limited inventory of both consonants and vowels and its limitation essentially to syllables made up of a vowel alone or a single consonant plus a vowel, has about seventy-five different syllables to be represented. The comparable figure for English would be in the thousands, both because English has roughly twice as many consonant phonemes and more than twice as many vowel phonemes as Japanese, and because English includes syllable-types with clusters of up to three consonants initially and four consonants finally.

As well-suited as Japanese is to a syllabic writing system, however, it is not written exclusively in that manner. Except in children's books, most nouns, verbs, and adjectives are represented by *kanji*, logographic characters originally borrowed from Chinese. Thus a written sentence of Japanese ordinarily includes two different writing systems intermixed, distinguishing content words from grammatical function words. In addition, two syllabaries are actually in use, one for native Japanese words (other than nouns, verbs, or adjectives), and the other primarily for foreign, mimetic, and cited words, rather like italics in English.

ALPHABETIC WRITING SYSTEMS

A third and last type of writing system is the alphabetic, with the phoneme being the unit basically represented. General-purpose writing systems, as opposed to systems specifically for phonetic representation, rarely if ever represent allophonic variation, since it is by definition not significant and therefore either totally free or totally predictable. Several alphabets besides the Roman are used, including the Cyrillic, Devanagari (Indic), and Arabic. For a given language, such a system necessarily uses a smaller character set and longer representations (in terms of number of characters) than either the syllabic or the logographic. Note, however, that the twenty six characters of the conventional typewriter-Roman alphabet are not sufficient to represent uniquely the phonemes of many languages, so that the set of spellings must include digraphs, diacritics, or contextually varying sound/spelling correspondences.

Alongside variation in the alphabet and set of graphemes employed, there is great variation in the degree to which the orthography represents phonemes only and not more-inclusive units. It is frequently pointed out that English orthography often represents larger units, while Finnish, Dutch, and Spanish, for instance, are nearly exclusively phonemic. It is true that orthographies vary greatly in this respect, and that English is a fairly extreme case of an orthography which, while unquestionably phonemic at root, represents larger units as well (morphemes and morphophonemes). Two example of this sort will suffice, though hundreds could be adduced:

phonemically different vowels are in many instances spelled alike (or at least similarly), with the vowels being paired in such a way that a given morpheme is spelled consistently, even when pronounced differently, as in *wide/width* or *sane/sanity*. Second, certain morphemes are spelled in a single manner, even though they are pronounced in phonemically varying ways and the variants would not generally be spelled alike. The past tense ending of weak (regular) verbs is spelled *-ed*, even though it is pronounced variously [t], [d], or [əd], according to the segment which precedes it. Conversely, most homophones like *steel* and *steal* are distinguished in spelling. Chomsky and Halle (1968), Venezky (1970), and Gleitman and Rozin (1977) have elaborated on this characteristic of English spelling.

That said, however, it should be noted that probably no orthography is perfectly phonemic, even with respect to segmental phonemes only, not even the often-cited Finnish. It is doubtful that such an orthography could exist for all the speakers of a language simultaneously, since, again by definition, the phonemic system will vary from one dialect to another. If there is a single orthography for a language, one can be fairly certain that it is not perfectly 'phonemic' for all speakers. Obviously, no such pan-dialectal phonemic representation could exist for a widely-varying world language like English; that fact is one of the major problems confronting spelling reformers. The developers of the initial teaching alphabet (i.t.a.) faced it explicitly and decided to represent phonemic contrasts, even those made in only one or a few dialects (Pitman and St. John, 1969). One result is that i.t.a. represents distinctions that no single speaker makes; another result is that it resembles standard spelling more closely than a phonemic representation for a single dialect would.

By far the more frequent kind of failure of orthographies to represent precisely the phonemic contrasts of a language is the tendency to represent larger units consistently, ignoring a phonemic contrast between two forms of a given morpheme, as in English. Having noted the overwhelming tendency to design alphabetic orthographies for those (thousands of) languages that do not yet have a standard orthography, Grimes and Gordon (1980, p. 94) nonetheless note that

> there is no known writing system that has been in use for long that symbolizes all the phonemic distinctions all the time. There seems to be a conventional wisdom that recognizes some differences as functionally less critical than others in certain contexts.

It is also relevant that most phonemically regular orthographies are for languages spoken by comparatively small numbers of people, primarily within a single geographical area and under the control of a relatively centralized political authority. Dutch and Finnish are such cases, though

Spanish is not; Dutch spelling has undergone several reforms in this century in order to achieve and maintain its near-regularity.

In this discussion of alphabetic orthographies we have considered together two properties of writing systems that are actually independent of one another: the level of the linguistic units represented and the representation of predictable detail. In fact, not only phonemes but also syllables, morphemes, and words may be predictable in context and may be omitted in writing. Just as there is perhaps no writing system that is entirely consistent in the size of the units that it represents, neither is there likely to be one which consistently includes or consistently omits predictable units.

This section has surveyed very briefly three main levels at which writing systems represent language. We have seen that although writing systems can be classified on this basis, few if any are entirely consistent. Like Chinese, Japanese, and English, most languages are written at two or more levels simultaneously. Many commentators have decried this fact, particularly in English, and some authorities on writing systems at least imply that consistent representations would be more satisfactory; Gleitman and Rozin (1977), on the other hand, argue that the representation of multiple levels provides the reader with useful information; distinctions between content and function words in Japanese and morphological information in English.

THE CHARACTER SET

Perhaps the most obvious demand which a writing system makes on would-be writers is a productive mastery of its character set. In fact, a child's first efforts in writing can be facilitated by easing or by-passing the production problem. Some children begin to write messages at age 3 and 4, using preformed characters, such as alphabet blocks or other movable-alphabet toys (Read, 1970). Such representations have serious drawbacks in portability and permanence, but they are surely writing. Manipulating a pencil on paper develops months later, after the child has explored, played with, and conquered the basic challenge of representing language alphabetically.

Across writing systems presently in use, the number of characters varies by a factor of about 2500, with some languages using only about 20 of the Roman letters, while Chinese has approximately 50,000 characters. In addition, there are large differences in difficulty of production. Learning to write the Roman alphabet fluently but legibly can be a substantial task for an English-speaking child, but learning to produce Chinese characters, which is considered an art form, can take years or even decades. There are mechanical means of producing Chinese characters, but they are hardly as easy to master as alphabetic typing, and for cultural as well as economic reasons, they are neither widely available nor widely accepted.

From these considerations it might be supposed that Chinese orthography is at best a difficult system for the learner, whatever it may be for the skilled user. Likewise, the development of alphabetic orthographies for Chinese and occasional movements toward reform may suggest that the prevailing system is not totally satisfactory, although one of the uses of Romanized writing is simply for communicating with foreigners. In fact, it is not easy to estimate the demands of a morphemic–syllabic writing system.

First, it is obviously not necessary for the average person to recognize, let alone produce, all of the characters. In conversations with leaders of the People's Republic of China's national educational system during October 1980, Dr Marshall Smith was told (personal communication) that a literate person recognizes from 1500 to 2500 characters, and that these make up about 90 percent of the tokens in everyday reading matter. Wang estimates (1973) that 'a knowledge of 4,000 to 7,000 characters is sufficient for, say, reading a newspaper'. These two estimates appear to conflict, but both are substantially smaller than the total number of characters.

Moreover, the characters have internal structure which aids recognition and production. Each is made up of strokes from an inventory of twenty possibilities; an average character has five or six strokes. At a second level of structure, each character is made up of one basic constituent from a set of 189. This radical may occur as an independent character but in most instances is combined with another element. For about 90 percent of Chinese characters today, that element is a 'phonetic', which indicates the pronunciation of the character, either fully or through a partial similarity such as rhyming. This kind of internal structure makes it possible for a reader to infer the interpretation of unfamiliar characters (see Wang, 1973, p. 54). While writers may not freely compose new characters on this basis, the internal structure undoubtedly aids recall and look-up; characters are arranged in dictionaries according to their radicals, and then by the number of strokes in the remainder (Wang, 1973).

In practice, then, the number of elementary characters that a writer must produce does not range quite so widely as was suggested at the beginning of this section; there are not 50,000 independent characters in Chinese but perhaps closer to a few thousand elements, as compared with about forty-six basic signs in a Japanese syllabary and smaller numbers of characters in the Roman, Cyrillic, Arabic, Greek, or Hebrew alphabets, for instance. Still, mastery of the character set itself can be an important variable in learning to write, at least if one compares Chinese with the alphabetic and syllabic systems.

Another psychologically important variable among writing systems is their ability to span time and space. These capabilities, after all, most centrally distinguish writing from speech. On this score, Chinese has amply demonstrated the virtues of a writing system that is relatively independent of pronunciation. Writings from a millenium ago in China are still relatively understandable, even though the spoken language has changed greatly. Wang (1973, p. 55) notes that 'the writing of Confucius [from the fifth century B.C.] is more intelligible to a modern Chinese than, say, a page of *Beowulf* is to an American' even though Beowulf was written about 1500 years more recently. The writing system itself has helped to give China a cultural heritage that can be traced back more than 3500 years.

Similarly, it is the writing system that makes it possible for 500 million Chinese to read the same documents, even though many of them speak dialects unintelligible to the others. Precisely because of the dialect variation in this enormous country, one can be sure that an alphabetic orthography will not find easy acceptance. Through its writing system, too, China has influenced the culture of all of Southeast Asia, including that of Japan. Many Japanese *kanji* represent the same meanings as the Chinese forms from which they are derived, even though the pronunciation is often totally different.

Even alphabetic orthography, while representing phonemes, usually manages not to represent dialectal variation. Certainly for a language like English, spoken and read around the world, it would be disadvantageous to develop local spellings. Orthographies are notoriously conservative, but not all of this conservatism is mere inertia. Some of the puzzles which orthography presents to the beginning writer arise from the effort to maintain a single representation across dialects, so that, for instance, children in Great Britain have been learning for centuries to spell post-vocalic /r/'s that they pronounce, if at all, as vowels.

Among the beginning spellers whom I have studied closely (Read, 1971, 1975), one 5-year-old, whom I will call Frank, had come from Atlanta to the Boston area, bringing with him the trait of raising /ɛ/ to [ɪ] before nasals; that is, Frank regularly pronounced *stem* as (stɪm), and *pen* as [pɪn]. In his early invented spelling, Frank spelled these words as *he* pronounced them, not as his Boston schoolmates did, producing spellings such as WIN (when), FINS (fence), and BIN (Ben). In this respect, Frank was not especially disadvantaged; every child must learn that English orthography does not represent his or her dialect, whatever it is, though some children encounter the problem more frequently than others. This source of difficulty in spelling is to be distinguished from structural properties, such as representing diverse levels of language simultaneously, and from idiosyncratic features of the spelling of individual words.

Another potentially difficult lesson for the writer as well as the reader has to do with aspects of speech which are poorly represented in virtually every orthography, namely the prosodic or suprasegmental characteristics:

intonation, stress, and duration. Both alphabetic and non-alphabetic writing systems fail to represent these aspects of speech, and yet they can be important to comprehension. One example is the ambiguity of sentences such as 'The hostess greeted the girl with a smile' in their written form. Recently investigators have begun to suspect that prosody may play a role in the comprehension of all spoken sentences, not merely the ambiguous ones.

An essential part of comprehension is identifying the major phrases of sentences, in order to relate them to each other. So, for example, in 'Mommy and Daddy are going out to dinner' the listener or reader must discern that the subject phrase is *Mommy and Daddy* and that the rest of the sentence is related to that phrase as predicate. In speech, the end of this major phrase is signalled by a slight lengthening of *Daddy*, primarily in its first vowel. No such signal of a clause boundary occurs, or even may occur, in writing. Punctuation in English sets off whole sentences from each other, marks off items in a series of parenthetical phrases, and demarcates some clauses, but otherwise, no overt indication of the internal structure of a sentence is allowed in writing.

Languages with similar orthographies vary somewhat in the representation of such structural information. In German, even common nouns are capitalized, and since almost all noun phrases end with nouns, this practice indirectly (and imperfectly) reflects structure. In Dutch, words that would receive contrastive stress in speech are written with accent marks, even in formal prose. Thus in the Dutch counterpart to 'The problem is not that he doesn't know; the problem is that he knows too *much*', the Dutch word corresponding to *much* would be written with accent marks (véél). In English, underlining such words is considered informal and is deliberately minimized by editors. Similarly, pairs of Dutch words that differ only in stress, such as ′voorkomen (appear in court) and voor′komen (prevent) are distinguished by accent marks in writing where ambiguity would otherwise result. The numerous English pairs, such as ′contract (noun) and con′tract (verb), are never marked for stress in writing.

There is some evidence that as listeners, children depend more heavily on prosodic cues than adults do (Read and Schreiber, 1980). A reasonable inference might be that, as readers, they must learn to comprehend without written counterparts to these prosodic cues. Certainly as writers, children have to learn that intonation, stress, and duration are not systematically reflected in punctuation, and that devices such as making letters larger or bolder, underlining, inserting additional spaces or ellipsis marks, and using exclamation points are all considered informal and used sparingly if at all in formal writing. What is difficult about punctuation may be not that it exists within a generally segmental orthography, but that it bears such an incomplete and indirect relationship to the suprasegmental cues which are often important to the understanding of speech. This issue has received little attention in research, though it is basic to an understanding of the developmental and educational challenges posed by orthography.

RELATIVE ACCESSIBILITY

A question which has received more attention, though not enough, is that of the relative accessibility of the units which are represented orthographically, from the word to the phoneme, that is, the relative ease with which a learner or a user can grasp and manipulate these units. Some awareness of language as an object that can be manipulated (e.g., segmented, classified, reordered) on several levels seems to be important to writing, not only in the beginning stages but also in skilled writing (cf. Baker, 1980; Read, 1978). That writing is fundamentally a manipulation of language is apparent not only in the drafting and redrafting which skilled writers go through at the levels of syntax, semantics, and discourse, but also at the orthographic core. In order to preserve and transmit language across time and space, we have contrived to represent, not the meanings which are apparent to consciousness as we speak and listen, nor the physical sounds which strike our ears, but intermediate units which vary substantially in their accessibility, especially to young children.

These units, from words to morphemes to syllables to phonemes, do not vary monotonically in the ease with which we can become aware of them and manipulate them. Words and syllables are relatively more accessible; morphemes and phonemes less so. The former are units of everyday parlance, which have proven rather difficult to define formally; the latter are creatures of linguistic analysis. That this is true for words as opposed to morphemes hardly requires demonstration to a reader of English; our basically phonemic orthography, like most others, also sets off words. That it represents morphemes as well, in pairs like *wide/width*, is not so apparent to the average reader.

The accessibility of syllables versus phonemes has been demonstrated by Liberman *et al.* (1977) in segmentation experiments with children and by Rozin and Gleitman (1977) in teaching disadvantaged inner-city children to read a syllabary. Rozin and Gleitman candidly admit that their syllabary curriculum was 'no panacea' for these children's reading difficulties, but there is little doubt that the syllabic writing was easier than the alphabetic. Also relevant here is a paper by Rozin *et al.* (1971), which briefly reports success in teaching American children to read Chinese characters. Those characters are not a syllabary, but the morphemes that they represent are almost all monosyllabic.

Liberman *et al.* (1977) and Rozin and Gleitman (1977) both indicate a probable reason that a syllable is more accessible than the phonemes that make it up; within a syllable, the individual phonemes overlap and affect each other. That is, in a syllable like *bag*, aspects of both the initial and final consonant are encoded in the vowel; there is no way of slicing the acoustic signal into three parts corresponding uniquely to the three phonemes. Because speech sounds affect their neighbors, there is no such thing as an invariant signal for /b/ or /æ/ or /g/.

This property helps to account for the relative obscurity of the phoneme; it is ironic that, over the centuries, writing has developed toward representing phonemes rather than words or syllables, with the result that considerable instruction in the linguistic basis of the orthography (rather than the character set or the assignment conventions) is necessary. But a few qualifications are in order.

First, the influence of speech sounds upon their neighbors is not limited to the syllable. As Kent and Minifie (1977) show, coarticulation extends beyond the boundaries of the syllable and even the word. Second, while syllables are easier for children to identify than phonemes, some puzzles remain in a language with complex syllable structure like that of English. It is easier to count syllables than to define their boundaries in words like *butter*; it is not clear that the syllable boundary corresponds with the morpheme boundary in a word like *helping* or *mixup*; it is not even clear how many syllables there are in words like *girl, seal*, or *chasm*. Thus the difference in accessibility between the syllable and the phoneme is only relative, and there would be problems in devising a syllabary for English, beyond the sheer number of characters required.

A special instance of the difficulty in isolating phonemes within syllables can be seen in young children's spelling. Both in pre-school and in the primary grades, children frequently give no representation for the nasal sounds in words like *pump, bent,* and *sink* (Read, 1971, 1975). This persistent pattern is all the more puzzling in that the children usually have no difficulty in spelling the 'same sound' in other positions – the /m/ in *come*, or the /n/ in *Ben*, or the /ŋ/ in *sing*, for instance. In my sample of spelling from children younger than 6 years, for example, /m/ in a word like *pump* is omitted 45 percent of the time, but in other positions (not before a consonant but before a vowel or at the end of a word), it is omitted less than 1 percent of the time.

The explanation for this anomaly is that for good phonetic reasons, the /m/ of *bum* and the /m/ of *bump* are to children's ears *not* the same sound; the former is about six times longer than the latter, and in fact, in most American pronunciation of *bump*, there may be no nasal consonant at all, the nasality being 'encoded' on the vowel (Malécot, 1960). That is, the longest, most intense, and most reliable difference between *bet* and *bent* is the occurrence not of a nasal consonant, but of a nasalized vowel. Given no special symbol for this vowel, beginners spell it with the same symbol as its non-nasalized counterpart. Except for this omission, BET is actually not a bad phonetic representation of *bent*.

Though this example gives rise to a frequent, persistent, and puzzling spelling pattern it is not really exceptional. Up to a point, it is analogous to the situation with *bag*, where the cues for /b/ are of very brief duration and encoded on the vowel. Identifying units smaller than the syllable is no trivial matter, however obvious it may appear to adults who have mastered an alphabetic orthography.

The question of accessibility applies not only to levels of language considered as a whole, but also to levels of structure within particular words. The fact that orthographies (and writing systems generally) characteristically represent different levels of language in different contexts can be explained on the assumption that some phonological and morphophonemic processes are transparent to the user, so that their effects may be ignored in orthography. For example, if the relation between /t/ in *Egypt* and /š/ in *Egyptian* is transparent in this sense, then it will be ignored in orthography. That is to say that *Egypt* within *Egyptian* is accessible to the speaker of the language and is displayed orthographically. If the similar relationship between *delude* and *delusion* were transparent, then the latter might be spelled *deludion*. Klima (1972) explores a number of assumptions about what is accessible, and the letter assignment conventions (orthographies) that would follow from these assumptions, in relation to the criteria of expressiveness (avoidance of ambiguity), versus economy.

An apparent problem with this way of looking at things is that it makes claims about the accessibility of various levels of structure, a quality which surely varies from one person to another, while the orthography is standardized. At the moment we must simply ignore that problem, since if we limited ourselves to invariant aspects of language we could say very little about how orthography relates to language. A genuine problem is that of saying what is meant by 'accessible' in this context; what precisely must hold between *Egypt* and *Egyptian* in order for the latter spelling to be a good one? The fact that the phonological process is a general one is not sufficient, and an awareness of the relationship in meaning is not necessary. This question, of what is accessible about linguistic structure, goes beyond orthography and can be answered only by a better understanding of how languages are structured and how they are used.

It has been suggested (e.g., in Chomsky and Halle, 1968) that the general principle of not representing predictable phonetic alternation accounts for the non-representation of prosodic features mentioned above. But the prosodic form (stress, intonation, and duration) is predictable only if the syntactic form of the sentence is given. That is, it is not predictable from the point of view of the reader, who must recover the syntactic (and semantic) relationships within the sentence. There is a substantial difference between using a uniform representation of the plural morpheme, knowing that the reader can predict its phonetic realization, if that is even necessary, and using a uniform representation for 'The large square blocks ...' regardless of whether the subject/predicate boundary comes before or after *blocks*, for example, whether the continuation is 'the opening.' or 'are on the table.'. The parsing of this sentence, and therefore the appropriate prosodic pattern, can be inferred only from the type of phrase which follows *blocks*, whereas the appropriate pronunciation of the *s* of *blocks* is inferable from the preceding phoneme. In English orthography (and others), the failure to distinguish phonetic alternants may be a help to the reader, but the failure to represent prosodic features may be a hindrance.

Though orthographies may sometimes seem contradictory and chaotic, their intricacies may also possess a certain elegance. Gelb (1963, p. 87) and Martin (1972, p. 86) cite representations of foreign names in Chinese, in which characters are sometimes chosen to suggest *both* the sound of the name and its connotation. Such examples may seem like elaborate word games to those of us who do not participate in them. English, however, may give somewhat the same appearance to outsiders with its trick of using the same letter, within different patterns, to represent the vowels of historically and morphologically related words, as in *wide/width, sane/sanity*, and *appeal/appellate*. Such pairings create spellings for six vowels from three vowel letters and at the same time represent relationships in derivation and in meaning. They adapt the Roman alphabet to the English language, while providing information to the reader and the vocabulary-learner.

An interesting variant on this practice is created by young children, some of whom rather consistently pair vowel spellings on a different basis. Turning again to my collection of spellings by children younger than six years, we find a tendency to spell the vowel of *bed*, /ɛ/, with the letter A. This spelling occurred in more than 40 percent of the 371 cases, barely fewer than the standard spellings, and far more frequent than any other non-standard spelling.

The other vowels which these children spelled *A* were those of *cake* and *bat* (/eɪ/ and /æ/), that is, essentially standard spellings, with the former also being the name of the letter *A*. Now these three vowels make up the mid and low front vowels of English; they are closely related in articulatory, perceptual, and acoustic form. The effect, then, is that the children spelled alike a family of vowels that *are* alike in sound.

On the basis of children's spelling of other groups of phonetically related vowels, and studies of their ability to recognize these phonetic relationships, I have suggested that it is indeed the phonetic similarities which influence young children's spelling, or at least the spelling of some young children at a certain stage in their development. They accept the notion that different vowels may be spelled with the same letter, but the vowels that they spell alike are those which are similar in sound, not those which are related historically and morphologically. This seems altogether reasonable, considering that young children have a considerable sensitivity to speech sounds (as in acquiring native pronunciation of one or more languages) but little or no acquaintance with derivational morphology. What is remarkable is that the children who created these patterns in their beginning spelling were already participating in the orthographic game of adapting the alphabet to the language on a principled basis.

REGULARITY

We have approached the end of this treatment of orthographic variables with little explicit mention of regularity, the consistency with which representations correspond to linguistic units within a writing system. One reason for this apparent neglect is that regularity needs no introduction; as teachers and researchers think about orthography, they are sure to consider regularity and likely to recall repeated criticisms of English spelling on this score. Another and somewhat contradictory reason, however, is that regularity is a good deal more complex than it appears and can be understood only in relation to other variables discussed above. Implicit in the recognition that most orthographies represent different units of language in different contexts is that these orthographies must be inconsistent when seen at any one level. But regularity at a single level may not be important. It is true but not revealing to say that *ed* may represent /ed/, /d/, and /t/ in English; a more revealing statement is that regular past tense is spelled uniformly.

With respect to reading, there is some evidence that consistency in orthography helps children learn to decode, as might be expected (van Rijnsoever, 1979; Kyöstiö, 1980), though these studies are informal and only implicitly comparative. With respect to writing, it has been noted that one of the chief effects of the (rather regular) initial teaching alphabet (i.t.a.) is to stimulate children's spontaneous writing. Vera Southgate summarized her interviews with nearly 400 individuals as follows:

(1) An overwhelming majority of infant teachers who had used i.t.a. expressed their pleasure in the increase in the quantity and quality of

children's free writing; many of them rating this as the chief advantage of i.t.a.

2. It was particularly emphasized that this free writing arose spontaneously, at an earlier stage than when t.o. [traditional orthography] was used, and that children were able to pursue this form of expression almost independently of the teacher (Warburton and Southgate, 1969, p. 146)

Even assuming that these effects are adequately and reliably measured through Southgate's interviews, however, they may be attributed not only to the regularity of i.t.a. but also to an increased emphasis on writing in i.t.a. classrooms, greater freedom from concern over errors, and the stimulation inherent in using an experimental technique.

Most basically, there is the problem of what regularity means. If it means representing only one kind of linguistic unit in a one-to-one mapping, then few writing systems approach regularity, and many major ones are wildly and inexplicably irregular. If we allow for representations at more than one level, then regularity becomes a complex notion indeed. Even given a working notion of regularity in this sense, there is the problem of what kinds of regularity facilitate reading and writing, bearing in mind that what is regular for the reader may be irregular for the writer. For example, English /n/ has two main spellings, *n* and *ng*, as in *sink* and *sing*. If these spellings represented no other phonemes, then the many–one mapping of spellings to sounds would be regular (in the sense of unique without reference to context) for the reader and not for the writer. Conversely for one–many mappings of spellings to sounds, such as *x* in English, which may represent /ks/ or /gz/ (as in *extend* and *exhaust*), the actual situation is far more complex than these examples suggest because *n* can represent other phonemes and /ks/ can be spelled in other ways. That is, there is really a many–many relationship, but the possibility of asymmetry remains.

Those of us concerned with writing must face the likelihood that regularity in writing systems, whatever forms it takes, may tend to favor the reader over the writer; these are, after all, primarily *reading* systems. In Chomsky and Halle's view of English orthography regularity is seen from the reader's point of view, and Householder (1971, pp. 253–256) shows as an example that the rules for pronouncing *-tion* are far simpler than those for spelling /šen/.

Since the 1950s various researchers have asked which kinds of regularity and structure in orthography the reader makes use of. Recently, Massaro and his colleagues (Massaro, 1980; Massaro *et al.*, 1980a) have compared the *frequency* of spellings with their phonological and orthographic *permissibility*. For example, is *lohuds* (legal structure but low-frequency bigrams) easier to read than *dhouls* (illegal structure but relatively frequent bigrams), where 'easy to read' is defined (a) as the accuracy of a search for a letter within these words (under time constraint) and (b) as a judgment of how closely the letter string resembles an English word? Massaro *et al*.s, (1980b) recent report suggests that the most important factors are whether a string is an English word and the permissibility of that string according to certain phonological and orthographic rules. The frequency of the bigrams (expressed as a logarithm) according to their position in the string accounts for some detail, while the frequency of a real word accounts for very little. It appears, in other words, that it is possible to state orthographic rules that have a greater effect on a reader's letter search than does frequency. As Massaro and his colleagues emphasize, it is also likely that these rules as presently stated are not yet optimal. With further research, we can probably come closer to saying just what counts as orthographic regularity. This work drives home the observation that regularity is no simple concept, even when limited to its effect on reading.

CONCLUSIONS

What we have come down to, then, is that there are numerous variables in orthography that are likely to affect performance in writing. These include the level of linguistic units which are represented (both the selection of levels and the variety of them), the degree of redundancy or representation of predictable detail, the way in which the orthography responds to language variation across time and geography, the relative accessibility to both learner and user of the units which are represented, the role of these units in comprehension, and the consistency of an orthography relative to the levels of language which it represents.

We have also seen that the writing system of a language does not evolve arbitrarily. The original borrowing of a character set with some assignment conventions, the adaptation of the writing system to the new language, and the evolution of this system over centuries all depend on the phonemic, syllabic, and morphemic structure of the language, on the dialect variety and historical change which must be accommodated, and on the cultural and political setting, such as the writing systems of culturally influential neighbors. What appears to be resistance to change is often the pull of linguistic, cultural, and political roots. What appears to be a bizarre writing system may in fact be well-suited to the language which uses it.

Within this framework, not only is regularity just one variable among several, but it cannot be understood without reference to the others. Nonetheless, the relevance of orthographic regularity to writing development is one major question for research. Another issue is accessibility: we do not really know the conditions under which larger or smaller units are especially salient to the learner or to the skilled user, to the reader or to the writer. The role of prosodic features in comprehension and their representation in writing is also ripe for investigation. Given a writing system which represents more than a single level of language, it is important to know how to introduce children to this multiplicity; how to move from the phonemic to the morphemic correspondence in English, or from the syllabic to the logographic in Japanese, for instance. Most basically, perhaps, there is the interesting and important question of the relationship between maturation and the accessibility of orthographic units. For example, it is more or less clear that children must achieve a certain level of maturation in order to identify within words and syllables the (more obscure) phonemes which alphabetic orthography generally represents; for some children this step is a major stumbling point (Liberman *et al.*, 1977). What is not clear is how this ability relates to an underlying cognitive function; is there a cognitive prerequisite for success with alphabetic spelling? Does acquaintance with the orthography promote this cognitive development, or do the two stimulate each other? To oversimplify, which comes first, the ability to read and write or the analysis of language which this ability implies?

Because writing cannot exist without a writing system, in the sense outlined here, and because all writing systems reveal complexities, neither the teaching of writing nor research on writing can afford to ignore the writing system itself, especially as we attempt to facilitate the initial stages of learning.

ACKNOWLEDGMENT

I want to thank my colleague, John Street, for his helpful advice on several points.

REFERENCES

Baker, R. G. (1980). Orthographic awareness. In *Cognitive Processes in Spelling* (ed. U. Frith), pp. 51–68. Academic Pres, London.

Chao, Y. R. (1968). *Language and Symbolic Systems*, Cambridge University Press, New York.

Chomsky, N. and Halle, M. (1968). *The Sound Pattern of English*. Harper & Row, New York.

Frase, L. T. (1982). Writing, text, and the reader. In *Writing: the Nature, Development, and Teaching of Written Communication* (eds. C. H. Frederiksen, M. F. Whiteman, and J. F. Dominic). Lawrence Erlbaum Associates, Hillsdale, N.J.

Gelb, I. J. (1963). *A Study of Writing*, The University of Chicago Press, Chicago.

Gleitman, L. R., and Rozin, P. (1977). The structure and acquisition of reading: Relations between orthographies and the structure of language. In *Toward a Psychology of Reading: The Proceedings of the CUNY Conference* (eds. A. S. Reber and D. L. Scarborough). Lawrence Erlbaum Associates, Hillsdale, N.J.

Grimes, J. E., and Gordon, R. G., Jr. (1980). Design of new orthographies. In *Orthography, Reading, and Dyslexia* (eds. J. F. Kavanagh and R. L. Venezky), pp. 93–104. University Park Press, Baltimore.

Hockett, C. F. (1958). *A Course in Modern Linguistics*, Macmillan, New York.

Householder, F. W. (1971) *Linguistic Speculations*, Cambridge University Press, London.

Kavanagh, J. F., and Mattingly, I. G. (eds.) (1972). *Language by Ear and by Eye*. MIT Press, Cambridge, Mass.

Kavanagh, J. F., and Venezky R. L. (eds.) (1980). *Orthography, Reading, and Dyslexia*. University Park Press, Baltimore.

Kent, R. D., and Minifie, F. (1977). Coarticulation in recent speech production models. *Journal of Phonetics,* **5**, 115–133.

Klima, E. S. (1972). How alphabets might reflect language. In *Language by Ear and by Eye* (eds. J. F. Kavanagh and I. G. Mattingly), pp. 57–80. MIT Press, Cambridge, Mass.

Kyöstiö, O. K. (1980). Is learning to read easy in a language in which the grapheme–phoneme correspondences are regular? in *Orthography, Reading, and Dyslexia* (eds. J. F. Kavanagh and R. L. Venezky), pp. 35–50. University Park Press, Baltimore.

Ladefoged, P. (1975). *A Course in Phonetics*. Harcourt Brace Jovanovich, New York.

Liberman, I. Y., Shankweiler, D., Liberman, A. M., Fowler, C., and Fischer, F. W. (1977). Phonetic segmentation and recoding in the beginning reader'. In *Toward a Psychology of Reading: The Proceedings of the CUNY Conference* (eds. A. S. Reber and D. Scarborough). Lawrence Erlbaum Associates, Hillsdale, N.J.

Malécot, A. (1960). Vowel nasality as a distinctive feature in American English'. *Language,* **36**, 222–229.

Martin, S. E. (1972). Nonalphabetic writing systems: some observations'. In *Language by Ear and by Eye* (eds. J. F. Kavanagh and I. G. Mattingly), pp. 81–102. MIT Press, Cambridge, Mass.

Massaro, D. W. (1980) How does orthographic structure facilitate reading? In *Orthography, Reading, and Dyslexia* (eds. J. F. Kavanagh and R. L. Venezky), pp. 193–209. University Park Press, Baltimore.

Massaro, D. W, Jastrzembski, J. E., and Lucas, P. (1980b). Frequency, orthographic regularity, and lexical status in letter and word perception. Technical Report no. 550, Wisconsin Research and Development Center, Madison.

Massaro, D. W., Taylor, G. A., Venezky, R. L., Jastrzembski, J. E., and Lucas, P. A. (1980a). *Letter and Word Perception: Orthographic Structure and Visual Processing in reading*. North Holland, Amsterdam.

Pitman, J. and St John, J. (1969). *Alphabets and Reading: the initial teaching alphabet*. Sir Isaac Pitman & Sons, London.

Read, C. (1970). Children's Perceptions of the Sounds of English. Unpublished doctoral dissertation, Harvard University.

Read, C. (1971). Preschool children's knowledge of English phonology. *Harvard Educational Review,* **41**, 1–34.

Read, C. (1975). *Children's Categorizations of Speech Sounds in English*. National Council of Teachers of English, Urbana, Illinois.

Read, C. (1978). Children's awareness of language, with emphasis on sound systems. In *The Child's Conception of Language* (eds. A. Sinclair, R. J. Jarvella, and R. J. Jarvella), pp. 65–82. Springer Verlag, Berlin.

Read, C., and Schreiber, P. (1980). Why short subjects are harder to find than long ones. In *Language Acquisition: the state of the art* (eds. L. Gleitman and E. Wanner). Harvard University Press, Cambridge, Mass.

Rozin, P., and Gleitman, J. M. (1977). The structure and acquisition of reading II: The reading process and the acquisition of the alphabetic principle. In *Toward a Psychology of Reading: The Proceedings of the CUNY Conference* (eds. A. S. Reber and D. L. Scarborough). Lawrence Erlbaum Associates, Hillsdale, N.J.

Rozin, P., Poritsky, S., and Sotsky, R. (1971). American children with reading problems can easily learn to read English represented by Chinese characters. *Science,* **171**, 1264–1267.

van Rijnsoever, R. J. (1979). Spellingen van voorschoolse kinderen en eersteklassers, *Gramma,* **3**, 169–96.

Venezky, R. L. (1970). *The Structure of English Orthography*. Mouton, The Hague.

Wang, W. S-Y. (1973). The Chinese language, *Scientific American,* **228** (2), 50–60.

Warburton, F. W. and Southgate, V. (1969). *i.t.a.: an independent evaluation*. John Murray and W. & R. Chambers, London.

The Psychology of Written Language
Edited by M. Martlew

CHAPTER 7

Psychological Strategies and the Development of Reading and Writing

PETER E. BRYANT AND LYNETTE BRADLEY

Psychologists have spent a great deal more time on children's reading than on their writing, and their comparative neglect of the children's written output is probably due to a widespread assumption that children draw on much the same processes to read and to write. There are now several reasons for rejecting this assumption (Frith, 1980), and the strong possibilities that children often read in one way and write in another raises some interesting questions about the kind of hypotheses one might have about the development of reading and spelling.

One question concerns the kind of barriers children have to surmount when they make any intellectual progress. Broadly speaking there seem to be two possibilities. One is couched in terms of *deficits*: the idea, which is a very common one, is that children initially lack certain skills or strategies and have to acquire them. This idea is extended to children in difficulty of one sort or another: for example it would explain the problems of backward readers as being due to the lack of some ability or skill or strategy. They cannot at first, it is often argued, tell certain letters apart or link heard patterns with seen patterns (Birch and Belmont, 1964) or dissect words into phonemes (Liberman *et al.*, 1977; Bruce, 1964; Marcel, 1980).

The second possibility is that the central question is one of the proper deployment of *strategies*. Here the idea is that children usually possess in one form or another the strategies which are needed to master the intellectual task at hand and that any difficulty they have is in realizing the appropriate time to employ that strategy. Extended to backwardness in reading, emphasis of this approach would be that some children are slow to learn to write or to read because they do not organize and consolidate their existing skills profitably enough.

Of these two alternative approaches the first is by far the more popular. It seems natural, if something is wrong with a child, to look for a gap in his intellectual armour. However the recent work which we mentioned in our first paragraph on the relationships between reading and spelling suggests that the second approach might be at least as successful, at any rate as far as written language is concerned.

Let us turn first to a particular example of Tom C, an intelligent 11-year-old boy whom we saw recently and who is at the moment experiencing a great deal of difficulty with reading and writing. These he is only managing at the 7½–8 year old level in contrast to his progress in other subjects, like mathematics, where his performance equals the average for his age.

It is reasonably well attested that at least two major skills (and probably many more) are involved in coping with written language. The first can be called phonological, and involves using the alphabetic code. Written words are constructed from symbols, that is, letters or groups of letters which represent the word's constituent sounds. The second can loosely be called visual and involves the visual recognition of whole words or sequences of letters.

How did Tom fare on these two fronts? First he showed definite signs of phonological proficiency. He was, for example, able to write out some meaningless words which were dictated to him like 'pring' and 'blim' and 'wug', and it is difficult to see how he could have managed that without knowing quite a lot about phonological segments (His phonological skills are not perfect, to be sure, as the sample of a piece of his writing, in Figure 1 about go-carts shows.) He also showed definite signs of some visual prowess. He could read words like 'bicycle', 'picture', and 'shepherd' straight off, and since these are words which it would be very difficult to construct on a purely phonological basis we must conclude that he managed to do so by some form of visual recognition. Indeed some of his reading errors seem to suggest a misapplied memory for the shapes of words: he read 'sauce' as 'square', 'imagine' as 'magazine', 'attracts' as 'anorak', for example.

One cannot, of course, say from this that his visual and phonological skills are normal, but they are there at least in some form, and it is certainly difficult to explain some of his difficulties in terms of absence of any skill or weakness in it. For example he wrote the words 'went' and 'down' correctly in the sample given in Figure 1. Because of this we asked him later to write the words 'bent' and 'frown'. He wrote 'bedet' and 'fran'.

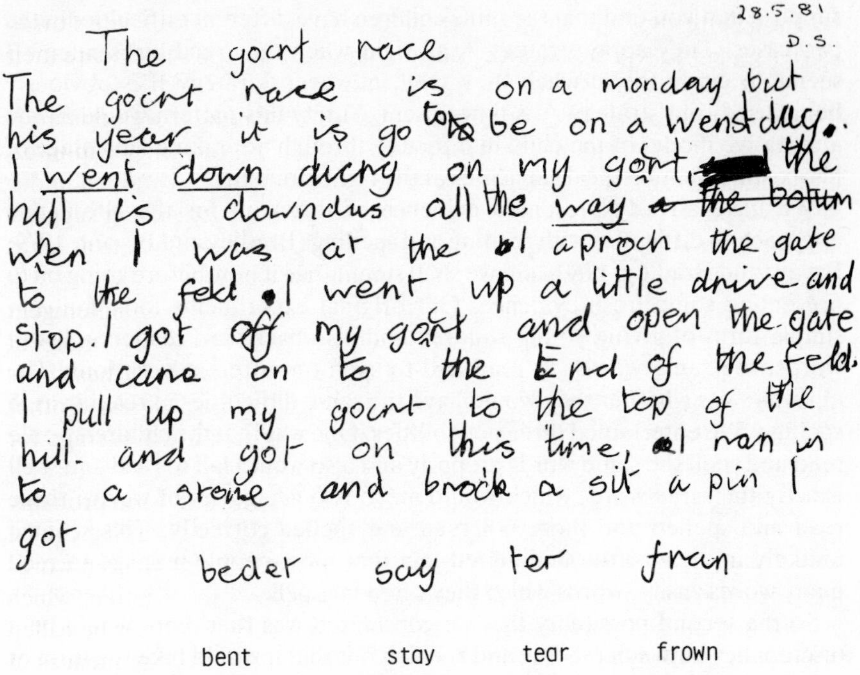

28.5.81
D.S.

The gocnt race

The gocnt race is on a monday but
his year it is go to be on a Wenstday.
I went down ducry on my gont, the
hill is downdus all the way ~~a the botum~~
wen I was at the aproch the gate
to the feld I went up a little drive and
stop. I got off my gont and open the gate
and cane on to the End of the feld.
I pull up my gocnt to the top of the
hill. and got on this time, I ran in
to a stone and brock a sit a pin I
got

beder say ter fran

bent stay tear frown

FIGURE 1 A written account of a go-cart race

Our argument is that these last mistakes cannot be dismissed as mere phonological failures. If he can construct words like 'pring' phonologically he is surely in principle capable of replacing the 'w' of 'went' with 'b' to make 'bent'. But he did not and we can ask why not. Our answer is that he probably remembered 'went' as an unsegmented whole when he wrote the word. We think that his failure to use this memory to make the word 'bent' was due to his not recognizing that here was a chance to use his existing phonological skills.

This was a particular case. Can we also say that the same problems about the correct deployment of strategies occur quite widely? Our argument is that they do, and it centres around the differences between learning to read and learning to spell.

Both these activities are complex enough, and may demand a set of different strategies. Suppose you look at the children's difficulties with both things and find that the difficulties take much the same form in reading and spelling: in both cases the child does not seem to be able to use strategy A. Such a discovery would fit in with the deficit approach: strategy A looks as though it is missing, and that is why the child cannot read or write well. But suppose that you find that the same children have different difficulties in the two cases. They apply strategy A all right when they read but strategy B seems to elude them: when they spell, however, strategy B is obviously being used, but strategy A is now absent. Surely this pattern would fit the alternative model of the child in difficulty through not taking advantage of his existing phonological capacities at the right moment.

We have already presented evidence of this kind for the alternative approach to difficuties with reading and spelling (Bradley and Bryant, 1979; Bryant and Bradley, 1980) and we shall summarize it now before going on to presenting some fresh evidence. Our original experiments took the very simple form of giving young children and also backward readers a list of words, the same words, to read and to spell on different occasions. The question was whether they would have the same difficulties in reading as in spelling. We entertained three possibilities. One was that the children would read and spell the same words properly and also would fail to read and spell exactly the same word, which would mean two categories of words: those read and spelled and those not read and spelled correctly. This seemed unlikely in view of the undoubted fact that most people manage to read many words easily, words which they often misspell.

So the second possibility that we considered was that there would be a discrepancy between reading and spelling but that it would take the form of children reading some words but not spelling them correctly, thus adding a third category: words read but not spelled.

The third possibility was of a two-way discrepancy, which in effect would add a fourth and rather surprising category, words spelled correctly but not read properly. If children read some words which they cannot spell, and also spell other words without being able to read them properly, we surely would be able to argue for our alternative to the deficit approach. Such a pattern would suggest that they read and spell in different ways and also that they neglect particular strategies when they read but take them up when they spell, and vice-versa.

In fact we found consistent evidence for this last possibility among children and also among backward readers. The two-way discrepancy, that is, some words read but not spelled, other spelled but not read, did appear. From this we conclude a certain independence between the way children learn to read and to spell.

Two further points need to be made about this independence. First it seems to be confined to the early stages of learning to read and to write. On the whole the two-way discrepancy has dropped out by the time the normal reader is roughly at an 8-year reading level. This might be the reason why Tom C, in whom the discrepancy is still marked, is stuck at the 7½–8 year old level in reading and in spelling. Secondly the discrepancy is greater among backward readers than with normal readers *of the same reading level*. This is important because it seems to show that the independence between reading and spelling is particularly marked among poor readers, and therefore that their problems might at least be partly the result of failing to take advantage of strategies which are available to them and which they do use in some situations.

But such a claim has little value put in such an abstract way. What are these strategies which they apparently do use, but all too selectively? Our contention is that the children in question, backward readers and young normal readers, tend to deal in phonological segments (c–a–t) when they spell words but to abandon it when they read. In reading, they concentrate on recognizing visual chunks or sequences of letters which signify either whole words or common sounds, like '-ight', as we have already suggested in the case of Tom C.

Our evidence for this comes partly from the kind of words which fall into the different categories. Those which children spelled but did not read tended to be easy to construct on a letter-by-letter basis, that is to say phonologically. These were words like 'bun' and 'mat'. The fact that children sometimes spelled but did not read such words certainly suggests that they were prepared to use their knowledge of phonological segments when they spelled. On the other hand the words which they spelled but did not read were difficult to construct in such a way, and might easily have demanded some kind of knowledge of 'chunks'. These were words like 'school' and 'light', very familiar but impossible to construct letter by letter, sound by sound.

Another part of our evidence comes from a form of intervention. We encouraged children to adopt a phonological strategy (i.e. to build up words sound by sound when reading), and found that this had virtually no effect on the words which they had neither read nor spelled before, but did considerably improve their performance with words which hitherto they had spelled correctly but had not managed to read. This certainly suggests that they could manage these words phonologically (and therefore could spell them) but had not managed to read them because they were not taking advantage of their existing phonological capacities.

So here is evidence for our alternative hypothesis of children failing because they do not take advantage of their own capacities. But the evidence is somewhat indirect because it comes mainly from a post hoc analysis of words which were either misread or misspelled. We can now turn to some later evidence from experiments which examine the processes of reading and spelling.

If our idea is right, that young children concentrate on phonological segments when they spell but get by without them when they read, interfering with the phonological code should have a much more serious effect on the way they spell than on their reading. Several psychologists, most notably Barron and Baron (1977), Martin (1978), Kleiman (1975), Hitch and Baddeley (1976) have suggested a way of producing this kind of interference. The technique is often called 'articulatory suppression' or more recently 'concurrent vocalization'. It consists of making people repeat a word aloud over and over again while doing some other task. The assumption is that this repetitive vocal activity will make phonological and articulatory activities more difficult. The assumption is a controversial one, and we shall return to the controversies after we have reported our experiments; but first we must describe one other major study which did use this technique which we shall from now on refer to as concurrent vocalization.

This was the study carried out by Barron and Baron (1977). They gave children from 6 years upwards two tasks; one which they called *sound task* dealt directly with phonological segments. the children were given several picture–word pairs, some of which rhymed (horn–corn), while others did not. Their task was to mark the rhyming pairs. The other task was called the *meaning task* and roughly approximated to reading. The child was again given picture–word pairs and had to mark those where the word meant the same as the picture.

Both tasks were given to all the children under two conditions. In one they did the tasks silently; in the other they 'vocalized concurrently': in fact they had to go on saying 'double, double, double' till the task was over.

The results were striking at all age levels. Even among the younger children concurrent vocalization had no effect on the meaning task, where children apparently worked out the meaning of the written words as well and as quickly when they were saying 'double double' as when they were not. Yet this same demand had a considerable effect on the rhyming task, which children managed much worse when they had to say 'double double' than when they did the task silently. Since rhyming involves some kind of phonological analysis, it seems that concurrent vocalization might impede the phonological strategy, and yet it does not seem to mess up young children's reading. Such a result obviously does agree quite well with our contention that children might often read without constructing words phonologically.

So we adopted the technique and used it in three experiments. The aim of the first was to check that the concurrent vocalization does indeed make it difficult for children to deal in phonological segments. The second experiment was to check Barron and Baron's claim that the technique leaves children's reading unscathed. The aim of the third was to examine our hypothesis by testing the prediction that concurrent vocalization will harm young children's spelling grievously. Our purpose then was to demonstrate once again the early independence of reading and writing by showing that concurrent vocalization affects the two activities quite differently.

EXPERIMENT I: CONCURRENT VOCALIZATION AND PHONOLOGICAL SEGMENTS

Since the criterion is that vocalization affects a child's capacity for dealing with phonological segments, we gave all the children tasks in which they had to detect whether pairs of words shared a phonological segment.

The aim of the experiment was to see whether concurrent vocalization, in this case 'bla–bla–bla, would make such tasks more difficult.

Children

The same children were seen in all three experiments. There were forty, divided into two age groups: (1) *Younger*, mean age 6 years 10 months (range 6 years 6 months – 7 years 3 months); (2) *Older*, mean age 7 years 8 months (range 7 years 3 months – 8 years 0 months). Both groups consisted equally of boys and girls. All the children had reading and spelling ages, as measured by Schonell tests, roughly in line with their chronological age. The mean reading and spelling ages of the Younger group were respectively 6 years 11 months and 6 years 9 months. The equivalent figures for the Older group were 7 years 10 months and 7 years 9 months. The children came from two local First Schools.

Method

Material

There were four sets of ten pairs of pictures of very familiar objects. Each pair of pictures was on a separate card. In two of these sets (Opening sound) five of the pairs had names whose opening consonant was the same (e.g. man–mouse, dog–door) and five did not. In the other two sets (Closing sound) five of the pairs had names with the same vowels and final consonants (e.g. cat–hat, red–bed) and five did not.

Procedure

After checking that the child used the same names for the picture as the experimenter, the four sets were given to the child in four separate trials. In each trial the ten cards were presented separately and the child had to mark those which began with the same sound in the opening sound trials or ended with the same in the closing sound trials. The mark was a line drawn connecting the two pictures.

In one trial in each condition the child had to do this silently; in the other he had to start saying 'bla–bla' before he was handed each card and go on saying it until he had decided whether to make a mark or not.

The experimenter demonstrated how and when to make the mark before each trial, and also what the child had to do in the interference trials. The order of the four trials, and the actual pictures presented in each condition, were systematically varied between children.

Results

The interference did indeed quite radically disrupt this phonological task, as the mean scores in Table 1 show. An analysis of variance in which there were three main terms – Age, Conditions (Opening versus Closing scores) and Interference (Concurrent Vocalisation versus Silent) produced a significant Interference term (F 41.18: $d.F.$ 1,38: $p < 0.001$). This confirms that saying "bla–bla" does have a significant damping effect on the child's ability to categorize words on the basis of common phonological components. There was also an Age term (F 7.1: $d.F.$ 1,38; $p < 0.05$).

TABLE 1 Mean correct scores (out of ten) in judging whether or not words began or ended with the *same sounds*

	Opening sound		End sound	
	Silent	Concurrent vocalization	Silent	Concurrent vocalization
6-year-olds	6.9	4.9	8.5	5.8
7-year-olds	8.1	6.7	9.4	7.4

Conclusion

Repeating a sound does appear to make it more difficult for young children to analyse words into phonological components.

EXPERIMENT 2: READING WORDS AND LETTERS

Our hypothesis is that the 'bla–bla' interference should not stop children reading whole words if they depend on, non-phonological strategy in reading. If, however, they have to read not whole words but single letters, to see if they represent phonological segments of a word, they should be seriously held back by concurrent vocalization. We decided therefore to look at the effects of phonological interference on tasks which involved reading either the whole word or part of it.

Method

Material

Whole words. Two groups of twenty picture–word pairs were selected for each group. The words in one group were relatively easy to read (milk, egg) and in the other relatively hard (eye, picture). The difficult words were designed to be as difficult to read as the difficult words were to spell in Experiment 3. Pilot tests confirmed that both age groups made more errors with the difficult words.

Each group of picture–word pairs was divided into two sets of ten. In each set, five of the picture–word pairs were correct in that the words were the correct names of the pictures, as for example, man (picture), man (word). In the other five cases they were not, for example, man (picture), mouse (word). Pilot tests had suggested that when children cannot read the word and can only guess whether a picture–word pair is correct, they rely on the first letter. To prevent this happening, in the majority of the incorrect pairs the incorrect word started with the same letter as the name of the picture.

Single letters. As well as the four sets of picture–word pairs, there were six sets of ten picture–letter pairs. Both age groups were given the same six sets. These pairs consisted of a picture and beside it a single letter which was either the first, the middle, or the final letter of a three-letter word. The child's task was to mark those pairs where the letter correctly stood for the appropriate part of the word.

First letter. In two sets of picture–word pairs, the letter was the first consonant. In five pictures, the first letter was the correct first letter of the name of the picture which it was beside; so if the picture was of a cat the letter was 'c'. If the picture–word pair was incorrect the letter might be 'm'. To emphasize that the letter was the first one in every case, it was presented to the left of two blacked-out letters, thus 'C ● ●'.

Middle letter. In two other sets, the letter was the middle letter, always a vowel. So the letter beside a picture of a cat would be '● a ●' in a correct pair and, for sample, '● e ●' in an incorrect pair.

Final letter. The remaining two sets related to the final consonants; Thus, the same cat picture, '• • t' would be the display in a correct picture letter pair and '• • s' could be an incorrect pair. Only twenty pictures were used, all of which had easy-to-read three-letter (CVC) names. They were combined into sets in different ways in the three different letter conditions. Each picture–word and picture–letter pair was put on a separate card.

Procedure

Throughout the experiment the child's task was to make the correct picture–word or picture–letter pairs by drawing a line between picture and word or letter. In every trial the children were given ten picture–word or picture–letter pairs.

All the children were given the four picture–word sets first. They had to make one easy and one difficult set silently and one of each saying 'bla–bla'. In the latter case they had to go on saying the sound from the moment they were given each of the ten cards until they had decided whether to mark it or not. The order of the four trials was systematically varied between children, and so was the assignment of the different sets to the various conditions.

Then the children were given the three kinds (first, middle, and last letter) of picture–letter sets. They marked one of each kind of set silently and the other saying 'bla–bla'. The order of the sets was again systematically varied.

Results

There was no difference at all between the silent and the bla–bla trials when

TABLE 2 Mean correct scores (out of ten) in the whole word and single-letter tasks

	Whole word		Single Letter		
	Easy	Difficult	First letter	Middle letter	End letter
6-year-olds					
Silent	9.2	6.5	8.5	6.9	7.1
Concurrent vocalization	8.9	6.8	6.4	4.9	4.9
7-year-olds					
Silent	9.6	7.5	9.9	7.5	7.8
Concurrent vocalization	9.6	7.9	7.2	5.1	5.8

the children were dealing with whole words. But, as Table 2 shows, there was a considerable difference when the children had to deal with single letters. This was not a product of the relative difficulty of the single-letter tasks, because the first letter condition was actually easier than the easy picture–word condition. Phonological interference spoiled the former, however, but not the latter. So it seems that phonological interference does not stop children reading whole words, but does make it difficult for them to recognize segments.

The word and letter tasks were analysed separately. Since the younger and older children were given different words, their results were subjected to different analyses of variance. The mean terms in their analyses were Material (Easy vs. Hard) and Interference. Both analyses showed a significant Materials term (Younger group F 34.05: $d.F.$ 1,18: $p < 0.001$, Older Group F 24.87; $dF.$ 1,18: $p < 0.001$) as would be expected and nothing else. Thus they confirm the absence of interference.

Since the same picture–letter sets were given to both groups these scores were analysed together. The main terms were Age, Conditions (first, middle, and last letter) and Interference. The analysis produced a significant Age term showing that the older children were better, and a significant Conditions term (F 88.7; $d.F.$ 1,38: $p < 0.001$) which was due, as Tukey tests showed, to the first letter condition being easier than the other two ($p <$ 0.01). There was also a significant interference effect (F 82.21: $d.F.$ 1,38: $p < 0.001$), which confirmed that concurrent vocalization impairs the single letter tasks. There were no interactions.

Conclusion

Concurrent vocalization impedes a child when he is matching pictures and letters but not when he matches pictures and words. This supports the idea that when children are reading they tend neither to construct words from their segments, nor to analyse them phonologically.

EXPERIMENT 3: SPELLING

Our hypothesis is that children spell primarily by constructing words from phonological segments. It follows that the interference which made a phonological task harder for children in the previous experiment should spoil their spelling too.

Method

Material

Two collections of twelve pictures were prepared for each age group; one whose names were easy to spell and one whose names were relatively hard to spell. Since the two groups had different spelling skills, they were given different sets of pictures. Pilot tests had shown that the children in each age group would be able to spell very nearly all the words in the easy set and roughly 60 percent of the words in the difficult set.

Each collection of pictures were divided into two sets of six pictures. Each picture was on a card by an empty space large enough for its name.

Procedure

Each child was given four trials of cards in each trial. In each trial he was given a set of six cards successively and asked to write the picture's name beside it. He did this silently in two trials, one with easy material and the other with difficult material. In the other two trials he had to repeat the sound 'bla–bla' from the time that he was given each card until the time he had finished writing the word.

The order of the four trials and of the individual cards within each trial was systematically varied between children. The allocation of the four sets of cards to the different conditions was also varied systematically.

Results

Both groups made many more spelling mistakes with phonological interference than without, as Table 3 shows.

TABLE 3 Mean correct spelling scores (out of ten)

	Easy	Difficult
6-year-olds		
Silent	4.9	3.4
Concurrent vocalization	2.0	0.7
7-year-olds		
Silent	5.2	3.1
vocalization	3.9	1.4

The two groups' scores were analysed separately because they were given different material. The main terms in each analysis of variance were Materials (Easy versus Difficult) and Interference. Both analyses produced significant Interference terms (Younger group F 131.23: $d.F.$ 1,18 $p <$ 0.001; Older group F 23.74: $dF.$ 1,18, $p < 0.01$) confirming that the children found the spelling task harder with phonological interference than without. In both analyses the Materials term was also significant (Younger group F 41.53: d.F. 1,18: $p < 0.001$; Older group F 26.38; *d.F.* 1,18; $p < 0.001$).

Conclusion

We have shown that phonological interference does impair children's spelling though it leaves their reading of whole words intact. This suggests that they do write words by building up phonological segments. This seems to be generally true of younger children, but true only of the older children's spelling of the more difficult words. The older children may not rely on the phonological strategy to spell easy words.

The very strong effect here on children's spelling contrasts sharply with the report that this sort of interference does not affect children's reading.

DISCUSSION OF THE EXPERIMENTS

Our recent results seem to provide clear evidence for the hypothesis that children use different strategies in reading and in spelling, and therefore that much of their performance depends not on their possession of particular strategies but on the way they choose to apply them.

But this of course turns on the assumption that concurrent vocalization does specifically attack the analysis of words into their phonological constituents. This assumption can be questioned (Besner, in press). How can we be sure that a task which is unimpaired by concurrent vocalization does not depend on phonological segments or that a task which is impaired does? Simply to appeal to our findings from Experiment 1 and Barron and Baron's (1977) rhyming data is not enough. It could be that children were having difficulty not because they could not take the words apart into segments but because they could not, for example, summon up the name of the pictures in the first place while they were saying 'bla–bla'.

However there are two further pieces of evidence, both of them cross-cultural, which seem to support our analysis of the effects of concurrent vocalization. In one, Kwee Young tested a group of Chinese children in schools in Singapore in which the teaching is in English as well as in Chinese. She gave these children reading and spelling tasks like ours, either silently or under concurrent vocalization. All the children were given both Chinese and English versions of these tasks. The point of the comparison lies in the difference between the two orthographies. English is alphabetic and depends heavily on the phoneme. Chinese is ideographic: particular symbols indicate particular names, and they are not constructed phonetically.

Like us, Kwee Young found that concurrent vocalization impaired spelling in English but had no effect on reading. And she also showed that it had no effect either on reading or on writing in Chinese. The difference, then, is in the Chinese and English writing tasks. The effect of concurrent vocalization on writing seems to be confined to a language which deals in phonological segments. Here is good evidence that concurrent vocalization affects spelling because it impairs phonological analysis.

A very similar result comes from Japan. The Japanese write in two different kinds of script. One, *kanji*, is ideographic and derived from the Chinese script. The other, *kana*, is phonological in that it works by dividing words up into syllables. Recently Yuko Kimura has demonstrated with Japanese children, ranging in age from 6 to 9 years, that concurrent vocalization impairs writing *kana*, the syllables, but has no effect on *kanji*, the ideographs. Again the effect is confined to the orthography which deals in phonological segments.

So we conclude that it is likely that our work, as well as the Barron and Baron study, demonstrates that the two skills of written language, reading and spelling, do often follow different routes, and that this is because of a specialization of strategies in reading and writing. We now have to look at the implications of this kind of specialization.

GENERAL DISCUSSION

Comparisons of input and output, in this case of reading and writing, give us a good opportunity to distinguish between the two main approaches that have been mentioned. Our evidence suggests that the two different sides of written language are managed in very different ways by young children and even more so by backward readers. What is more, their difficulties in reading may very well be partly due to their reluctance to use strategies, such as the phonological strategy, which they nevertheless eagerly adopt when they write words. And, *mutatis mutandis*, their spelling difficulties might be the result of their unwillingness to deal in chunks or sequences when they write, despite the fact that these same chunks form the backbone of their reading.

In the case of normal readers and spellers, this specialization is probably a transitory phenomenon. The data described at the start of the chapter suggest that the original separation between the two activities vanishes after 2 or 3 years or so of experience in reading and writing. What probably happens is that children begin to deal in whole words and sequences of letters when they write, and to use phonological segments to construct words, particularly strange new words, when they read.

It has been demonstrated that backward readers, in whom the specialization lasts more stubbornly, can also bring the two strategies together. A recent experiment (Bradley, 1981) shows the signal success of a method called Simultaneous Oral Spelling which relies heavily on children writing out words at the same time as they spell them. With this method backward readers are able to remember and reproduce the spelling of difficult and irregular words quite successfully and over a long period of time. Our suggestion is that establishing writing patterns helps them to remember spelling, and thus in this book on writing we suggest that writing provides the bridge between reading and spelling.

We conclude with Tom C with whom we started. His ability to reproduce sequences of letters in cursive script provided that needed bridge. For people like him we recommend a written approach to reading.

REFERENCES

Barron, R. W., and Baron, J. (1977). How children get meaning from printed words. *Child Development,* **48**, 587–594.

Besner, D. (in press). Concurrent articulation and phonological encoding in reading for meaning. Paper presented to the Experimental Psychology Society meeting at the University of York, April 1979.

Birch, H. and Belmont, L. (1964). Auditory–visual integration in normal and retarded readers. *American Journal of Orthopsychiatry,* **34**, 852–861.

Bradley, L. (1981). The organisation of motor patterns for spelling: an effective remedial strategy for backward readers. *Developmental Medicine and Child Neurology,* **23**, 83–91.

Bradley, L., and Bryant, P. E. (1978). Difficulties in auditory organisation as a possible cause of reading backwardness. *Nature,* **271**, 746–747.

Bradley, L., and Bryant, P. E. (1979). The independence of reading and spelling in backward and normal readers. *Developmental Medicine and Child Neurology,* **21**, 504–514.

Bruce, D. (1964). Analysis of word sounds by young children. *British Journal of Educational Psychology,* **34**, 158.

Bryant, P. E., and Bradley, L. (1980). Why children sometimes write words which they cannot read. In U. Frith (Ed.): *Cognitive Processes in Spelling*. Academic Press, London.

Frith, U. (1980). Unexpected spelling problems. In (ed.), U. Frith: *Cognitive Processes in Spelling*. Academic Press, London.

Hitch, G., and Baddeley, A. D. (1976). Verbal reasoning and working memory. *Quarterly Journal of Experimental Psychology,* **28**, 603–621.

Kleiman, G. M. (1975). Speech recoding in reading. *Journal of Verbal Learning and Verbal Behaviour,* **14**, 323–339.

Liberman, I. Y., Shankweiler, D., Liberman, A., Fowler, C., and Fischer, F. (1977). Phonetic segmentation and recoding in the beginning reader. In A. Reber, and D. Scarborough, (eds.), *Toward a Psychology of Reading*, pp. 207–226. Laurence Erlbaum Associates, New Jersey.

Marcel, A. J. (1980). Phonological awareness and phonological representation: investigation of a specific spelling problem. In U. Frith (ed.), *Cognitive Processes in Spelling*. Academic Press, London.
Martin, M. (1978). Speech recoding in silent reading. *Memory and Cognition*, **6**, 108–114.

The Psychology of Written Language
Edited by M. Martlew

CHAPTER 8

The Development of Handwriting

ARNOLD J. W. M. THOMASSEN AND HANS-LEO H. M. TEULINGS

The present chapter is concerned with the development of handwriting as a perceptual-motor skill. A principal task in studying the development of skill is to examine the nature of both hardware and software changes which occur. This implies the discovery of the basic structures and processes operating at different stages, and the factors involved in their modification in the course of development (Connolly, 1970). This is by no means a simple matter. It is not merely a question of assessing the availability of skills or subroutines for children of various ages. It requires also that we consider the necessary cognitive and physical aspects associated with performing certain tasks. Furthermore, skill development is not a continuous process; there appear to be steps which constitute transitions from one stage to the next. In order to describe a child's behaviour at a certain developmental stage it may be necessary to postulate the existence of different control procedures at different stages in development. Following Bruner (1970) the problem becomes one of finding the transformation rules whereby the child goes from one form of organization to the next.

Skills which have been mastered are characterized by the economical division of attention between external and internal signals. Because of the redundancy in both types of signals, there is spare attentional capacity which can be employed in monitoring higher-order levels of performance. The question is how such a skill develops. In various forms (e.g. Kay, 1970; Bruner, 1970) it has been suggested that the micro-structure of a skill or the relevant subroutines are gradually incorporated into an overall plan or action programme, or what Kay called the macro-strategy.

The child especially has great difficulty in detecting regularities in the stimulus input. But, more important and perhaps causal to this, is the difficulty in producing reliable and stable responses. The detection of regularities is thus made much more difficult because the child's performance is much more variable. This makes skilled behaviour difficult to attain. Kay (1970) therefore emphasizes the need for a child first to acquire control over his own responses, preferably in sequential units of considerable size. This constitutes a precondition, he must be able to attend to the external requirements and fit the motor sequence in phase with them whilst also taking into account any other relevant stimuli. Bruner (1970) comments on these statements that the regularities involved in skill learning are not just probabilities but a supporting structure of rules of a highly generic kind. These can convert encounters with the environment into rules for processing information and for signalling the requirements of a response (p. 152). When discussing schemata below we shall encounter similar notions. We shall see also that a beginning has been made in answering some of the questions related to the development of graphic skills.

SPECIAL FEATURES OF HANDWRITING AS A DEVELOPING SKILL

As a skill, handwriting is plainly a complex perceptual-motor task. This expresses the fact that writing is a flowing task, not one of discrete responses, although there are interruptions, for example, at word boundaries. It deals with a large variety of different, co-ordinated movements and it is subject to visual guidance, or at least to visual monitoring. In Poulton's (1957) terminology, handwriting should perhaps be classed as a closed skill because it is relatively little affected by the environment. Skilled writing movements are so commonplace that one is inclined to overlook their complexity. However, that they are one of the most advanced achievements of the human hand cannot be overlooked. The hand is an extremely complex and delicate mechanism, containing 27 bones and being controlled by over 40 muscles. These muscles are mainly situated in the lower arm and they are connected to the fingers by an intricate set of tendons. Their activity is precisely co-ordinated by some timing system under neural control. As with many other skills, writing involves strict requirements with respect to the timing and the force control of co-ordinated movements of arm, hand, and fingers. The precise ordering and timing of the movements determine the structure of the movement pattern. The development of certain skills can be characterized reasonably well by reference to the abilities, in Fleishman's (1966) sense, required for their performance. However, this is difficult in the case of handwriting (cf. Søvik, 1975). There may be a stage where aiming, or wrist–finger speed, or arm–hand steadiness are abilities contributing to proficiency in writing. As in most skills there will be an early stage in which non-motor abilities (e.g. verbal, visual, spatial) play a part, as well as a later stage in which a factor specific to the writing task itself is particularly important. The development of handwriting is, however, especially complex because it is culture-dependent.

The present state of our knowledge is summarized in a number of reviews. The older skill literature has been reviewed by Welford (1968) and Bilodeau (1969). More recent developments in the study of motor control are reported in three volumes edited by Stelmach (Stelmach, 1976, 1978; Stelmach and Requin, 1980). Developmental aspects of skill are treated in Connolly (1970), Connolly and Bruner (1974), Holt (1975) and Kelso and Clark (1982). For the literature on handwriting a number of sources are available. A comprehensive bibliography of handwriting in the form of a classified list of 1754 publications, covering a wide range of topics and extending over the 70-year period 1890–1960, has been produced by Herrick (1960). Some of the more important of these and later references receive thorough attention in Herrick (1963) and in the most recent monograph on handwriting as a skill by Søvik (1975). Work on handwriting through the 1960s has been reviewed by Askov *et al.* (1970) and that during the 1970s by Peck *et al.* (1980).

MOTOR CONTROL THEORY AND THE DEVELOPMENT OF HANDWRITING

A typical feature of skilled performance, and certainly of handwriting, is that it involves the smooth execution of a structured sequence of co-ordinated movements, in which each movement occurs at its proper time in the sequence. The two major theoretical interpretations of how skilled performance is achieved are both concerned with the role of feedback. These are the closed-loop and the open-loop theory of motor performance. They will now be discussed.

Feedback, Programming, and Schema Theory Applied to the Development of Skill

The closed-loop position has been formulated by Adams (1976) roughly as follows. An intended movement is selected from long-term motor memory, where it resides as a memory trace. This trace determines the start of the movement. Its further performance is dependent on a continuous comparison between the memory representation of the residue of the same movement made on previous occasions, its perceptual trace, and the kinaesthetic feedback from the movement actually being made. An error signal resulting from this comparison acts as the stimulus for correction movements. The perceptual trace is gradually shaped by feedback information from repeated performances, until finally it represents the sensory consequences of the correctly performed movement.

The open-loop theory postulates that skilled performance is under the control of central motor programmes, which are autonomously responsible for the sequencing and timing of the movement pattern. The motor programme, which contains all the information necessary for the correct performance of this pattern, is built up by practice. Ultimately, it will encompass a set of muscle commands that is structured before the movement sequence begins, and that allows the entire movement to be carried out uninfluenced by peripheral feedback (Keele, 1968, p. 387). Thus, a smooth and accurate performance of the movement is possible without the necessity of peripheral feedback from one part of the sequence to trigger the execution of the next part.

To be sure, the open-loop theory does accept the presence of feedback, but in view of the information contained in the motor programme, it stresses the fact that in many instances feedback is redundant. Some of the more recent discussions of motor control (e.g. Keele and Summers, 1976; Glencross, 1977) have emphasized the need for an interactive contribution of both ready-made programmes and on-line processing of feedback in both the development and the performance of a skill. It is now generally accepted that skilled movements are possible without kinaesthetic feedback, but it may be that this only holds for certain highly practised skills such as walking, which appears to develop without special tutoring, and not for skills involving precise manipulation, such as writing. Reviews of the motor-programme concept are provided by Klapp (1977) and Keele (1981).

A specific form of central motor-programme theory has been proposed by Schmidt (1975, 1976) under the name of schema theory. Whilst giving full consideration to the role of feedback it provides an alternative to the closed-loop theory and also to earlier forms of the open-loop theory. The closed-loop interpretation is inadequate, first because in many forms of skilled performance feedback from one element is too slow (100–150 ms) to determine the execution of the next element, and second because it appears that skilled performance of some tasks (mainly well-practised movement patterns) is to a certain extent possible without feedback from the limbs. On the other hand fully programmed execution of a motor task, as suggested by the earlier open-loop interpretations, is also inadequate. Too many different movements, as defined by a different sequences of muscle contractions, would impose immense demands on storage and present very difficult retrieval problems. Furthermore, novel, unpractised movement

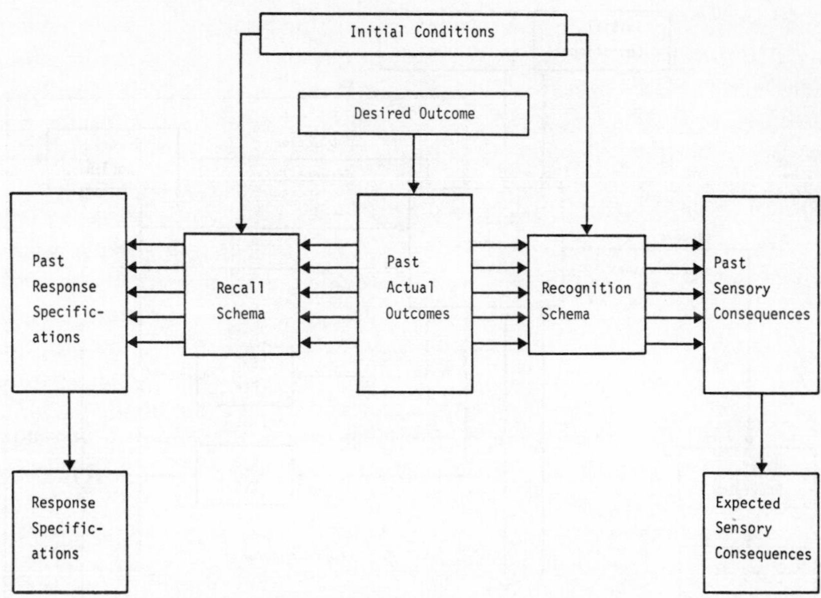

FIGURE 1 The recall and recognition schema in relation to various sources of information (from Schmidt, 1975)

patterns can sometimes be performed skilfully; how is this possible if no programme is available?

Schmidt proposes the schema concept for the control of discrete movements. His theory does not require a separate motor programme for every movement; moreover, it is able to explain the generation of novel movements. Schema theory assumes that movements are organized by means of a generalized motor schema, comprising a recall and a recognition part (see Figure 1). A motor schema is developed on the basis of experience in the execution of movements belonging to the same class of tasks. It represents an abstraction of the relation between four sources of information that are stored for every movement; viz., information on initial conditions, information on response specifications, information on sensory consequences, and information on the desired outcome of the response. The strength of the relation among these sources is increased with increasing precision of feedback. The recall schema contains the relationship between past outcomes and past response specifications; it selects the response specifications for novel movements. The recognition schema contains the relation between past outcomes and past sensory consequences; it predicts the sensory consequences for the intended movement and its effect. The actual feedback, both proprioceptive and exteroceptive, is evaluated

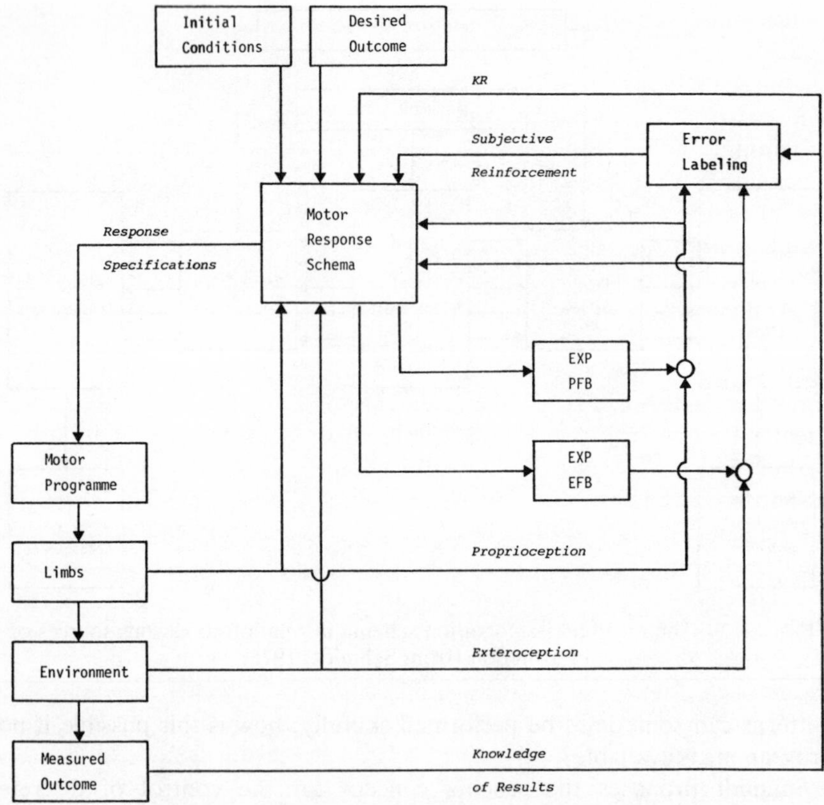

FIGURE 2 The motor response schema (in which recall and recognition schema are combined for clarity) in relation to events occurring within a trial. Abbreviations: KR = knowledge of results; EXP PFB = expected proprioceptive feedback; EXP EFB = expected exteroceptive feedback (from Schmidt, 1975).

against the predicted feedback. Any deviations are fed back as error to the motor schema and are identified by an error-labelling system. Corrections, however, are not possible within a reaction time of 200 ms after the errors are made. Learning is achieved by an updating of the motor schema through its incorporation of the error corrections so that the schema is better equipped for its next activation (see Figure 2).

Thus, a schema in this sense is a generalized, abstract motor programme for a class of movements. In the case of writing, such a class may represent a letter, a high-frequency cluster of letters, a signature, or a frequent word. It does not contain all the muscle commands but, instead, a set of rules specifying how, setting out from an initial starting position, a specific desired outcome can be obtained. In a schema certain variables are specified, such as the sequence of individual movements, their relative timing, and their relative force. Other variables are left unspecified in the programme to enable the adaptive execution of any member of the class of movements. The variables adjusted for any specific execution of the generalized programme are, for example, movement time, force, and the muscles involved. In the case of handwriting it has been pointed out by Merton (1972) that a word in someone's pencil handwriting on paper looks very similar to the same word in that person's writing, much larger, in chalk on a blackboard; and this in spite of the differences in execution (muscles and joints involved, as well as the force levels applied). This suggests that both productions are based on the same abstract programme in which the relative space and time components are invariant, but to which specific muscles and force parameters can be applied. Increase in the force level will overcome greater friction or produce bigger writing, or both, but the relationships within the product remain constant and therefore the products look essentially the same.

The motor programme for a written letter in a person's handwriting could conceivably contain the relative timing (phasing) of forces, applied with relative ampitudes or for relative durations, by two antagonist pairs in two orthogonal directions. Attempts to specify handwriting in these terms have been made in models by Wing (1978), Viviani and Terzuolo (1980), and Hollerbach (1981), and in a simulation study by Vredenbregt and Koster (1971). They support the possibility that this kind of motor programming exists for handwriting. Schema theory itself was not developed to cover continuous tasks, but it would seem capable of handling a skill like writing. Here discrete letters or letter clusters may be generated on the basis of schemata which are retrieved, programmed, and executed sequentially, perhaps in an overlapping fashion, making use of a short-term buffer to enhance the system's efficiency and flexibility. Research designed to investigate these possibilities is presently carried out in our laboratory.

The existence of abstract motor programmes has important consequences for the preparation of discrete movements as well as for the smooth performance of continuous movements which are an essential feature of most skills. Preparation, or programming, involves the performance of operations translating the abstract programme retrieved from long-term motor memory into a neural code that directly controls the muscles. In discrete tasks it has been shown that the required accuracy, duration, length, and complexity of a movement all have an affect on the amount of time required for such programming (cf. Klapp, 1978). This time is an important component of the latency preceding the movement in a reaction-time situation. It is suggested by Klapp and Greim (1979) that this latency mainly reflects the organization of the timing aspect of the movement. In the case of initiating a pre-cued speech sequence, moreover, it has been shown that the time needed to start the first word of a string of words increases with the length of the string (Sternberg *et al.*, 1978).

In the case of writing, similar observations have been made in our laboratory (Hulstijn and Van Galen, 1982) which tentatively show that the addition of an element (stroke or letter) to a well-practised and pre-cued letter adds 10 ms to its initiation following a 'go' signal. It has also been shown in our laboratory (Knippenberg *et al.*, 1978; Van Galen, 1980) that children and adults take less time to prepare the same letter or letter-like grapheme for a second or third time in succession. This may reflect recency effects in the programming activity, probably due to increased retrieval efficiency. The motor time necessary for performing the movement was indeed insensitive to repetitions. From a developmental point of view it is interesting to note that for children age 4–6, those with proximal motor control showed a much smaller decrease of programming time on repetitions than did children with the more advanced distal motor control.

Another consequence of the existence of abstract motor programmes is that certain aspects of a movement can be prepared even before the complete set of specifications defining the movement is known to the subject. Rosenbaum (1980) has shown that aspects such as the extent of the movement, its direction, and the arm with which it is to be performed, can be prepared upon their pre-cuing by the experimenter. Such preparation results in a shortened latency compared to the latency of initiating a non-pre-cued movement. Moreover, in our laboratory it was found that the content of the letter sequence to be written is in part independent of the size that is required. All subjects initiated an expected letter sequence more rapidly than an unexpected letter sequence (150 ms). However, an expected size of writing resulted in much smaller savings (50 ms) and was absent in about half the subjects (Stelmach and Teulings, 1982).

For the fluid and rapid performance of a continuous task, the preprogramming of movement sequences is of essential importance. By a skilled performer, a programme can be retrieved well in advance, and its translation into the appropriate neural motor commands may be postponed. Of course the skill also requires the correct perception and identification of stimuli, situations, and internal states to which the various programmes that he has built up apply. This constitutes the perceptual aspect of the skill. Its motor aspect may be described as a flexible and adaptive overlap of retrieval, translation, and execution of successive programmes which require little attention during performance. If an efficient perceptual interpretation of the environment takes place, and if the required motor sequence is efficiently delegated to motor programmes, attention to the performance of a skill can be limited to general monitoring of the progress of the movements. Remaining attentional capacity can be directed to higher-order levels of control, and to specific deviations from expected internal or external states. Regrettably, there is very little experimental research on continuous tasks; support for these views on the modularity of behaviour with respect to writing is lacking altogether.

NOTES ON THE ORIGIN OF MOTOR SCHEMATA AND THEIR DEVELOPMENT

Connolly (1977) has put the schema concept into a developmental perspective. Moreover, he has stressed the fact that the development of a skill involves the construction of a programme of action intentionally directed at a specific goal (Connolly, 1975). For example, a child learning to write would not only learn a sequence of muscle contractions, but he would also acquire the skill in terms of temporal and spatial sequences of strokes. According to Connolly, the basic units of the skill are subroutines of this general kind, embedded in a more complex, hierarchically organized sequence. Following Bruner, Connolly regards skill as modular in the sense that subroutines are relatively independent units, each dealing with a limited aspect of the problem to which the motor skill provides a solution. In this view, the software changes, brought about as a consequence of cognitive development, may be the acquisition of new subroutines and of novel rules for their combination. With respect to hardware changes in the developing organism, Connolly suggests that certain components of action programmes may be wired in. He points out, for example, that timing is an essential aspect of all skills and makes the suggestion that endogenous rhythms may be the basic timing references in movement control. Preadapted subroutines may thus in the course of development be differentiated and integrated into action programmes.

In various developmental studies of children aged between 5 and 11 years (the age range in which writing is normally learned) it appears that, under favourable conditions, they are able to perform accurately programmed arm movements. Schmidt (1980) quotes a study by Gallagher and Thomas who administered a ballistic linear slide task to children aged 7–10 years, and to adults. The observed differences in accuracy between these groups were greatly reduced and no longer significant when the intervals between successive trials (presumably necessary for the processing of feedback) were increased from 3.6 to 12 s. A developmental study on programming versus feedback in pointing movements by children and 5–11 years has been reported by Hay (1979). She observed mainly ballistic pointing movements in 5-year-old children. However, between 5 and 7 years the occurrence of ballistic movements declined in favour of movements guided by feedback.

When these were first introduced, there was a disturbance of the overall pattern, probably due to a temporary lack of integration between the new closed-loop and the old open-loop system. Integration betwen the two was achieved only from the age of 9 onwards. Similar findings were obtained in a later study involving prismatic distortion of the visual field. Pointing movements were always begun in the direction of the virtual position of the target. They were readjusted after the children had seen their hand in the distorted visual field. Five-year-olds were very late with their corrections, which suggests that their movements were ballistic in nature. Seven-year-olds were very early with their corrections, indicating their feedback-dependent, closed-loop approach. The 9- and 11-year-olds showed a more flexible approach in which the ballistic movement was monitored visually, but not disturbed until the trajectory was almost complete. From these results it appears that relatively gross movements can be, and in pointing behaviour initially are, programmed accurately by children in the age groups studied. The function of feedback, which was shown to be necessary in both studies, can be interpreted as shaping the relevant schema. The development of schemata in writing has also been studied, albeit in a somewhat different framework. A few examples are discussed below.

VISUAL AND MOTOR SCHEMATA AND THE DEVELOPMENT OF HANDWRITING

A specific hypothesis with respect to schemata in reading and writing has been tested by Frith (1974). She assumed that experienced readers and writers would have schemata available for existing letter shapes but not for unfamiliar letter-like graphemes. Frith hypothesized that perceptual schemata would show tolerance for spatial deviations but that motor schemata would lack such tolerance. This is indeed what she found when presenting letters and letter-like shapes, both in their normal and in a reversed orientation. Adults and good- and poor-reading children were given instructions either to copy or to reverse the stimuli. Copying a reversed letter takes a considerable amount of extra time and gives rise to many errors in adults as well as children. Letter-like shapes for which neither perceptual nor motor schemata are available are always more difficult to reverse than to copy. Reversing a reversed letter, however (i.e. writing a normal letter in response to the letter in its reversed orientation), is no more difficult than copying it. Frith also found that younger poor readers have only weak schemata, and that the writing effects obtained also held for writing with the non-preferred hand. This indicates not only that muscle commands are represented in the motor schema, but that some more abstract representation must also be stored.

Copying, as we shall see below, is a sequential process requiring the analysis of the visual form, which is initially perceived as a structured whole into segments. Moreover, when copying the form the child is required to draw these segments in their relation to the whole which is as yet absent. His production implies the reconstruction of the model starting from its segments. Rand (1973) found that in the case of young children the visual and motor aspects of copying are by no means parallel. Children have far less difficulty analysing than reconstructing the forms. They can be taught how to analyse the forms without a positive effect on their copying performance, or they can be taught how to copy the forms without improving their discrimination ability. Similar findings were obtained by Williams (1975) in a study on discriminating and writing letter-like graphemes by children aged 4 and 5 years. Copying letters is apparently based on an ability distinct from that for discriminating between letters.

An interesting case study of a 2.5-year-old girl, who learnt how to write the letters of the alphabet, unaware of any symbol–sound relationship, is provided by McCarthy (1977). It appeared that Sarah learned the letters, in a specific order, determined by common distinctive features: circular letters first, followed by straight-line letters, then by line-and-loop letters, and finally by diagonal letters. This development suggests that a general schema is gradually differentiated with practice and then supplemented by a new one. It was noted, furthermore, that the learning of a new letter caused regression in discriminating between letters. This indicates that motor schemata are independent from visual schemata also at this early stage of development.

Obviously there is not a single schema mediating both reading and writing. This confirms the visual-motor distinction made by Frith (1974). Both types of schema are developed, the visual schemata to some extent independently from the motor schemata. With respect to the latter complex motor representation, it is important to note that the effective drawing instruction employed by Rand (1973) consisted of teaching children to plan their copy, that is, where to start, which direction to take, when to change direction, and when to stop. These organizing principles are very similar to the syntactic rules discussed below. Rand's results underline the essential developmental progress made by the child when he acquires these rules of syntax for the autonomous guidance of his own graphic behaviour.

A CLOSED-LOOP INTERPRETATION OF THE DEVELOPMENT OF HANDWRITING

We shall now briefly examine a closed-loop approach to handwriting development that is rather different from the programming and schema approach above, but which leads to a compatible conclusion. An impressive amount of research on handwriting, both theoretical and applied, has been carried out by Søvik (1975, 1981). His work involves a cybernetic interpretation of handwriting development in which diverse forms of feedback are crucial. Søvik bases his research on the older neurogeometric theory developed by Smith (1962), in which the neural system is hypothesized to control behaviour through the functioning of difference detectors. These operate both within and between the various receptor systems, and between the efferent innervation of a movement and its afferent feedback information. In this light, immediate, detailed and accurate feedback is seen by Søvik as the most essential feature for the development and performance of the handwriting skill. Not only 'reactive' feedback from the performing hand is processed, but also 'instrumental' feedback from the pen, and 'operational' feedback obtained through visual inspection of the product.

According to the theory, the co-ordinated feedback operating in perceptual-motor tasks may involve very complex motor systems. In the case of handwriting they reach from shoulder to fingers. Feedback from these sytems is integrated with with postural and transport movements and with information from the senses. The brain receives information about any differences which are detected and generates a motor outflow based on them. The motor outflow specifies the required movement pattern of the handwriting. Much of the research by Søvik demonstrates the role of feedback in the development and performance of the handwriting skill.

Moreover, the theory also allows for the integration of external visual information, such as that of an observed movement, into the control of a self-generated movement (Søvik, 1981). The feedback theory thus also incorporates a dynamic cross-yoking of the motor mechanisms of several individuals, so that their movements constitute a mutual source of feedback-controlled sensory input. In an individualized instruction experiment general support was obtained for the effectiveness of following the movements which were made by the teacher. The specific relationship between normal proprioceptive and visual feedback and the feedback involved in the latter kind of dynamic imitation is, however, left unspecified. What appeals to us is that there is an interesting correspondence with the effectiveness of teaching a child how to approach a copying task by instructing him with respect to certain principes (cf. Rand, 1973). This indicates that observation and reference to one's own motor system can lead to a more implicit but equally effective insight in how to set out and proceed in writing.

THE DEVELOPMENT OF PERFORMANCE ASPECTS OF HANDWRITING

Task Demands of Handwriting as a Motor Skill

Handwriting is a complex activity requiring many component sub-skills. If we disregard the visual components for a moment, they may be summed up as follows. First, the writer must be seated in a suitable way with a proper support for his writing arm; at the same time the contralateral hand holds the paper stable. Second, the writer must hold the writing instrument in such a way that he can easily move horizontally across the paper and see the tip of the pen during this traverse. This implies a suitable grip between thumb and middle and index fingers and a proper support of the shaft or barrel of the instrument between thumb and index finger. The hand, moreover, should be rotated slightly so that it rests on the two other fingers. Third, the writer must be able to make movements with the pen in a 'writing-like' fashion. This implies a suitable grip between thumb and middle and index fingers and a proper support of the shaft or barrel of the instrument between thumb and index finger. The hand, moreover, should be rotated slightly so that it rests on the two other fingers. Third, the writer must be able to make movements with the pen in a 'writing-like' fashion. This implies a succession of small movements of the instrument's tip superimposed on progressive horizontal (transport) movements along the line from left to right. These small movements should be of more or less constant size, or of a limited set of sizes, and result in lines, curves, waves, angular transitions, and loops, which go to form letters and words.

These multiple and widely varying motoric requirements must be learned in a process of training. To them must be added, of course advanced requirements regarding the visual analysis of examples of the specific letters and those regarding the ability to reconstruct the examples motorically. The best measure of achievement is the quality of the finished product, writing itself. To write satisfactorily requires the ability to distinguish visually between graphic forms and to judge their correctness. Learning to write also requires that the individual is able to distinguish the kinaesthetic feedback associated with correct responses from that associated with incorrect or inadequate movements. Certain aspects of these abilities have been studied in some detail, for example, cross-modal integration (Birch and Lefford, 1967; Connolly and Jones, 1970).

The Manipulation of the Writing Tool

Writing is a tool-using skill, and writing instruments have to be grasped and held stable in the hand before writing can be produced by appropriate movements of the tool. A detailed analysis of the manipulation of a paint brush by children has been made by Connolly and Elliott (1972) in the context of an extremely interesting account of the evolution and the ontogeny of hand function. These authors distinguished seven types of grip, five of which they classified, following Napier (1956), as power grips, and two as precision grips. An example of the former type of grip pattern is the palmar grip. The frequency with which precision grips were used by their

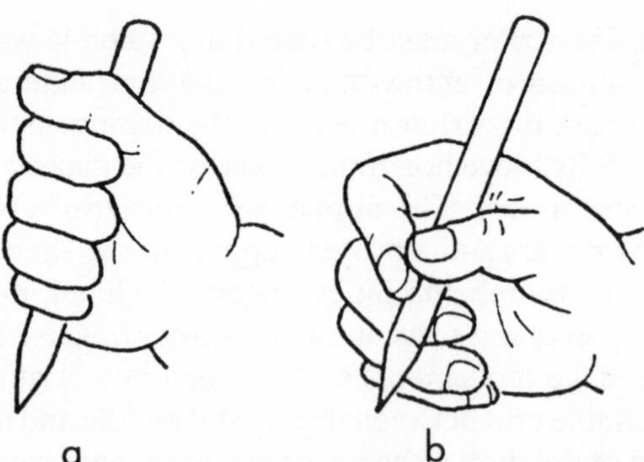

FIGURE 3 Two representative examples of grip patterns on a pencil. (a) Palmar grip; (b) adult grip (by kind permission of Kevin Connolly)

sample increased with age. By far the most frequently occurring grip was the (precision) adult grip (see Figure 3).

An account of the development of grasping and manipulating a crayon has been given by Gesell (1940). A complementary account, concerned with the development of writing posture (also involving the non-writing hand) and of location of writing on the sheet of paper, has been provided by Ames (1948). A more recent study of developmental stages in writing-tool manipulation was performed by Rosenbloom and Horton (1971) using British Children. This study served as a reference for Saida and Miyashita (1979) who examined pencil grips of Japanese children; the latter authors observed similar patterns but a more rapid development in Japanese children (especially girls) than in British children, probably due to cultural factors. Recently, Lundberg (1979) introduced a drawing test for the assessment of arm–hand function in young children. The most important changes seem to occur between the ages of 2 and 4 years. One significant change concerns the manner in which the instrument is picked up; this is a major step which clearly displays anticipation of the use to which the instrument is to be put.

Gesell (1940) describes how at about 12 months a child, though able to manipulate a narrow object with the fingertips, grasps it firmly with the palm of his hand when using the object for poking, tapping, or brushing. This also happens with the crayon. The child at this age waves the tool about, banging it onto the table and brushing it at arm's length in mainly lateral movements. At about 18 months, the child picks up the crayon, grasps one end firmly in the palm of the hand (see Figure 3a) and draws the other end across the paper, largely by shoulder movements. For these observations the pencil was always presented with its point directed away from the child. Around the age of 24 months the child picks up the crayon by placing the thumb parallel to it at its left, and the fingers to the right. The necessary adjustment of the crayon for writing is subsequently done with the left hand. At this stage there are awkward attempts to extend the index and middle fingers toward the point of the writing instrument. There is still a firm hold on the crayon, but now the child begins to manipulate it with the fingers. The pressure exerted through the crayon is very variable, often leading to lifting the crayon off the paper. At about 30 months there is, according to Gesell, a peculiar interest in finger movements, and in imitating the writing movements made by others. By the time the child is about 3 years old the adult grip on the crayon is approached by resting its shaft at the junction of the thumb and the index finger. The middle finger is extended towards the point of the crayon, while the thumb is in opposition to the index finger higher up the shaft. At this age there is an increased use of the fingers in drawing.

Gesell (1940) describes a transitional stage in picking up a pencil at about 4 years. The index and middle fingers are now placed to the left of its shaft and the thumb to its right. After having lifted the pencil, the child rotates its point under the palm of his hand, and he adjusts it for writing, sometimes with with the aid of his left hand. The pencil is held with the tip of the thumb, index, and middle finger, the latter being extended most. The crayon or pencil is handled with greatly increased skill; it is firmly grasped and moved mainly by flexion and extension of the fingers. At about 5 years the child is really skilled, both in picking up the pencil in the adult fashion and in handling it for adjustment and for writing. The adult grip on the pencil is now almost attained. The middle finger supports it near its point, and the thumb and index are applied at varying points on the shaft. The child now handles the pencil with considerably greater precision. Finally, at about 6 years, the adult grip is reliably assumed; the thumb and index finger are flexed slightly more than the middle finger, and their movements together with those of the wrist are responsible for the writing product (see Figure 3b).

The Development of Graphic Skills

The grip used on the writing instrument may facilitate or inhibit certain types of strokes, but there is more to it. Just as grips have a developmental history (cf. Connolly and Elliott, 1972), so too have the types of scribbles or strokes made (Kellogg, 1969). Gesell (1940) noted that the course of development in writing follows the general maturational direction from proximal to distal. There is a gradual improvement in control, especially of the more precise finger movements. This is reflected by a reduction in the size of drawing and writing and by a reduction in superfluous movements, both in number and extent.

At the age of 18 months, scribbling occurs spontaneously and the infant also imitates scribbling vigorously. Gibson (1969) has suggested that these scribbles provide an excellent opportunity for the child to become familiar with the relationship between his movements and the resulting feedback. At this age the child begins to make definite strokes for the first time and he differentiates these from scribbles. When about 2 years, the child makes smaller marks, and he can imitate vertical and circular strokes. Over the next 6 months his ability to imitate the writing movements of others is increased, and this will lead to the expansion of his repertoire of strokes. The eyes, which initially followed the movements of the hand, gradually guide the hand as a result of an increased eye–hand co-ordination (Lurçat and Kostin, 1970). The child now flexes both elbow and wrist, and the subtlety of the line patterns is greatly increased (Spielman, 1976). By 3 years the strokes are better controlled, more varied (waves, zigzags, circles, loops) and less repetitive. Smaller units are now achieved, according to various authors (e.g. Bender, 1938; Piaget and Inhelder, 1948), owing to the ability to interrupt larger scribbles or repetitive movements; circles from repeated loops, angles from zigzags, lines from curves or zigzags (cf. Spielman, 1976). Visual guidance, according to Lurçat and Kostin (1970), is, however, not sufficiently developed for drawing spirals. The size of the drawings is continually reduced. Piaget and Inhelder (1948) observed that children now produce drawings which are more similar to the models; their open or closed nature is now represented. Somewhat later the copies also represent the topological features of the models, for example, a square as a circle with four marks. By about 4 years, circles which are more rounded can be produced (usually in a clockwise fashion by right-handed children). Both cross and square can now typically be copied. The child still has difficulty in drawing oblique lines, but the path of a diamond can be traced between parallel lines 1 cm apart, with few errors. It appears that at this age there is an increase in the ability to trace, almost irrespective of direction. Around the age of 4 years, according to Gesell, the child enters the stage of beginning graphic representation in which for the first time objects are represented in a manner which is similar to adult representations.

Kellogg's (1969) analysis of a large number of free drawings by children has led her to suggest that some twenty different basic scribbles can be identified in the products of the youngest children. These she regards as the result of movements produced without visual guidance and serving as basic elements in the various forms of graphic art. They include dots and curves, single and multiple lines, single and multiple loops, and circles. Following this initial stage, according to Kellogg, children start drawing single diagrams (circle, square, cross, triangle, closed irregular forms, and X shapes) and later combinations of two diagrams, or aggregates of three or more. These designs appear to be produced for their own sake rather than as attempts at the representation of objects, even if the results are sometimes similar to objects. The environment does not really provide any visual models for children drawing until they are about 4 years (Kay, 1969).

Copying is a more complex task than producing either unconstrained scribbles or spontaneously drawn designs such as those mentioned above. Copying, as the sequential representation of a visual pattern, involves perception and analysis, imagery and motor abilities, and the integration of these. A specific developmental order in the geometric patterns that children are able to copy has been reported by a number of authors (e.g. Ames and Ilg, 1951; Birch and Lefford, 1967; Connolly, 1968; Rand, 1973). There is a good measure of agreement about this order; circles at 3 years of age, squares at 4, triangles at 5, and diamonds at 7 years, are the general findings.

A 5 year old usually has no difficulty in drawing easily recognizable forms. He quite skilfully copies a square and a triangle. The child has increased control over straight strokes produced in a downward direction, not only vertical but also oblique, and in a left–right horizontal direction. Diamonds are traced without error. The accuracy of copying increases quite sharply between 5 and 6 years. This may be facilitated by an increasing ability around that age to integrate visual and kinaesthetic information (Birch and Lefford, 1967). If the child draws rather than copying from a model, his drawing activity may be guided by a visual image. Drawing then may be regarded as moving the pencil along the projected contours of the imagined object. It is proposed by Spielman (1976) that the production of a drawing in which the lines represent contours (i.e., boundaries or edges of solid forms) requires a higher level of perceptual and cognitive achievement than the production of a drawing in which the lines represent the solid forms themselves (e.g., single lines for legs, or scribbled patches for water in a jar). Drawings of the latter type are obviously made earlier in development.

The Speed of Handwriting: Age and Size as Independent Variables

In studying the development of handwriting it is important to examine not only qualitative but also quantitative changes. Of the variables that can be measured, speed is probably the simplest overall measure of proficiency in writing. A sharp increase in speed of writing as a function of increasing age has been described (Cormeau Velgh-Lenelle *et al.*, 1970; Essing, 1965). This effect is observed when subjects are writing at their normal speed and when responding to the instruction to write as quickly as they can. The rate of increase is greatest between 7 and 9 years, after which it tapers off until about 13 years when there is little further increase. At that age more than two letters are written per second.

The fact that the size of writing is not directly proportional to the time required for its production has been observed by several authors (Katz, 1951; Denier van der Gon and Thuring, 1965; Michel, 1971; Wing, 1978; De Jong, 1979). In the case of adults, considerable size increases result in relatively small increases in the time required. Apparently the same letters are written with a minimal change in their temporal patterning but with varying force amplitude. Higher force amplitude levels result in greater speeds when larger sizes are required. From a developmental point of view it is of interest to know to what extent such schema-like, relatively constant temporal patterns are already present in the repertoire of young children. We have been investigating this question in our laboratory.

In a study with thirty six right-handed boys and girls aged 6;5, 8;5 and 11;4 years and with 12 adults we examined (De Jong, 1979; Teulings *et al.*, 1980) the maximum speed of writing loops and circles of various sizes (5, 10, 20, 40, 80 mm) produced in clockwise and counterclockwise directions. The spatial and temporal characteristics of the movements were digitized and stored in a computer (see Teulings and Thomassen, 1979). It appeared that both age and size differences were very significant, but that there was no significant interaction between age and size. This indicated that the modest increase in writing time (up to a factor of 16) was comparable for the three age groups. The greatest increase in writing time was in size increases between 40 and 80 mm, which may reflect the fact that for 80 mm letters, which is outside the range of normal writing, more of the writing limb is involved so that inertial factors may play a greater role. The main question was thus answered unambiguously: children, writing loops and circles at maximum speed, show similar, very modest time increases when the size of the letters is greatly increased. These increases, moreover, are similar to those of adults, which suggests near-constant schema-like timing characteristics in these simple patterns, even for the youngest groups.

Two subsidiary findings should also be mentioned. First, the direction means favoured counterclockwise writing movements for all age groups, but they were significant only in the 8-year-old group. This confirms the instruction-bound behaviour observed by other authors (e.g. Goodnow *et al.*, 1973) at an early stage of practice: our alphabet is predominantly written in a counterclockwise direction. Only the largest loops, which fall outside the range of normal pencil-on-paper writing, were performed more rapidly in a clockwise fashion by the 6- and 8-year-olds. Second, the most interesting interaction with age was concerned with the difference between producing repeated circles while remaining on the same spot and producing loops in a continuous progressive left-to-right transport movement. It appears that 6-year-olds almost double their writing time when they have to progress linearly. They need some 450 ms extra for each loop if the loop is not made on the same spot but placed progressively to the right of the preceding loop, as in writing successive letters. Eight-year-olds need only 150 ms extra; 11-year-olds take about 100, and adults use hardly any extra time for progression. This indicates that writing loops in a progressive movement constitutes a different task for untrained children in whom the transport movement is not yet integrated with the circular movements, and thus adds to overall task difficulty. It is only during the course of development and practice that the transport movement appears to take on an automatized character so that the circular movements can be superimposed on it without an increase in the speed of performance of the latter. It should be pointed out that these progression data do not include any movement times of the hand over the paper: the task was such that the subjects wrote several loops at once without moving their hand along; any hand shifts still occurring during the task were excluded from the analysis.

Notes on Copying Difficulty, Especially of Obliques.

We now return to copying. We shall consider some of the variables affecting the degree of difficulty encountered by children of different ages. Graham *et al.*, (1960) suggest that the difficulty of a drawing is determined by the number of constituent parts, defined as discontinuities, or changes of direction, and the angles of the direction change. They drew up a list of eighteen patterns ordered from easy to difficult, the easiest being the vertical line (followed by the horizontal line and the circle), the most difficult being the diamond (preceded by the V shape and upright and inverted triangles).

The well-known special difficulty of drawing obliques as present in diamonds, V shapes, triangles, and diagonals has been interpreted in various different ways. One is that the child may orient himself on the horizontal and vertical edges of the paper (e.g. Berman *et al.*, 1974), but not on any cue facilitating diagonal movements. Another interpretation is that the vertical body axis serves as a reference, also for the horizontal lines, which have a simple orthogonal relationship to this axis (Berman, 1976). A third interpretation is that children are deficient in their perceptual analysis (Piaget and Inhelder, 1948); but this has not been supported by later research (Gibson *et al.*, 1962; Maccoby and Bee, 1965). A specific difficulty in any pattern to be copied may be its incompatibility with directional preferences in the drawing of a child at a given age (cf. Ames and Ilg, 1951; Thomassen and Teulings, 1979; see below), or conflict with syntactic rules describing higher-order preferences of graphic behaviour (cf. Goodnow and Levine, 1973).

De Swart (1979) in our laboratory has attempted to define the complexity of writing movements in motor terms; that is in terms of the number of antagonist pairs involved in their performance. The greater difficulty of oblique compared with vertical or horizontal lines may be described as resulting from the involvement of two orthogonally arranged antagonist pairs instead of one. Two groups of children were investigated, both aged 4–5 years, one group having proximal, the other distal, motor control. It was hypothesized that only the distal group would show the oblique effect because only in a distal mode does the involvement of two antagonist pairs apply. By using a writing tablet (see Teulings and Thomassen, 1979) it was possible to investigate the speed and accuracy of performance in drawing straight lines in four directions (rightward, downward, and the two diagonals that can be drawn from left to right). Accuracy was defined as the variance around the least-squares regression line fitted through samples points of the writing trace.

The results showed that right-handed children aged 4–5 years with proximal motor control drew the horizontal (left-to-right) and vertical (downward) lines faster than did children employing distal motor control. However, the accuracy with which these lines were drawn was significantly less in the proximal group. The two diagonals, both left-to-right, one upward, the other downward, were drawn less accurately but with equal speed by both groups. An interesting interaction was noted with respect to accuracy. The distal group not only drew the diagonals more accurately, but showed only a slight difference in accuracy between the two diagonals in favour of the upward diagonal. The proximal group, in contrast, showed a large difference between the two oblique directions, the upward diagonal being by far the least accurately drawn.

These data can be interpreted as follows. The assignment of greater complexity to diagonals in terms of a greater number of antagonist pairs does not apply in the case of proximal children. To the extent that they draw from the shoulder, they will have less difficulty with the downward diagonal than with the upward if they are right-handed as in our sample. They can proceed simply by pulling outwards. Right-handed distal children, however, in command of a more refined system, will draw diagonals with the antagonist pairs mentioned above. But larger strokes in the direction of the upward diagonal can also be produced with a single antagonist pair moving the fingers or the wrist, so that the latter diagonal is then favoured by them. McAllister (1900) presented a diagram showing that the upward left-to-right diagonal is about the fastest (the easiest) to draw, both by finger and by wrist movements, as opposed to the downward left-to-right diagonal, which is the slowest (most 'difficult'). These data confirm our expectations that there are many levels at which the copying difficulty, especially of obliques, can be discussed. moreover, if perceptual and structural factors are minimized, it may still appear that easy and difficult directions in writing change or alternate, dependent on development and the motor system involved. Other directional preferences are considered below.

HIGHER-ORDER PRINCIPLES IN THE DEVELOPMENT OF GRAPHIC SKILLS

In the discussion of the component skills of handwriting it has been implicitly assumed that these are organized in a hierarchical fashion. We shall now focus upon the various types of higher-order principles of organization that are involved in drawing and writing. For example, the production of particular forms, the drawing of lines in various directions, the order of copying the different segments of a model, and the occurrence of certain errors in writing are all governed by systematic tendencies. These may include relatively straightforward motor biases, sequential rules for graphic behaviour, and principles related to language processing.

Developing Biases in Handwriting and their Possible Causes

That writing is a culture-bound activity has been emphasized. Not only language and its orthography, but also motor aspects of handwriting are greatly influenced by culture and education. This is sometimes ignored, as is illustrated by reference to the 'Three Rs'. Writing should perhaps be represented twice, once in respect of spelling and once for its perceptual-motor features. These constitute two quite different educational problems that just happen to be tackled at the same time. Teaching a child even the motor preliminaries to writing often involves the introduction of cultural standards (e.g. regularity, neatness), cultural biases (e.g. a specific slant, counterclockwise rotations, left-to-right transport) and constraints (as regards posture, grip, and the hand used for writing).

In a later stage of development these cultural standards, biases, and restrictions are difficult to disentangle from any natural tendencies. If natural tendencies are established they may be idiosyncratic or they may reflect a general trend. Any such general trend may be perceptual or motor in nature. They may even be of a 'higher order', reflecting universal principles of behaviour analogous to syntactic principles in language. Thus, the development of any recurring principles in the organization of graphic skills should be carefully examined in respect to their generality, culture-dependence, and degree of abstractness. Some of the regularities which appear to govern the performance aspects of handwriting are discussed below. The results are not conclusive as to their cause but certain general motor features seem to be involved.

Directionality in Handwriting

In many tasks, such as describing a visual array, placing pegs in a board, drawing or copying a design, most people display marked directionality.

This tendency of processing the details of a task in a specific spatial order, which is in general dependent on age, may result from a number of factors, such as a lateral asymmetry of one type or another, motor preferences related to flexion and extension, spatial factors related to optimal viewing and manipulation, and cultural factors including reading and writing habits. Developmental trends are probably present in most of these, and specific combinations of such factors may affect particular tasks.

It has been known for many years that the general pattern of copying simple figures by children and adults is to some extent stereotyped. If children of a given age are asked to copy a simple geometrical design they tend to start at a location and proceed in a direction typical for their age (Gesell, 1940; Gesell and Ames, 1946). Age changes in the starting location and the direction in which a circle is drawn provide an example (Ames and Ilg, 1951). It is not clear whether these changes in directional preference are due to physiological, visuomotor, or cultural influences. Indeed, we have speculated (Thomassen and Teulings, 1979) that two semi-independent systems are involved. The first system, having a 'peripheral' character and slowly developing from an adduction or flexion preference to an abduction or extension preference, would serve scribbling, high-rate, and non-representative graphic behaviour. The second system, being of a 'central' nature, would follow a more rapid development, especially between the ages of 5 and 7 years. It is, in our culture at least, biased towards a counterclockwise writing direction, and perhaps related to the way in which children are taught to write the alphabet.

In a cross-cultural study allowing comparisons across age and experience with left-to-right processing of verbal materials, it is possible to clarify certain cultural aspects of the complex problem of directionality. Such a study has been performed by Goodnow *et al.*, (1973). They asked American and Israeli children, aged from 5 to 7 years, and adults, to copy simple geometrical designs and observed the subjects' adherence to six of the sequential rules decribed by Goodnow and Levine (1973). The results show significant developmental effects for all of the six directional rules in both cultural groups and significant cultural differences for five of the rules. The Israeli subjects showed a slightly lower observance of the rules in most designs, but not in all of them. The differences between these two groups could be reduced to generalizations from their experience with specific letter shapes. The tendency for such generalization appears to be greatest in the early stage of writing instruction. From a detailed analysis of these shapes Goodnow *et al.* (1973) also concluded that some differences between the two groups may have been caused by a difference between English and Hebrew with respect to their directional consistency. Hebrew words and sentences are read from right to left, but many letters are built up from left to right. The letter effects may be especially influential on copying. Thus, the value of this cross-cultural comparison appeared to be limited principally to any effects above the level of individual letters; these effects were significant but small.

In a similar cross-cultural context Lieblich *et al.* (1975) noted that the Arab environment seems to be more homogeneously right–left oriented than the Jewish. Speculations by these authors include the suggestion that the 'natural' strokes of horizontal lines for right-handed subjects are left–right in all cultures, and that it requires 'stable modelling' to shift this tendency into a right–left one, as is achieved in the second or third grades of the Arab school. We shall encounter similar tendencies in Japanese children below.

Syntactic Aspects of Graphic Behaviour

The study of higher-order systems involved in graphic skills has attracted much interest since the work by Goodnow and Levine (1973). These authors studied the copying of rectilinear designs by children of various ages and by adults, and noted systematic regularities with respect to the start point and the sequence of successive movements. Goodnow borrowed Bruner's (1971) term 'grammar of action' for the syntactic principles she uncovered. The observed starting rules refer to a tendency to start at the topmost point, or at the leftmost point, or to start with a vertical line or, given a design with an apex, to start coming down the left oblique. The derived progression rules describe a bias towards drawing all horizontal lines from left to right and all vertical lines from top to bottom and a tendency towards drawing the design in a single, continuous line. Adherence to these rules is in a systematic way dependent upon compatibility or conflict amongst the different rules that might at any one monent be applied in the case of a specific design. Thus, copying an L-shape need not involve a conflict among any of the rules, whereas copying an inverted or reversed L-shape would always be in conflict with at least one of the rules. However, the most important factor is age. With development there is in general an increased conformity to the rules, but the strength of one rule (e.g. start with a vertical line) may decline while that of another rule (e.g. start at the top) increases, or shows a curvilinear relationship (e.g. draw with a continuous line).

An extension of Goodnow and Levine's (1973) rules has been suggested by Ninio and Lieblich (1976). They observed that the younger children copy a shape with the smallest number of unspecified starting points, or in their terminology with the smallest number of degrees of freedom. The letter T, for example, can be copied in many ways. One is to begin in a downward direction from the top of the vertical, followed by a short leftward and a short rightward horizontal, always beginning at the same starting point; this is an example of a copy with zero degrees of freedom. Another way of producing a T is to start at the left end of the horizontal, followed by the vertical, going downwards from the middle of the horizontal; this represents one degree of freedom. A third way is to start at the top of the vertical, followed by the horizontal starting from the left and touching the top of the vertical in its course; this is an example of a copy with two degrees of freedom. Ninio and Lieblich (1976) observed a steady increase in degrees of freedom with increasing age. They suggest that during the acquisition of a skill the degrees of freedom are kept low, whereas mastery of the skill is characterized by greatly enhanced degrees of freedom.

In our laboratory the drawing ability of a group of 4-year-olds was related to distal versus proximal movement strategies (De Swart, 1979). In a free drawing task, given to children of the same age, distally performing children were found to draw more straight lines (especially obliques), more closed contours, and more complex patterns such as spirals, than the proximally performing children. The straight lines were always drawn from left to right or from top to bottom, except when they were attached to lines drawn earlier. These earlier lines then served as a starting point for the lines which followed. This confirms the general tendency mentioned above, and underlines the fact that age is but one variable. Predictions about a child's drawing abilities and preferences should be based on his stage of motor development, as assessed by an independent measure such as the degree of distal control of movements.

In view of our earlier comments on cultural factors involved in the development of higher-order preferences, it is interesting to look at Japanese children. In Japan a mixture of writing systems is used, the characters of which, moreover, may be arranged vertically, or from right to left, or from left to right. For initial teaching purposes, however, the left–right arrangement of *kana* characters is employed. These are quite different from the Roman alphabet. Japanese children, however, display developmental changes in the sequential organization of their copying behaviour that are very similar to those observed in western cultures. Nihei (1980) reports the following developmental trend in copying by Japanese children. At 5 years there is a stage where the same point or line serves as a starting point for various further strokes of the pattern; Nihei called this fixed anchoring. It is followed at 6 years by a stage where the entire pattern is drawn in a continuous line, which is called fluid anchoring. It is only subsequent to this age that the next stage begins; a start is now made from points not connected to the preceding stroke; it is called ballistic starting. The latter stage, requiring imagery as a guide to drawing, is seen as the last developmental stage. These developmental changes show close correspondence with those described by Ninio and Lieblich (1976). To be sure, they are independent of directionality as such. Nihei (1980) notes that the general left–right and top-down directional principles implied in Goodnow's first two progression rules are the dominant principle also for Japanese adults. Young Japanese children seem first to apply these principles to single lines; when they go on to make more complex figures, the principles give way, temporarily, to the fixed-anchoring and fluid-anchoring strategies.

An interesting aspect of the approach made by Goodnow and Levine (1973) is its capacity to explain certain biases in the errors made by children learning to write. Lewis and Lewis (1965) have reported that the pattern of reversals in attempts to write the letters b, d, p, and q is highly asymmetrical; two or three times as many reversals occur at d and q than at b and p. Interestingly, the former pair is in conflict with the progression rule of continuing from left to right. The authors suggest that the predominant d–b and q–p reversals may in this light be regarded as 'regularizing' errors akin to those occurring in spoken language. Nihei (1980) makes a similar observation with regard to the fact that 88 percent of the reversal errors made by Japanese children correspond with the left-to-right direction which prevails in their writing.

A direct test of the predictive value of the grammar of action for stroke patterns preferred by children is provided by Simner (1981). He asked kindergarten and 1st and 2nd grade children to copy letters and digits. Most kindergarten children, who had not received any formal instruction, preferred the same specific stroke pattern for most of the letters and digits. The large majority of the patterns, moreover, were in agreement with the starting and progression rules. Simner also found, however, that a child's adherence to a rule in copying a geometric shape does not always imply his use of that rule in copying a letter. This means that there are limits to the generalization of the syntactic principles across different types of shapes. A further important finding by Simner was that formal writing instruction does not have a strong effect on the use of alternative stroke patterns. It is suggested by him that it is unlikely, therefore, that instruction produces new motor rules which in turn would transfer to other copying tasks, as has been suggested by Goodnow *et al.* (1973). Finally, Simner reported that in those cases where conflicts exist between several rules of the grammar of action, the latter grammar does not always predict the solution adopted. The author suggested that the child first takes the entire figure into account and then decides which strokes require least effort and which are likely to produce the least amount of error. This seems to be a valuable further expansion of the above suggestion made by Ninio and Lieblich (1976) that subjects attempt to reduce uncertainty as much as possible.

The restricted number of general patterns observed does not lead necessarily to the conclusion that the child's entire spatial knowledge or his attempts at graphic representation are restricted to this set of rules. It may well be that even an expanded grammar of action as specified in rules of the type discussed applies only to writing and to schematically copying geometrical designs. Indeed it might be appropriate to regard these as belonging to a broad class of writing-like behaviours, ranging from the production of more or less familiar strokes and letters, through the copying of geometrical designs, to the drawing of certain conventional simplified representations such as of a house, a person, a tree, which may be acquired by the child as quasi-symbolic, schematic, or pictographic, representations.

Handedness and the Development of Handwriting

We shall not discuss the causes or development of handedness since excellent reviews are available (Lenneberg, 1967; Satz, 1976; Lebrun and Zangwill, 1981). We will restrict ourselves here to briefly mentioning a few implications of left-handedness for the directional aspects of handwriting. It is obvious that the horizontal movements involved in carrying the pencil across the page are reversed motorically when they are performed with the opposite hand. A left–right stroke results from an adduction movement by the left hand but from an abduction movement by the right hand. As one might expect, this difference is reflected in the development of slightly different shapes or different directional biases in the production of strokes (Goodnow, 1977). Such differences may shed light on the relative importance of anatomical and cultural influences on the issue of directionality; they may also yield principles for teaching the alphabet in a sequence that is natural to left-handers. To the best of our knowledge, however, these specific differences have not been systematically observed. To Goodnow's (1977) and Nihei's (1980) statements that left-handers show a slightly smaller rightward directionality than right-handers, we add our own informal observation that a larger proportion of left-handers than of right-handers tend to write the digit zero in a clockwise fashion. The latter observation is in line with findings reported by Connolly and Elliott (1972) on directionality in painting 3–5 year olds. They found that left-handers drew horizontals from right to left and tended to make clockwise curves.

Further obvious sources of difference between the writing movements of left-handers and.right-handers are the required tilt of the point of the writing instrument (which must be prevented from piercing the paper) and the need for an unobstructed view of the trace left behind by the pen. The left–right direction of normal writing, both within letters and between letters and words, greatly favours the normal right-handed writing grip, in which the pen is pulled away from its trace, leaving the trace to the left of the pen-point unsmudged and unobstructed for visual inspection. Such a favourable condition cannot be achieved so naturally by left-handers. In general, one of the two following postures is normally adopted. A left-hander can either hold the pen so that its point is directed away from him while his hand is held below the writing line and his elbow close to his side. This is the non-inverted writing posture. The left-hander can also sharply bend his wrist such that the pen-point is directed towards him while his hand is held above the writing line and his elbow pointing outwards. Levy (1973) and Levy and Reid (1976, 1978) have suggested that the latter, inverted, posture is indicative of an ipsilateral cerebral control of writing. Attempts to replicate these findings and reconcile them with population statistics remain inconclusive (Weber and Bradshaw, 1981). It is obvious, however, that these grips will result in different movement patterns, and therefore in the development of different letter shapes even within the left-handed part of the population.

An Integrated model of Spoken and Written Language

Thus far, we have not given any attention to the fact that writing involves words. Since language itself is the principal higher-order system governing writing, a comprehensive model of writing should also incorporate the linguistic structures determining the selection of the words to be written, the required letters, and their order of production. A comprehensive model of the kind we have in mind should be able to explain the orderly execution of the correct schemata for letters, letter clusters, and words and how these are influenced by sequential probabilities, the rules of orthography and linguistic context. To the best of our knowledge the only model which includes some consideration of the motor aspects of handwriting, and which links up with current models of language processing (e.g. Morton, 1980) has been proposed by Ellis (1982). The author makes an attempt to explain a large variety of writing errors (as distinct from spelling errors) on the basis of the model. These slips of the pen, all at the level of letters or letter sequences, include anticipations, perservations, letter masking (omission of one of a pair of repeated letters), haplography (omission of one of a pair of repeated letters plus the letters occurring between the two repeated letters), reversals, substitutions, and scale errors. For each of these a specific locus in the model is held responsible. In the model the cognitive system has an auditory and a visual input logogen system and a speech as well as a graphemic output logogen system (see Figure 4). The latter system is a lexical memory for written words. It receives various types of information, for example, about the meaning of the word to be written, in the form of a semantic code from the cognitive system itself. It makes available the

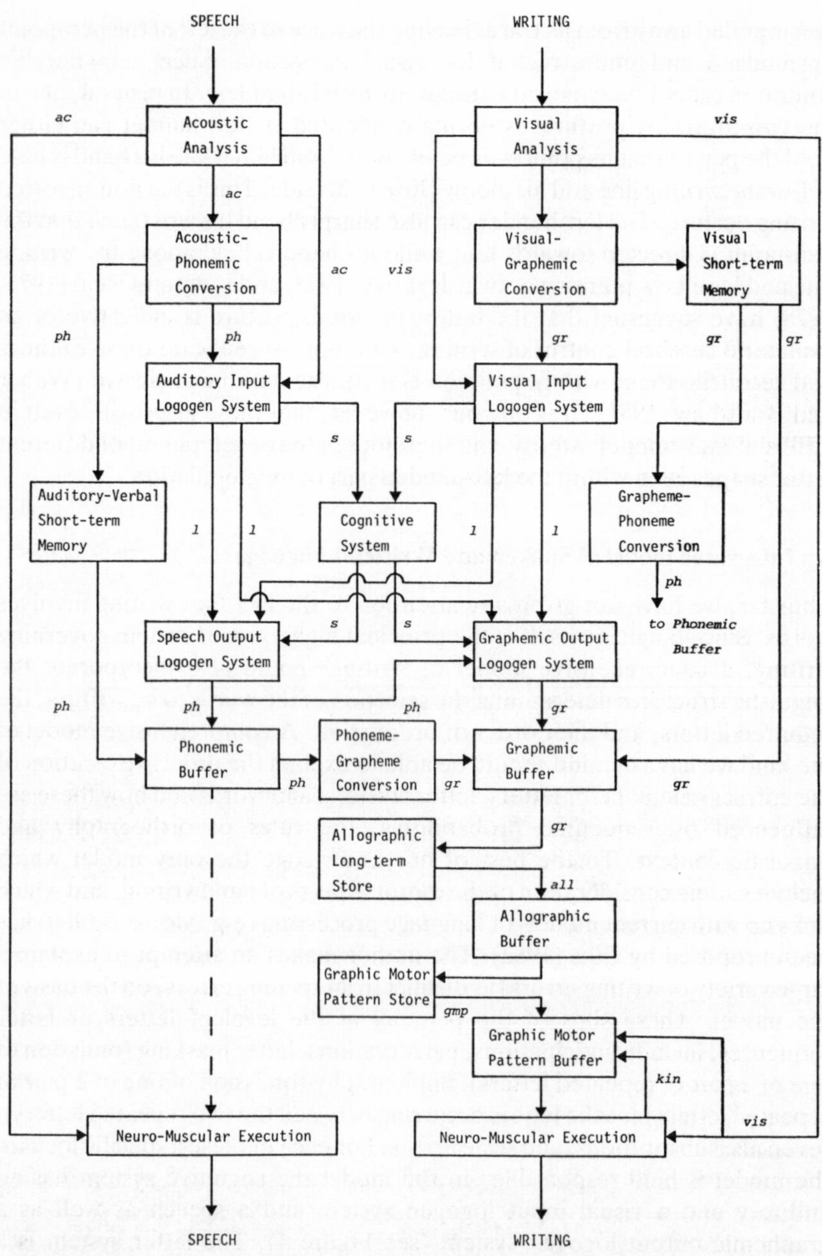

FIGURE 4 A model for spelling and writing (and reading and hearing). Abbreviations: *ac* = acoustic code; *all* = allographic code; *gpm* = graphic motor pattern code; *ph* = phonemic code; *s* = semantic code; *vis* = visual code (from Ellis, 1982)

spelling of a written word and thus produces a graphemic code in terms of the letters to be written. This code is fed to an allographic long-term store, where the letters receive their spatial descriptions in terms of upper and lower case and their specific types or form (allographs), the selection of which depends on a number of context variables. The resulting allographic code, though spatial, is still relatively abstract. It specifies the selected letter shape neither in terms of organization of strokes nor in terms of its size or of the muscle system involved in its execution. The spatial description is used to select from a store the appropriate motor pattern in terms of the sequence of the strokes to be made, including their direction and relative sizes. The resulting coded motor pattern is transmitted to a neuromuscular execution system which specifies the absolute size of the letters and finally produces them.

Ellis' (1982) model, which can be seen as a representation of a system operating at the level of letters, seems reasonably effective in explaining a variety of writing errors. The execution part of the model is of special interest in the present context. It is concerned with the production of allographs or letters, but in its present form it is not capable of explaining, for example, the frequent d–b reversals made by children. This would require the assumption of weakly represented grapheme schemata on the one hand and of overruling tendencies like the progression rules discussed above, on the other. Furthermore it is reasonable to assume that sequential probabilities and context effects lead to a chunking of programmes, for example, for frequent word endings if larger size than single letters. On the other hand there are various kinds of writing errors which involve strokes or sequences of strokes at levels lower than whole letters. For example, counting errors, which are manifested by under-performance or over-performance in letters with repeated strokes (m, n, u, v, w) or substitutions between letters having certain strokes in common (e.g. b-p, d-g, h-n), which tend to occur under experimental conditions involving a secondary task.

Such errors would require a specification of the neuromuscular execution part of the model other than the autonomous realization of selected allograph schemata in an all-or-none fashion. Counting errors would seem to require that certain schemata (or all schemata if they are insufficiently established) are subject to kinaesthetic or visual monitoring to keep account of the number of completed similar strokes. Substitutions among similar letters would imply the need for a procedure to reduce the probability of intrusions of letters with a similar start or build-up. The obvious developmental implication of this discussion is that the system outlined by Ellis becomes increasingly complete and efficient. A specific difficulty in the earliest stage of writing may be caused by verbal interference in children if they name the letters to be written and at the same time verbalize their self-instructions for producing them. It need not be argued that kinaesthetic and visual feedback are of great importance during early learning. Elementary strokes, and certainly schemata for graphemes, acquire stability only in the course of prolonged practice; allographs of graphemes and their clusters come at a later stage in the development of writing.

CONCLUSION

A start has been made on the analysis of how handwriting develops, but where do we go from here? In our view there are several interesting lines of enquiry to pursue. First it is important to provide a full descriptive account of the development of the graphic abilities which underlie handwriting. A further question concerns how schemata are built up in the course of development. We do not know what the original response units are and how they develop; nor do we understand how they are organized into programmes of increasing size. An attempt should be made to separate the effects of specific training from those of general development. Effective forms of training also need to be identified and analysed; a question here is how specific training should be. A further issue requiring consideration is the developing role of imagery in writing and copying; are visual images in the planning of writing movements gradually replaced by motor images? The changing roles of time and space as constant parameters of writing movements during development should also be the subject of experimental investigation. Although there has been a good deal of work on the rules governing graphic skills, more remains to be done. It is not known as yet to what extent such rules, and their development, are a function of anatomical biases such as flexion and extension, or of imaged spatial relationships. An important question concerns the aspects of writing, both manuscript and cursive, which are compatible or incompatible with these syntactic principles. Such information would obviously be of educational significance.

Finally, it would be very rewarding to devise a model of handwriting which not only encompassed letter shapes, but also took some account of the constraints of language, at least up to the word level. This would involve the study of timing similarities among similar and dissimilar letters, the examination of production characteristics of frequent and infrequent letter sequences, and a comparison of correct productions of a given letter or word with productions which are inadequate. Comparisons of the latter kind should give us insights into the final stage of the development of handwriting upon which to build the use of writing as a mode of communication and expression.

REFERENCES

Adams, J. A. (1976). Issues for a closed-loop theory of motor learning. In G. E. Stelmach (ed.), *Motor control: Issues and trends*. Academic Press, New York.

Ames, L. B. (1948). Postural placement orientations in writing and block behavior: Developmental trends from infancy to age ten. *Journal of Genetic Psychology,* **73**, 45–52.

Ames, L. B., and Ilg, F. L. (1951). Developmental trends in writing behavior. *Journal of Genetic Psychology,* **79**, 29–46.

Askov, E., Otto, W., and Askov, W. (1970). A decade of research in handwriting: Progress and prospect. *Journal of Educational Research,* **64**, 100–111.

Bender, L. (1938). A visual motor Gestalt test and its clinical use. *New York American Orthopsychiatric Association Research Monograph,* **3**.

Berman, P. W. (1976). Young children's use of the frame of reference in construction of the horizontal, vertical and oblique. *Child Development,* **47**, 259–263.

Berman, P. W., Cunningham, J. G., and Harkulich, J. (1974). Construction of the horizontal, vertical and oblique by young children: failure to find the 'oblique effect'. *Child Development,* **45**, 474–478.

Bilodeau, E. A. (ed.) (1969). *Principles of Skill Acquisition*, Academic Press, New York.

Birch, H. G., and Lefford, A. (1967). Visual differentiation, intersensory integration, and voluntary motor control. *Monograph of the Society for Research in Child Development,* **32**, 1–87.

Bruner, J. S. (1970). The growth and structure of skill. In K. Connolly (ed.), *Mechanisms of Motor Skill Development*. Academic Press, London.

Bruner, J. S. (1971). Competence in infants. Paper presented at the meeting of the Society for Research in Child Development, Minneapolis, 1971. (Cited by Goodnow and Levine, 1973).

Bruner, J. S. (1973). Organization of early skilled action. *Child Development,* **44**, 1–11.

Connolly, K. (1968). Some mechanisms involved in the development of motor skills. *Aspects of Education,* **7**, 82–100.

Connolly, K. (ed.) (1970) *Mechanisms of Motor Skill Development*. Academic Press, London.

Connolly, K. (1975). Action, movement and skill. In K. S. Holt (ed.), *Movement and Child Development*. W. Heinemann Medical Books Ltd., London.

Connolly, K. (1977). The nature of motor skill development. *Journal of Human Movement Studies,* **3**, 128–143.

Connolly, K., and Bruner, J. S. (eds.) (1974). *The Growth of Competence*. Academic Press, London.

Connolly, K., and Elliott, J. (1972). The evolution and ontogeny of hand function. In N. Blurton Jones (ed.), *Ethological Studies of Child Behaviour*. Cambridge University Press, Cambridge.

Connolly, K., and Jones, B. (1970). A developmental study of afferent–reafferent integration. *British Journal of Psychology,* **61**, 259–266.

Cormeau Velghe-Lenelle, M., Distrait, V., Toussaint, J., and Bidaine, E. (1970). Normes de vitesse d'écriture. Étude statistique de 1844 écoliers Belges de 6 à 13 ans. *Psychologica Belgica,* **10**, 247–263.

De Jong, A. M. L. (1979). De schrijfbeweging: Experimenteel-psychologisch onderzoek en enige klinische ervaringen m.b.t. ontwikkelingsaspecten van het schrijfgedrag opgevat als motorische vaardigheid. Master's Thesis, University of Nijmegen.

Denier van der Gon, J. J., and Thuring, J. Ph. (1965). The guiding of human writing movements. *Kybernetik*, **2**, 145–148.

De Swart, S. (1979). Komplexe motoriek: Uitvoering en ontwikkeling. Master's thesis, University of Nijmegen.

Ellis, A. W. (1982). Spelling and writing (and reading and speaking). In A. W. Ellis (ed.), *Normality and Pathology in Cognitive Functions*. Academic Press, London.

Essing, W. (1965). Untersuchungen über Veränderungen in der Schreibmotorik im Grundschulalter. *Human Development,* **8**, 194–221.

Fleishman, E. A. (1966). Human abilities and the acquisition of skill. In: E. A. Bilodeau (ed.), *Acquisition of Skill*. Academic Press, New York.

Frith, U. (1974). Internal schemata for letters in good and bad readers. *British Journal of Psychology,* **65**, 233–241.

Gesell, A. (ed.) (1940). *The First Five Years of Life*. Harper, New York.

Gesell, A., and Ames, L. B. (1946). The development of directionality in drawing. *Journal of Genetic Psychology,* **68**, 45–61.

Gibson, E. J. (1969). *Principles of Perceptual Learning and Development*. Meredith, New York.

Gibson, E. J., Gibson, J. J., Pick, A. D., and Osser, H. (1962). A developmental study of the discrimination of letter-like forms. *Journal of Comparative and Physiological Psychology,* **55**, 897–906.

Glencross, D. J. (1977). Control in skilled movements. *Psychological Bulletin,* **84**, 14–29.

Goodnow, J. (1977). *Children Drawing*. Harvard University Press, Cambridge, Mass.

Goodnow, J., Friedman, S. L., Bernbaum, M., and Lehman, E. B. (1973). Direction and sequence in copying: the effect of learning to write in English and Hebrew. *Journal of Cross-Cultural Psychology,* **4**, 263–282.

Goodnow, J. J., and Levine, R. A. (1973). The grammar of action: sequence and syntax in children's copying. *Cognitive Psychology,* **4**, 82–98.

Graham, F. K., Berman, P. W., and Ernhart, C. B. (1960). Development in preschool children of the ability to copy forms. *Child Development,* **31**, 339–359.

Hay, L. (1979). Spatial–temporal analysis of movements in children: motor programs versus feedback in the development of reaching. *Journal of Motor Behavior,* **11**, 189–200.

Herrick, V. E. (1960). *Comprehensive Bibliography of Handwriting and Related Factors, 1890–1960*. Handwriting Foundation, Washington, D.C.

Herrick, V. E. (ed.) (1963). *New Horizons for Research in Handwriting*. University of Wisconsin Press, Madison.

Hollerbach, J. M. (1981). An oscillation theory of handwriting. *Biological Cybernetics,* **39**, 138–156.

Holt, K. S. (1975). *Movement and Child Development*. W. Heinemann Medical Books Ltd., London.

Hulstijn, W., and Van Galen, G. P. (1982). Reaction time and movement time in letter writing: The effects of stimulus repetition and complexity. Paper presented at the Workshop on the Motor Aspects of Handwriting, Nijmegen, July.

Katz, D. (1951). *Gestalt Psychology: Its Nature and Significance*. Methuen, London.

Kay, H. (1969). The development of motor skills from birth to adolescence. In E. A. Bilodeau (ed.), *Principles of Skill Acquisition*. Academic Press, New York.

Kay, H. (1970). Analysing motor skill performance. In K. Connolly (ed.), *Mechanisms of Motor Skill Development*, Academic Press, London.

Keele, S. W. (1968). Movement control in skilled motor performance. *Psychological Bulletin,* **70**, 387–403.

Keele, S. W. (1981). Behavioral analysis of movement. In V. B. Brooks (vol. ed.), *Handbook of Physiology*: Section I: The Nervous System. Volume II: Motor Control, Part 2. American Physiological Society, Baltimore.

Keele, S. W., and Summers, J. J. (1976). The structure of motor programs In G. E. Stelmach (ed.), *Motor Control: Issues and Trends*. Academic Press, New York.

Kellogg, R. (1969). *Analyzing Children's Art*. National Press Books, Palo Alto, Calif.

Kelso, J. A. S., and Clark, J. E. (eds.) (1982). *The Development of Movement Control and Co-ordination*. Wiley, New York.

Klapp, S. T. (1977). Response programming, as assessed by reaction time, does not establish the commands for particular muscles. *Journal of Motor Behavior,* **9**, 301–312.

Klapp, S. T. (1978). Reaction time analysis of programmed control. In R. S. Hutton (ed.), *Exercise and Sport Sciences Reviews*. Journal Publishing Affiliates, Santa Barbara, Calif.

Klapp, S. T., and Greim, D. M. (1979). Programmed control of aimed movements revisited: the role of target visibility and symmetry. *Journal of Experimental Psychology: Human Perception and Performance,* **5**, 509–521.

Knippenberg, H., Aerle, E. and van Galen, G. P. (1978). Ambiënte vs. focale informatieverwerking, motorische controle en ontwikkeling van complexe motoriek. Master's thesis, University of Nijmegen.

Lebrun, Y., and Zangwill, O. (eds.) (1981). *Lateralization and Language in Children*. Swets & Zeitlinger, Lisse.

Lenneberg, E. H. (1967). *Biological Foundations of Language*. Wiley, New York.

Levy, J. (1973). Lateral specialization of the human brain. Behavioral manifestion and possible evolutionary bias. In J. Kiger (ed.), *The Biology of Behavior*. Oregon State University Press, Cornwallis.

Levy, J., and Reid, M. (1976). Variations in writing posture and cerebral organization. *Science,* **194**, 337–339.

Levy, J., and Reid, M. (1978). Variations in cerebral organization as a function of handedness, hand posture in writing, and sex. *Journal of Experimental Psychology: General,* **107**, 119–144.

Lewis, E. R., and Lewis, H. P. (1965). An analysis of errors in the formation of manuscript letters by first-grade children. *American Educational Research Journal,* **2**, 25–35.

Lieblich, A., Ninio, A., and Kugelmass, S. (1975). Developmental trends in directionality of drawing in Jewish and Arab Israeli children. *Journal of Cross-Cultural Psychology,* **6**, 504–510.

Lundberg, A. (1979). The drawing test: a tool for assessment of arm–hand function in children 1–3 years of age. *Neuropaediatrie,* **10**, 1–6.

Lurçat, L., and Kostin, E. (1970). Study of graphical abilities in children. *Perceptual and Motor Skills,* **30**, 615–630.

Maccoby, E. E., and Bee, H. L. (1965). Some speculations concerning the lag between perceiving and performing. *Child Development,* **36**, 367–377.

McAllister, C. N. (1900). Researches on movements used in handwriting. *Yale Psychological Laboratory Studies,* **8**, 21–63.

McCarthy, L. (1977). A child learns the alphabet. *Visible Language,* **11**, 271–284.

Merton, P. A. (1972). How we control the contraction of our muscles. *Scientific American,* **226** (May), 30–37.

Michel, F. (1971). Etude experimentale de la vitesse du geste graphique. *Neuropsychologia,* **9**, 1–13.

Morton, J. (1980). The logogen model and orthographic structure. In U. Frith (ed.), *Cognitive Processes in Spelling*. Academic Press, London.

Napier, J. R. (1956). The prehensile movements of the human hand. *Journal of Bone and Joint Surgery,* **38B**, 902–913.

Nihei, Y. (1980). Developmental change in motor organization: Covert principles for the organization of strokes in children's drawing. *Tohoku Psychologica Folia,* **39**, 17–23.

Ninio, A., and Lieblich, A. (1976). The grammar of action: 'phrase structure' in children's copying. *Child Development,* **47**, 846–849.

Peck, M., Askov, E. N., and Fairchild, S. H. (1980). Another decade of research in handwriting: Progress and prospect in the 1970s. *Journal of Educational Research,* **73**, 283–298.

Piaget, J., and Inhelder, B. (1948). *La réprésentation de l'espace chez l'enfant*. Presses Universitaires de France, Paris.

Poulton, E. C. (1957). On prediction in skilled movements. *Psychological Bulletin,* **54**, 28–32.

Rand, C. S. W. (1973). Copying in drawing: the importance of adequate visual analysis vs. the ability to utilize drawing rules. *Child Development,* **44**, 47–53.

Rosenbaum, D. A. (1980). Human movement initiation: specification of arm, direction and extent. *Journal of Experimental Psychology: General*, **109**, 444–474.

Rosenbloom, L., and Horton, M. E. (1971). The maturation of fine prehension in young children. *Developmental Medicine and Child Neuroogy,* **13**, 3–8.

Saida, Y., and Miyashita, M. (1979). Development of fine motor skill in children: Manipulation of a pencil in young children aged 2 to 6 years old. *Journal of Human Movement Studies,* **5**, 104–113.

Satz, P. (1976). Cerebral dominance and reading disability. In R. Knights and D. Bakker (eds.), *The Neuropsychology of Learning Disorders*. University Park Press, Baltimore.

Schmidt, R. A. (1975). A schema theory of discrete motor skill learning. *Psychological Review,* **82**, 225–260.

Schmidt, R. A. (1976). The schema as a solution to some persistent problems in motor learning theory. In G. E. Stelmach (ed.), *Motor Control: Issues and Trends*. Academic Press, New York.

Schmidt, R. A. (1980). On the theoretical status of time in motor program representations. In A. E. Stelmach and J. Requin (eds.), *Tutorials in Motor Behavior*. North-Holland, Amsterdam.

Simner, M. L. (1981). The grammar of action and children's printing. *Developmental Psychology,* **17**, 866–871.

Smith, K. U., (1962). *Delayed Sensory Feedback and Behavior*. Saunders, Philadelphia.

Søvik, N. (1975). *Developmental Cybernetics of Handwriting and Graphic Behavior*. Universitetsforlaget, Oslo.

Søvik, N. (1981). An experimental study of individualized learning instruction in copying, tracking, and handwriting based on feedback principles. *Perceptual and Motor Skills*, **53**, 195–215.

Spielman, K. S. (1976). Development of the perception and production of line forms. *Child Development*, **47**, 787–793.

Stelmach, G. E. (ed.) (1976). *Motor Control: Issues and Trends*. Academic Press, New York.

Stelmach, G. E. (ed.) (1978). *Information Processing in Motor Control and Learning*. Academic Press, New York.

Stelmach, G. E., and Requin, J. (eds.) (1980). *Tutorials in Motor Behavior*. North-Holland, Amsterdam.

Stelmach, G. E., and Teulings, J. L. H. M. (1982). Programming of expected and unexpected movements. Paper presented at the Workshop on the Motor Aspects of Handwriting, Nijmegen, July.

Sternberg, S., Monsell, S., Knoll, R. L., and Wright, C. E. (1978). The latency and duration of rapid movement sequences: comparisons of speech and typewriting. In G. E. Stelmach (ed.), *Information Processing in Motor Control and Learning*. Academic Press, New York.

Teulings, J. L. H. M., and Thomassen, A. J. W. M. (1979). Computer-aided analysis of handwriting movements. *Visible Language*, **13**, 219–231.

Teulings, J. L. H. M., Thomassen, A. J. W. M., and Van Galen, G. P. (1980). Schrijfsnelheid als functie van schrijfgrootte en leeftijd. *Technical Report*, Psychology Laboratory, University of Nijmegen.

Thomassen, A. J. W. M., and Teulings, J. L. H. M. (1979). The development of directional preference in writing movements. *Visible Language*, **13**, 299–313.

Van Galen, G. P. (1980). Storage and retrieval of handwriting patterns: a two-stage model of complex motor behavior. In G. E. Stelmach and J. Requin (eds.), *Tutorials in Motor Behavior*. North-Holland, Amsterdam.

Viviani, P., and Terzuolo, C. (1980). Space–time invariance in learned motor skills. In G. E. Stelmach and J. Requin (eds.), *Tutorials in Motor Behavior*. North-Holland, Amsterdam.

Vredenbregt, J., and Koster, W. G. (1971). Analysis and synthesis of handwriting. *Philips Technical Review*, **32**, 73–78.

Weber, A. M., and Bradshaw, J. L. (1981). Levy and Reid's neurological model in relation to writing hand/posture: An evaluation. *Psychological Bulletin*, **90**, 74–88.

Welford, A. T. (1978). *Fundamentals of Skill*. Methuen, London.

Williams, J. (1975). Training children to copy and to discriminte letterlike forms. *Journal of Educational Psychology*, **67**, 790–795.

Wing, A. M. (1978). Response timing in handwriting. In G. E. Stelmach (ed.), *Information Processing in Motor Control and Learning*. Academic Press, New York.

PART IV

Early Approaches To The Acquisition Of Written Language

Epitectus: *Discources*.	If you wish to be a good writer, write.
Horace: *Ars Poetica.*	Knowledge is the foundation and source of good writing.
Emerson: *Journals*.	Writing is more and more a terror to old scribes.
Marie Clay (Jenny aged 5;9)	I can do The alphabet. can you do The al pha bet.

The Psychology of Written Language
Edited by M. Martlew

CHAPTER 9

Young Children's Approach to Literacy

CECILIA DE GÓES AND MARGARET MARTLEW

Long before children receive formal instruction in reading and writing, the process of acquiring the component skills necessary for these activities has already begun. Children have normally, for instance, had a fair amount of experience in drawing and outlining shapes as well as having contact with printed texts in their day-to-day experience. As Downing (1969) has stressed, this comes from contact with written labels on boxes, road signs, shops, etc., as well as from more conventional encounters with books. Young children therefore have some notion or expectation, be it adequate or not, about written language, and the systematic training that comes from instruction in school adds other kinds of experience to what the child has already acquired.

Acquiring written language introduces the child to a complex, abstract system in which the conventions of the system have to be consciously mastered from the beginning. This differs from the acquisition of speech which children acquire in a highly motivating social context without awareness of the mechanisms of production. Vygotsky (1978; Chapter 11, this volume) highlights this by pointing to the difference between the child's linguistic ability and his early attempts at writing. The specific characteristics of writing make it necessary for the child to master a more differentiated syntax. Although initially mediated by speech, this is reduced or disappears in the sense that the social roles of the two systems are very different. Related to these differing social demands are the specific formal features which the child gradually acquires, so moving from writing down speech to writing written language (Bereiter, 1980).

Taking into account young children's considerably ability in the use of spoken language and their rudimentary experience with written language, there are many questions to be asked about their growing awareness of the symbolic function of writing, and of its characteristics and functions.

When analysing the origins of written language, Vygotsky (1978) proposed that gesture marks the starting point, so initial scribbles would be taken as gestures rather than intended drawings. This has parallels with play, where the child first performs representational gestures with objects and toys. In fantasy play, however, objects are used to stand for something other than what they physically or immediately represent. Fantasy play is then a progression to second-order symbolism, as is writing, and in this sense is a preliminary stage of it. Written language he conceives of as second-order symbolism deriving from the first-order symbolism of speech. In this way, Vygotsky connects the processes of drawing, play, and writing, to explain the child's progress towards the higher-order symbolism involved in writing.

Luria (1978; Chapter 10 this volume) believed that in order to be able to write, the child has to develop the use of cues as auxiliary functional signs, as the recording of symbols in writing allows the recall and transmission of ideas and concepts. He conducted some studies in which he analysed the marks made on paper by children who were as yet unable to read or write. He persuaded them to 'write' to help them to recall phrases that were dictated to them. He was able to identify progressive changes in the marks which these children produced, showing that initially dictations were depicted pictographically but that the signs used moved progressively towards the use of symbols.

The work of Vygotsky and Luria is still of enormous interest and significance. They offer insights into the preliminary stages of literacy and suggest ways of exploring different aspects of early literacy. In particular, they show that we cannot assume that the acquisition of literacy only begins with formal instruction.

Studies by Reid (1966) and Downing (1969) show that children do not have clear notions about the activity of reading, or about the basic vocabulary that is used; such terms, for example, as *word* or *sound*. We need to extend our knowledge of the notions that children have about the written word, how they begin to decode as well as produce it, and how they react to the distribution of words in the text, the presence of punctuation marks and so on. The strategies which children use to approach written language are directly related to educational practice. Teachers have long been entangled in controversies about the most adequate methods of instruction, proponents defending particular approaches as ones which take account of the natural or necessary sequence of processes that children undergo in learning.

Despite the variety of available methods, the major debate hinges on the emphasis on code as opposed to emphasis on meaning. Chall (1967) summarizes this polarization as a divergence between those who believe initial learning must imply a mastery of the alphabetic code and those who assume that meaning has priority from the beginning. The dispute is by no means resolved, although few teaching programmes are illustrations of only one point of view. Analysing research findings bearing on this issue, Bryant and Bradley (1980) suggested that children learn to write by different routes. Both segmentation skills and the ability to perceive 'chunks' are important, and they report findings indicating the predominance of phonological cues in writing, compared with the importance of visual cues in reading (Bradley and Bryant, 1979).

Frith (1980) referred to teachers' expectancy of a natural transfer of one of these abilities to the other. Currently reading is emphasized, but other schemes have introduced writing instruction first, from which point children were expected to end up being able to read. However, Frith also argues for a relative dissociation between the two abilities. This indication of relatively independent processes operating at the beginning of reading and writing has only recently been highlighted, and it leads to interesting new perspectives on the controversial question of teaching methods. As well as investigating learning strategies, it is also important to consider what the child *knows* about language. Although there has been an increasing interest in children's awareness or intuitions about language, few conceptual or empirical attempts have yet been made to relate various metalinguistic abilities to one another or to general aspects of cognitive development (Hakes, 1980).

Generally, children beginning to write have only a limited awareness of the nature and function of acting upon sounds and letters. This requires an ability to reflect on language itself which few children of this age have, though Gleitman *et al.* (1972) report the 'a/an' distinction from a 4 year old who asked, 'Mummy, is it AN adult or A-NUHdult?'. This is an interesting query, considering the original form of a newt (an ewt) and an orange (a narange). It is also interesting because this child's ability to talk about segmentation was not carried over into her spontaneous usage until two years later. She had, in other words, an awareness of segmentation, but not the ability to act on this awareness. Liberman and Shankweiler (1979) believe that young children have a tacit awareness of phonological segmentation in that they can distinguish subtle phonological differences in the flow of speech. However, they add that reading and writing require a finer ability to analyse words into phonemes, an ability which has to be acquired in the initial stages. This may represent the nucleus of linguistic awareness necessary for reading and writing but other aspects are also essential for developing young children's capacity to cope with the written system. Initially, words are confused with what they represent. For instance, the response to the question, 'Why is pencil a word?' was 'Because it writes' (Papandropoulou and Sinclair, 1974), and 'Why is cow a word?', 'Because it has horns' (Vygotsky, 1962). Children operating under this confusion, therefore, fail to accept function words or abstract words as words, there being no concrete image to relate them to. Children's reasons for not accepting function words are diverse, some responses to 'the' as a word, for instance, produced the following responses from 4–6-year-old children: 'It isn't with another word', 'It doesn't sound like one', and 'No people say it' (Templeton and Spivey, 1980). Preschool children also have no real concept of the relationship of the length of the sound of a word to its written equivalent (Rozin *et al.*, 1974).

Hakes (1980) points out that language is normally treated in an instrumental manner rather than as an end in itself, that is language is treated as 'transparent' (something to be seen through) rather than 'opaque' (something to be focused on in its own right). The central issue of language awareness, according to Lundberg (1978), is the shifting of attention from content to form. Whereas initially words bear direct relationships to what they designate, this attention shift allows them to become opaque. At a time when young children are beginning to read and write, they show an increasing ability to act and think deliberately, and of being able to distance themselves from a situation and reflect upon it. In a more general framework, Piaget's interpretation of children's consciousness of their acts is relevant to the growth of metalinguistic awareness (Piaget, 1976). To become aware of an act is not a process that merely adds to the performance of the act. The cognizance of it modifies the situation and implies a passage from a practical assimilation of an object to a conceptual assimilation, thus leading to higher conceptualization. Questions as to how children progress in their initial stages of mastering the written language have to be set in terms of learning and development. When analysing the interaction between learning and development, Vygotsky (1978; Chapter 11 this volume) proposed that language creates what he called 'the zone of proximal development', which refers to the distance between what the child is already able to perform and what he is potentially capable of. Learning is converted into development.

YOUNG CHILDREN'S CONCEPTUALIZATIONS OF WRITTEN LANGUAGE

Even very young children will write, either spontaneously or in response to a request. They will do this by drawing, or by making marks or using letters. What they produce will depend on their developmental level and the specific experience they have had with written language. There are some children who can write before they can read. They can compose sentences using an idiosyncratic orthography, which, although it differs from conventional orthography, is decodable, even though the young writer cannot read it. After studying such children, Chomsky (1979) suggested that they should be encouraged to write without regard for conventional spelling to encourage their awareness of the symbolic functions of written communication.

The symbolic function of written language can be examined, however, at an earlier stage than the time when children are recognizing and writing some words. Children go through a long period of differentiation in relation to their eventual ability to recognize and produce texts. Luria's investigations on children's early attempts at writing showed that initially the act of writing appears to be an end in itself and unrelated to linguistic meaning. Children asked to write down a dictation, for instance, will start to make marks, before a word or phrase has been given. Following this, writing is undifferentiated in its appearance but the position and relationship of marks on the page serve the function of mnemonic aids, helping the child to recall phrases. Increasing differentiation is observable in these marks, in the features of the word forms, and in what they refer to. Children's writing at this stage has pictographic characteristics, and the change from this to symbolic representation is apparent when the writing sustains a systematic correspondence with what is said.

Ferreiro and her colleagues (1979) investigated children's awareness of written language by studying 4–6 year old children from different socioeconomic levels. They looked at the way the children approached text in books and symbols written on cards, and examined how they responded to instructions to write different words, words and their respective diminutives, etc. For each of these situations the children's behaviour was categorized and these category groups showed how performance reflected the children's increasing comprehension in their attempts to cope with the abstract nature of writing and the conventions of the written system. The diminutive in Spanish, for instance, provides an excellent opportunity for analysing a child's tendency to retain a direct relationship between the size of the object referred to by a word and its written form. The diminutive in Spanish is formed by adding a suffix to the original word which makes the smaller object correspond to a larger word. Ferreiro *et al.* identified a first level of performance where completely different or exactly the same written representations were given for both words. At the next level there appeared to be a reconciliation of the similarities and the differences between the two words in that the writing was equivalent for both words but smaller marks were used for the diminutive, or one letter was omitted, or letter positions changed. The third level showed an increase in the number of marks used to represent the diminutive.

These investigations focus on the processes which precede the comprehension and production of written language. Following these approaches we developed a study to extend our knowledge of the progressive levels of the young child's awareness of what written language is. The study was designed to examine the patterns of writing in young children. In order to consider what understanding the children had of the marks that they made on the paper, situations were devised which required free writing, dictation and copying. thirty-four children, aged 3–6 years, were involved in the study. They all attended either a nursery or a first school. The children were interviewed individually in their classroom and the sessions were divided into two parts. Initially, children were asked to write anything they wished. As generally the first word children learn to write is their name, they were specifically asked to write their first name if they did not do so spontaneously. Following this, they were asked to write phrases of two words (one dress; two books; four flowers), each phrase being presented separately. The second part of the session consisted of copying and rewriting isolated words. These words were presented as letters painted on wooden blocks (tree; pencils; balls). The word was read, the children asked to repeat it and then to copy it. The fact that the word was built up from various individual letters was emphasized to encourage the children to include all of them in their copies. When the children had finished their attempts at copying each word from the letter blocks, these were taken away and the children were asked to write the word again, no mention being made of the copy they had just completed. The important element of the copying and rewriting situation was not the quality of the reproduction of the word but the children's ability to regard the word as a unit and to take their own copy as a model for rewriting.

The children's responses to these tasks were classified on the basis of this

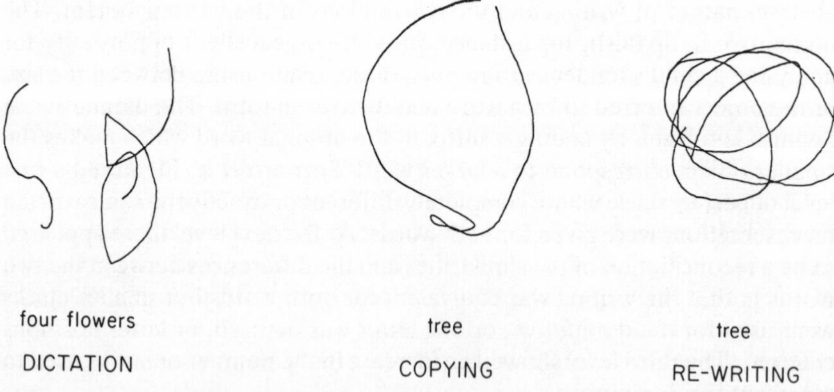

FIGURE 1 Level one: representative responses to three writing tasks. In level one there is no resemblance between the marks and the objects referred to

into the category system described below. In the first level (Figure 1) there is no distinction between the scribbles produced in either session. The marks produced on the paper bear no resemblance to a depiction of the objects referred to, either when writing or copying. These marks tended either to be circular and elliptical shapes or to be straight lines which frequently went from one edge of the paper to the other. When children labelled these marks, they did so only when they had completed them. Some children scribbled continuously and did not stop until asked to. It seemed that the action or gestures involved were as important as the marks being produced. Children at this level, when they were about to copy the words, might examine the letter blocks before writing but they did not look at them while they were copying. When they were asked to rewrite the word, they would not have any regard for their own 'copy' but made new scribbles.

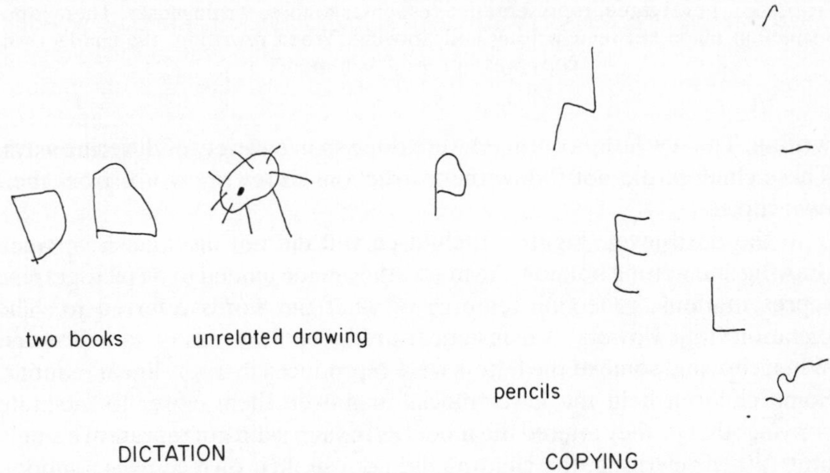

FIGURE 2 Level two: representative responses to two writing tasks. The marks made during the dictation bear some resemblance to the objects referred to but no distinction is made between drawing and writing. Not all the letters were reproduced when copying, and no attempt was made at rewriting

Children in the second level (Figure 2) were those who could make marks which reflected a depiction of the objects represented by the words. The marks they made were not merely scribbles, but tended to take the form of units or closed shapes. They still lacked, however, the distinctive features of the objects referred to. During the dictation there were refusals to write, taken in the sense of 'make' or 'draw', the reason given was that they were not able to. When copying, the children reproduced only some of the letters and then not in a linear fashion. Nor was a left-to-right orientation observed either when visually examining the model words or when sequencing in

FIGURE 3 Level three: representative responses to three writing tasks. There is no distinction made between writing and drawing. When rewriting, the child's own copy was not used as a model

writing. The few letters outlined were done so in a variety of differing ways. These children did not follow the instructions to rewrite words from their own copies.

In the third level (Figure 3), children still did not distinguish between drawing and writing but now the marks they made tended to be pictographic representations, reflecting features of what the words referred to. The dictation 'four flowers', for instance, produced drawings of four flowers. When copying, some of the letters were reproduced in a non-linear manner. Some children held the letter blocks or moved them closer to facilitate copying; that is, they altered the model as though it did not represent a single unit. When rewriting, the children did not use their own copy as a model. Random drawings and unrelated letter shapes were also likely to occur. To these children writing was a matter of drawing, and the model word was conceived of as a set of shapes to be copied.

The fourth level (Figure 4) was defined by children who showed a partial distinction between drawing and writing. When engaged in free writing, the children used letters to write their own names, and in a few cases other people's names as well, though these were not always written correctly. The dictation was still taken down as a pictographic representation. The copying task results in a fairly good reproduction of letters in the correct sequence, and when rewriting, after the letter blocks had been removed, these children used their own copies as models for the task. The set of letters corresponding to an identified word still represented that word, at least for a short period of time.

FIGURE 4 Level four: representative responses to three writing tasks. Dictation is still represented pictographically but copies are now used as models for rewriting

The fifth level (Figure 5) marks children's awareness of the distinction between drawing and writing. These children wrote their own names, some also wrote other people's names, and in the dictation task they wrote strings of letters. These generally had no correspondence to the sounds of the words, apart from a few cases where the first letter was appropriate. Words were copied easily and usually without distortions. When asked to rewrite the words without the original model, these children did not hesitate to reproduce their own copy.

FIGURE 5 Level five: representative responses to three writing tasks. This marks the child's awareness of the difference between drawing and writing in the dictation although there is little correspondence between sounds and letters

In the sixth level (Figure 6), as in the preceding one, the children distinguished between drawing and writing. They differed, however, in that they refused to write, justifying their refusal on the grounds that they could not, despite repeated encouragement. This refusal suggests that these children recognized that writing is a system of marks which follow a set of

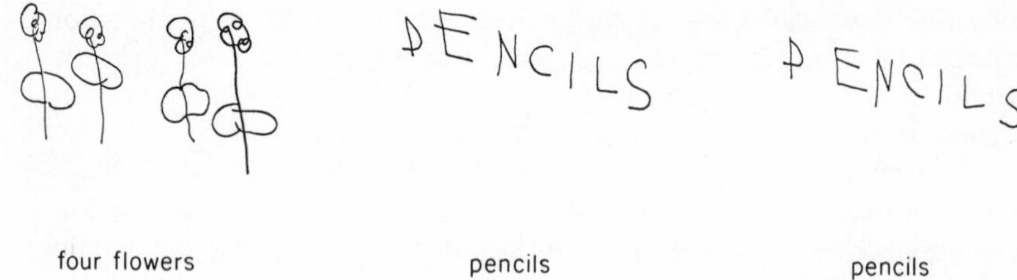

FIGURE 6 Level six: representative responses to three writing tasks. These children refused to write anything for the dictation, on the grounds that they were unable to, but they agreed to draw. This suggests they recognized that writing follows certain conventions

conventions and that not any string of letters will stand for a given word. Copying and rewriting followed the same pattern as children in level five, but some showed surprise that they were asked to copy the same word again.

Only one child was classified as being in level seven (Figure 7). His manner of writing showed that he had already acquired several of the rules of the written language system and had mastered several letter/sound correspondences. He stayed within the limits of what he could write correctly in the free writing task, while in the dictation, although there were deviations from acceptable sequences, the words were identifiable. Children in the preceding levels had shown some awareness, in varying degrees, of the possibility of representing speech graphically, but this child seemed to be aware of the symbolic function of written language, even though he could not be properly termed either a writer or a reader. The level

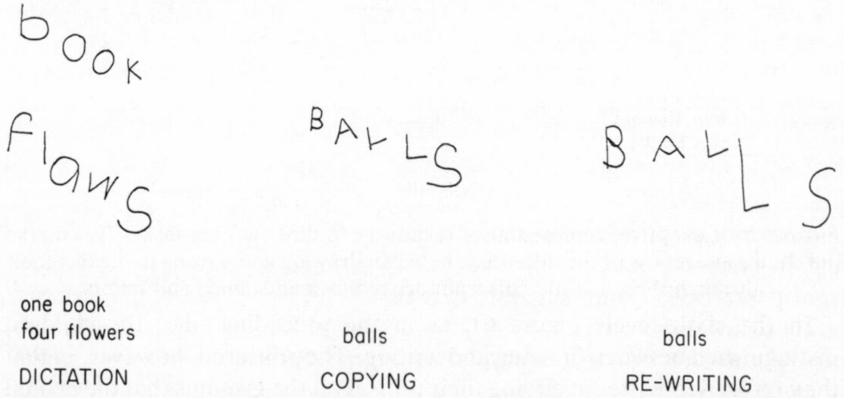

FIGURE 7 Level seven: responses to three writing tasks. This child produced identifiable words and seemed aware of the symbolic nature of written language

following this would be when the child is able to understand the functional aspects well enough to produce very simple written texts. This would show a rcognition of phoneme/grapheme correspondences and a clear notion of second-order symbolism where the written word stands for the spoken word which represents objects and events in the world (Vygotsky, 1962). This is not to say that the child at this stage would be a fluent writer or would know conventional spelling rules. It does mean, however, that the basic functions have been grasped and can be applied in various situations, as for instance the children cited by Chomsky (1979). In principle, it shows an understanding of the role of written language. What characterizes the progression to this level is the developing capacity to use marks, not as an end in themselves, but as a signal for the spoken word. Following this is the ability to differentiate these marks so that these bear a systematic relationship to a conventional set of rules.

Analysis of the data in terms of age showed, as expected, that the younger children are in the lower levels. Most of the children were in the intermediate levels, with only the 5–6 year olds reaching the advanced levels (Table 1). In terms of the tasks, copying and rewriting served most effectively for characterizing the initial levels, while writing and dictation were more significant for the advanced levels.

TABLE 1 Number of subjects as a function of age, and levels of conceptualization of written language

Age	Levels of conceptualization							
	1	2	3	4	5	6	7	
3;0–3;6	1							
3;6–4;0	2	1			1			
4;0–4;6	2	1	1	1				
4;6–5;0			5	3				
5;0–5;6			4	1	2 1			
5;6–6;0			2	3	1	2		
Total	5	+ 2	+ 12	+ 7	+ 3	+ 4	+ 1	= 34

Additional data on this were collected from another group of children of higher socio-economic level. Comparing the original findings with those from this second group suggests that these children reached the different levels of awareness at an earlier age. The difference lay in the rate of progress, not in the quality of the writing performance. In their investigation of children's writing of different words, Ferreiro *et al*. (1979) identified a developmental trend which they analysed into seven levels. These were an initial lack of differentiation between writing and drawing; initial differentiation, with, for example, a letter inserted in the drawing to represent the word; clear differentiation which was reflected in the use of letters or letter-like shapes but there was a global correspondence of spoken/written words; correspondence between parts of the word in its written and spoken forms, without a conventional sound/letter correspondence but with an indication that different marks stand for different parts of the word; using a letter to stand for a syllable (syllabic hypothesis); alphabetic writing which shows regard for the sound value of at least some letters; correct alphabetic writing.

The general trend of the differentiation process appears to have the same fundamental points of progress in the study undertaken by us and that conducted by Ferreiro *et al.*, although the seven levels do not fully coincide with the levels reported here. Some of our subjects were younger than 4 years and showed certain behaviours at quite low levels, whereas our more advanced subjects had not yet achieved correct alphabetic writing. The suggestion of a difference in development as a function of socioeconomic level accords with the conclusions of Ferreiro.

The levels of awareness have been described sequentially to reflect the children's progress towards realizing the symbolic nature of written language and the nature of the code that requires the acquisition of a set of rules. The development from scribbling to drawing, then to pictographic representation and to something we would call *logographic depiction* before the emergence of symbolic marks, supports the suggestions put forward by Luria and Vygotsky (Chapters 10 and 11, this volume). These trends might be differentially affected by factors such as written language representations, as, for instance, alphabetic or non-alphabetic systems or the specific instructional programmes which children receive.

Some of the findings may require further investigation. The distinction between level five and level six, for instance, was made on the basis of children in level six refusing to write. This was interpreted as a recognition that there were specific conventions attached to writing which the children were aware they had not yet mastered. For these children, random letter strings would not suffice as representing a specific word. This reflected a certain inflexibility in relation to the writing task they were being encouraged to perform. Frith and Frith (1980) suggest that flexibility may be a feature of reading acquisition but inflexibility is important for writing. In these terms the refusal to write can be seen as indicating a more advanced level of awareness. On the other hand, children's refusal could be attributable to the interview situation or personality characteristics. More observations are needed to clarify this point.

In this study the children were able to give pictographic representations to the dictated phrases because they all referred to concrete objects. To investigate children's responses to phrases that had no concrete representation, a complementary study was devised. In a similar situation, Luria (1978; Chapter 10 this volume) observed children's attempts to draw something related to the content of what was presented and their use of arbitrary marks to record the phrase. Fourteen new children took part in this study and four categories of writing resulted from the investigation. Children in the first category gave pictographic representations for content phrases, but not for abstract phrases (e.g. I am all right). Most of the children came in the next category. They took down the dictation by writing numbers, letters or letter-like shapes, forming repetitive patterns using similar 'writing' for different words. The phrase was recorded by a few letters, and neither the length of the spoken word nor the number of words in the phrase matched the comparative lengths of the written marks. The third category was marked by a refusal to write; these children protested that they were not able to, although they would always agree to draw the content phrases when asked to do so. In the final category the marks showed a partial correspondence with the sounds of the words, although the children did not record separate strings of letters to stand for separate words.

This complementary study serves to reflect the progressive mastery of the early stages of written language reflected in the first study; the initial inability to distinguish between drawing and writing is replaced by the use of letters or letter-like sequences to depict spoken words. Again, the refusal to write was interpreted as showing the child to be at a more advanced level but the sample size does not allow for a clear interpretation of this performance. The ability to record some sound/letter correspondence and show rudimentary signs of separating words marked the most advanced level. These patterns are equivalent to the fourth through to the seventh stages of the previous study, the age range being narrower in the latter case, which explains the more contracted categorization.

CHILDREN'S NOTIONS OF BASIC METALINGUISTIC TERMS

When children begin to learn to read and write, they encounter a new set of terms. Children are taught, for instance, to copy letters, or to read words or complete sentences. Papandropoulou and Sinclair (1974) found that children of 4–5 years did not conceptualize differences between word, object, or action, thereby showing no distinction between reflecting on and using language. Children from 5 to 7 years would react to the word as a name and confound the word with the act of speaking it. Functional words, such as articles and propositions, were not considered to be words when they were presented in isolation. Over 7 years, children showed a further step in differentiation, treating words as units in terms of meaning, although dependent on the global context in which they occurred. Non-content words were now accepted as words, and also these children were able to produce long and short words in terms of phonological extension without this assessment being biased by the meaning of the word and whether it referred to large or small objects. Children above 8 years considered words to be autonomous units, independent of insertion in a global utterance, and would indicate that words are made up of letters, so referring more to the visual rather than the phonological components of word forms.

Templeton and Spivey (1980) conducted a similar study, adding an explicit attempt to correlate the word conceptualization process with levels of cognitive functioning. Their results replicated, in general terms, those of Papandropoulou and Sinclair (1974). The authors also emphasized that the child's verbal formulations about words are influenced by his experience with print, a point also made by Berthoud-Papandropoulou (1978). Children classified as concrete operational, for example, reflected their perception of print in their answers by saying, 'It's something you write, and you tell something. You spell them.' These remarks about the influence of print, as well as the conclusions drawn from studies by Reid (1966) and Downing (1969) suggest further steps should be taken in the analysis of children's linguistic awareness when they begin to encounter written language.

As part of their investigations, Ferreiro *et al.* (1979) presented subjects with a task in which they had to classify cards with different symbols written on them. These included different types of writing (handwriting, print, etc.), repetitive and non-repetitive patterns, letter-like shapes, etc. The children were instructed to classify the cards in terms of what 'can be read'. In performing the task, the children used several criteria: quantity of symbols; variety of patterns; distinction of letter as opposed to non-letter; distinction of separate as opposed to linked writing (the latter being rejected); and a distinction between letter and number. Children coming from a higher socioeconomic group tended to apply more simultaneous criteria than those in a lower group. Continuing these investigations, we looked at children's responses to different written symbols to examine how, and using what criteria, children identify written 'words', 'letters', and 'numbers'. As, in this study, we were interested in children's ability to detect differences, rather than in their verbalizations, we used a sorting task. This avoided having to depend on children's attempts to express difficult abstract notions (Downing, 1969). This was not merely a perceptual discrimination task, for the emphasis was on the criteria used for the identification of three categories. These were being looked at in purely graphical terms without any relation to spoken equivalents. Nor were the symbols used presented in text in this instance, though this could also be explored. There were forty children, aged from 4 to 6 years, who sorted out cards which they thought had words on, from cards with other things on them. There were twenty cards in all, with different symbols printed on them; real words, isolated letters, strings of vowels, strings of consonants, numbers, and strings of symbols which appear in printed text (e.g. commas, dashes, etc.). After sorting cards with words on, they were asked to select cards which had numbers on. Following this, they were shown pairs of cards, one with a letter on, the other with a word, and they were asked to say which category each belonged to.

Again, the children's responses could be differentiated into progressive categories. The most primitive response reflected strategies probably unrelated to the task. For example, alternation tactics were used, where one card was said to have a word, but not the next, etc., with no account being taken of the symbols on the cards. Another tactic was to say that only the first card had a word on it. A different criterion was to choose any string of symbols (including those which were different from numbers and letters) as words. A third category included children who would only accept written symbols of a certain length as being words. This excluded, therefore, isolated letters, but included numbers and non-letter strings. A fourth group of children included only numbers and letters, either in isolation or in strings. The fifth criterion used was to accept strings of letters independent of the length of the letter string. The final group suggested that selection was made on the basis that words consist of strings of letters of a certain length so cards with only one or a few letters on were rejected. As none of these children was yet able to read, none of them chose only the cards which had real words on them. Some of the children who did not show any ability to distinguish between printed words and other symbols were asked questions about the terms 'word', 'letter', and 'picture' while they were looking at a book. A similar lack of differentiation could be observed in their use of the terms 'picture' and 'word', and also between 'letter' and 'word', although there was no confusion between the terms 'letter' and 'picture'. The choices that the children made in the selection task reflected this confusion of letter and word, with few children making consistent responses. Numbers, on the other hand, were clearly differentiated by 50 per cent of the children. The rest adopted a variety of criteria for making choices, some including all printed symbols, others accepting letter for number, etc.

These findings indicate that, although children use and respond to these metalinguistic terms, close examination shows an undifferentiated application. In this respect these results accord with the findings of Downing (1969), Reid (1969), and Templeton and Spivey (1980). However, they also show that children to have rudimentary abilities in identifying printed symbols and the existence of adequate conceptualizations is not an all-or-nothing matter. With the group we studied, we identified six ways of sorting the cards. The first two might be regarded as qualitatively equivalent; the first reflected strategies unrelated to graphic symbols, while the second showed acceptance of any graphic symbol. Both reflect a lack of concern with discrimination between the variations of printed symbols. Length requirements were the criterion for the third category, while, in the fourth, only certain types of symbols were selected. In the last two categories, which comprised 50 per cent of the children, words were taken as consisting of letters, the only difference between the two groups being the attention paid to the length of the words.

It appears, therefore, that the acceptance of a set of symbols as a word is differentiated developmentally in terms of the shape of the symbols and the string length. While shape is crucial, length is not an effective guide to word identification. Operating on this criteria, children will reject words such as 'I', 'to', 'or', etc., words in fact which are generally function words. As has already been pointed out, children are also likely to reject these as words because they do not refer to observable objects (Templeton and Spivey, 1980).

YOUNG CHILDREN'S AWARENESS OF PUNCTUATION

Almost nothing is known about the acquisition of punctuation skills, or indeed to what extent even adults have or have not mastered the range of conventions and their appropriate use. One interesting example of an unusual early awareness of the need for punctuation in a 7-year-old, however, has been cited by Gleitman *et al.* (1972).

Child (writing):	They call Pennsylvania Pennsylvania because William Penn had a (Penn) in his name.
Mother:	Why did you put those marks round the word 'Penn'?
Child:	Well, I wasn't saying Penn, I was just talking about the word.

Examining the distinction made between letters and punctuation marks, Ferreiro *et al.* (1979) found that the children initially made no distinction at all between the two types of symbols. They then move to making very clear discriminations but with no real notion of the functions of either, particularly the punctuation marks. Children who showed a partial discrimination tended to include the exclamation mark and the question mark in their letter categories.

When children begin to read, sentences in the texts they encounter are demarcated by full stops and capitalization. What children's perceptions of these punctuation marks, and others which they come across, might be, is generally unclear. Their initial writing, particularly narratives which adopt a continuous 'and then' flow of ideas, suggest a random use of a system not fully understood even at the simplest level. In conjunction with the other studies, therefore, we also looked at children's responses to punctuation marks as graphic symbols which they encounter in texts but which they may or may not be aware of. We examined the responses of twenty children, aged 5;9 to 6;8 years, to a copying task and individual interviews. A passage from a story was read to each child, after which he was asked to copy some lines from the text. These lines included several punctuation marks; a full stop, comma, question mark, exclamation mark, and ellipsis points. When the copying was finished the child was asked questions about the spaces between words and the punctuation marks in the passage.

Most of the copies did retain the spaces between words, though some children ignored them either totally or partially. When questioned, most did state the need for spaces as otherwise 'the words would squash up', or 'would get mixed up', or 'you couldn't read them'. Some children suggested that the space signalled the end of a word and the beginning of another. There were a few children who were unable to produce any consistent reason for the existence of spaces between words, and even tried to explain them within the specific content of the story, that is they put them into an immediate contextual situation.

The punctuation marks most frequently reproduced were the question mark and the exclamation mark. Fewer than 50 per cent of the children copied the full stop and comma. The ellipsis points did not appear in any of the copies. Children's responses in the interviews suggested that they had very diffuse ideas about the function of punctuation marks. Most of them thought that the marks were not to be read in the way that words are, but they did not know what their purpose was. The full stop was thought 'to finish the line' or 'to finish the story' so they did have a concept of it terminating something. The other marks, however, were neither labelled nor was their function indicated. When asked to give reasons why the marks were different, most of the children could provide no answer at all. A few characterized the differences in terms of their perceptual features and they described or compared the shapes. Asked whether the marks should be read in different ways, some children answered affirmatively, contradicting their previous assertions, because the question was framed in a different way, that the marks 'are not there to be read'. Some went so far as to suggest that the use of different marks was a matter of preference.

In the children's copies, the marks that were most frequently reproduced were the question mark and exclamation mark, whereas the full stop, whose function seemed to be more or less grasped, was generally omitted. While copying, the children appear to have been dominated by the salient perceptual features of these more obvious punctuation marks, so they were included almost as graphemes. The function of the smaller marks went unrecognized and they were ignored. Copying seemed to be treated as a purely visual representational task while the interview concentrated the children's attention on different aspects of the use of punctuation. This would account for the discrepancy between children's performance when copying and their responses to questions.

RECAPITULATION

Our investigations have centred on examining the development of linguistic awareness in the preliminary stages of literacy. The studies are exploratory and aimed at instigating developmental approaches rather than establishing normative data. These investigations are based on suggestions stemming from Vygotsky and Luria, which can be complemented and advanced by our present knowledge of the development of cognitive and linguistic awareness.

Downing (1979) argues that those who study reading and writing, without taking account of linguistic awareness, are overlooking the fact that the human being does reflect on his own and others' behaviour. To reflect on one's own behaviour disrupts automaticity and modifies action (Piaget, 1976). This slows down performance but provides opportunities for insightful learning. Children beginning to read and write can produce and comprehend spoken language. Our concerns must be to ensure that they have opportunities for learning about language as well as teaching written language skills. Lundberg (1978) reminds us that linguistic awareness is not a well-defined field. There are many issues to be resolved and clarified, and he urges the need to investigate ways of stimulating linguistic awareness and relating it to cognitive development in general.

In broadening the spectrum of this approach, it is worth remembering what Resnick (1979) has to say when analysing the difficulties there are in passing from theory to practice in reading. She criticizes cognitive and learning theorists, arguing that cognitive investigators have tended to study stable states even when undertaking so-called developmental research, although they are now becoming more concerned with the transitional stages of developing competence. Learning investigators, on the other hand, have analysed behavioural change, or events related to it, but have frequently overlooked developmental and cognitive aspects. Because of this, Resnick concludes, we know little about the acquisition and development of reading despite so much research having been done in this area.

The line of analysis undertaken here suggests that considerable attention should be given to exploring the way children's abilities progress, be it gradual or saccadic, in the process of developing written language. The question is not one of attempting to define accuracy or readiness in discerning the stage of when to start to read. Following suggestions made originally by Vygotsky and Luria, as well as from the more recent research discussed in this chapter, the child's preliterate period is enhanced by experiences which encourage the 'drawing of speech', playing with the sounds of language, separating form from content, exploring from the beginning the communicative function of written language. In other words, to develop the child's symbolic awareness in both general and specifically literate, communicative ways.

REFERENCES

Bereiter, C. (1980). Development in Writing. In L. E. Gregg and E. R. Steinberg (eds.),, *Cognitive Processes in Writing*. Lawrence Erlbaum, Hillsdale, N.J.

Berthoud-Papandropoulou, I. (1978). An experimental study of children's ideas about language. In A. Sinclair, R. T. Jarvella, and W. T. M. Levelt (eds.), *The Child's Conception of Language*. Springer Verlag, Berlin.

Bradley, L., and Bryant, P. E. (1979). Independence of reading and spelling in backward and normal children. *Developmental Medicine and Child Neurology,* **21**, 504–514.

Bryant, P. E., and Bradley, L. (1980). Why children sometimes write words which they do not read. In U. Frith (ed.), *Cognitive Processes in Spelling*. Academic Press, London.

Chall, J. S. (1967). *Learning to Read: the Great Debate*. McGraw Hill, New York.

Chomsky, C. (1979). Approaching reading through invented spelling. In L. B. Resnick and P. A. Weaver (eds.), *Theory and Practice of Early Reading*. Lawrence Erlbaum, Hillsdale, N.J.

Downing, J. (1969). How children think about reading. *Reading Teacher,* **23**, 217–230.

Downing, J. (1979). *Reading and Reasoning*. Chambers, Bath.

Ferreiro, E., Palacio, M. G., Guajardo, E., Rodriquez, B., Vega, A., and Cantu, R. L. (1979). *El nino preescolar y su comprension del sistema de escritura*. Organizacion de los Estados Americanos, Mexico.

Frith, U. (1980). Unexpected spelling problems. In U. Frith (ed.), *Cognitive Processes in Spelling*. Academic Press, London.

Frith, U., and Frith, C. (1980). Relationships between reading and spelling. In J. F. Kavanagh and R. L. Venezky (eds.), *Orthography, Reading and Dyslexia*. University Park Press, Baltimore.

Gleitman, L. R., Gleitman, H., and Shipley, E. F. (1972). The emergence of the child as grammarian. *Cognition,* **1**, 137–164.

Hakes, D. T. (1980). *The Development of Metalinguistic Abilities in Children*. Springer-Verlag, Berlin.

Liberman I. Y., and Shankweiler, D. (1979). Speech, the alphabet and teaching to read. In L. B. Resnick and P. A. Weaver (eds.), *Theory and Practice of Early Reading*, vol. 2. Lawrence Erlbaum, Hillsdale, N.J.

Lundberg, I. (1978). Aspects of linguistic awareness related to reading. In A. Sinclair, R. J. Jarvella, and W. J. M. Levelt (eds.), *The Child's Conception of Language*. Springer-Verlag, Berlin.

Luria, A. R. (1978). The development of writing in the child. In M. Cole (ed.), *The Selected Writings of A. R. Luria*. M. E. Sharp Inc., New York.

Papandropoulou, I., and Sinclair, H. (1974). What is a word? Experimental study of children's ideas on grammar. *Human Development,* **17**, 241–258.

Piaget, J. (1976). *The Grasp of Consciousness – Action and Concept in the Young Child*. Routledge & Kegan Paul, London.

Reid, J. F. (1966). Learning to think about reading. *Educational Research,* **9**, 56–62.

Resnick, L. B. (1979). Toward a usable psychology of reading instruction. In L. B. Resnick and P. A. Weaver (eds.), *Theory and Practice of Early Reading*. Lawrence Erlbaum, Hillsdale, N. J.

Rozin, P., Bressman, B., and Taft, M. (1974). Do children understand the basic relationship between speech and writing? The mow-motocycle test. *Journal of Reading Behavior,* **6**, 327–334.

Templeton, S., and Spivey, E. M. (1980). The concept of word in young children as a function of level of cognitive development. *Research in the Teaching of English,* **14**, 265–278

Vygotsky, L. S. (1962). *Thought and Language*. MIT Press, Cambridge, Mass.

Vygotsky, L. S. (1978). The prehistory of writing. In M. Cole, V. John-Steiner, S. Scribner, and E. Souberman (eds.), *Mind in Society – The Development of Higher Psychological Process*. Harvard University Press, Cambridge, Mass.

The Psychology of Written Language
Edited by M. Martlew

CHAPTER 10

The Development of Writing in the Child

ALEXANDRIA R. LURIA

I

The history of writing in the child begins long before a teacher first puts a pencil in the child's hand and shows him how to form letters.

The moment a child begins to write his first school exercises in his notebook is not actually the first stage in the development of writing. The origins of his process go far back into the pre-history of the development of the higher forms of a child's behavior; we can even say that when a child enters school, he has already acquired a wealth of skills and abilities that will enable him to learn to write within a relatively short time.

If we just stop to think about the surprising rapidity with which the child learns this extremely complex technique, which has thousands of years of culture behind it, it will be evident that this could come about only because during the first years of his development, before reaching school age, a child has already learned and assimilated a number of techniques leading up to writing that have already prepared him and made it immeasurably easier for him to grasp the concept and technique of writing. Moreover, we may reasonably assume that even before reaching school age, during this individual 'prehistory', as it were, the child has already developed a number of primitive techniques of his own that are similar to what we call writing and perhaps even fulfill similar functions, but that are lost as soon as the school provides the child with the culturally elaborated, standard, and economical system of signs, but that these earlier techniques served as necessary stages along the way. The psychologist is faced with the following important and intriguing problem: to delve deeply into this early period of child development, to ferret out the pathways along which writing developed in its prehistory, to spell out the circumstances that made writing possible for the child and the factors that provided the motive forces of this development, and, finally, to describe the stages through which the development of the child's primitive writing technique pass.

The developmental psychologist therefore concentrates his attention on the preschool period in the child's life. We begin where we think we shall find the beginnings of writing, and leave off where educational psychologists usually begin: the moment when the child begins to learn to write.

If we are able to unearth this 'prehistory' of writing, we shall have acquired a valuable tool for teachers, namely, knowledge of what the child was able to do before entering school, knowledge on which they can draw in teaching their pupils to write.

II

The best way to study this prehistory of writing and the various tendencies and factors involved in it is to decribe the stages we observe as a child develops his ability to write and the factors that enable him to pass from one stage to another, higher stage.

In contrast to a number of other psychological functions, writing may be described as a culturally mediated function. The first, most fundamental condition required for a child to be able to 'write down' some notion, concept, or phrase is that some particular stimulus or cue, which in itself has nothing to do with this idea, concept, or phrase, is employed as an *auxiliary sign* whose perception causes the child to recall the idea, etc., to which it referred. Writing therefore presupposes the ability to use some cue (e.g., a line, a spot, a point) as a functional auxiliary sign with no sense or meaning in itself but only as an auxiliary operation. For a child to be able to write or note something, two conditions must be fulfilled. First, the child's relations with the things around him must be differentiated, so that everything he encounters will fall into two main groups: either things that represent some interest of the child's, things he would like to have, or with which he plays, or instrumental objects, things that play only a utilitarian, or instrumental role and have sense only as aids for acquiring some object or achieving some goal and therefore have only functional significance for him. Second, the child must be able to control his own behavior by means of these aids, in which case they already function as cues he himself invokes. Only when the child's relationships with the world around him have become differentiated in this way, when he has developed this functional relationship with things, can we say that the complex intellectual forms of human behavior have begun to develop.

The use of material tools, the rudiments of this complex, mediated adaptation to the external world, is observable in apes. In his classic experiments Köhler (1917) demonstrated that under certain conditions things may acquire a functional significance for apes and begin to play an instrumental role. When an ape takes a long stick to get a banana, it is quite obvious that the banana and the stick are psychologically of different orders for the animal: whereas the banana is a goal, an object toward which the animal's behavior is directed, the stick has meaning only in relation to the banana, i.e., throughout the entire operation it plays only a functional role. The animal begins to adapt to the given situation not directly, but with the aid of certain tools. The number of such instrumental objects is still few, and in the ape their complexity is minimal; but as behavior becomes more complex, this instrumental inventory also becomes richer and more complex, so that by the time we reach man, the number of such objects playing an auxiliary functional role in the life of a human being, who is a cultural animal, is enormous.

At a certain stage in evolution, external acts, handling objects of the external world, and internal acts as well, i.e., the utilization of psychological functions in the strict sense, begin to take shape indirectly. A number of techniques for organizing internal psychological operations are developed to make their performance more efficient and productive. The direct, natural use of such techniques is replaced by a cultural mode, which relies on certain instrumental, auxiliary devices. Instead of trying to size up quantity visually, man learns to use an auxiliary system of counting; and instead of mechanically committing things to, and retaining them in, memory, he writes them down. In each case these acts presuppose that some object or device will be used as an aid in these behavioral processes, that is, that this object or device will play a functional auxiliary role. Such an auxiliary technique used for psychological purposes is writing, which is the functional use of lines, dots, and other signs to remember and transmit ideas and concepts. Samples of florid, embellished, pictographic writing show how varied the items enlisted as aids to retaining and transmitting ideas, concepts and relations may be.

Experiments have shown that the development of such functional devices serving psychological ends takes place much later than the acquisition and use of external tools to perform external tasks. Köhler (1917] attempted to set up some special experiments with apes to determine whether an ape could use certain signs to express certain meanings, but was unable to find any such rudiments of 'record keeping' in apes. He gave the animals paint, and they learned how to paint the walls, but they never once tried to use the lines they drew as signs to express something. These lines were a game for the animals; as objects they were ends, never means. Thus, devices of this sort develop at a much later stage of evolution.

In what follows we shall decribe our efforts to trace the development of the first signs of the emergence of a functional relation to lines and scribbles in the child and his first use of such lines, etc., to express meanings; in doing so we shall hopefully be able to shed some light on the prehistory of human writing.

III

The prehistory of writing can be studied in the child only experimentally, and to do this the skill must first be brought into being. The subject must be a child who has not yet learned to write; he must be put into a situation that will require him to use certain external manual operations similar to writing to depict or remember an object. In such a situation we should be able to determine whether he has acquired the ability to relate to some device that has been given to him as a sign or whether his relation to it still remains 'absolute', i.e., unmediated, in which case he will be unable to discover and use its functional, auxiliary aspect.

In the ideal case the psychologist might hope to force a child to 'invent' signs by placing him in some difficult situation. If his efforts are more modest, he can give the child some task that is easier for the child to cope with and watch the successive stages the child goes through in assimilating the technique of writing.

In our preliminary experiments we followed this second course. Our method was actually very simple: we took a child who did not know how to write and gave him the task of remembering a certain number of sentences presented to him. Usually this number exceeded the child's mechanical capacity to remember. Once the child realized that he was unable to remember the number of words given him in the task, we gave him a sheet of paper and told him to jot down or 'write' the words we presented. Of course, in most cases the child was bewildered by our suggestion He would tell us that he did not know how to write, that he could not do it. We would point out to him that adults wrote things down when they had to remember something and then, exploiting the child's natural tendency toward purely external imitation, we suggested that he try to contrive something himself and write down what we would tell him. Our experiment usually began after this, and we would present the child with several (four or five) series of six or eight sentences that were quite simple, short, and unrelated to one another.

Thus, we ourselves gave the child a device whose intrinsic technique was unfamiliar to him and observed to what extent he was able to handle it and to what extent the piece of paper, the pencil, and the scribbles the child made on the paper ceased being simple objects that appealed to him, playthings, as it were, and became a tool, a means for achieving some end, which in this case was remembering a number of ideas presented to him. We think our approach here was correct and productive. Drawing on the child's penchant for imitation, we gave him a device to use that was familiar to him in its outward aspects but whose internal structure was unknown and strange. This allowed us to observe, in its purest form, how a child adapts spontaneously to some device, how he learns how it works and to use it to master a new goal.

We assumed that we would be able to observe all the stages in a child's relationship to this device, which was still alien to him, from the mechanical, purely external imitative copying of an adult's hand movements in writing to the intelligent mastery of this technique.

By giving the child merely the external aspects of the technique to work with, we were able to observe a whole series of little *inventions* and discoveries he made, within the technique itself, that enabled him gradually to learn to use this new cultural tool.

It was our intention to provide a psychological analysis of the development of writing from its origins and, within a short period, to follow the child's transition from the primitive, external forms of behavior to complex, cultural forms. Let us now examine our results. We shall try to describe how children of different ages responded to this complex task and to trace the stages of development of writing in the child from its beginnings.

IV

Not surprisingly, at the outset we encountered a problem that could have presented a considerable obstacle. It turned out that 4–5 year olds were totally unable to understand our instructions. On closer analysis, however, we found that this 'negative' finding actually reflected a very essential and fundamental charcteristic of this age group: 3, 4, and 5 year old children (it was impossible to fix a definite dividing line; these age demarcations depend on a multitude of dynamic conditions having to do with the child's level of cultural development, his environment, etc.) were still unable to relate to writing as a tool, or means. They grasped the outward form of writing and saw how adults accomplished it; they were even able to imitate adults; but they themselves were completely unable to learn the specific psychological attributes any act must have if it is to be used as a tool in the service of some end.

If we asked such a child to note (or write) on paper the sentences presented to him, in many instances the child would not even refuse with any special insistence, simply referring to his inability to perform the task.

Little Vova N. (5 years old), for the first time in our laboratory, in response to the request to remember and write down the sentence 'Mice have long tails', immediately took a pencil and 'wrote' a number of scrawls on the paper

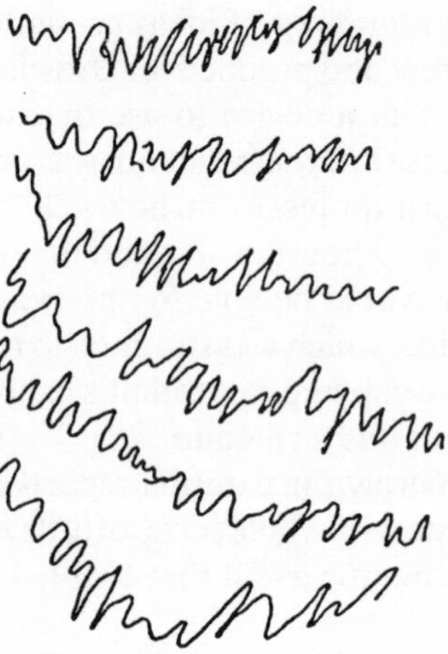

FIGURE 1 Vova N., aged 5 years, 'writing' the dictated sentence, 'Mice have long tails'

(Figure 1). When the experimenter asked him what they were, he said, quite confidently, 'That's how you write.'

The act of writing is, in this case, only externally associated with the task of noting a specific word; it is purely imitative. The child is interested only in 'writing like grown-ups'; for him the act of writing is not a means of remembering, of representing some meaning, but an act that is sufficient in its own right, an act of play. But such an act is by no means always seen as an aid to helping the child later remember the sentence. The connection between the child's scrawls and the idea it is meant to represent is purely external. This is especially evident in cases in which the 'writing' is sharply and noticeably divorced from the sentence to be written and begins to play a completely independent and self-sufficient role.

We frequently observed one peculiar phenomenon in small children: a child whom we had asked to write down the sentences we gave him would not limit himself to ordinary 'writing down', as in the case just described; he would sometimes invert the normal order of writing and begin to write without hearing out what we had to say.

In these cases the function of 'writing' had become dissociated from the material to be written; understanding neither its meaning nor its mechanism, the child used writing in a purely external and imitative way, assimilating its outer form, but not employing it in the right way. Here is a graphic example from an experiment with Lena L., 4 years old. Lena was given some sentences and told to remember them, and to do this she had to 'write them down'. Lena listened to the first three sentences and after each began to write down her scribbles, which were the same in each case, i.e., they were indistinguishable from one another. Before the fourth sentence I said to her: 'Listen, this time write, ...'. Lena, without waiting until I finished, began to write. The same thing happened before the fifth sentence.

The results are the undifferentiated scrawls in Figure 2, characteristic of this phase of development. There are two points that stand out especially clearly here: 'writing' is dissociated from its immediate objective, and lines are used in a purely external way; the child is unaware of their functional

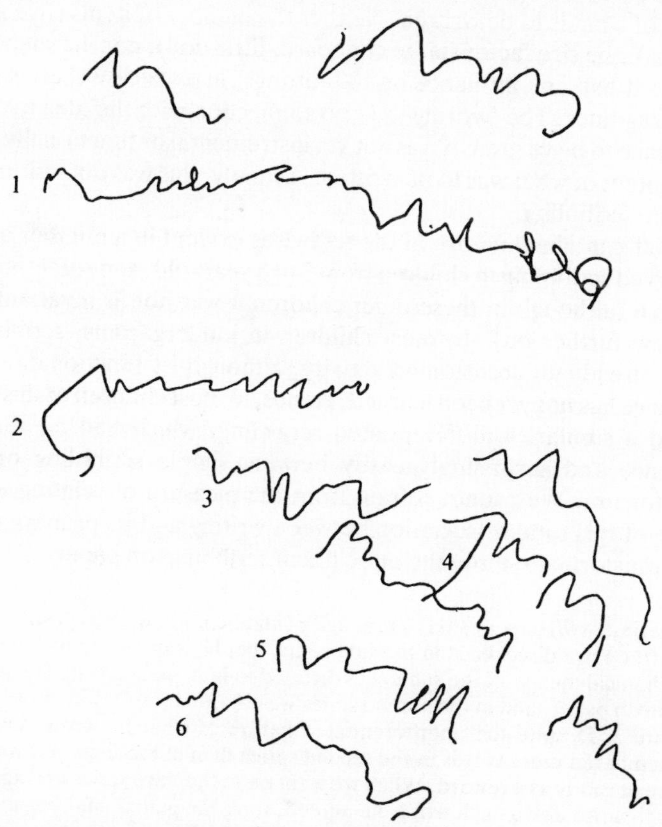

FIGURE 2 Lena L., aged 4 years, 'writing' from dictated sentences:
1. There are five pencils on the table.
2. There are two plates.
3. There are many trees in the forest.
4. There is a column in the yard.
5. There is a large cupboard (written prematurely)
6. The little doll (written prematurely)

significance as auxiliary signs. That is why the act of writing can be so completely dissociated from the dictated sentence; not understanding the principle underlying writing, the child takes its external form and thinks he is quite able to write before he even knows what he must write. But a second point is also clear from this example: the child's scrawls bear no relationship to the meaningful sentence dictated to him. We have deliberately presented an example with quite explicit features that would be reflected in the mere outward form of writing if only the child understood the actual purpose and mechanism of writing things down, and its necessary connection with the meaning of what is to be written. Neither the number of items (five pencils, two plates), the size factor (large cupboard, little doll), nor the shape of the object itself had any influence on the jottings; in each case there were the same zigzag lines. The 'writing' had no connection with the idea evoked by the sentence to be written; it was not yet instrumental or functionally related to the content of what was to be written. Actually, this was not writing at all, but simple scribbling.

This self-contained nature of the scrawls is evident in a number of cases: we observed scribbling in children from 3 to 5 years old, and sometimes even as old as 6 (although in these older children it was not as invariant, as we shall show further on). In most children in kindergartens, scribbling on paper is already an accustomed activity, although its functional, auxiliary significance has not yet been learned. Hence, in most children of this age, we observed a similar, undifferentiated scrawling, which had no functional significance and surprisingly easily became simple scribbling on paper merely for fun. We cannot refrain from the pleasure of relating a typical example of this total dissociation between writing and its primary purpose and its transformation into the mere fun of scribbling on paper.

Experiment 9/III, series III, Yura, age 6 (middle kindergarten group).

After Yura discovered in the first series that he was unable to remember by mechanical means all the sentences dictated to him, we suggested he note them down on paper; and in the second series we obtained results like those shown in Figure 2. Despite the undifferentiated nature of what he wrote down, Yura remembered more words in the second series than in the first, and was given a piece of candy as a reward. When we went on to the third series and again asked him to write down each word, he agreed, took the pencil, and began (without listening to the end of one sentence) to scribble. We did not stop him, and he continued to scribble until he had covered the whole page with scrawls that bore no relation to his initial purpose, which was to remember the sentences. These scrawls are shown in Figure 3. Everything on the right side (A) was done before the sentences were presented; not until later, after we stopped him, did he begin to 'write down' the sentences shown on the left side (Nos. 1–7).

Complete lack of comprehension of the mechanism of writing, a purely external relation to it, and a rapid shift from 'writing' to self-contained fun

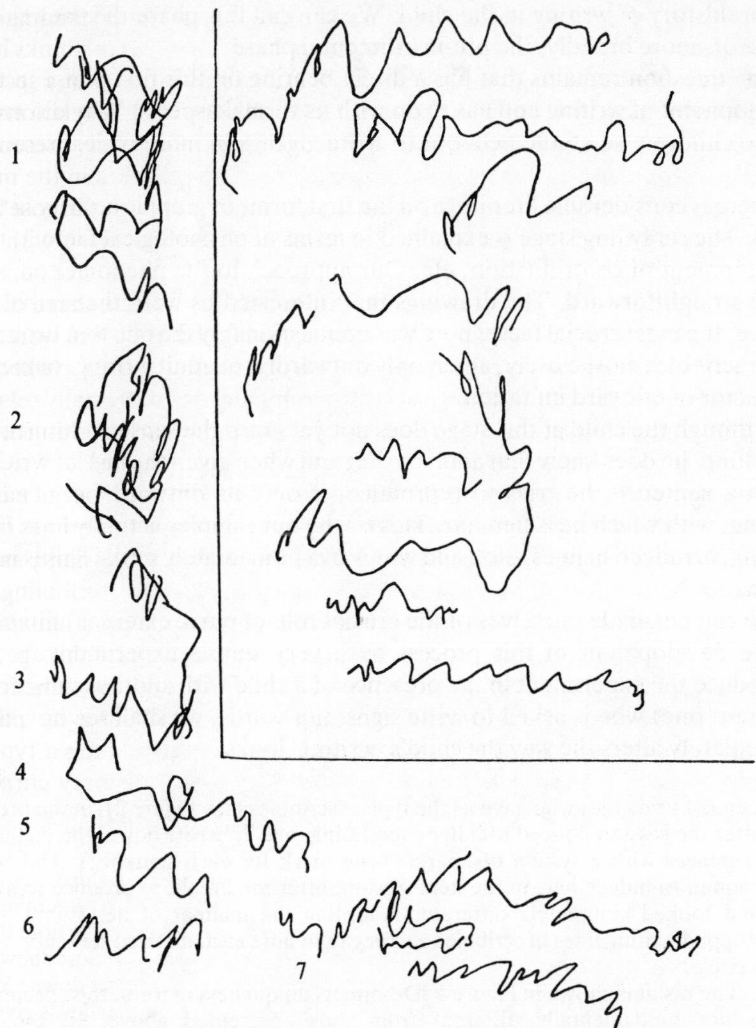

Figure 3 Yura, aged 6 years, 'writing' from dictated sentences;
1. There are many stars in the sky.
2. There is one moon.
3. I have thirty teeth.
4. Two hands and two legs.
5. A large tree.
6. The car runs.
The scrawls within the border were written before the dictation

bearing no functional relation to writing are characteristic of the first stage in the prehistory of writing in the child. We can call this phase the prewriting phase or, more broadly, the pre-instrumental phase.

One question remains that has a direct bearing on this first phase in the development of writing and has to do with its formal aspects: Why did most of the children we studied choose to write zigzags in more or less straight lines?

There is considerable literature on the first forms of graphic activity in the child. The scrawling stage is explained in terms of physiological factors, the development of co-ordination, etc. Our approach to the phenomenon was more straightforward. The drawings that interested us were the scribbles. Hence, the most crucial factor here was unquestionably the one that brought these scribbles most closely, albeit only outwardly, to adult writing, namely, the factor of outward imitation.

Although the child at this stage does not yet grasp the sense and function of writing, he does know that adults write; and when given the task of writing down a sentence, he tries to reproduce, if only its outward form, adult writing, with which he is familiar. This is why our samples actually look like writing, arranged in lines, etc., and why Vova immediately said, 'This is how you write.'

We can persuade ourselves of the crucial role of pure, external imitation in the development of this process by a very simple experiment: if we reproduce the experiment in the presence of a child with another subject (a different one) who is asked to write signs, not words, we shall see how this immediately alters the way the child's 'writing' looks.

> Lena, 4 years old, who gave us the typical scribbles (see Figure 2), in the break after the session noticed that her friend Lina, age 7, 'wrote down' the dictated sentences with a system of 'marks' (one mark for each sentence). This was enough to induce her, in the next session, after the break, to produce scrawls that looked completely different. Adopting the manner of her friend, she stopped writing lines of scribbles and began to note each dictated sentence with a circle.
>
> The result is shown in Figure 4. Despite its uniqueness of form, this specimen is not fundamentally different from those presented above. It, too, is undifferentiated, random, and purely externally associated with the task of writing; and it, too, is imitative. Just as in the previous examples, the child was unable to link the circles she drew with the ideas conveyed in the sentence and then to use this circle as a functional aid. This phase is the first phase of direct acts, the phase of pre-instrumental, precultural, primitive, imitative acts.

V

Does 'writing' help a child, at this stage, to remember the meaningful message of a dictated sentence? We can answer 'no' in almost all cases, and

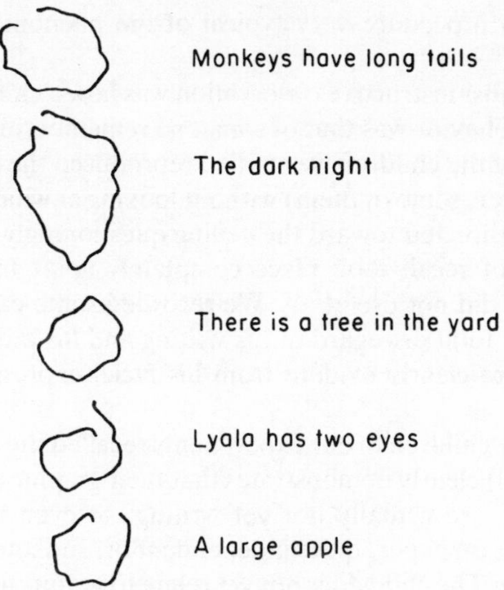
Monkeys have long tails
The dark night
There is a tree in the yard
Lyala has two eyes
A large apple

FIGURE 4 Lena, aged 4 years, 'writing' from dictated sentences

that is the characteristic feature of this prewriting stage. The child's writing does not yet serve a mnemonic function, as will become obvious if we examine the 'sentences' written by the child after dictation. In most cases the child remembered fewer sentences after 'writing' them down in this way than he did without writing; so writing did not help, but actually hindered, memory. Indeed, the child made no effort to remember at all; for in relying on his 'writing', he was quite convinced that it would do his remembering for him.

Let us, however, take a case in which the child remembered several sentences even in a writing experiment. If we observe how these sentences were recalled, we shall see clearly that 'writing' had nothing at all to do with this remembering, that it took place independently of the child's graphic efforts.

The first thing a psychologist studying memory notices is that a child mobilizies all the devices of direct mechanical memory, none of which are found in reading. The child fixes and recalls; he does not record and read: some of his jottings are quite beside the point, and without effect. In our experiments we frequently observed that a child would repeat the sentence after writing it down, to nail it down, as it were; when we asked him to recall what he had written, he did not 'read' his jottings from the beginning, but would go right to the last sentences, to catch them while they were fresh in his memory – a procedure very typical of the phenomenon of making a mental note.

Finally, the most instructive observation was how a child would behave in recalling. His behavior was that of someone remembering, not of someone reading. Most of the children we studied reproduced the sentences dictated to them (or rather, some of them) without looking at what they had written, with their gaze directed toward the ceiling questioningly; quite simply, the entire process of recall took place completely apart from the scribbles, which the child did not use at all. We recorded some cases of this sort on film; the child's total disregard of his writing and his purely direct form of remembering are clearly evident from his facial expressions recorded on film.

Thus, the way children in our experiments recalled the dictated sentences (if they did at all) clearly demonstrates that their graphic efforts at this stage of development are actually not yet writing, or even a graphic aid, but merely drawings on paper, quite independent of, and unrelated to, the task of remembering. The child does not yet relate to writing as a tool of memory at this stage of development. This is why in our experiments the children almost always cut a poor figure: of a total of six to eight sentences, most of which they were able to remember by mechanical means, they could remember only two or three at most if asked to write them down, which indicates that if a child has to rely on writing without the ability to use it, the efficiency of memory is considerably reduced.

Nevertheless, our findings also include some cases that a first glance are rather surprising in that they are completely at variance with all we have just described. A child would produce the same meaningless scribbles and lines, yet he would still be able to recall perfectly all the sentences he had written down. Moreover, as we observed him, we had the impression that he was actually making use of his writing. We checked this and indeed discovered that these scribblings actually were more than just simple scrawls, that they were in some sense real writing. The child would read a sentence, pointing to quite specific scrawls, and was able to show without error and many times in succession which scribble signified which of the dictated sentences. Writing was still undifferentiated in its outward appearance, but the child's relation to it had completely changed: from a self-contained motor activity, it had been transformed into a memory-helping sign. The child had begun to associate the dictated sentence with his undifferentiated scribble, which had begun to serve the auxiliary function of a sign. How did this come about?

In some sessions we noted that the children would arrange their scribblings in some pattern other than straight lines. For instance, they would put one scribble in one corner of the paper and another in another, and in so doing begin to associate the dictated sentences with their notations; this association was further reinforced by the pattern in which the notations were arranged, and the children would declare quite emphatically that the scribble in one corner meant 'cow', or that another at the top of the paper meant 'chimney sweeps are black'. Thus, these children were in the process of creating a system of technical memory aids, similar to the writing of primitive peoples. In itself no scribble meant anything; but its position, situation, and relation to the other scribbles, i.e., all these factors together, imparted to it its function as a technical memory aid. Here is an example:

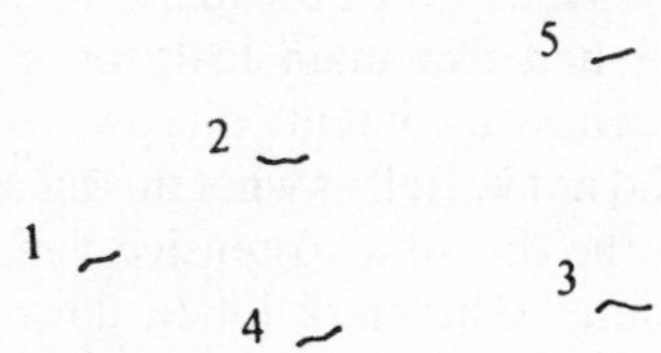

FIGURE 5 Brina, aged 5 years, 'writing' from dictated sentences:

1. Cow.
2. A cow has legs and a tail.
3. Yesterday evening it rained.
4. Chimney sweeps are black.
5. Give me three candles.

Brina, age 5 (first time in our laboratory), was asked to write down a number of sentences dictated to her. She quickly learned how to proceed and after each word (or sentence) had been dictated, she would make her scribble. The results are shown in Figure 5. One might think that our little subject had made these marks without any connection with the task of remembering the dictated sentences, just as most of the children discussed above. But not to our surprise, she not only recalled all the dictated sentences (true, there were not many, only five) but also correctly located each sentence, pointing to a scribble and saying: 'This is a cow' or 'A cow has four legs and a tail', or 'It rained yesterday evening', etc. In other words, she recalled the dictated sentences by 'reading' them. It is clear that Brina understood the task and employed a primitive form of writing, writing by means of topographical markings. These markings were quite stable; when she was questioned directly, she did not mix them up, but rigorously distinguished one from the other, knowing exactly what each one meant.

This is the first form of 'writing', in the proper sense. The actual inscriptions are still undifferentiated, but the functional relation to writing is unmistakable. Because the writing is undifferentiated, it is variable. After using it once, a child may a few days later have forgotten it, and revert back to mechanical scribbling unrelated to the task. But this is the first rudiment of what is later to become writing in the child; in it we see for the first time the psychological elements from which writing will take shape. The child now recalls the material by associating it with a specific mark rather than just mechanically, and this mark will remind him of the particular sentence and help him to recall it. All this and the presence of certain techniques of undifferentiated topographical writing in primitive peoples spurred our interest in this undifferentiated technical aid to memory, the precursor of real writing.

What role actually is played by the little mark the child makes on a piece of paper? We saw that it had two main features: it organized the child's behavior, but did not yet have a content of its own; it indicated the presence of some meaning, but did not yet tell us what this meaning was. We could say that this first sign plays the role of an ostensive sign or, in other words, the primary sign to 'take note'. The mark jotted down by the child creates a certain set and serves as an additional cue that some sentences have been dictated, but provides no hints as to how to discover the content of those sentences.

An experiment demonstrated that this interpretation of a primary sign was unquestionably the right one. We can describe a number of cases to prove this. A child at this stage of development in his relationship to a sign tries to use the marks he has made to guide him in recalling. Frequently, these 'sentences' have nothing in common with those dictated, but the child will formally fulfill his assignment and for each cue find the 'matching word'.

> Here is an example of this relation of the child's to a primitive sign (we omit the actual drawing as it is very similar in structure to the preceding illustrations). We gave a child 4 years, 8 months old a series of words:
> 'picture–book–girl–locomotive'.
>
> The child noted each of these words with a mark. When she had finished her writing, we asked her to read it. Pointing to each mark in succession, the girl 'read':
> 'girl–doll–bed–trunk'.
>
> We see that the words recalled by the child have nothing in common with the words given; only the number of words recalled was correct; their content was determined completely by the emotional sets and interests of the child (R. E. Levin's experiment).

This illustration enables us to get to the psychological structure of such a primary graphic sign. It is clear that a primary, undifferentiated, graphic sign is not a symbolic sign, which discloses the meaning of what has been written down; nor can it yet be called an instrumental sign in the full sense of the word, as it does not lead the child back to the content of what was written down. We should rather say that it is only a simple *cue* (although one artificially created by the child) that conditionally evokes certain speech impulses. These impulses, however, do not necessarily direct the child back to the situation he has 'recorded'; they can only trigger certain processes of association whose content, as we have seen, may be determined by completely different conditions having nothing at all to do with the given cue.

We might describe the functional role of such a cue as follows:

Let us imagine the process of writing (alphabetic, pictographic, or conventionally agreed on) in an adult. A certain content A is written with the symbol X. When a reader looks at this symbol, he immediately thinks of the content A. The symbol X is an instrumental device to direct the reader's attention to the initial written content. The formula:

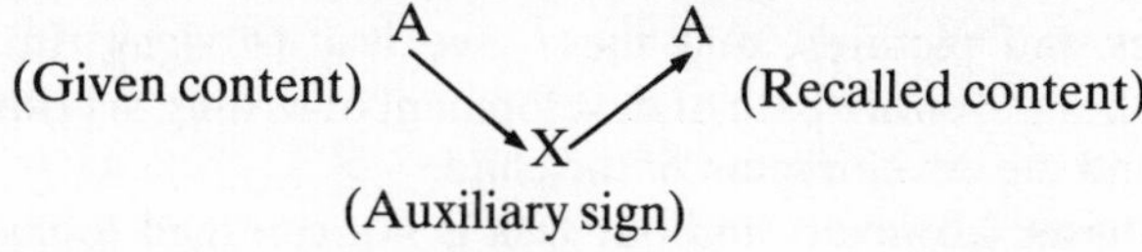

is the best expression of the structure of such a process.

The situation with respect to a primitive mark such as we have just been discussing is completely different. It only signals that *some* content written down by means of it exists, but does not lead us to it; it is only a cue evoking some (associative) reaction in the subject. We actually do not have in it the complex instrumental structure of an act, and it may be described by the following formula:

(Given content) A→X
X→N (Recalled association)
(Primitive mark)

where N may not have any relation to the given content A, or, of course, to the mark X.

Instead of an instrumental act, which uses X to revert attention back to A, we have here two direct acts: (1) the mark on the paper, and (2) the response to the mark as a cue. Of course, in psychological terms this is not yet writing, but only the forerunner of it, in which the most rudimentary and necessary conditions for its development are forged (Werner, 1926).

VI

We have already discussed the insufficient stability of this phase of undifferentiated, memory-helping writing. Having taken the first step along the path of culture with it, and having linked, for the first time, the recalled object with some sign, the child must now go on to the second step: he must differentiate this sign and make it really express a specific content; he must create the rudiments of literacy, in the truest sense of the word. Only then will the child's writing become stable and independent of the number of elements written down; and memory will have gained a powerful tool, capable of broadening its scope enormously. Finally, only under these conditions will any steps forward be taken along the way toward objectivization of writing, i.e., toward transforming it from subjectively coordinated markings into signs having an objective significance that is the same for everyone.

Our experiments warrant the assertion that the development of writing in the child proceeds along a path we can describe as the transformation of an undifferentiated scrawl into a differentiated sign. Lines and scribbles are replaced by figures and pictures, and these give way to signs. In this sequence of events lies the entire path of development of writing in both the history of nations and the development of the child.

We are psychologists, however, and our task is not confined to simple observation and confirmation of the sequence of individual phases: we should like also to describe the conditions that produce this sequence of events and to determine empirically the factors that facilitate for the child the transition from a stage of undifferentiated writing to the level of meaningful signs expressing a content.

Actually, one can say there are two pathways by which differentiation of the primary sign may take place in a child. On the one hand, the child may try to depict the content given him without going beyond the limits of arbitrary, imitative scrawling; on the other hand, he may make the transition to a form of writing that depicts content, to the recording of an idea, i.e., to pictograms. Both paths presuppose some jump that must be made by the child as he replaces the primary, undifferentiated sign with another, differentiated one. This jump presupposes a little invention, whose psychological significance is interesting in that it alters the very psychological function of the sign by transforming the primary sign, which merely establishes ostensively the existence of a thing, into another kind of a sign that reveals a particular content. If this differentiation is accomplished successfully, it transforms a sign-stimulus into a sign-symbol, and a qualitative leap is thereby effected in the development of complex forms of cultural behavior.

We are able to follow the elementary inventions of a child along both these paths. Let us examine each of them separately.

The first signs of differentiation we were able to observe in the small child occurred after several repetitions of our experiment. By the third or fourth session, a child of 4 or 5 years would begin to link the word (or phrase) given him and the nature of the mark with which he distinguished the word. This meant that he did not mark all the words in the same way; the first differentiation, as far as we could judge, involved reflection of the rhythm of the phrase uttered in the rhythm of the graphic sign.

The child quite early begins to show a tendency to write down short words or phrases with short lines and long words or phrases with a large number of scribbles. It is difficult to say whether this is a conscious act, the child's own invention, as it were. We are inclined to see other, more primitive mechanisms at work in this. Indeed, this rhythmic differentiation is by no means always stable. A child who has written a series of sentences given him in a 'differentiated' manner in the next session (or for that matter even in the same session) will revert to primitive undifferentiated writing. This suggests that in this rhythmically reproductive writing some more primitive mechanisms, not an organized and conscious device, are at work.

But what are these mechanisms? Are we not dealing here with simple coincidence, which leads us to see a pattern where there is only the play of chance?

An example drawn from one of our experiments may serve as material for a concrete analysis of this problem.

> Lyuse N., age 4 years, 8 months. We gave her a number of words: mama, cat, dog, doll. She wrote them all down with the same scrawls, which in no way differed from one another. The situation changed considerably, however, when we also gave her long sentences along with individual words: (1) girl; (2) cat; (3) Zhorzhik is skating; (4) Two dogs are chasing the cat; (5) There are many books in the room, and the lamp is burning; (6) bottle; (7) ball; (8) The cat is sleeping; (9) We play all day, then we eat dinner, and then we go out to play again.
>
> In the writing the child now produced, the individual words were represented by little lines, but the long sentences were written as complicated squiggles; and the longer the sentence, the longer was the squiggle written to express it.

Thus, the process of writing, which began with an undifferentiated, purely imitative, graphic accompaniment to the presented words, after a period of time was transformed into a process that on the surface indicated that a connection had been made between the graphic production and the cue presented. The child's graphic production ceased being a simple accompaniment to a cue and became its reflection – albeit in very primitive form. It began to reflect merely the rhythm of the presented phrase: single words began to be written as single lines, and sentences as long, complicated scribbles, sometimes reflecting the rhythm of the presented sentence.

The variable nature of this writing suggests, however, that perhaps this is no more than a simple *rhythmic* reflection of the cue presented to the subject. Psychologically, it is quite comprehensible that every stimulus perceived by a subject has its own rhythm and through it exerts a certain effect on the activity of the subject, especially if the aim of that activity is linked to the presented stimulus and must reflect and record it. The primary effect of this rhythm also produces that first rhythmic differentiation in the child's writing that we were able to note in our experiments.

Below we shall discuss the very intimate relationship that we believe exists between graphic production and mimicry. Functionally, graphic activity is a rather complex system of cultural behavior, and in terms of its genesis may be regarded as expressiveness materialized in fixed form. It is just this sort of reflection of mimicry we see in the example given above. The rhythm of a sentence is reflected in the child's graphic activity, and we quite frequently encounter further rudiments of such rhythmically depictive writing of complex speech clusters. It was not invention, but the primary effect of the rhythm of the cue or stimulus that was at the source of the first meaningful use of a graphic sign.

VII

This first step along the way of differentiation of primitive, imitative, graphic activity is still very weak and impoverished, however. Although a child may be able to reflect the rhythm of a sentence, he is still unable to mark the content of a term presented to him graphically. We must await the next step, when his graphic activity begins to reflect not only the external rhythm of the words presented to him but also their content; we await the moment when a sign acquires meaning. It is then that we shall doubtless be dealing with inventiveness.

Actually, when undifferentiated, imitative, graphic activity first acquires expressive content, is this not a tremendous step forward in the child's cultural behavior? But even here, again, it is not enough merely to show invention. Our task must be to ascertain what factors are responsible for the shift to a meaningful, depictive sign; and to show what they are means to discover the internal factors determining the process of invention of expressive signs in the child.

The task of the experimenter in this case is consequently to test certain inputs into an experiment and determine which of them produces the primary transition from the diffuse phase to the meaningful use of signs.

In our experiments there was one serious factor that could influence the development of writing in the child: this was the content of what was presented to him; and in varying this, we might ask, What changes in the content we presented were conditions for inducing a primary transition to differentiated, depictive writing?

Two primary factors can take the child from an undifferentiated phase of graphic activity to a stage of differentiated graphic activity. These factors are number and form.

We observed that number, or quantity, was perhaps the first factor to break up that purely imitative, unexpressive character of graphic activity in which different ideas and notions were expressed by exactly the same sort of lines and scribbles. By introducing the factor of number into the material, we could readily produce differentiated graphic activity in 4–5 year old children by causing them to use signs to reflect this number. It is possible that the actual origins of writing are to be found in the need to record number, or quantity.

Perhaps the best thing to do is to reproduce a protocol showing the process of differentiation of writing as it took place under the influence of the factor of quantity.

> Lena L., 4 years old, in her first attempt to write sentences produced an undifferentiated scrawl for each sentence, with completely identical scribbles (see Figure 2). Of course, since these scribbles were totally unrelated to the ideas, they did not even give the effect of writing, and we concluded that this kind of mechanical graphic production hindered rather than helped memory.
>
> We then introduced the factor of quantity into a number of experiments to determine how the altered conditions would affect the development of graphic activity. We were immediately able to note the beginnings of differentiation (Figure 6).
>
> Indeed, graphic production changed sharply under the influence of this factor (especially if one compares it with the sample in Figure 2). We now see a clear differentiation, linked to the particular task. For the first time each scrawl reflects a particular content. Of course, the differentiation is still primitive: what differentiates 'one nose' from 'two eyes' is that the scribbles representing the former are much smaller. Quantity is still not clearly expressed, but relations are. The sentence 'Lilya has two hands and two legs' was perceived and recorded in a differentiated fashion: 'two hands' and 'two legs' each had their own scribble. But most important, this differentiation appeared in a child who had just produced some totally undifferentiated scribblings, not betraying even the least indication that they might have anything at all to do with the sentences dictated.

This example brings us to the following observation: quantity was the factor that broke up the elementary, mechanical, undifferentiated, graphic production and for the first time opened the way toward its use as an auxiliary device, hence raising it from the level of merely mechanical imitation to the status of a functionally employed tool.

Of course, the graphic production itself is still muddled; and the technique has not yet assumed precise, constant contours: if we again dictated material having no reference to quantity, we would again obtain an undifferentiated

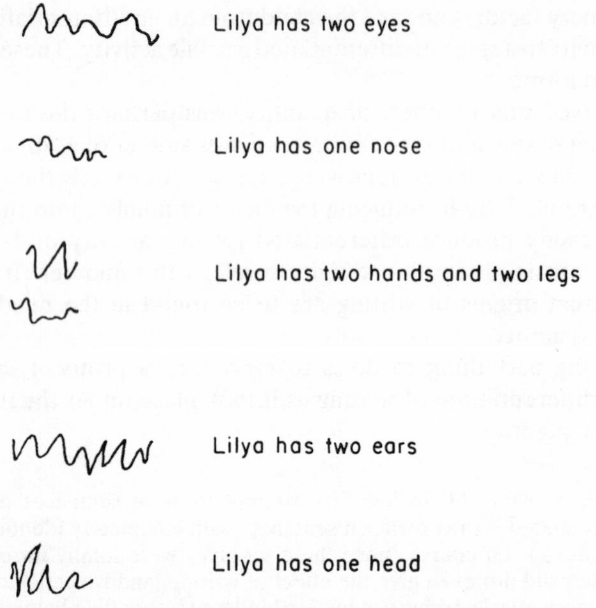

FIGURE 6 'Writing' from dictated sentences, Lena L., aged 4 years

scribbling by the same child, with no attempt on her part to represent a particular content with a particular mark. But now that the first step had been taken, the child was, for the first time, able really to 'write' and, what is most important, to 'read' what she had written. With the transition to this primitive but differentiated graphic activity, her entire behaviour changed: the same child who had been unable to recall two or three sentences was now able to recall all of them confidently and, what is more, for the first time was able to read her own writing.

Thanks to the quantity factor, this differentiation was achieved in children 4–5 years old. The influence of the factor of quantity was especially strong in cases in which the factor of contrast was added – when, for example, the sentence 'There are two trees in the yard' was followed by the sentence 'There are many trees in the forest', the child tried to reproduce the same contrast, and hence could not write both sentences with the same markings and instead was forced to produce differentiated writing.

Having noted this, let us go on immediately to the second factor defining and accelerating the transition from undifferentiated play writing to real, differentiated, expressive, graphic activity.

In our experiments we observed that differentiation of writing could be considerably accelerated if one of the sentences dictated concerned an object that was quite conspicuous because of its color, clear-cut shape, or size. We combined these three factors into a second group of conditions that would promote the child's learning to put a specific content into his writing and make it expressive and differentiated. In such cases we saw how graphic production suddenly began to acquire definite contours as the child attempted to express color, shape, and size; indeed, it began to have a rough resemblance to primitive pictography. Quantity and conspicuous shape lead the child to pictography. Through these factors the child initially gets the idea of using drawing (which he is already quite good at in play) as a means of remembering, and for the first time drawing begins to converge with a complex intellectual activity. Drawing changes from simple representation to a means, and the intellect acquires a new and powerful tool in the form of the first differentiated writing.

Here is a protocol illustrating the guiding role played by the factor of form in the child's discovery of the mechanism of writing; this protocol also shows clearly the process of differentiation as it progresses.

> Vova N., 5 years old, first time in our laboratory. The subject was asked to write sentences dictated to him in order to remember them. He began immediately to produce scribbles, saying, 'This is how you write' (see Figure 1). Obviously, for him the act of writing was purely an external imitation of the writing of an adult without any connection with the content of the particular idea, since the scribbles differed from one another in no essential way. Here is the record:
>
> 1. The mouse with a long tail. — Subject (writes:) This is how you write.
> 2. There is a high column. — Subject (writes:) Column ... This is how you write.
> 3. There are chimneys on the roof. — Subject (writes:) Chimneys on the roof ... This is how you write. ...
>
> Now we give the subject a picture in bright colors, and the reaction immediately changes.
>
> 4. Very black smoke is coming out of the chimney. — Subject: Black. Like this! (Points to the pencil and then begins to draw very black scribbles, pressing hard.)
> 5. In the winter there is white snow. — Subject: (Makes his usual scribbles, but separates them into two parts, apparently unrelated to the idea of 'white snow'.)
> 6. Very black coal – — Subject: (Again draws heavy lines.)

Both the protocol and the writing itself in Figure 7 show that the generally undifferentiated writing acquires an expressive character in only two cases

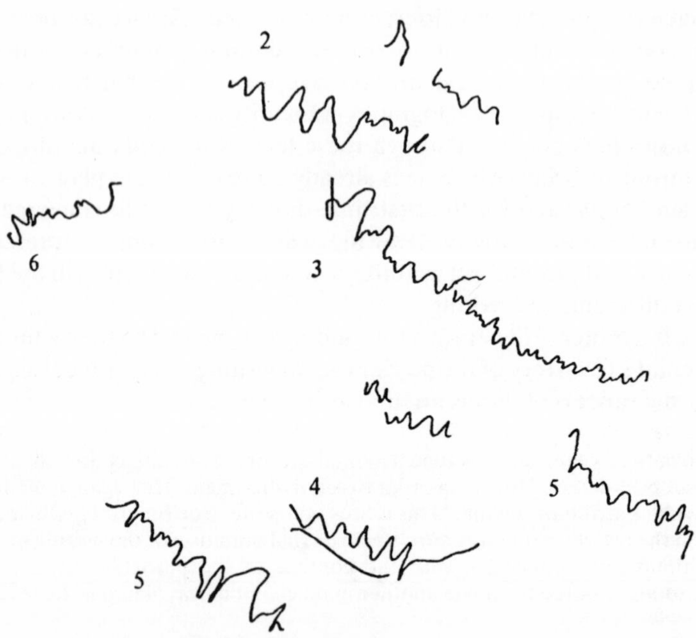

FIGURE 7 'Writing' from dictation, Vova N., aged 5 years

(4 and 6), in which 'black smoke' and 'black coal' are depicted with heavy black lines. For the first time the scrawls on paper assume some of the features of true writing.

The effect becomes clear when we see how the subject recalls what he has written. When asked to recall what he has written, he refuses to recall anything at all. It seems that he has forgotten everything, and his scribblings tell him nothing. But after examining the scrawls, he suddenly stops at one of them and says, spontaneously: 'This is coal.' This is the first time such spontaneous reading occurs in this child, and the fact that he had not only produced something differentiated in his graphic activity but also was able to recall what it represented fully confirms that he had taken the first step toward using writing as a means of remembering.

This sort of differentiation was achieved in 4 and 5 year olds, and it is quite possible that in some cases it can occur even much earlier. The most important thing about all this is that the emergence of the conditions necessary for writing, the discovery of pictographic writing, the first use of writing as a means of expression, occurred before our eyes. We can say with assurance that after observing with our own eyes, in our laboratory, how a child gropingly repeated the first primitive steps of culture, many elements and factors in the emergence of writing became incomparably clearer for us. Sometimes, in the same experiment, we were able to observe the sequence of a whole series of inventions carrying the child forward to one new stage after another in the cultural use of signs.

The best thing to do, perhaps, is to present a protocol from one of our experiments in its entirety. We have therefore selected a record for a 5 year old girl in which we may follow step by step her discovery of cultural signs. We have purposely chosen a subject whose undifferentiated, mnemotechnical writing we have presented earlier (Figure 5).

> Brina Z., age 5. The experiment was done in a number of consecutive sessions in each of which five or six sentences were dictated with the instruction to write them down in order to remember them.
>
> 1st session. The experimenter dictated five sentences: (1) The bird is flying. (2) The elephant has a long trunk. (3) An automobile goes fast. (4) There are high waves on the sea. (5) The dog barks.
>
> The subject made a line for each sentence and arranged the lines in columns (see Figure 8, I). The lines were identical. In the recall test, she remembered only three sentences, i.e., the same number she remembered without writing anything down. She recalled spontaneously, i.e., without looking at her scribblings.
>
> 2nd session. The experimenter dictated five sentences, which included quantitative elements: (1) A man has two arms and two legs. (2) There are many stars in the sky. (3) Nose. (4) Brina has 20 teeth. (5) The big dog has four little pups.
>
> The subject drew lines arranged in a column. Two hands and two legs were represented by two discrete lines; the other sentences were represented by one line each (Figure 8, II). In the recall test the subject declared that she had forgotten everything and refused to try to remember.
>
> 3rd session. The experimenter repeated the second series 'to help her write down and remember what was dictated a little better'. He then dictated the second series again with a few changes: (the subject's scribblings are given in Figure 8, III):

1. Here is a man, and he has two legs.	Subject: Then I'll draw two lines.
2. In the sky there are many stars.	Subject: Then I'll draw many lines.
3. The crane has one leg.	(Makes a mark) ... The crane is on one leg ... There you are ... (Points) The crane is on one leg.
4. Brina has 20 teeth.	(Draws several lines.)
5. The big hen and four little chicks.	(Makes one big line and two small ones; thinks a little, and adds another two.)

> In the recall test, she remembered everything correctly except for sentence

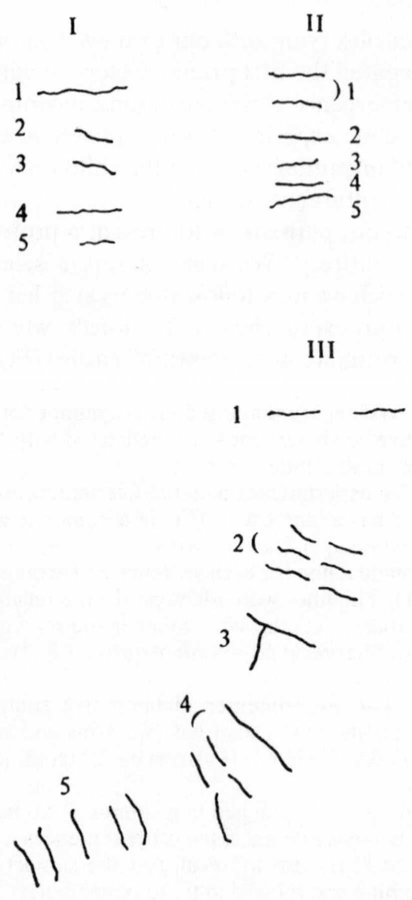

FIGURE 8 Brina, Z., aged 5 years, 'writing' from dictation (see text)

No. 2. When the experimenter dictated this sentence to her and asked, 'How can you write this so as to remember it?' she answered, 'Best with circles.'

4th session. The experimenter again dictates sentences and the subject writes them down.

1. The monkey has a long tail.	Subject: The monkey (draws a line) has a long (draws another line) tail (yet another line).
2. The column is high.	Okay, so I'll draw a line. The column came broken.
3. The bottle is on the table.	Now I can draw the table and then the bottle. But I can't do it right.

4. There are two trees. (Draws two lines.) Now I'll draw the branches.

5. It's cold in winter. Okay. In the winter (draws line) it's cold (draws line).

6. The little girl wants to eat. (Draws a mark.) [Experimenter:] Why did you draw it like that? [Subject:] Because I wanted to.

In the recall test she remembered correctly Nos. 2, 3, 5, and 6 (see Figure 9.) About No. 4 she said: 'This is the monkey with the long tail.' When the experimenter pointed out that this sentence was No. 1, she objected: 'No, these two long lines are the monkey with the long tail. If I hadn't drawn the long lines, I wouldn't have known.'

FIGURE 9 Brina, Z., aged 5 years, 'writing' from dictation (see text)

This experiment began with completely undifferentiated writing. The subject would jot down lines without relating to them in any way as differentiated signs referring to something. In the recall test she did not use these lines and recalled directly, as it were. It is understandable that the failure in the first two experiments depressed her somewhat, and she tried to refuse to go on, declaring that she couldn't remember anything and that she 'didn't want to play any more'. At this point, however, a sudden change occurred, and she began to behave completely differently. She had discovered the instrumental use of writing; she had invented the sign. The lines she had drawn mechanically became a differentiated, expressive tool, and the entire process of recall for the first time began to be mediated. This invention was the result of a confluence of two factors: the interjection of the factor of quantity into the task, and the experimenter's insistent requirement that she 'write so that it could be understood'. Perhaps even without this last condition the subject would have discovered the sign, maybe a little later; but we wanted to accelerate the process and restore her interest. This we were able to do; and the subject, after switching to a new technique and finding it successful, continued to co-operate for another hour and a half.

In the third session, which we shall now discuss, she discovered for the first time that a sign, by means of numerical differentiation, had an expressive function: when asked to write 'The man has two legs' Brina immediately declared, 'Then I'll draw two lines'; and once having discovered this technique, she continued to use it. She then combined this device with a rough schematic representation of the object: the crane with one leg she depicted with a line with another meeting it at right angles; the large dog with four pups became a large line with four smaller ones. Thus, in the recall test she no longer proceeded completely from memory, but read what she had written, each time pointing to her drawing. The only case of failure was 'There are many stars in the sky.' In the test session this was replaced with a new drawing in which the stars were represented by circles, not lines.

Differentiation continued in the fourth session, in which the length of the column was represented by a long line and the tree and bottle were drawn directly. Of particular interest is her attempt to differentiate her writing in another direction, mentioned above: when Brina had difficulty expressing a complex formulation, she wrote down the dictated sentence semimechanically, rhythmically breaking it down into words, each of which was represented by a line (monkey – long – tail, winter – cold). She continued to use this technique for some time; we have observed the same technique in 7–8 year old children. This technique was less successful than the technique of real, differentiated writing, however, and hence is a special case. After writing 'It is cold in winter' with two long lines, the subject began to recall them as the 'monkey with the long tail', declaring that she had purposely drawn the long line and that without it she would have been unable to remember the monkey's long tail. We see here how a technique that has been used ineffectively is reworked and acquires an attribute corresponding to one of the ideas; the line is then interpreted differently and is transformed into a sign.

After having started with undifferentiated play writing, before our very eyes the subject discovered the instrumental nature of such writing and worked out her own system of expressive marks, by means of which she was able to transform the entire remembering process. Play was transformed into elementary writing, and writing was now able to assimilate the child's representational experience. We have reached the threshold of pictographic writing.

VIII

The period of picture writing is fully developed by the time a child reaches the age of 5 or 6 years; if it is not fully and clearly developed by that time, it is only because it already begins to give way to symbolic alphabetic writing, which the child learns in school – and sometimes long before.

If it were not for this factor, we should have every reason to expect that pictography would achieve a flourishing development; and this is what we actually see everywhere that symbolic writing is not developed or does not exist; pictography flourishes among primitive peoples (there have been many interesting studies of pictography). The richest development of pictography is found in retarded children, who are still preliterate; and we should, without reserve, recognize that their fine and colorful pictographic writing is one of the positive accomplishments of retarded children. (In Figure 10 we show some drawings by a retarded child that are quite impressive in their vividness and grace.)

The pictographic phase in the development of writing is based on the rich experience of the child's drawings, which need not in themselves serve the function of mediating signs, in any intellectual process. Initially drawing is play, a self-contained process of representation; then the perfected act can be used as a device, a means, for recording. But because the direct experience of drawing is so rich, we often do not obtain the pictographic phase of writing in its pure form in the child. Drawing as a means is very frequently blended with drawing as a self-contained, unmediated process. Nowhere in such material can one discern any sign of the difficulties the child experiences in going through the differentiation of all these processes into means and ends, objects and functionally related techniques, which, as we saw above, are the necessary condition for the emergence of writing.

We shall not dwell in detail on all the characteristic features of this pictographic phase in the development of writing in the child, since this phase has been studied much more than all the others. We shall merely underscore the distinction between pictographic writing and drawing, and once again draw on an actual experimental record to illustrate our point.

Marusya G., 8 years old, is a mentally retarded child. She cannot write, and has poor command of speech. Her Binet–Bert IQ is 60. Despite this handicap, however, she has remarkable representational gifts. Her drawings are an excellent example of how drawing may not be an indicator of intellectual aptitude, but may in compensation develop in people whose intellectual (especially verbal) aptitudes are impaired.

We performed our usual experiment with Marusya. In the first natural series, she remembered only one of the six words. After noting this, we went directly on to the writing experiment. Here is the record:

Experiment: Now I shall tell you a number of things, and you should write them down on the paper so you can remember them better. Here is a pencil.

Subject: How should I write it? House and girl, right? (Begins to write 'girl'; see Figure 10, 1)

FIGURE 10 Marusya, G., aged 8 years, 'writing' from dictation (see text).

Experimenter: (1) Listen. Write that a cow has four legs and a tail.

Subject: A little cow, a real little cow. I think I'd better draw the girl instead.

Experimenter repeats the instructions.)

I don't know how (draws the girl).

(2) Chimney sweeps are black.

Black. A little box. I don't know how to draw a chimney (draws a box, then begins to draw a flower). (Figure 10, 2 and 3a ["This is a flower."])

(3) Yesterday evening at rained.

It was wet. I put on my galoshes. There was a little drizzle. Here it is (makes a few light lines on the paper [Figure 10, 3]). I can draw snow, too. Here it is (draws a star, Figure 10, 3a).

(4) We had a tasty soup for lunch.

Soup, tasty (Figure 10, 4); they go together.

(5) The dog is running about the yard.

Dog, little (draws a dog).

(6) The boat is sailing the sea.

Here's the boat (draws).

At this point a bright light was turned on so that we could film the process, and the experimenter called the subject's attention to it: 'Look at our little sun.' The subject then proceeded to draw a circle and declared: 'Here is the sun' (Figure 10, 2a).

In the recall test, the subject named all the figures she had drawn, regardless of whether they depicted what had been dictated or were spontaneous drawings: (1) Girl, (2) Soup, (3) The boat is sailing, (4) The black box, (5) Here is a flower, (6) The dog. ... She then took the pencil and drew a road and said, 'Here is a road' (Figure 10, 7).

Our record gives a good, detailed description of the development of pictographic writing in the child. What is especially noteworthy is the extraordinary ease with which the child took up this kind of writing yet dissociated the depicted figures from the writing task and turned it into spontaneous, self-contained drawing. It was with this tendency to draw pictures, not to write with the aid of pictures, that our experiment began, when Marusya at our request to pay attention to everything said to her immediately answered: 'How should I write? A house, a little girl, right?' The process of the functional use of writing was incomprehensible to her; and if she learned it later, it would remain a shaky acquisition. Several times during the course of the experiment, Marusya reverted to spontaneous drawing, with no function related to remembering the dictated material.

This dual relationship to drawing remained with our subject throughout all the following experiments, and the agility with which she would switch from pictographic writing back to spontaneous drawing was something observed in many preschoolers and, especially, in older retarded children. The more outstanding the pictography, the easier it was for these two principles of picture writing to be mixed.

A child may draw well but not relate to his drawing as an auxiliary device. This distinguishes writing from drawing and sets a limit to the full development of pictographic literacy in the narrow meaning of the term. The more retarded the child, the more marked is his inability to relate to drawing other than as a kind of play and to develop and understand the instrumental use of a picture as a device or symbol, though his drawing skills may be well developed.

But now we have come to the problem of the development of the symbolic phase of writing; and in order not to lose the connection with what has been said, we should pause for a moment on a very important factor at the borderline between pictography and symbolic writing in the child.

IX

Let us imagine a case in which a child who can write pictographically must put down something that is difficult (or even impossible) to express in a picture. What does the child then do?

This situation, of course, forces the child to find ways around the problem, if he does not simply refuse to perform the task. Two such detours, very similar to each other, are possible. On the one hand, the child instructed to record something difficult to depict may instead of object A put down object B, which is related in some way to A. Or, he may simply put down some arbitrary mark instead of the object he finds difficult to depict.

Either way leads from pictographic writing to symbolic writing, except that the first still operates with the same means of pictographic representation whereas the seond makes use of other qualitatively new devices.

In experiments with mentally retarded children we often observe the development of indirect means of the first type; school and school instruction provide ample opportunities for the second type.

Let us imagine that a small child or a retarded child is able to draw well, and we suggest to him some picture that, for some reason, he finds difficult to draw. How does he proceed in this case?

We can analyze the indirect means a child devises in such a case in their purest form on the basis of one of our experiments. Let us first take a subject whom we have already discussed earlier – Marusya G.

FIGURE 11. Marusya, G., aged 8 years, 'writing' from dictation (see text)

In a fourth sesson we again gave her a series of sentences that were not all equally easy to write down. Here is an extract from the record (see Figure 11).

1. Two dogs on the street.	Subject: Two dogs (draws) ... and a cat (draws a cat). Two big dogs.
2. There are many stars in the sky.	What stars ... here is the sky (draws a line). Here is some grass below (draws) ... I see them from the window (draws a window).

What does this extract tell us? The subject has difficulty in representing pictographically the sentence 'There are many stars in the sky', and she creates her own unique way to get around the problem: she does not draw the image given her, but instead portrays an entire situation in which she saw stars. She depicts the sky, the window through which she saw the stars, etc. Instead of the part, she reproduces the entire situation, and in this way solves the problem.

A similar situation was encountered with another subject, Petya U., 6½ years old. Here is an extract from the record.

Session III, (2) There are 1,000 stars in the sky.	Subject: I can't draw 1,000 stars. If you want, I'll draw an airplane. This is the sky (draws a horizontal line) ... Oh, I can't. ...

We see here the difficulty of an image that does not lend itself well to graphic representation, so that the subject tries to get around the problem by depicting other, related objects.

These children had insufficient ability to use drawing as a sign or a means, and this was complicated by their attitude toward drawing as a self-contained game. Hence, the representation is extended from a single image to a whole situation in which this image was perceived; it is given new roots. In this situation, however, the indirect path is purely of the most primitive sort. The whole instead of the part is the first indirect device used in early childhood; we shall be able to understand it if we take into account the diffuse, holistic, poorly differentiated nature of a child's perceptions (Werner, 1926). At the very last stages, these indirect means acquire another, more differentiated and more highly developed nature.

It is hardly necessary to present all the instances in which a child chooses an indirect means and, instead of a whole that he finds difficult to depict, draws some part of it, which is easier. These features of all infantile drawing that is already at a more differentiated stage have been described many times, and are well known to all. Two tendencies are characteristic of the pictographic writing of a child at a relatively advanced stage: the object to be depicted may be replaced either by some part of it or by its general contours or outline. In either case the child has already gone beyond the aforementioned tendency to depict an object in its entirety, in all its details, and is in the process of acquiring the psychological skills on whose basis the last form, symbolic writing, will develop. Let us give just one more example of the first appearance of this kind of representational drawing in a child. This is the 'part instead of the whole' device we observed in the experiments involving writing a number.

> Shura, N., 7½ years old. The child is instructed to write the sentence we presented above: 'There are 1,000 stars in the sky.' The subject first draws a horizontal line ('the sky'), then carefully draws two stars, and stops. Experimenter: 'How many do you still have to draw?' Subject:
> 'Only two. I'll remember there are 1,000.'

Clearly, the two stars here were a sign for a large quantity. It would be wrong, however, to assume that such a small child was capable of using the 'part for the whole' device. We had occasion to observe a number of children who wrote the sentence about 1,000 stars with so many 'stars', i.e., marks, that after demurring several minutes, we finally had simply to stop this procedure, which looked as though it were going to end with a thousand stars. A considerable degree of intellectual development and abstraction are necessary to be able to depict a whole group by one or two representatives; a child who is capable of this is already at the verge of symbolic writing.

> Let us consider briefly some experiments we ran in this regard on adults. An adult audience was asked to represent concrete or abstract concepts graphically; these adults invariably depicted one attribute of the whole (e.g., 'stupidity' was represented as donkey ears, 'intelligence' by a high forehead, 'fear' by raised hair or big eyes, etc.). Graphic representation by means of a particular attribute, however, is not at all easy for a child, whose discriminating and abstracting powers are not very well developed.

We have arrived at the question of a child's symbolic writing, and with this will have reached the end of our essay on the pre-history of a child's writing. Strictly speaking, this primitive period of infantile literacy, which is so interesting to the psychologist, comes to an end when the teacher gives a child a pencil. But we should not be completely correct in saying such a thing. From the time a child first begins to learn to write until he has finally mastered this skill is a very long period, which is of particular interest for psychological research. It is right at the borderline between the primitive forms of inscription we have seen above, which have a prehistoric, spontaneous character, and the new cultural forms introduced in an organized fashion from outside the individual. It is during this transitional period, when the child has not completely mastered the new skills but also has not completely outgrown the old, that a number of psychological patterns of particular interest emerge.

How does a child write who, although he is still unable to write, knows some of the elements of the alphabet? How does he relate to these letters, and how does he (psychologically) try to use them in his primitive practice? These are the questions that interest us.

Let us first describe some extremely interesting patterns we observed in our material. Writing by no means develops along a straight line, with continuous growth and improvement. Like any other cultural psychological function, the development of writing depends to a considerable extent on the writing techniques used and amounts essentially to the replacement of one such technique by another. Development in this case may be described as a *gradual improvement in the process of writing, within the means of each technique, and sharp turning points marking a transition from one such technique to another*. But the profoundly dialectical uniqueness of this process means that the transition to a new technique initially sets the process of writing back considerably, after which it then develops further at the new and higher level. Let us try to see what this interesting pattern means, since without it, in our opinion, it would be impossible for such cultural psychological functions to develop.

We saw that the prehistory of infantile writing traces a path of gradual differentiation of the symbols used. At first the child relates to writing things without understanding the significance of writing; in the first stage, writing is for him not a means of recording some specific content, but a self-contained process involving imitation of an adult activity but having no functional significance in itself. This phase is characterized by undifferentiated scribblings; the child records any idea with exactly the same scrawls. Later – and we saw how this develops – differentiation begins; the symbols acquire a functional significance and begin graphically to reflect the content the child is to write down.

At this stage the child begins to learn how to read: he knows individual letters, and he knows that these letters record some content; finally, he learns their outward forms and how to make particular marks. But does this mean that he now understands the full mechanics of their use? Not at all. Moreover, we are convinced that an understanding of the mechanisms of writing takes place much later than the outward mastery of writing, and that in the first stages of acquiring this mastery the child's relation to writing is purely external. He understands that he can use signs to write everything, but he does not yet understand how to do this; he thus becomes fully confident in this writing yet is still totally unable to use it. Believing completely in this new technique, in the first stage of development of symbolic alphabetic writing the child begins with a stage of undifferentiated writing he had already passed through long before.

Here are some examples from our records for different subjects obtained under different conditions.

> Little Vasya G., a village boy 6 years old, could not yet write, but knew the individual letters A and I. When we asked him to remember and write down some sentences we dictated, he easily did so. In his movements he showed total confidence that he would be able to write down and remember the dictated sentences. The results are shown in the following record.

1. A cow has four legs and a tail.	Subject: I know he has four legs, and this (writes) is 'I'.
2. Chimney sweeps are black.	(Writes) and this is 'A'.
3. Yesterday evening it rained.	Here's rain. Here's 'I' (writes).
4. There are many trees in the woods.	Subject: (writes) Here is 'U'.
5. The steamer is sailing down the river.	The steam goes like this (makes a mark). Here's 'I'.

The result was a column of alternate I's and A's having nothing to do with the dictated sentences. Obviously, the subject had not yet learned how to

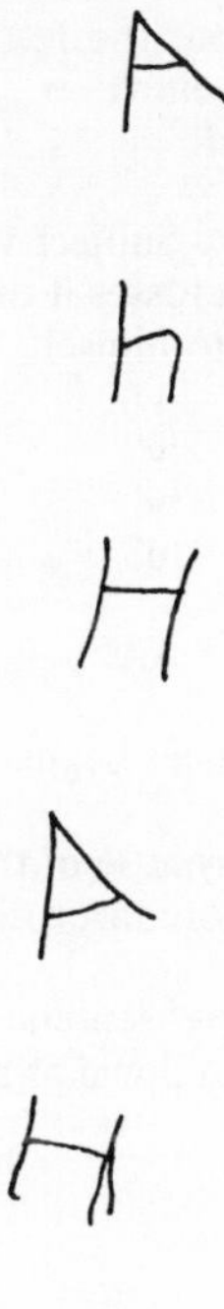

FIGURE 12 Vasya, G., aged 6 years, individual letters written for dictated sentences

make such a connection, so that in the task in which he was to read what he wrote, he read the letters (I and A) without relating them at all to the text.

In this case the letters were completely non-functional; the child was at a stage fully analogous with the stage studied earlier.

But one may object: the child had obviously not yet learned the function of writing, and psychologically the letters were totally analogous to the earlier scribbles. He had not yet gone beyond the stage of primary, undifferentiated, graphic activity. This observation is quite true, but it does not vitiate the law we wished to demonstrate. We can present data showing that this inability to use letters, this lack of understanding of the actual mechanism of alphabetic writing, persists for a long time. To study the psychological underpinnings of automatized writing skills rather than these skills themselves we selected a somewhat different approach; the children were instructed not to write each word in a sentence completely. The results of this test gave us a deeper insight into a child's attitude toward writing. Here is an example:

Vanya Z., 9 years old, a village boy, wrote the letters well, and willingly participated in our experiment. The results, however, showed a very unique attitude toward his writing. Here is the record:

1. Monkeys have long tails.	Subject writes first 'n' and then crosses it out and writes 'i' (saying to himself: u obezyan-*i*).
2. There is a tall tree.	'v'
3. It's dark in the cellar.	'v'
4. The balloon soars.	'v'
5. The big dog gave birth to four pups.	'u'
6. The boy is hungry.	'm'

[Translator's note: Each of the Russian sentences begins with the letter the boy wrote down.]

Of course, the subject was able to recall very little of the written words on the basis of what was written here. The way he wrote three different sentences (2, 3, and 4) induced us to do the following test.

In a second session was gave the boy six sentences beginning with the preposition "u". All six sentences were written down as six completely identical letters 'u' (see Figure 13).

FIGURE 13 Vanya, Z., aged 9 years, individual letters written for dictated sentences

These data show that the ability to write does not necessarily mean that the child understands the process of writing and that a child who can write may, under certain conditions, display a totally undifferentiated attitude toward writing and a lack of comprehension of the basic premises of it, namely, the need for specific distinctions to record different contents.

We obtained even clearer results when we asked a schoolchild who had recently learned how to write to write some idea with any marks (or graphic designs); he was forbidden only to use letters. The most conspicuous result of these experiments was the surprising difficulty the child had in reverting to the phase of pictorial, representational writing through which he had already passed. Our expectation, which seemed quite reasonable, that given the conditions of our experiment, the child would immediately revert to simple drawings proved wrong. The child whom we had forbidden to use letters did not revert to the picture stage, but remained at the level of symbolic writing. He worked out his own signs and, using them, tried to do the assignment. Finally, what was most interesting of all was that in using these signs he started with the same undifferentiated phase with which he began the development of writing in general, only now he gradually developed differentiated techniques for this higher level of development.

Here is a record of an experiment done with Shura I., a city schoolboy 8½ years old. We asked him to note each sentence we dictated with marks to remember it. The subject quickly consented to the experiment, and in the first session used a very simple system. He marked each sentence with crosses, each element of the sentence being noted by one cross. Here is what he produced:
Session I:

1. A cow has four legs and a tail. XXX
(Cow – four legs – tail.)
2. Negroes are black. XXX
(Negroes – are – black.)
3. It rained yesterday evening. XXX
(It rained – yesterday – evening.)
4. There are many wolves in the forest. XXX
(There are – many wolves – in the forest.)
5. House. X
6. Two dogs, a large one and a small one. XXX
(Two dogs – large one and – small one.)

The completely undifferentiated nature of this writing shows with graphic clarity that the subject had not yet grasped the mechanism of symbolic writing and used it only externally, thinking that these marks in themselves would be of assistance to him.

The effect of such writing was quite expected; the subject remembered only three of the six sentences, and moreover was completely unable to indicate which of his markings represented which sentence.

FIGURE 14 Shura, I., aged 8½ years, pictographic writing to dictated sentences

To follow the process in its purest form, we forbade our subject to make crosses. The result was a transition to a new form, marks that were not as undifferentiated but that he continued to use in a purely mechanical fashion. In this second trial, however, we were already able to achieve some differentiation; the subject discovered pictographic writing and resorted to it after a number of failures with his marks. Here is the record (see Figure 14).

Session II

1. Monkeys have long tails.	(Makes two marks.)
2. There is a high column on the street.	(Two marks.)
3. The night is dark.	(Two marks.)
4. There is one bottle and two glasses.	(I'll write down a bottle.)
5. One big dog and one small dog.	(Makes two marks.)
6. Wood is thick.	(I'll write down wood.)

We see that at first this writing was undifferentiated; but then, in cases that were especially conducive to pictography, the subject went over to a graphic depiction of the objects. He was not consistent in this, however, and at even the slightest difficulty in depicting something would again revert to undifferentiated use of signs.

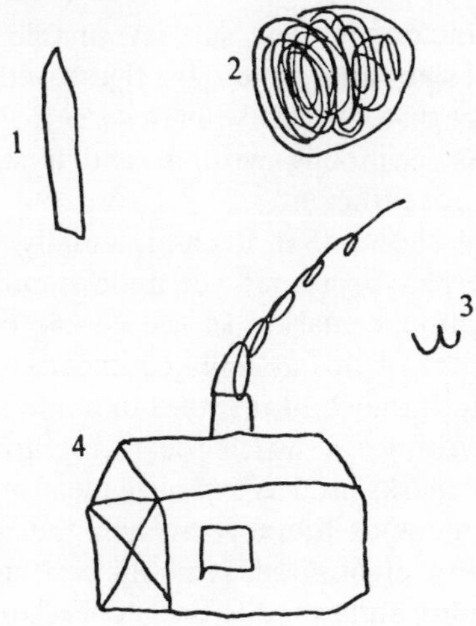

FIGURE 15. Shura, I., aged 8½ years, use of signs to identify abstract terms when 'writing' dictated sentences

But in this case, we were able to advance one step in our inquiry into the most difficult problem of our study, namely, the mechanisms by which this arbitrary conventional sign is created. Session III shows this mechanism.

We gave the subject a number of concrete images with a word between them identifying the situation. Figure 15 shows the interesting process of generation of a sign to identify an abstract term.

Session III

1. There is a column.	(The subject draws something.)
2. The night is dark.	(I'll put a circle for the night (draws a filled-in circle).
3. The bird is flying	(The subject draws something.)
4. Smoke is coming from the chimney.	I'll draw a house with smoke (draws).
5. The fish is swimming.	Fish ... fish. ... I'll draw a fish.
6. The girl wants to eat.	I'll draw a girl. ... She wants to eat (makes a mark) – there it is – she wants to eat (Figure 15, 6, 7)

The last is very characteristic. The subject, unable to draw 'hunger', reverted to his system of signs and, next to the figure of the little girl, placed a mark meant to signify that the girl wanted to eat. Pictography here is combined with arbitrary symbolic writing, and a sign is used where pictographic means are not sufficient.

Our example clearly shows that a child initially assimilates school experience purely externally, without yet understanding the sense and mechanism of using symbolic marks. In the course of our experiment, however, a positive aspect of this assimilated experience emerged; when conditions were restricted, the child reverted to a new, more complicated form of pictographic writing, in which the pictographic elements were combined with symbolic marks used as technical means for remembering.

The further development of literacy involves the assimilation of the mechanisms of culturally elaborated symbolic writing and the use of symbolic devices to simplify and expedite the act of recording. This takes us beyond our topic, and we shall explore the psychological fate of writing further in another study of adults who are already cultural beings. We have come to the end of our essay, and may sum up our conclusions as follows.

One thing seems clear from our analysis of the use of signs and its origins in the child: it is not understanding that generates the act, but far more the act that gives birth to understanding – indeed, the act often far precedes understanding. Before a child has understood the sense and mechanism of writing, he has already made many attempts to elaborate primitive methods; and these, for him, are the prehistory of his writing. But even these methods are not developed all at once: they pass through a number of trials and inventions, constituting a series of stages with which it is very useful for an educator working with school-age children and preschoolers to be acquainted.

The 3 or 4 year old first discovers that his scribblings on paper can be used as a functional aid to remembering. At this point (sometimes much later) writing assumes an auxiliary instrumental function, and drawing becomes sign writing.

At the same time as this transformation takes place, a fundamental reorganization occurs in the most basic mechanisms of the child's behavior; on top of the primitive forms of direct adaptation to the problems imposed by his environment, the child now builds up new, complex, cultural forms; the major psychological functions no longer operate through primitive natural forms and begin to employ complex cultural devices. These devices are tried in succession, and perfected, and in the process transform the child as well. We have observed the engrossing process of the dialectical development of complex, essentially social forms of behavior that after traversing a long path, have brought us finally to the mastery of what is perhaps the most priceless tool of culture.

REFERENCES

Kohler, W. (1917). *Intelligenzprüfungen an Menschenaffen.*

Werner, H. (1926). *Einführung in die Entwicklunspsychologie.*

The Psychology of Written Language
Edited by M. Martlew

CHAPTER 11

The Prehistory of Written Language

LEV S. VYGOTSKY

Until now, writing has occupied too narrow a place in school practice as compared to the enormous role that it plays in children's cultural development. The teaching of writing has been conceived in narrowly practical terms. Children are taught to trace out letters and make words out of them, but they are not taught written language. The mechanics of reading what is written are so emphasized that they overshadow written language as such.

Something similar has happened in teaching spoken language to deaf-mutes. Attention has been concentrated entirely on correct production of particular letters and distinct articulation of them. In this case, teachers of deaf-mutes have not discerned spoken language behind these pronunciation techniques, and the result has been dead speech.

This situation is to be explained primarily by historical factors: specifically, by the fact that practical pedagogy, despite the existence of many methods for teaching reading and writing, has yet to work out an effective, scientific procedure for teaching children written language. Unlike the teaching of spoken language, into which children grow of their own accord, teaching of written language is based on artificial training. Such training requires an enormous amount of attention and effort on the part of teacher and pupil and thus becomes something self-contained, relegating living written language to the background. Instead of being founded on the needs of children as they naturally develop and on their own activity, writing is given to them from without, from the teacher's hands. This situation recalls the development of a technical skill such a piano-playing: the pupil develops finger dexterity and learns to strike the keys while reading music, but he is in no way involved in the essence of the music itself.

Such one-sided enthusiasm for the mechanics of writing has had an impact not only on the practice of teaching but on the theoretical statement of the problem as well. Up to this point, psychology has conceived of writing as a complicated motor skill. It has paid remarkably little attention to the question of written language as such, that is, a particular system of symbols and signs whose mastery heralds a critical turning-point in the entire cultural development of the child.

A feature of this system is that it is second-order symbolism, which gradually becomes direct symbolism. This means that written language consists of a system of signs that designate the sounds and words of spoken language, which, in turn, are signs for real entities and relations. Gradually this intermediate link, spoken language, disappears, and written language is converted into a system of signs that directly symbolize the entities and relations between them. It seems clear that mastery of such a complex sign system cannot be accomplished in a purely mechanical and external manner; rather it is the culmination of a long process of development of complex behavioral functions in the child. Only by understanding the entire history of sign development in the child and the place of writing in it can we approach a correct solution of the psychology of writing.

The developmental history of written language, however, poses enormous difficulties for research. As far as we can judge from the available material, it does not follow a single direct line in which something like a clear continuity of forms is maintained. Instead, it offers the most unexpected metamorphoses, that is, transformations of particular forms of written language into others. To quote Baldwin's (1895) expression regarding the development of things, it is as much involution as evolution. This means that, together with processes of development, forward motion, and appearance of new forms, we can discern processes of curtailment, disappearance, and reverse development of old forms at each step. The developmental history of written language among children is full of such discontinuities. Its line of development seems to disappear altogether; then suddenly, as if from nowhere, a new line begins, and at first it seems that there is absolutely no continuity between the old and the new. But only a naive view of development as a purely evolutionary process involving nothing but the gradual accumulation of small changes and the gradual conversion of one form into another can conceal from us the true nature of these processes. This revolutionary type of development is in no way new for science in general; it is new only for child psychology. Therefore, despite a few daring attempts, child psychology does not have a cogent view of the development of written language as a historical process, as a unified process of development.

The first task of a scientific investigation is to reveal this prehistory of children's written language, to show what leads children to writing, through what important points this prehistorical development passes, and in what relationship it stands to school learning. At the present time, in spite of a variety of research studies, we are in no position to write a coherent or complete history of written language in children. We can only discern the most important points in this development and discuss its major changes. This history begins with the appearance of the gesture as a visual sign for the child.

GESTURES AND VISUAL SIGNS

The gesture is the initial visual sign that contains the child's future writing as an acorn contains a future oak. Gestures, it has been correctly said, are writing in air, and written signs frequently are simply gestures that have been fixed.

Wurth pointed out the link between gesture and pictorial or pictographic writing in discussing the development of writing in human history. He showed that figurative gestures often simply denote the reproduction of a graphic sign; on the other hand, signs are often the fixation of gestures. An indicating line employed in pictographic writing denotes the index finger in fixed position. All these symbolic designations in pictorial writing, according to Wurth, can be explained only by derivation from gesture language, even if they subsequently become detached from it and can function independently.

There are two other domains in which gestures are linked to the origin of written signs. The first concerns children's scribbles. We have observed in experiments on drawing that children frequently switch to dramatization, depicting by gestures what they should show on the drawing; the pencil-marks are only a supplement to this gestural representation. I could cite many instances. A child who has to depict running begins by depicting the motion with her fingers, and she regards the resultant marks and dots on paper as a representation of running. When she goes on to depict jumping, her hand begins to make movements depicting jumps; what appears on paper remains the same. In general, we are inclined to view children's first drawings and scribbles rather as gestures than as drawing in the true sense of the word. We are also inclined to ascribe to the same phenomenon the experimentally demonstrated fact that, in drawing complex objects, children do not render their parts but rather general qualities, such as an impression of roundness and so forth. When a child depicts a cylindrical can as a closed curve that resembles a circle, she thus depicts something round.

This developmental phase coincides nicely with the general motor set that characterizes children of this age and governs the entire style and nature of their first drawings. Children behave in the same way in depicting concepts that are at all complex or abstract. Children do not draw, they indicate, and the pencil merely fixes the indicatory gesture. When asked to draw good weather, a child will indicate the bottom of the page by making a horizontal motion of the hand, explaining, 'This is the earth', and then, after a number of confused upward hatchwise motions 'And this is good weather.' We have had the occasion to verify more precisely, in experiments, the kinship between gestural depiction and depiction by drawing, and have obtained symbolic and graphic depiction through gestures in 5 year olds.

DEVELOPMENT OF SYMBOLISM IN PLAY

The second realm that links gestures and written language is children's games. For children some objects can readily denote others, replacing them and becoming signs for them, and the degree of similarity between a plaything and the object it denotes is unimportant. What is most important is the utilization of the plaything and the possibility of executing a representational gesture with it. This is the key to the entire symbolic function of children's play. A pile of clothes or piece of wood becomes a baby in a game because the same gestures that depict holding a baby in one's hands or feeding a baby can apply to them. The child's self-motion, his own gestures, are what assign the function of sign to the object and give it meaning. All symbolic representational activity is full of such indicatory gestures; for instance, a stick becomes a riding-horse for a child because it can be placed between the legs and a gesture can be employed that communicates that the stick designates a horse in this instance.

From this point of view, therefore, children's symbolic play can be understood as a very complex system of 'speech' through gestures that communicate and indicate the meaning of playthings. It is only on the basis of these indicatory gestures that playthings themselves gradually acquire their meaning – just as drawing, while initially supported by gesture, becomes an independent sign.

We attempted experimentally to establish this particular special stage of object writing in children. We conducted play experiments in which, in a joking manner, we began to designate things and people involved in the play by familiar objects. For example, a book off to one side designated a house, keys meant children, a pencil meant a nursemaid, a pocket watch a drugstore, a knife a doctor, an inkwell cover a horse-drawn carriage, and so forth. Then the children were given a simple story through figurative gestures involving the set objects. They could read it with great ease. For example, a doctor arrives at a house in a carriage, knocks at the door, the nursemaid opens, he examines the children, he writes a prescription and leaves, the nursemaid goes to the drugstore, comes back, and administers medicine to the children. Most 3 year olds can read this symbolic notation with great ease. Four or five year olds can read more complex notation: a man is walking in the forest and is attacked by a wolf, which bites him; the man extricates himself by running, a doctor gives him aid, and he goes to the drugstore and then home; a hunter sets out for the forest to kill the wolf.

What is noteworthy is that perceptual similarity of objects plays no noticeable part in the understanding of the symbolic notation. All that matters is that the objects admit the appropriate gesture and can function as a point of application for it. Hence, things with which this gestural structure cannot be performed are absolutely rejected by children. For example, in this game, which is conducted at a table and which involves small items on the table, children will absolutely refuse to play if we take their fingers, put them on a book, and say, 'Now as a joke, these will be children.' They object that there is no such game. Fingers are too connected with their own bodies for them to be an object for a corresponding indicatory gesture. In the same way, a piece of furniture in the room or one of the people in the game cannot become involved. The object itself performs a substitution function; a pencil substitutes for a nursemaid or a watch for a drugstore, but only the relevant gesture endows them with this meaning. However, under the influence of this gesture, older children begin to make one exceptionally important discovery – that objects can indicate the things they denote as well as substitute for them. For example, when we put down a book with a dark cover and say that this will be a forest, a child will spontaneously add, 'Yes, it's a forest because it's black and dark'. She thus isolates one of the features of the object, which for her is an indication of the fact that the book is supposed to mean a forest. In the same way, when a metal inkwell cover denotes a carriage, a child will point and say, 'This is the seat.' When a pocket watch is to denote a drugstore, one child might point to the numbers on the face and say, 'This is medicine in the drugstore'; another might point to the ring and say, 'This is the entrance.' Referring to a bottle that is playing the part of a wolf, a child will point to the neck and say, 'And this is his mouth.' If the experimenter asks, pointing to the stopper, 'And what is this?' the child answers, 'He's caught the stopper and is holding it in his teeth.'

In all these examples we see the same thing, namely, that the customary structure of things is modified under the impact of the new meaning it has acquired. In response to the fact that a watch denotes a drugstore, a feature of the watch is isolated and assumes the function of a new sign or indication of *how* the watch denotes a drugstore, either through the feature of medicine or of the entrance. The customary structure of things (stopper in a bottle) begins to be reflected in the new structure (wolf holds stopper in teeth), and this structural modification becomes so strong that in a number of experiments we sometimes instilled a particular symbolic meaning of an object in the children. For example, a pocket watch denoted a drugstore in all our play sessions, whereas other objects changed meaning rapidly and frequently. In taking up a new game, we would put down the same watch and explain, in accordance with the new procedures, 'Now this is a bakery.' One child immediately placed a pen edgewise across the watch, dividing it in half, and, indicating one half, said, 'All right, here is the drugstore, and here is the bakery.' The old meaning thus became independent and functioned as a means for a new one. We could also discern this acquisition of independent meaning outside the immediate game; if a knife fell, a child would exclaim, 'The doctor has fallen.' Thus, the object acquires a sign function with a developmental history of its own that is now independent of the child's gesture. This is second-order symbolism, and because it develops in play, we see make-believe play as a major contributor to the development of written language – a system of second-order symbolism.

As in play, so too in drawing, representation of meaning initially arises as first-order symbolism. As we have already pointed out, the first drawings arise from gestures of the (pencil-equipped) hand, and the gesture constitutes the first representation of meaning. Only later on does the graphic representation begin independently to denote some object. The nature of this relationship is that the marks already made on paper are given an appropriate name.

H. Hertzer (1926) undertook to study experimentally how symbolic representation of things – so important in learning to write – develops in 3–6 year old children. Her experiments involved four basic series. The first investigated the function of symbols in children's play. Children were to portray, in play, a father or mother doing what they do in the course of a day. During this game a make-believe interpretation of particular objects was given, making it possible for the researcher to trace the symbolic function assigned to things during the game. The second series involved building materials, and the third involved drawing with colored pencils. Particular attention in both these experiments was paid to the point at which the appropriate meaning was named. The fourth series undertook to investigate, in the form of a game of post office, the extent to which children can perceive purely arbitrary combinations of signs. The game used pieces of paper of various colors to denote different types of mail: telegrams, newspapers, money orders, packages, letters, postcards, and so forth. Thus, the experiments explicitly related these different forms of activity, whose only common feature is that a symbolic function is involved in all of them, and attempted to link them all with the development of written language, as we did in our experiments.

Hetzer was able to show clearly which symbolic meanings arise in play via figurative gestures and which via words. Children's egocentric language was widely manifest in these games. Whereas some children depicted everything by using movements and mimicry, not employing speech as a symbolic resource at all, for other children actions were accompanied by speech: the child both spoke and acted. For a third group, purely verbal expression not supported by any activity began to predominate. Finally, a fourth group of children did not play at all, and speech became the sole mode of representation, with mimicry and gestures receding into the background. The percentage of purely play actions decreased with age, while speech gradually predominated. The most important conclusion drawn from this developmental investigation, as the author says, is that the difference in play activity between 3 year olds and 6 year olds is not in the perception of symbols but in the mode in which various forms of representation are used. In our opinion, this is a highly important conclusion; it indicates that symbolic representation in play is essentially a particular form of speech at an earlier stage, one which leads directly to written language.

As development proceeds, the general process of naming shifts farther and farther toward the beginning of the process, and thus the process itself is tantamount to the writing of a word that has just been named. Even a 3 year old understands the representational function of a toy construction, while a 4 year old names his creations even before he begins to construct them. Similarly, we see in drawing that a 3 year old is still unaware of the symbolic meaning of a drawing; it is only around age 7 years that all children master this completely. At the same time, our analysis of children's drawings definitely shows that, from the psychological point of view, we should regard such drawings as a particular kind of child speech.

DEVELOPMENT OF SYMBOLISM IN DRAWING

K. Buhler (1930) correctly notes that drawing begins in children when spoken speech has already made great progress and has become habitual. Subsequently, he says, speech predominates in general and shapes the greater part of inner life in accordance with its laws. This includes drawing.

Children initially draw from memory. If asked to draw their mother sitting opposite them or some object before them, they draw without ever looking at the original – not what they see but what they know. Often children's drawings not only disregard but also directly contradict the actual perception of the object. We find what Buhler calls 'x-ray drawings'. A child will draw a clothed figure, but at the same time will include his legs, stomach, wallet in his pocket, and even the money in the wallet–that is, things he knows about but which cannot be seen in the case in question. In drawing a figure in profile, a child will add a second eye or will include a second leg on a horseman in profile. Finally, very important parts of the object will be omitted; for instance, a child will draw legs that grow straight out of the head, omitting the neck and torso, or will combine individual parts of a figure.

As Sully (1895) showed, children do not strive for representation; they are much more symbolists than naturalists and are in no way concerned with complete and exact similarity, desiring only the most superficial indications. We cannot assume that children know people no better than they depict them; rather they try more to name and designate than to represent. A child's memory does not yield a simple depiction of representational images at this age. Rather, it yields predispositions to judgments that are invested with speech or capable of being so invested. We see that when a child unburdens his repository of memory in drawing, he does so in the mode of speech – telling a story. A major feature of this mode is a certain degree of abstraction, which any verbal representation necessarily entails. Thus we see that drawing is graphic speech that arises on the basis of verbal speech. The schemes that distinguish children's first drawings are reminiscent in this sense of verbal concepts that communicate only the essential features of objects. This gives us grounds for regarding children's drawing as a preliminary stage in the development of written language.

The further development of children's drawing, however, is not something self-understood and purely mechanical. There is a critical moment in going from simple mark-making on paper to the use of pencil-marks as signs that depict or mean something. All psychologists agree that the child must discover that the lines he makes can signify something. Sully illustrates this discovery using the example of a child who haphazardly drew a spiral line, without any meaning, suddenly grasped a certain similarity, and joyfully exclaimed, 'Smoke, smoke!'

Although this process of recognizing what is drawn is encountered in early childhood, it is still not equivalent to the discovery of symbolic function, as observations have shown. Initially, even if a child perceives a similarity in a drawing, he takes the drawing to be an object that is similar or of the same kind, not as a representation or symbol of the object.

When a girl who was shown a drawing of her doll exclaimed, 'A doll just like mine!' it is possible that she had in mind another object just like hers. According to Hetzer, there is no evidence that forces us to assume that assimilation of the drawing to an object means at the same time an understanding that the drawing is a representation of the object. For the girl, the drawing is not a representation of a doll but another doll just like hers. Proof of this is provided by the fact that for a long time children relate to drawings as if they were objects. For example, when a drawing shows a boy with his back to the observer, the child will turn the sheet over to try to see the face. Even among 5 year olds we always observed that, in response to the question, 'Where is his face and nose?' children would turn the drawing over, and only then would answer, 'It's not there, it's not drawn.'

We feel that Hetzer is most justified in asserting that primary symbolic representation should be ascribed to speech, and that it is on the basis of speech that all the other sign systems are created. Indeed, the continuing shift toward the beginning in the moment of naming a drawing is also evidence of the strong impact of speech on the development of children's drawing.

We have had the opportunity of observing experimentally how children's drawing becomes real written language by giving them the task of symbolically depicting some more or less complex phrase. What was most clear in these experiments was a tendency on the part of school-age children to change from purely pictographic to ideographic writing, that is, to represent individual relations and meaning by abstract symbolic signs. We observed this dominance of speech over writing in one school child who wrote each word of the phrase in question as a separate drawing. For example, the phrase 'I do not see the sheep, but they are there' was recorded as follows: a figure of a person ('I'), the same figure with its eyes covered ('don't see'), two sheep ('the sheep'), an index finger and several trees behind which the sheep can be seen ('but they are there'). The phrase 'I respect you' was rendered as follows: a head ('I'), two human figures, one of which has his hat in hand ('respect') and another head ('you').

Thus, we see how the drawing obediently follows the phrase and how spoken language intrudes into children's drawings. In this process, the children frequently had to make genuine discoveries in inventing an appropriate mode of representation, and we were able to see that this is decisive in the development of writing and drawing in children.

SYMBOLISM IN WRITING

In connection with our general research, Luria (1929) undertook to create this moment of discovery of the symbolics of writing so as to be able to study it systematically. In his experiments children who were as yet unable to write were confronted with the task of making some simple form of notation. The children were told to remember a certain number of phrases that greatly exceeded their natural memory capacity. When each child became convinced that he would not be able to remember them all, he was given a sheet of paper and asked to mark down or record the words presented in some fashion.

Frequently, the children were bewildered by this suggestion, saying that they could not write, but the experimenter furnished the child with a certain procedure and examined the extent to which the child was able to master it and extent to which the pencil-marks ceased to be simple playthings and became symbols for recalling the appropriate phrases. In the 3–4 year old stage, the child's notations are of no assistance in remembering the phrases; in recalling them, the child does not look at the paper. But we occasionally encountered some seemingly astonishing cases that were sharply at variance with this general observation. In these cases, the child also makes meaningless and undifferentiated squiggles and lines, but when he reproduces phrases it seems as though he is reading them; he refers to certain specific marks and can repeatedly indicate, without error, which marks denote which phrase. An entirely new relationship to these marks and a self-reinforcing motor activity arise: for the first time the marks become mnemotechnic symbols. For example, the children place individual marks on different parts of the page in such a way as to associate a certain phrase with each mark. A characteristic kind of topography arises – one mark in one corner means a cow, while another farther up means a chimney-sweep. Thus the marks are primitive indicatory signs for memory purposes.

We are fully justified in seeing the first precursor of future writing in this mnemotechnic stage. Children gradually transform these undifferentiated marks. Indicatory signs and symbolizing marks and scribbles are placed by little figures and pictures, and these in turn give way to signs. Experiments have made it possible not only to describe the very moment of discovery itself but also to follow how the process occurs as a function of certain factors. For example, the content and forms introduced into the phrases in question first break down the meaningless nature of the notation. If we introduce quantity into the material, we can readily evoke a notation that reflects this quantity, even in 4 and 5 year olds. (It was the need for recording quantity, perhaps, that historically first gave rise to writing.) In the same way, the introduction of color and form are conducive to the child's discovery of the principle of writing. For example, phrases such as 'like black', 'black smoke from a chimney', 'there is white snow in winter', ' a mouse with a long tail', or 'Lyalya has two eyes and one nose' rapidly cause the child to change over from writing that functions as indicatory gesture to writing that contains the rudiments of representation.

It is easy to see that the written signs are entirely first-order symbols at this point, directly denoting objects or actions, and the child has yet to reach second-order symbolism, which involves the creation of written signs for the spoken symbols of words. For this the child must make a basic discovery – namely that one can draw not only things but also speech. It was only this discovery that lead humanity to the brilliant method of writing by words and letters; the same thing leads children to letter writing. From the pedagogical point of view, this transition should be arranged by shifting the child's activity from drawing things to drawing speech. It is difficult to specify how this shift takes place, since the appropriate research has yet to lead to definite conclusions, and the generally accepted methods of teaching writing do not permit the observation of it. One thing only is certain – that the written language of children develops in this fashion, shifting from drawings of things to drawing of words. Various methods of teaching writing perform this in various ways. Many of them employ auxiliary gestures as a means of uniting the written and spoken symbol; others employ drawings that depict the appropriate objects. The entire secret of teaching written language is to prepare and organize this natural transition appropriately. As soon as it is achieved, the child has mastered the principle of written language and then it remains only to perfect this method.

Given the current state of psychological knowledge, our notion that make-believe play, drawing, and writing can be viewed as different moments in an essentially unified process of development of written language will appear to be very much overstated. The discontinuities and jumps from one mode of activity to another are too great for the relationship to seem evident. But experiments and psychological analysis lead us to this very conclusion. They show that, however complex the process of development of written language may seem, or however erratic, disjointed, and confused it may appear superficially, there is in fact a unified historical line that leads to the highest forms of written language. This higher form, which we will mention only in passing, involves the reversion of written language from second-order symbolism to first-order symbolism. As second-order symbols, written symbols function as designations for verbal ones. Understanding of written language is first effected through spoken language, but gradually this path is curtailed and spoken language disappears as the intermediate link. To judge from all the available evidence, written language becomes direct symbolism that is perceived in the same way as spoken language. We need only try to imagine the enormous changes in the cultural development of children that occur as a result of mastery of written language and the ability to read – and of thus becoming aware of everything that human genius has created in the realm of the written word.

PRACTICAL IMPLICATIONS

An overview of the entire developmental history of written language in children leads us naturally to three exceptionally important practical conclusions.

The first is that, from our point of view, it would be natural to transfer the teaching of writing to the preschool years. Indeed, if younger children are capable of discovering the symbolic function of writing, as Hetzer's experiments have shown, then the teaching of writing should be made the responsibility of preschool education. Indeed, we see a variety of circumstances which indicate that in the Soviet Union the teaching of writing clearly comes too late from the psychological point of view. At the same time, we know that the teaching of reading and writing generally begins at age six in most European and American countries.

Hetzer's research indicates that 80 percent of 3 year olds can master an arbitrary combination of sign and meaning, while almost all 6 year olds are capable of this operation. On the basis of her observations, one may conclude that development between 3 and 6 years involves not so much mastery of arbitrary signs as it involves progress in attention and memory. Therefore Hetzer favors beginning to teach reading at earlier ages. To be sure, she disregards the fact that writing is second-order symbolism, whereas what she studied was first-order symbolism.

Burt (1917) reports that although compulsory schooling begins at age 5 years in England, children between 3 and 5 are allowed into school if there is room and are taught the alphabet. The great majority of children can read at 4½. Montessori (1965) is particularly in favor of teaching reading and writing at an earlier age. In the course of game situations, generally through preparatory exercises, all the children in her kindergartens in Italy begin to write at 4 and can read as well as 1st-graders at age 5.

But Montessori's example best shows that the situation is much more complex than it may appear at first glance If we temporarily ignore the correctness and beauty of the letters her children draw and focus on the content of what they write, we find messages like the following: 'Happy Easter to Engineer Talani and Headmistress Montessori. Best wishes to the director, the teacher, and to Doctor Montessori. Children's House, Via Campania', and so forth. We do not deny the possibility of teaching reading and writing to preschool children; we even regard it as desirable that a young child enter school if he is able to read and write. But the teaching should be organized in such a way that reading and writing are necessary for something. If they are used only to write official greetings to the staff or whatever the teacher thinks up (and clearly suggests to them), then the exercise will be purely mechanical and may soon bore the child; his activity will not be manifest in his writing and his budding personality will not grow. Reading and writing must be something the child needs. Here we have the most vivid example of the basic contradition that appears in the teaching of writing not only in Montessori's school but in most other schools as well, namely, that writing is taught as a motor skill and not as a complex cultural necessarily entails a second requirement: writing must be 'relevant to life – in the same way that we require a 'relevant' arithmetic.

A second conclusion, then, is that writing should be meaningful for children, that an intrinsic need should be aroused in them, and that writing should be incorporated into a task that is necessary and relevant for life. Only then can we be certain that it will develop not as a matter of hand and finger habits but as a really new and complex form of speech.

The third point that we are trying to advance as a practical conclusion is the requirement that writing be *taught* naturally. In this respect, Montessori has done a great deal. She has shown that the motor aspect of this activity can indeed be engaged in the course of children's play, and that writing should be 'cultivated' rather than 'imposed'. She offers a well-motivated approach to the development of writing.

Following this path, a child approaches writing as a natural moment in her development, and not as training from without. Montessori has shown that kindergarten is the appropriate setting for teaching, reading and writing, and this means that the best method is one in which children do not learn to read and write but in which both these skills are found in play situations. For this it is necessary that letters become elements of children's life in the same way, for instance, that speech is. In the same way as children learn to speak, they should be able to learn to read and write. Natural methods of teaching reading and writing involve appropriate operations on the child's environment. Reading and writing should become necessary for her in her play. But what Montessori has done as regards the motor aspects of this skill should now be done in relation to the internal aspect of written language and its functional assimilation. Of course, it is also necessary to bring the child to an inner understanding of writing and to arrange that writing will be organized development rather than learning. For this we can indicate only an extremely general approach; in the same way that manual labor and mastery of line-drawing are preparatory exercises for Montessori in developing writing skills, drawing and play should be preparatory stages in the development of a children's written language. Educators should organize all these actions and the entire complex process of transition from one mode of written language to another. They should follow it through its critical moments up to the discovery of the fact that one can draw not only objects but also speech. If we wished to summarize all these practical requirements and express them as a single one, we could say that children should be taught written language, not just the writing of letters.

REFERENCES

Baldwin, J. M. (1895). *Mental Development in the Child and the Race*. Macmillan, New York.

Buhler, K. (1930). *Mental Development of the Child*. Harcourt Brace, New York.
Burt, C. (1917). *Distribution of Educational Abilities*. P. S. King and Sons, London.
Hetzer, H. (1926). *Die Symbolische Darstelling in der fruhen Windhert*. Deutscher Verlag fur Jugend und Volk, Vienna.
Luria, A. R. (1929). Materials on the development of writing in children. *Problemi Marksiskogo Vospitaniya,* **1**, 143–176.
Montessori, M. (1965). *Spontaneous Activity in Education*. Schoken, New York.
Sully, J. (1896). *Studies of Childhood*. Appleton, London and New York.
Wurth. Reference not available.

PART V

Difference And Deficit In Written Language

Jonson: *Explorata: Consuetudo.*	I will like and praise some things in a young writer which yet, if he continue in, I cannot but justly hate him for.
Jonson: *Explorata; De Stylo.*	Ready writing makes not good writing: but good writing brings on ready reading.
Pope: *Eassy on Criticism.*	Whoever thinks a faultless piece to see Thinks what n'er was, nor is, nor e'er shall be. In every work regard the writer's end Since none can compass more than they intend; And if the means be just, the conduct true, Applause, in spite of trivial faults, is due.

The Psychology of Written Language
Edited by M. Martlew

CHAPTER 12

Problems and Difficulties: Cognitive and Communicative Aspects of Writing

MARGARET MARTLEW

Producing prose that is both interesting and informative is a highly complex enterprise. It is hardly surprising therefore that many find writing difficult. An awareness of difficulty is potentially present at all stages of development, from beginners' initial problems in forming and spacing letters to professional writers' struggle to select the best words and order for their thoughts. The degree of difficulty experienced is related to the particular type of writing and to the writer's awareness of what the writing task requires. The level of writing ability does not necessarily alleviate the experience of difficulty, it merely alters its focus. Experienced writers, freed from having to give conscious attention to the mechanics of writing, shift their focus to higher-order skills and the cognitive awareness of different orders of difficulty from those experienced by beginning writers. Galbraith (1980) points this out, for instance, when he suggests that what we write often appears impoverished compared with what we wanted to write. This is reflected in one of the themes running through *The Four Quartets*, which Eliot expresses as;

> Trying to use words, and every attempt
> Is a wholly new start, and a different kind of failure
> Because one has only learned to get the better of words
> For the thing one no longer has to say, or the way in which
> One is no longer disposed to say it.
> (T. S. Eliot: *East Coker*)

One of the major problems is that of sustaining coherence between topic, audience and communicative goals. New ideas evolve in the course of writing and these, even for experienced writers, can create a separation between the goals governing modes of expression and those relating to ideas. It is all too easy to adopt a pretentious style, as, for example, the obscurantism and verbosity that fill pages of academic journals and official documents (Wason, 1980a).

While fluent prose may not always be easy to produce, however, many writers can still express themselves with reasonable competence, their finished texts not generally revealing the difficulties that were encountered in the process of composition. This is not the case with poor and beginning writers. Their writing reflects deviations from the accepted conventions of formal written text. These deviations can occur at all levels, from illegible handwriting and aberrant spelling to revealing a lack of organization or awareness of the reader's requirements for understanding what has been written.

Questions as to what a writer needs to know, and how he acquires and utilizes this knowledge, have been the subject of recent insightful theoretical and empirical approaches (Bereiter and Scardamalia, 1980, 1981; Scardamalia and Bereiter, 1980; Gregg and Steinberg, 1980; Olson, 1977a,b,c; Wason, 1980b; Matsuhashi, 1981). Beginning writers develop an awareness of the skills and knowledge needed to overcome their problems at various stages in their acquisition of written language skills. Poor writers, on the other hand, retain many of the characteristics of beginning writers, and leave school, despite years of enforced literacy, with a poor grasp of written language. There is obviously no one simple answer why this should be so. Motivational factors can be as important as cognitive or linguistic difficulties. External factors, such as teaching environments, will also create differential effects.

Poor writers, despite their maturity and different world experience, can remain as beginning writers at one or many of the component skills and levels of written language. Observations of the written products of poor writers characterize them as writing as they speak (Olson, 1977a), this being connected to certain cognitive states and social conditions which leads to a failure to be explicit or to be aware of the 'decontextualized' nature of written language (Elasser and John-Steiner, 1977). Ideas are put down as they arise, so planning is at a local rather than at a global level (Bereiter, 1980) and little time is spent in prewriting activities (Stallard, 1974). Reference is unclear and unspecified in a way that is more appropriate to spoken than written language (Collins and Williamson, 1981). Conceptually, Flower and Hayes (1980) suggest, poor writers may have an inadequate schema. Having failed to automatize skills, they cannot concentrate on composing: 'For the inexperienced or remedial writer, the rules of grammar and the conventions of usage and syntax may make enormous demands on time and attention.'

Why these generalizations typify poor writers requires explanation. These can be explored by examining the similarities and differences of spoken and written language and considering the knowledge and awareness that is needed for competent written discourse. Poor writers themselves provide evidence of failures in performance and it is often the case that a system in error can provide useful insights into the characteristics of the production system itself. The question also needs to be set in a developmental context. Poor writers fail to show progressive mastery and co-ordination of skills in writing. Is this because the task demands are too complex or because they adopt habitual ways of approaching the task and thereby remain unaware that they have problems in writing? To effect a change, the writer has to realize that change is desirable. Professional authors can find writing difficult but paradoxically some poor writers may have the problem of not finding certain aspects of writing difficult and so persist in habits detrimental to communicative effectiveness: 'What is written without effort is in general read without pleasure' (Samuel Johnson, *Miscellanies*, Volume 2). It is possible that some poor writers do not fully realize in what ways their writing is inadequate, or that they do not realize how to effect a change. Alternatively, some may fail at other levels because they cannot maintain their goals when faced with the total complexities of the writing task.

Following a general examination of the differences between spoken and written language, I wish therefore, in this chapter, to consider poor writers in the context of the development of communication skills, conceptual knowledge, and cognitive awareness. I shall conclude with a discussion of the writing processes of poor and better writers based on inferences made from pausing during the production of written essays.

SPOKEN AND WRITTEN LANGUAGE

Language, whether spoken or written, is a highly evolved, adaptive, and complex system for communicating a vast range of meaning. Both spoken and written language are engagements in discourse, their essential function is communication. Although these systems are obviously interlinked, effective written discourse cannot, however, be construed as simply transcribed speech. The strategies for claiming a reader's active participation depend on different skills and knowledge from verbal conversation, operations which require more conscious awareness and complex integration than those needed for spoken discourse.

The close affinities of these two systems of communication create difficulties in distinguishing real differences from those which are more immediately apparent. The more apparent are those manifested by transcription skills (handwriting, spelling, and punctuation), whereby concepts are translated into conventionalized visible marks rather than acoustic signals. The real differences, I suggest, lie in the cognitive and linguistic processes utilized in composing text as opposed to engaging in spoken discourse. This reflects the functional difference between the two systems. From a linguistic viewpoint, Vachek (1973) defined the norm of written language as 'a system of graphically manifestable language elements whose function is to react to a given stimulus (which is not an urgent one) in a static way, i.e. in a preservable and easily surveyable manner, concentrating on the purely communicative aspect of the approach of the reacting language users'. From this definition, and an equivalent one for spoken norms, Vachek goes on to argue that some situations are more appropriate for one form of expression than the other and that, in cultured language communities, it is essential to have a command of both to fully exploit the potential of language.

Development of Speech and Writing

When children start to write they already have a good knowledge of how to use spoken language in ordinary conversational exchanges. They have acquired these communicative skills from social interactions which go back to the preverbal period, before they could produce even one word. Spoken language is acquired in a highly motivating social context (Bates, 1976; Bruner, 1978; Snow and Ferguson, 1977; Waterson and Snow, 1978) and children find it a very effective way of achieving communicative goals. Normally, it is acquired with very little effort, the initial production and recognition of sounds probably being facilitated by biological mechanisms which enable children to make phonological distinctions in the early months of life (Eimas and Tartter, 1979). By the time children start formal schooling they have generally, and apparently with little conscious effort, acquired all the basic structures of the adult language and a flexible and adaptive functional range.

Children come to written language, therefore, with a concept of spoken language as a rewarding social reciprocity, attained with apparent ease. Compared with speech, however, the acquisition of writing is slow and more effortful, removed from immediate communicative purposes. Apart from the few children who write before they can read (Chomsky, 1979) and produce text for their own enjoyment (Britton, 1981), most children acquire written language from classroom tuition, as a solitary activity with no immediate feedback. As Vygotsky (1962) puts it, writing is an abstraction, a means of representing language through secondary symbolism, where the sign stands for words which in turn stand for objects and events in the real world.

Children starting to write have to cope with segmentation problems and realize that words are built up from letters which are not neccessarily isomorphic with the sounds of a language. They also have to demarcate sentence boundaries, connecting words into fully formed grammatical sentences using appropriate punctuation markers. Concepts of what constitutes a sentence do not need to be made explicit in speech. What constitutes an acceptable grammatical sentence in formal written language, therefore, has to be dissociated from what is acceptable as a spoken utterance. In Sheffield, we investigated the awareness of a group of 16–17 year old poor writers as to what would constitute an acceptable, fully formed sentence in a written text. We found a 90 per cent error rate in their acceptance of familiar expressions such as 'Two pints of bitter, please' as complete, formal sentences. The usual reason given for acceptance, particularly also for descriptive noun phrases (for example, 'a bright red skirt'), was that they could have been answers to questions ('What did you buy?'). This is interesting when comparisons are made with a 7-year-old's responses in a game played to assess the grammatical acceptability of sentences (Gleitman *et al.*, 1972)

Adult: How about this: *know the answer*.
Child: That's the only way to say it I think.
Adult: The only way to say what?
Child: You better *know the answer*.

This segment, 'know the answer', was accepted because it could be attached to another segment of a spoken utterance, a link that was being made by the 16–17 year old poor writers.

Some who did recognize that certain constructions would be inappropriate as sentences in a written composition, showed that they confused the concept of sentence with truth value. For instance, a reason for 'students sitting on the stairs' being unacceptable, was that it was wrong for students to sit on the stairs. The phrase was given the same kind of contextual reality that young children give to the concept of words, Vygotsky (1962), for example, asking 'Why is cow a word?' received the answer 'Because it has horns.' They failed to calculate the logical implicature of the sentence, assimilating it instead into what they know (Olson, 1977a; Chapter 2, this volume). If poor writers are at this level in their conceptualization of what a sentence is, then it is not surprising that their syntactic expression resembles transcribed speech.

Speech and Writing; Production Features

Speech, as Olson (1977b) says, is a flexible, all-purpose instrument, unconstrained by the conventions that characterize written language.

Speech is transient and fades rapidly, so when we listen, we concentrate on extracting meaning and soon forget the original form of the utterance (Jarvella, 1970; Sachs, 1967; Bransford *et al.*, 1972). Disfluencies and errors largely pass unnoticed unless one has a scientific interest in speech production or a quick response to certain Freudian slips of the tongue. Pronunciation is by no means standard, but this rarely interferes with comprehension. Gross unconventional spelling or literal transcriptions can make comprehension almost impossible ('tin tin tin', for example, roughly represents the Sheffield sound equivalent for 'it isn't in the tin'). Nor would a run of unfinished or inadequately constructed utterances, which characterize many conversations, conform to the requirements for complete grammatical sentences in written language.

The act of writing creates a visible artefact that is separated from the writer as well as the reader. Because it is a visible and permanent creation, unlike speech, it can be reworked, manipulated, and altered. This is important, for while mistakes and misrepresentations in speech may pass unnoticed in writing they remain to confuse the reader and remind the writer of his inadequacies. In writing, the surface features convey the meaning, so text has to be legible, grammatical, explicit, and unambiguous in a more rigorous way than is required in speech. The reader has to be guided by the context created by the writer to the subtle differences of meaning which, in speech, can be conveyed by pitch, intonation, and tone. Punctuation provides an impoverished equivalent for such features. In formal written language this is particularly so; a heavy splattering of exclamation marks, dashes, and underlining to achieve emphasis, for example, would be inappropriate. Punctuation can substitute for intonation to a certain extent, by demarcation, as in 'My friend decided the doctor was lying.' as opposed to 'My friend, decided the doctor, was lying.' It can also serve, in a limited and not wholly desirable way, to disambiguate badly constructed sentences, as in 'For sale; bath, for a baby, with a non-slip bottom.' It is really the question mark which stands out as an accepted marker for registering changes in pitch or intonation, otherwise changes of expression of meaning have to be written into the text.

Producing written marks as opposed to sounds, involves different parts of the body, oral/aural as opposed to visuo/motor mechanisms, though it is possible that aural processes are implicated in writing more than in reading (Frith, 1980). Handwriting is slower and requires more physical effort than speech, particularly for the inexperienced writer. For instance, while it took approximately 12 minutes to produce a written sample of 200 words, 200 spoken words took only 2 minutes (Horowitz and Newman, 1964), or, alternatively, approximately two spoken items are produced per second, as opposed to six written syllables (Newman and Nicholson, 1976). But although writing is generally associated with making visible marks on paper, either by handwriting or typing, this is not a necessary distinguishing feature which differentiates it from speech. Text of all kinds, from letters to novels, can be produced from dictation. Gould (1978a) has shown that inexperienced subjects could learn to dictate letters which were indistinguishable from handwritten ones, with very little practice. Also speeches can be written as though they were spontaneous productions of the moment, and dramatic conversations transcribed to simulate free exchanges of discourse.

In practical terms, however, writing in school generally involves handwriting. Handwriting, the forming of letters with conventional shapes and their combination into accepted spelling patterns, requires the development of complex visuo-motor skills (Thomassen and Teulings, Chapter 8, this volume), so that familiar words can be run off from available lists without conscious attention having to be given to the process. Also, in order to communicate, handwriting needs to be legible. Though many take a perverse pride in having illegible handwriting, illegibility can have detrimental consequences, affecting such things as spelling achievement and teachers' assessment of the content of essays (Graham and Miller, 1980).

Conceptual Differences between Speech and Writing

The major distinguishing characteristics between speech and writing lie more in the conceptualization and expression of meaning than in the mode of execution of ideas. In conversation, listeners can infer what is meant from how and where comments are made, as much as from the words used. If there is any doubt or confusion, the speaker can repeat or rephrase, and ideas are generated mutually. Conversations are shared engagements where the primary intention to get ideas across is not necessarily curtailed by grammatical disfluency. As Chafe (1980) says:

> 'the speaker's chief goal is to get across what he has in mind, and he is not likely to be interested in grammaticality unless there is good reason to think of it and usually there is not. ... After someone has said something, it would not be a damaging criticism to tell him 'You spoke ungrammatically', I doubt if the average person would care. But it would be damaging to say 'You didn't get across what you had in mind.'

Written language, because it is permanent, lays us open to scrutiny and assessment in the way we record our thoughts, opinions, and feelings. Evaluation is associated with written language from the early stages of acquisition, throughout the school years, and for some it extends through a lifetime. Children progress through school scanning pages returned to them with corrective red marks showing where they offended, several days or weeks previously, against certain written conventions. Or, as Shuy (1980) wryly points out, passages are designated as 'awk', or 'monot.', comments frequently ignored by the children and which teachers themselves often find difficult to enlarge on.

The effectiveness of spoken discourse, on the other hand, is rarely subjected to close analysis. We converse without giving a lot of conscious attention to the processes which result in rapidly articulated utterances. The occasional reflection that 'I could have phrased that in a better way' or the careful planning of a deliberated utterance are not frequent occurrences in the give-and-take of normal discourse. Conversations generally take place without conscious reflection, without thought processes themselves being the object of higher-order cognitive processes, in a metacognitive manner, which is the case with most formal written language.

Both the cognitive and linguistic demands of written language generate complexities greater than those encountered in speech. Writers, unaided by the facilitative prompts available in the context of spoken discourse, have to formulate their ideas and translate them into visible, highly conventionalized language; to reflect, in form, function, and content, a meaningful discourse with a reader distanced from them in space and time. Meaning has to be made explicit by the choice and ordering of words, inference being constrained by the lack of an immediate and shared context (Olson, 1977b). In everyday language we do not tend to use language in a strictly logical way. Logical discourse involves the use of linguistic forms in a relatively inflexible manner for postulating relationships. Children's developing awareness of the logical aspects of language use can be observed in many of their jokes when they realize that the idiomatic intention of an utterance differs from the literal meaning (Shultz and Robillard, 1980). This deliberate mismatch of idiomatic and logical use of language is the basis of much of the humour in *Alice Through The Looking Glass*, as the following extract illustrates:

> 'There's nothing like eating hay when you're faint', he remarked to her, as he munched away.
> 'I should think throwing cold water over you would be better', Alice suggested, 'or some sal-volatile.'
> 'I didn't say there was nothing *better*', the King repied. 'I said there was nothing *like* it' which Alice did not venture to deny.

In writing, the text creates the context and the writer has to develop from this, carefully assessing what can be assumed knowledge extending beyond the given text and what has to be explicitly stated and elaborated within it.

Shared context and reciprocity have another important advantage in speech that is lacking in writing. If a speaker runs out of ideas, someone else can take the floor and can in turn stimulate further developments to the conversational theme. Composing in isolation can be very difficult for many, who experience initial problems in retrieving related ideas from memory and then in organizing and developing them. Children have to learn to provide their own prompts to enable them to retrieve material to write about (Bereiter, 1980). Isolation also makes it difficult to keep the reader in mind, though this is differentially affected by the type of discourse being produced. Discursive text, for instance, which encourages the reader to concentrate on the topic of the essay, is more likely to cause the writer to ignore the reader's needs than persuasive writing where the task is audience-centred (Crowhurst and Piché, 1979).

In summary, then, dissociating written language from spoken expression requires a different way of thinking about, and being aware of, language. It is, however, perhaps misleading to discuss the differences in terms of 'spoken' and 'written', terms which can be misleading in their apparent focus on the mode of production. Written language is used to define a use of language where compositional goals are achieved using a highly conventionalized form of language. The mode of production is to a certain extent immaterial. As Gould (1978b) discovered, for instance, his letter-writing experiments, good authors were good authors whether dictating or writing, compositional factors were more important than output modality factors. The nature of the kind of cognition needed, and the knowledge and skills involved, can be traced in terms of both specific and general linguistic and cognitive development in relation to composing text.

WRITING: COMMUNICATION AND COGNITION

When composing text, effective communication requires fulfilment of the goals of the writing task by the application of appropriate cognitive procedures at all levels through sustained awareness of what is involved. These three aspects of the writing task are listed in Figure 1. This gives a broad schematic representation of the interactive aspects of the linguistic and cognitive processes and procedures operative during the writing process, but does not attempt to model these in detail.

Writing: Process and Product

The complexities of what the production of text involves is best considered from the extensive discussion given to this question by Cooper and Matsuhashi (Chapter 1, this volume). The broad outline here focuses on the cognitive and linguistic strategies interactive during the process.

Theoretically, the writing task presents the writer with a communicative goal whereby, through a series of integrated strategies, he attempts to

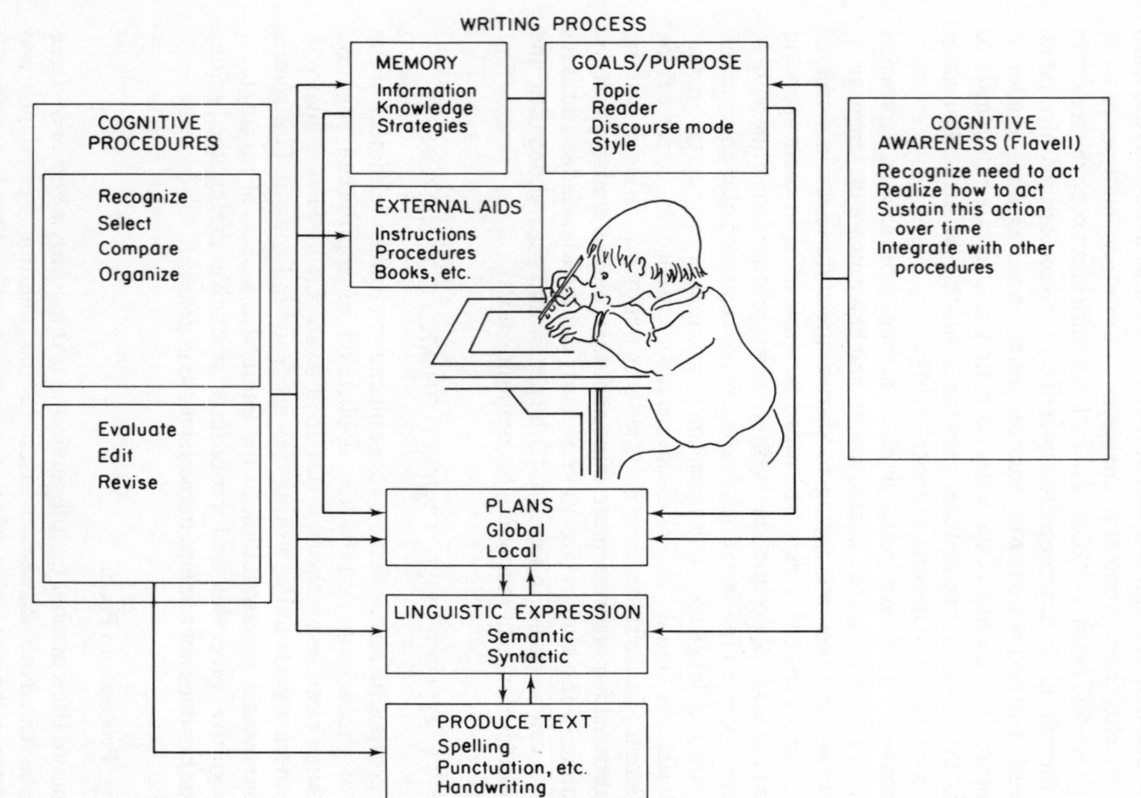

FIGURE 1 Schematic representation of cognitive processes in writing

achieve his recognized aims. These are to write on a particular topic, for an envisaged reader, in a selected mode and appropriate style. This involves the utilization of a series of complex procedures which should be operative at all levels of the writing task from, for example, checking spelling to revising global organization.

Initially, in the planning stage, the writer considers what relevant knowledge he has on a subject. This has to be retrieved from long-term memory or collected from external material, then structured to satisfy the needs of the material itself and possibly, the anticipated reader. During the planning operation the procedures of differentiating, selecting, evaluating, and revising lead to a general selection and ordering of the appropriate material. This plan has then to be translated into a linguistic representation, again with the writer calling these cognitive procedures into operation where appropriate, to select and evaluate particular semantic and syntactic choices. Thus the text is operated on, analysed, and revised in view of what has been written or is planned to follow and adapted to achieve topic and audience goals.

Each stage of the writing process is affected by constraints, both external and internal. The external may be trivial: a stuffy room, a leaky pen; or highly demanding: such as writing an examination script or creating a poem. The internal constraints relate to the individual's experience, vocabulary, ability to make experience available, to organize and integrate, etc. All these will affect the resulting text in relation to achieving interesting and effective communicative goals in respect of audience, topic, and mode of discourse. Writers vary in their approaches to writing (Wason, 1980a). Some spend a long time planning in detail what they will write, others prepare numerous rough drafts, and writers frequently find that ideas evolve in the process of writing. Experienced writers can pre-plan, plan, and execute this plan, switching their attention from the immediate sentence to other selected focal points. Their high level of skill gives them essential flexibility which ensures cohesion and intelligibility as their goals are sustained throughout the writing process.

Writing proficiency is advanced when writers successfully automate what could be termed the lower-order skills relating to the transcriptions aspects of writing. When the majority of words used can be run off without having to focus on spelling, and clause boundaries are automatically demarcated by appropriate punctuation and capitalization, the writer is relieved from having to devote conscious attention to these operations. The writer can then focus on the higher-level operations needed to maintain an awareness of overall global aims, either in accordance with a prespecified plan or integrating new ideas which evolve in the course of composition.

This level of expertise develops over time with children's increasing mastery of complex syntax (Harrell, 1957; O'Donnell *et al.*, 1967; Ingram, 1975) and semantics (Katz and Brent, 1968; Rosenthal, 1979; Ackerman, 1978). Complex syntax develops gradually matched by parallel cognitive progression as children move from the concrete operational level to logical awareness associated with formal operations. Loban (1976) noted a plateau in complexity of oral language at about 13 years followed a year later in written language. Having a varied range of syntactic constructions makes it possible for experienced writers to be precise and economic in their expression. This development can be seen even in the early stages of composition when relative clauses emerge and replace 'and' conjunctions, as Ingram (1975) illustrates:

> 'Once there was a kitten and its name was Cindy.'
> 'Once there was a kitten named Cindy.'
> 'Once there was a big scarry man and he had lots of faces.'
> 'Once there was a big scarry man with lots of faces.'

Experienced writers can express complex ideas in simple syntactic frames and also, as Hunt (Chapter 4, this volume) points out, condense a number of related ideas within a single sentence frame. Children's linguistic development therefore is integrated with the growth of their conceptual capacity which allows them to reflect on language and their own thought processes.

Metacognitive Awareness and the Utilization of Cognitive Procedures

Mature speakers of a language have the ability to reflect on and evaluate the language they use. Some of these metalinguistic skills are apparent even in very young children (Clark, 1978; Slobin, 1978; de Villiers and de Villiers, 1972; Gleitman *et al* 1972), but their awareness of language, as Hakes (1980) points out, differs from that of older children and adults. He suggests that young children seem to notice and comment on some aspect of an utterance almost as though without an intention of doing so. It happens spontaneously. Whereas adults and older children do the same thing, they also develop the capacity to deliberately reflect on language, which, he proposes, may relate to an increasing ability to engage in controlled cognitive processing operations.

Writing is a more deliberate and conscious act than speech, and requires the ability to reflect upon language in ways parallel to those discussed by Flavell (1979), Flavell *et al.* (1981). Metacognitive abilities reflect an ability to think and act deliberately, to be able to stand back from a situation and reflect upon it. Metalinguistic skills involve reflecting upon the properties of language and in communicative terms, being able to consciously select, evaluate, revise, and reject what is inappropriate in terms of given situations and listeners/readers. Effective communication depends on messages being formulated to satisfy specific needs of listeners/readers. Flavell (1974), in his model of role-taking skills, proposes that initially children have to recognize that such a need exists, recognize that action is required, and then find ways of acting upon their awareness of this need. The next step is to be able to maintain this awareness and appropriate action over time.

In ordinary conversation, even very young children seem, in their performance skills, to be able to role-take in the way outlined by Flavell. There is ample literature to show that children can adapt to the needs of different listeners (Martlew, 1979). For example, young children have demonstrated that they can change the content of their descriptions of events to listeners who were or were not present when an event took place (Menig-Peterson, 1975), or make allowances for constraints on listeners' comprehension abilities, adapting their utterances for listeners who cannot see (Maratsos, 1973), or for children younger than themselves as opposed to adults (Shatz and Gelman, 1973) and can do so without cues from another person, either in dramatic monologues (Martlew *et al.*, 1978) or talking to dolls (Sachs and Devin, 1976).

Children in ordinary conversations rely heavily on context to give semantic value to their communication. When spoken language has been assessed in situations where contextual reference has been curtailed, and precise verbal reference has been necessary for effective communication, young children have been found to be less adequate at making themselves understood than in normal spontaneous speech. In experimental situations, when deprived of contextual aids, or asked to give precise definitions which require selection and evaluation of relevant criteria, children of 7 and 8 years have been unable to communicate adequately. Either they fail to decentre from their own egocentric viewpoint (Glucksberg *et al.*, 1975) or they do not operate the necessary procedures to choose effective descriptions (Asher and Oden, 1976). It is also possible that young children are not aware that verbal messages do actually convey meaning (Robinson and Robinson, 1976). They lack an understanding of what communication is (Robinson, 1981) largely because they fail to conceptualize what messages mean to listeners because messages do not 'themselves become objects of cognitive scrutiny and evaluation' (Flavell, 1976).

These referential situations have parallels with written language in that the writer is removed from the reader, unable to rely on contextual aids, and has to make meaning specific.

In writing, an awareness of the reader, in relation to style and content, has to be sustained solely by internal prompts throughout the entire exercise. Maintaining this awareness of the reader may well be one of the most problematic aspects of writing. To what extent children can do this is unclear. Crowhurst and Piché (1979) found that 12 year olds differentiated their ways of writing persuasive arguments by using more complex syntax for a teacher than a friend; 15 year olds, however, showed little evidence of adaptation on a persuasiveness measure when writing for three audiences of different degrees of familiarity to the writer and there was no clear evidence of syntactic differences (Rubin and Piché, 1979).

When we asked groups of 11 year olds, 13 year olds, and adults to write stories for adults as opposed to children, an adaptation which even very young children can achieve in a social context, the 11 year olds failed to do this. The 13 year olds reflected a significant difference on only one measure; that is, they used more abstract nouns when writing for adults (Martlew, 1978). The adult group appeared to alter their way of writing on the syntactic and semantic measures taken but there may be some doubt as to whether all adults can change their way of writing as readily and as automatically as they can their way of speaking. Over a third of the adults in this study wrote very short, condensed stories for children. Further examination of this subgroup showed that there was no differentiation for the intended reader on any measure except one. This was the same as that found for the 13 year olds; they used significantly more abstract nouns in their stories for adults. Interestingly, the 11 year old showed an awareness of the need for adaptation but an inability to sustain action to achieve a difference in their writing. Almost 90 per cent began their stories for children, but not for adults, with the conventional opening 'Once upon a time'.

Writers failing to recognize that written language requires different strategies for achieving communicative goals compared with speech, will not be aware of the need to apply certain cognitive procedures at various stages and levels of the writing process. If writers remain unaware of problems – such as, for instance, their lack of cohesiveness or disregard for the listener's viewpoint – they will remain, to varying extents and for different modes of writing, as beginning writers; or rather, turn into poor writers at one or many levels of the writing process. The degree of impoverishment will depend on how far they have progressed in mastering some of the component skills. As poor, or impoverished writers, they will have formed habitual ways of writing which, unlike beginning writers, will have to be unlearned before they can progress. As Bereiter and Scardamalia (1980) point out, attention needs to be given to the coping strategies which children bring to tasks in making use of the knowledge that they have. They found, for instance, that children in 4th to 6th grade had difficulty in explicitly stating what topics they knew either a lot or only a little about. This reflected an inability to perform the necessary memory search and retrieval;

that is, to engage in metamemorial search. Children may continue to use strategies, even if they have not been very efficient. Because the strategies have worked to a certain extent, however, they continue to use them, thereby defeating instructional attempts to improve their written ability.

Knowledge and Skill

When composing, writers are calling on both their linguistic knowledge and knowledge of a more general kind and they are applying skills relevant to communication but which also have more general cognitive application. Ammon (1981) makes these distinctions between knowledge and skill in relation to communication and more general cognitive tasks. He highlights the point that children may have the ability to do something in one situation, such as make comparisons and select criteria on salient bases, or decentre from their own perspective, but be unable to do this in a communicative situation. Some writers therefore may face problems because they cannot utilize certain cognitive procedures, or some may be able to, but may not realize when it would be appropriate. Having knowledge is not sufficient; writers need to be able to make use of this knowledge.

The difficulty may be a fundamental one in relation to knowledge and skill in that competent writing reflects differences in organization and structure from spoken discourse. It may be the case that different knowledge structures are involved in the course of utilization processes operating on world knowledge and linguistic information in writing. Vygotsky (1962) saw written language as 'a separate linguistic function, differing from oral speech in both structure and mode of functioning' because 'the motives are more abstract, more intellectualized, further removed from immediate needs'. Similarly, Olson (1977a) talks about knowledge being relatively specific to the purposes for which it was acquired:

> Knowledge is the picture of reality constructed to sustain some pattern of action. Different patterns of action therefore result in different knowledge structure. I would suggest that written logical statements are not merely representations of knowledge but a particular form of activity that specifies reality in its own biased form.

The question of whether knowledge constructed through active and conscious awareness, as discussed by Flavell (1979), leads to the formulation of different knowledge structures in relation to written language, as posited by Olson, is open to investigation. In practical terms this metacognitive activity provides a basis for much of the empirical work undertaken by Scardamalia and Bereiter (Chapter 3, this volume) in their investigations aimed at improving performance. It also is implied in their interesting paper on inert knowledge (Bereiter and Scardamalia, 1980). They argue that the conscious attainment of generalizable knowledge is not a simple matter but depends on 'a great deal of mental effort expended in a context created by that effort itself'.

If writing necessitates this greater awareness of the utilization of knowledge and the structuring of language to meet the specific constraints of formal conventions, what parallels can be found that connect literacy and changes in cognition? Furthermore, can these illuminate the problems found in the compositions of beginning and poor writers? Cross-cultural studies, making comparisons across literate and non-literate cultures, offer one mode of investigation. Greenfield (1968) adopts an approach sympathetic to Olson, as do Elasser and John-Steiner (1977), supporting the view that written language has implications for cognitive development. They hypothesize that writing is conducive to abstract thought, entailing the mental separation of things from their context, as opposed to speech, which is tied up with context-dependent thought. Is context-dependent language tied up with context-dependent thought, so that once thought is freed from concrete situations, the way is clear for abstract symbolic manipulation of a qualitatively different kind? Scribner and Cole (1978), after examining cognitive abilities on various tasks in literate and non-literate members of the Vai tribe, treat such broad generalizations with qualification. It was apparent that the literate Vais were better at the organization of verbal material but not necessarily better on other tasks demanding the application of abstract cognitive skills. Ingram (1975), hypothesizing that transformational ability develops with writing, cites linguists' difficulties in eliciting complex sentences from non-literate cultures as supportive evidence.

Positing different knowledge structures or utilizing knowledge in specific ways, may also need a theory of how written language develops in the first instance. Vygotsky (1962) suggests that it derives initially from symbolic representation in play and drawing (de Góes and Martlew, Chapter 9, this volume). It then develops from inner speech, which is the language of self-direction and intrapersonal communication. Because of this, writing is initially vague, omitting or not clearly specifying referents. For writing to become effective communication, this predicative idiomatic structure has to be elaborated syntactically and semantically. Speech written down will have similar deficiencies if used as though directed at self as audience, and the reader is left to make inferences based on assumed shared knowledge or context.

Difficulty in Writing and the Problems of Poor Writers

The compositions of beginning writers do suggest a tendency to transcribe speech and to write in an idiomatic form for self. Farrel (1978) supports the notion that beginning writers may be doing little more than roughly transcribing the way they talk with little regard for the conventions of writing. He also assumes that students become beginning writers at different ages and remain at this stage for different lengths of time. Others also hold the view that the writing of novices is characterized by reliance on an oral repertoire. Shaughnessy (1977) noted, among other things, a lack of modification and elaboration of the subject elements of sentences, and also that poor writers assumed the reader knew what was going on in the writer's mind; therefore they omitted introductions, transitions, or explanations. This failure to give explicit information persisted, Collins and Williamson (1981) found, despite the total number of words used increasing with an increase in age. This semantic abbreviation, as they termed it, remained a feature of the compositions of poor writers. Cayer and Sacks (1979) noted that unpractised writers elaborated predicates more than subjects in both their oral and written language. They also retained surface phrases in their writing such as 'you know', 'you see', 'isn't it', etc. Local planning reflects features of unplanned discourse which shows a reduction in syntactic complexity as well as less economy in organization (Kroll, 1978; Ochs, 1979). It is interesting, however, to reflect on the somewhat equivocal findings of studies making comparisons between oral and written language. As mentioned earlier, Gould (1978b) found that good composers were good whether they dictated or wrote letters. There were no differences in sentence length or linguistic differences in their oral and written products, and there were fewer differences between output mode than there were between the speakers and writers. Similarly, Blankenship (1967) discovered more within-group differences between speech and writing than there were stylistic differences between spoken and written language products.

The way language is used habitually in day-to-day interactions may well influence the ease with which individuals can acquire written language. Spoken language may indeed interfere with written language production, but certain ways of speaking may also facilitate its acquisition. Olson (1977a) refers to the specialized form of language appropriate to written text which involves the translation of knowledge into essayist prose. It is this, he claims, that 'makes schooling difficult for most children and completely inaccessible for others, depending on the predominant use of language in the home'. The language generally associated, in broad terms, with the middle class is more similar to formal written language than the context-based language of the more closely knit lower class groups. Although this suggests class can have detrimental effects, if is not necessarily the case (Poole, Chapter 13, this volume) and requires investigation of psychological processes rather than broad sociological descriptions. Individual differences in communication are linked with differences in general cognitive styles, attitudes, awareness, and other interactive factors (Higgins, 1977). Overall group comparisons frequently mask differences between and within individuals, and possibly too much attention has been given to group differences (Mosenthal and Na, 1981). As Dickson (1981) points out when discussing the development of oral communication, more attention should be focused on techniques for measuring the production and receptive skills of the individual.

In summarizing the previous discussion, I wish to return to the question of difficulty in writing, which relates to an awareness of difficulty and the application of strategies, and the problems of poor writers. These, I suggested, may well stem from a lack of awareness of problems, a failure to automate appropriate techniques and to recognize errors and deviations. As writing is a difficult task to perform optimally, greater experience and ability, rather than creating feelings of ease and facility, may only sharpen the realization of the struggle to translate knowledge and experience into text. Realizing communicative aims and strategies for achieving them by manipulating knowledge and language at various levels, from initial conceptualization and global planning to the execution of surface structures, is an interactive process. There are many difficulties to overcome while focusing on the immediate linear output of visual symbols; concepts may evade easy capture by surface structures, or threaten to disrupt stylistic consistency; cohesiveness has to be retained with the previous text and what is to follow and a sense of audience and style maintained.

Language Production; Process and Product

Poor writers seem to perpetuate many of the characteristics of beginning writers, even though their world experience changes and they have generally been writing for many years. Perpetually doing more of the same can show practice perfecting the habitual errors of poor writers. Why should this be so, particularly in cases where children show academic ability in other subjects? Are, for instance, poor writers so aware of their problems that they are inhibited from producing text? Do they lack a realization that there are strategies which could be utilized for overcoming problems at various stages? At a more basic level, if a writer has difficulty in manipulating a pen to form legible letters, does this inevitably slow down the writing process to such an extent that the number of ideas held in short-term memory is curtailed? Alternatively, if the writer has to pause to consider spelling patterns, or when and where to use punctuation, is he then unable to think about higher-level composing processes? Where a writer is having difficulty in retrieving any ideas on a topic what chance is there for organizing material in a cohesive and interesting fashion? Furthermore, if habitual ways of speaking do not necessitate practice in explicitness, because of known context and stereotypic conversations, is there any notion of sustaining the concept of a separate and distant reader?

The questions just raised relate to the interaction of knowledge and skill, and to the awareness of the linguistic and cognitive demands of the writing task. If poor writers have inadequate knowledge structures and are either unaware or unable to apply appropriate procedures, continuing for many years to produce text in this way, they may be finding writing too easy to perform. Consequently, improvement is unlikely. Alternatively, though aware of their inadequacies, they may be unable to deal with them, as this *cri de coeur* from a 16-year-old school leaver suggests:

> I think children at school today dont seem to be taught to write properly because teachers dont learn you all they say is write this down but they never tell you how to write it down. I think you should be told how to do sentences properly, wear to put full stops and commers etc. Children these days write down things on how they talk but when I was at school I wanted to write down things but didnt know how to write it ~~down.~~ You seem to know what to put down but you dont know really how to set it down. You write down stories on how you talk and you end up ~~wr~~ missing words out.

Although this chapter summarizes many of the problems of poor writers, and we have examined ways in which they deviate from acceptable norms, assessment of writing is not an easy task, despite the numerous approaches available (Cooper and Odell, 1977). Generally assessments are made on finished texts. This does not necessarily lead to a greater understanding of the difficulties that writers have experienced in the process of production. There is the danger of ending up with descriptions of poor writers, equivalent to those abounding in the literature on social class, which define the characteristics but do little to delineate the processes. It is not always possible, for instance, to know whether poor writers are 'slow' writers, and therefore have difficulty in retaining ideas in short-term memory, or whether they do have to focus on spelling, thereby distracting attention from composing.

Examining the process of language production is notoriously difficult. Various methods have been used in both speech and written language. In written language, for example, Emig (1971) and Flower and Hayes (1980) asked writers to verbalize their thoughts while engaged in writing. The most prevalent approaches have been in spoken language using errors and pause locations to make inferences about the processes underlying production.

Models of speech production using error data (Fomkin, 1980) suggest stage models of production in which a general concept is retrieved from memory and a message formulated around the topic to be communicated. A syntactic structure is then assigned and syntactic markers inserted. A search is then made for lexical items, adjustments made to morphemes, and this serially ordered information is passed on to a motor control centre for articulation. The model is somewhat crude and by no means definitive, even though there is evidence from speech errors which do occur, and indeed from those which have never been observed to occur, which lend support to it. Evidence from speech errors also suggest that people generally plan their speech in clausal units, as errors do not usually cross clausal boundaries.

Research investment over the past 25 years looking for regularities of patterning in the location of hesitations in speech supports this, though other units of language encoding have been suggested. Hesitations in speech have been taken to indicate time spent in planning; frequent locations in specific positions are assumed to indicate functional units of planning because of the non-random distribution of such pauses. Initially, based on the theoretical orientation of the period, single words were taken to be the encoding units (Goldman-Eisler, 1958). Critical reassessments of this earlier work led to Boomer's (1965) proposals that speech was not integrated on a word-by-word basis but planning ranged forward to cover a structured unit of syntax and meaning. Boomer defined this as a phonemic clause, a phonologically marked segment with a primary stress (Trager and Smith, 1951). Regularities in the pattern of hesitations therefore should be more apparent in the more frequent occurrence of hesitations at the beginning of clause boundaries as speakers may not have finished formulating the next clause to be uttered. This Boomer found to be the case; 54.3 per cent of hesitations occurring at the beginning of clauses, though the modal position was after the first word as Boomer did not include pauses at terminal junctures in his analyses. When this was adjusted for (Barik, 1968), the modal position for hesitations was found to be before the first word.

Evidence for larger units of planning in speech was posited by Henderson *et al* (1966) who identified cycles of hesitant and fluent phases in speech. Their inferences that hesitant phases in speech were used for planning larger units than clauses was questioned by Jaffe *et al.* (1972) who generated random-pause phonations series and obtained similar cyclic effects. Butterworth (1975) also proposed longer planning sequences than the clause, relating idea units to the location of hesitations.

What is being planned during these periods of hesitation, whether they serve a cognitive or linguistic function, is open to debate, as is the whole notion that there is a single planning unit for language production. Three main types of pause location have been identified; lexical (those occurring within a clause, suggesting a lexical decision is being made); clausal, and suprasegmental, where both cognitive and linguistic decisions may be involved. Goldman-Eisler (1968) does not accept that pauses are related to linguistic decisions, claiming that syntactic planning is automatic and unconscious. She draws this conclusion from a comparison between pause times measured in descriptions and explanations of cartoons. In both, sentence complexity was high but pause times briefer when cartoons were described, description being assumed to be a less cognitively demanding task than explanation. Rochester and Gill (1973), however, found that disfluency was related to complexity. Fewer disruptions occurred in sentences with relative than with complement clauses, for which they offered both a syntactic and semantic explanation.

Taking a developmental approach and collating evidence collected from twelve studies conducted over a period of 8 years, Sabin *et al.* (1979) found a developmental decrease in the total length of pause time for the retelling of a preread passage, but a more significant decline in the frequency of pausing for reading passages. They infer from this that frequency is a sensitive measure of linguistic skill while length is more associated with cognitive processing.

Although pauses occurring during language production are used to draw inferences about linguistic and cognitive processing, obviously not all pauses are necessarily connected with these operations. In speech, for example, pauses can be used to assist the listener's comprehension; in writing they may result from adjustments to pen grip, or be time given to reading previous text. Not all clauses are preceded by pauses. Many proceed without any evidence in real time that the speaker is having to consider what he is going to say next. Planning for the next sequence is obviously taking place while the present unit is being produced, and it is only when the speaker is unsure of how he is going to proceed, that pauses occur. There is no reason why planning should not take place, in fact, at any point in the production process; and there are serious limitations and problems connected with the search for normative encoding units. Most work on hesitations in speech, for instance, takes overall measures of frequency or length without regard for content (Dechert and Raupach, 1980; Siegman and Feldstein, 1979; Butterworth, 1980). Butterworth (1975), however, used 'idea' boundaries when hypothesizing the existence of suprasegmental semantic planning. His investigation reflected the difficulty independent judges had in reaching consensus on what constituted such boundaries. But as Chafe (1979) says, when he proposes a change of attitude and approach.

> I realise that there is a research tradition which regards the interpretation of content as too subjective or intuitive to allow any reliable conclusions. I would argue on the contrary that it is only by looking in detail at what a subject is talking about at each point in the discourse that we can come significantly closer to an understanding of the production processes.

Danks (1977) also has lamented the lack of interest in semantic analysis in production research, particularly when this is compared with the complex analyses developed for text comprehension (de Beaugrande, 1980; Sanford and Garrod, 1980; Kintsch and Van Dijk, 1978). As Danks points out, production must involve some consideration for the way ideas are linked. Spittle and Matsuhashi (1981) adopted such an approach in an interesting propositional analysis on the written text of one subject. They confirmed their predictions, drawn from comprehension research, that higher-order propositions were preceded by longer pauses than lower-order propositions. Chafe (1979), defining larger to smaller planning units, equates cognitive processes (memory, episode, thought, focus) with linguistic expression (story, paragraph, sentence, phrase), proposing the phrase or focus as the central unit of production. A series of phrases can be produced with relatively little effort provided they lie within a single thought. There is likely to be more difficulty if a new thought has to be retrieved and considerable difficulty when switching to a new episode. Chafe also suggests that with more time for thinking, as in writing, the formulation may be different.

Time Intervals in Writing

Time measures were used to investigate writing processes as long ago as 1946 by Van Bruggen, who looked at the rate of 'flow' in compositions. He found, among other things, that it took longer to produce original compositions than to retell stories. Technical problems have made for difficulties in relating time intervals to written text, though various procedures have been suggested (Van Bruggen, 1946; Katz, 1948; Crashaw and Ottoway, 1977; Perl, 1980). Video, using a mirror and carbon, provides a way of linking time intervals with what is written (Matsuhashi, 1981), particularly if it is combined with a contact pen, but data are then very time-consuming to analyse. Measurements of time intervals reported here were made by linking a Summagraphics bit pad to a RM 380Z computer. This made it possible for more accurate recordings to be made of intervals when the pen was on or off the paper during writing. These data were read into a file and the whole text could be reproduced on a video monitor. By tracing the movement of a cursor across the reproduced text, time intervals could be accurately noted.

This system has been used in a small pilot study, to examine the location of short and long pauses in essays written by two groups of teenagers, five in each group. One group had passed public examinations at Ordinary level, including the English Language paper, and progressed to the sixth form to prepare for their Advanced level examinations. The other group had not been entered for the Ordinary English Language exams, as their written abilities were considered too poor. They were attending a pre-training course at a college of further education which would lead eventually to a skilled or semi-skilled job. There were very marked differences between the groups, therefore, in terms of past academic achievement and future life prospects. Conceptual, as well as linguistic, differences were therefore expected to be reflected in the quality of the texts produced.

The two groups were given essay topics which they agreed they could write on. All the Ordinary-level teenagers were happy to discuss the value of examinations. The further education college group were not interested in this topic and chose to discuss the value of the course they were attending.

Taking account of the characteristics of poor writers that have been discussed, that have been based on their completed written products, there were certain issues to be explored further by looking at the processes of this small group of poor writers in comparison with the group of better writers. These can be broadly expressed as the four points listed below, though the separation is artificial as the items listed are interactive:

(1) Are poor writers hindered in expressing their ideas because their handwriting is slow and they have to devote too much time to transcriptional aspects, such as spelling and punctuation because these have not been fully automated?
(2) Poor writers have been found to write as they speak. Transcribing speech would lead to the inclusion of idiomatic expression, non-explicit reference, etc. Would this kind of writing, being relatively unplanned, be executed with greater fluency and fewer pauses?
(3) The effort of finding something to write about and translating this into a linguistic form, will result in local planning and a lack of cohesiveness in the poorer writers, indicated by major pause intervals not occurring at sentence boundaries.
(4) The better writers will show a greater awareness of the demands of the writing task, pausing for longer intervals before idea units to ensure that the structure and content of their writing is appropriate to topic, audience, and preceding text. Poor writers, on the other hand, will show a lack of consistent planning.

Even though constrained to composing their essay within the limits of one page, the better group of writers, as expected, wrote more. The mean number of pause intervals for the better writers was 122 compared with 80.4 ($p < 0.01$). The mean pause length was slightly, but not significantly, longer for the poorer writers (1.29 s as opposed to 0.99 s) nor was there any difference in the total duration when related to the length of the compositions. In other words, the poor writers were not taking longer than the better writers to produce equivalent numbers of words. Writing did not appear to be a slower and more effortful task in physical terms. This is also borne out by the modal pause measures. Again there was no difference between the model pause times for the groups. The better writers showed a mean that was very slightly faster than the other group (0.40–0.45 as opposed to 0.46–0.54 s), though one writer in the better group wrote very quickly, her modal pause between words being in the range 0.25–0.30 s.

An arbitrary measure for short pauses assessed them as being twice the length of the modal pause assigned on an individual basis. Long pauses were taken as being more than three times the length of the modal pause. The relative occurrence of both long and short pauses was almost equivalent for both groups (better writers, long pause, 1.2; short pause, 0.70: poorer writers, long pause, 1.30; short pause, 0.90). The frequency with which these pauses occurred within the groups varied enormously, although the mean frequency does not reflect this and the difference was not significant (better writers, 5.58, range 3.36–7.65; poorer writers, 6.18, range 1.86–8.91). In the better writers, 38.88 per cent of their long pauses and 24.62 per cent of their short pauses occurred either at the beginning of sentences or main clauses. The equivalent distribution for the poorer writers was 40.2 per cent (long pauses) and 16.2 per cent (short pauses). In the better group, 36.6 per cent long and 26.3 per cent short pauses occurred at places other than subordinate clause or phrasal boundaries, where no obvious lexical choice was being made nor a clause being terminated. This percentage was slightly less for the poorer writers (14.6 and 27.5 per cent), but there were insufficient data to examine this more thoroughly.

The small number of subjects in this exploratory study limited a fuller analysis of the data and generalizability of the findings. What was apparent was the range of individual difference within the two groups and that more might be learnt of writing processes by examining individual scripts. This is particularly pertinent in view of the characteristics generally used to define poor writers. What was evident from these compositions was that these characteristics also occurred in the writing of the other group, in both the finished text and the way of writing, but other factors compensated. The poor writers had few or no compensatory factors in their writing at any level. I shall elaborate on this while discussing the texts, taking first two essays which reflect a tendency to transcribe speech. They do, however, reflect different ways of speaking in the two individuals, and the poorer writer disregards her lack of mastery over basic transcription skills.

Mary's script (figure 2) provides an interesting example of speed and fluency. Long and short pauses are relatively infrequent (mean pause frequency, 7.73) and some of the transitions between words in her fluent phases are very rapid, 11.8 per cent are less than 0.39 s. She achieves this ease in writing by writing down speech, showing no awareness of her

Line	
1	I .46 found .61 the .54 course .56 as .48 been
2	.94 very .4 intesting .8 and 3.81 easy
3	1.3 to .61 make .58 friends .31 it .47 as
4	1.04 stopped .38 me .31 from .41 getting
5	.96 board .32 for 1.69 a .78 start .93 , .59 and
6	1.06 also 1.92 I .67 have .40 learn't 1.48 alot .96 which
7	1.28 I .94 never .43 knew 1.12 before 1.8 . 3.17 I 3.71 can
8	.94 honestly .55 say .96 my .49 maths
9	1.24 and .59 spelling .58 as .72 improved
10	1.09 very .65 much .55 indeed .12 . 4.19 and .30 I
11	.83 can .77 honestly .55 say .55 I .78 have
12	1.25 been .35 very .49 happy .60 when .34 I
13	1.23 return .42 home 1.94 and .25 I .42 look-
14	.98 Forward .36 to .62 do .59 my .54 household
15	1.29 chores .64 . 1.97 Such .52 as .95 the .45 basic
16	1.67 routine .85 such .56 as .85 ironing
17	1.26 and 1.53 cooking .65 etc .30 .

FIGURE 2 Essay written by Mary, with time intervals between words given in seconds

problems with spelling, punctuation, or syntactic organization. As she progresses she also shows an increasing disregard for the given topic. She initially lists her ideas on the course, and the essay becomes more personal and idiomatic as it develops. Ten out of eleven of her long pauses occur before a transition to a new idea focus, a cluster of long pauses (line 7) marking a change from generalities to details and the longest pause (line 10) introducing a change of topic, despite the repetition of an idiomatic phrase. None of the pause intervals suggests she was giving any thought to her spelling, punctuation, or syntax.

Her first idea, that the course has been interesting, is produced with little difference in the time intervals between the words, the omitted 'h' reflecting a persistent and ignored dialect interference, as she persistently spells 'has' incorrectly. She commits herself to a co-ordinate construction, pauses (3.82 s) presumably to work out the following idea, for the idea is then put down with no regard for the lack of syntactic cohesion. This may well be because she was also concentrating on putting down the next idea focus, omitting meantime to mark the sentence boundary. This section was written rapidly and is followed by a more disjointed grouping of words in terms of distribution of pause intervals after a search for a way of finishing the first clause (line 5, 1.69 s before 'a start'). Presumably some vague formulation of an idea had taken place as the longest pause (line 6, 1.92 s) comes after 'and also' but the exact wording has not been decided on. The long pause before the full stop and the first word of the next sentence suggests a search for more information. She puts down 'I' and then has to formulate what she wants to say and slips into a conversational idiom with only a short pause before the complement clause (line 8). This section is terminated with a full stop but, following a long pause concentrating on the next focal idea, this mark is forgotten, and she continues with a conjunction, producing ideas about her emotional response fairly fluently. She pauses again for further local planning before the next conjunction, this section again being written fairly rapidly despite the grammatical error. She then ends the sentence, pauses, marks the next word with capitalization but continues with an attached phrase, listing elaborations to the previous sentence with a long pause before the last item.

This text supports the notion of the poor writer not having mastered the basic conventions of the written system but lacking an awareness of the problems she has in producing competent text. No indication is given by the pause intervals that she gives any thought to her deficiencies. Her composition is not constrained, therefore, by having to pay attention to lower-order skills. These have indeed been automated, albeit incorrectly. Her pauses indicate local planning, showing a disregard for preceding text in terms of either grammatical or topic cohesion. She writes fastest at the beginning of units that contain more than one idea (for example, lines 3, 4 and lines, 12, 13), the speed of execution resulting in disfluencies which are ignored. There is no evidence that she fully formulates what she was going to write as she frequently rushes into a particular construction and then has to pause to work it out. The topic is treated in a non-evaluative, subjective manner, and the style is that of speech being repetitive and containing many speech idioms which are redundant (for example, 'I can honestly say', 'very much indeed'), dialect intrusions ('as') and homophones ('board'). Because she changes plans, as she might in conversation, her constructions are frequently ungrammatical (lines 2–3), even though her sentences are short and not particularly complex.

Susan (Figure 3) is a representative of the better writers; indeed she obtained the top grade in her Ordinary level examination and her script was selected as being among the top of the better writers by two independent judges. I would contend, however, that it also bears the hallmarks of

I .75 personally .47 have .46 a .33 very .36 biased
1.02 view .41 on .32 the .34 relevance .39 of .69 exams .8 . 2.46 I
1.58 happen .31 to .29 find .29 that .4 I .32 never .34 get .65 exam
2.23 nerves .29 and .28 that .41 I .39 almost .47 invariably
1.18 'do' .41 better .33 in .48 exams .35 than .38 in .44 class .13 .
1.0 This .27 is .25 probably .33 because .36 I .27 am
.78 downright .36 lazy .31 in .47 class .34 and .24 if .3 I
.86 could .37 be .24 bothered .3 to .27 work .30 in .44 class
2.44 then 1.18 my .27 exams .41 results .29 would .25 be .20 the
.81 same .30 as .36 my .30 class .72 results .14 . 4.44 However
1.46 now .28 I .36 have .26 written .32 this .56 , .36 I .24 will
.85 probably .36 find .77 that .42 I .22 do .29 terribly
.82 in .28 my .32 exams .28 next .45 week .92 and
.72 everyone 1.86 will .45 laugh .26 at .29 me .14 .
1.26 I .35 always .48 dread .26 this .25 happening
1.83 but .26 I .28 have .21 been .30 very 2.3 lucky
.81 so .29 far .86 so .28 I .18 will .39 just
.79 pray .21 for .27 my .25 luck .25 to .18 hold
.66 out .40 because .43 I .26 have .24 done
.76 absolutely .27 no .23 revision .29 at .11 all .35 !
4.91 Overall .56 though .14 , .98 I .35 tend .28 to .27 think
.69 that .32 exams .29 are .26 good .21 because
1.0 they .28 do .25 test .43 ~~the~~ .50 what .40 a .46 person
.66 has .72 learnt 1.47 (or .56 not .31 learnt!).

FIGURE 3 Essay written by Susan, with time intervals between words recorded in seconds

transcribed speech, but of the educated speech of a receptive, intelligent 15-year-old with a skilful control of the conventions of written language.

Like Mary's composition there is little evidence of overall planning in relation to the evaluative nature of the topic set. She digresses, retaining only tenuous connection at times with the topic, but her ideas are linked, each connected with the preceding one. She also treats the topic in a non-evaluative, personalized manner, adopting a conversational style. Her linguistic expression contains redundancies and speech idioms but there is a marked difference between the scripts at the level of transcription skills. Her handwriting is more legible, her spelling is impeccable; her punctuation appropriate; and her syntax is varied, flexible, and without error. Furthermore, although she digresses, what she writes is lively and animated, she shows no lack of ideas, merely of disciplining them. As an essay supposedly evaluating examinations it almost fails in its purpose, a recognition of this being apparent in the last sentence. Most of the essay is a description of personal reactions which grow out of the situation created by the writer as she free-associates while composing.

At the beginning of her essay Susan's long pauses follow a similar pattern to Mary's. She pauses after her first general statement and goes on to link the next two sentences without a pause. There is one within-clause pause before 'nerves', presumably lexical. The pauses before the last clause in the third sentence (lines 8 and 9) seem to be used for ordering and expressing an already formulated plan as they follow a conditional clause. However, unlike Mary her fluent phases cover several idea units and the time intervals between words are very short, shorter than any other writers'. All her ideas in the first section relate to her attitude to exams and class work, and this takes her to the last clause of the sentence. The pause before the next section marks the transition to a new progression, suitably marked by its length (4.4 s). Not until the next transition (line 20) is there a pause of a similar length (4.91 s). This section is more disjointed at the beginning than at the end, where following a short pause in line 17 (0.86 s), the next two clauses are written with extremely short intervals between the words.

Although there is no overall global plan apparent in the essay, it is apparent from the pauses, and where they occur and do not occur, that Susan plans many units ahead and executes these plans fluently. Her fluency results from adopting a conversational style and ignoring the more cognitively demanding evaluative purpose of the essay. Her pauses do not, as Mary's, reflect the appending of extra phrases after pausing, suggesting local planning in discreet units. In this way her writing process differs from Mary's even though her product shows many of the features of idiomatic speech (for example, 'I will just pray that my luck holds out', 'I will probably find I do terribly').

Debbie's writing (figure 4) reflects the struggle of a poor writer to find something to write about. She paused more than any of the others, the numerous long pauses throughout indicating planning almost at the single-word level rather than even limited local idea units. Despite long pauses in places, which suggest ample time is given to plan and formulate a clausal unit (those occurring for instance before main clauses in line 1;

Line

Since$^{.90}$Post$^{.52}$September$^{13.56}$I$^{1.32}$have$^{2.23}$learn't
$^{7.92}$about$^{.68}$Literacy,$^{7.88}$I$^{.44}$have$^{1.21}$found$^{1.62}$this$^{1.04}$very
$^{1.05}$helpful$^{2.25}$but$^{2.9}$I$^{.63}$do$^{.54}$feel$^{.77}$I$^{.37}$need$^{8.03}$more
$^{1.28}$help$^{.81}$with$^{.72}$my$^{.96}$spelling$^{1.04}$,$^{3.17}$and$^{.25}$also$^{2.57}$with
$^{2.74}$my$^{.75}$commers$^{1.75}$and$^{.59}$full$^{.66}$stops$^{.22}$.
$^{3.58}$This$^{1.36}$is$^{1.13}$very$^{.51}$inportance$^{.83}$to$^{.4}$me$^{.98}$as
$^{1.19}$I$^{1.04}$hope$^{2.62}$to$^{.89}$take$^{.71}$my$^{2.39}$S.E.N.$^{8.62}$in$^{.39}$my
$^{.95}$Nursing$^{1.74}$Carree$^{.17}$,$^{13.9}$IN$^{1.03}$1981$^{.17}$.$^{5.03}$Febaury
$^{21.02}$I$^{.72}$am$^{1.17}$very$^{.56}$pleased$^{.92}$that$^{1.07}$I$^{.43}$was
$^{1.59}$accepted$^{2.16}$in$^{2.79}$the$^{1.41}$College$^{3.63}$.

FIGURE 4 Essay written by Debbie, with time intervals between words recorded in seconds.

13.56 s, line 2; 7.88 s, line 9; 21.02 s), the following sequences are broken up as information is appended after long time intervals. In line 7 and 8, for instance, she pauses for 8.62 s after writing 'S.E.N.', writes the next two words with fairly short time intervals, but then pauses before each word at the end of the sentence. Indeed, she concludes the sentence with a full stop, then ignores this and adds 'Febaury'. There is a further long pause while she tries to find another idea to focus on.

The content of Debbie's short essay reflects an awareness of her inadequacies and a strong motivation to improve. It also shows how far she has to go at both the transcriptional and conceptual level. The effort of producing text is obviously much more arduous and difficult for her than it was for Mary. However, the text, although the work of a poor writer, bears somewhat fewer of the elements of transcribed speech than Mary's did.

In complete contrast to Debbie's effortful writing, Josie (Figure 5) wrote very quickly, pausing less than any writer in either group. In terms of surface representation, however, there is little apparent difference between the problems that these two writers have. She has similar problems with spelling (for example, lines 3, 8, 12, 18), unmarked by pausal recognition. She also appends a phrase after a full stop (line 12) but omits the full stop and capitalization in lines 3–4. There are also two interesting slips of the pen in line 4 ('and' for 'has') and line 6 ('it' for 'I') which reflect a lack of attention to what has been written. Text is treated in the same way as speech. Once produced, it is ignored.

The main difference between Debbie's and Josie's texts lies in the greater fluency of the latter's essay. She can produce several ideas within a fluent run, particularly in the first paragraph. The length and frequency of pauses

I .36 have .33 found .45 this .70 course .74 very
.88 interesting .88 and .65 would .34 like
.89 to .32 conentiance .87 with .36 my .36 education
1.71 the .53 coure .48 and .89 made .60 a .56 good
.91 ground .61 base .66 for .28 me .72 to
.88 learn .62 and .71 it .44 feel .50 I .23 would .41 like
.97 to .38 carry .46 on .53 after .40 this .89 course .28 as
.82 finished .55 by .44 comming .78 to .37 night
.95 school .14 .
2.36 The .28 teachers .63 are .73 very .32 nice
1.1 and .77 helpful 1.92 but .59 one .53 or .63 two .77 are
.94 mechanincal .14 . 2.03 with .59 there .58 teaching
5.34 I .44 feel .46 I .22 have .45 gained .54 a .20 lot
.92 from .45 this 2.46 last .54 few .78 weeks 1.07 and
.99 hope .50 to .46 continue .78 with 2.64 my
1.33 education 4.04 I .30 hope 1.68 the .51 next
1.55 lot .55 of .49 people .53 gain .50 as .33 much
.88 enjoyment 1.47 from .92 this .72 coause
1.65 as .43 I .46 have.

FIGURE 5 Essay written by Josie, with time intervals between words given in seconds

increase towards the end as she becomes repetitive and begins to run out of ideas. She still retains fluent sections, however, notably the main clauses which are executed as uninterrupted units.

One of the most interesting essays was produced by one of the better group. This was particularly interesting because it highlights problems of a different kind from the ones just discussed in relation to the poor writers. This writer, Jane (Figure 6), has difficulties with writing, even though she has passed her Ordinary level English examination, is now in the sixth form and was therefore included in the group of better writers. Jane is verbally fluent in conversation, she talks quickly and easily. She is aware that she has organizational problems in writing, her main concern being with her spelling. She has worked very hard to counteract her difficulties, which are reflected in this essay.

Line

EXAms$^{1.98}$,$^{.96}$I$^{.63}$find$^{1.02}$are$^{.81}$really$^{1.0}$no
$^{1.88}$test$^{.96}$of$^{.91}$ones$^{.92}$abilaty$^{6.79}$. Many$^{.64}$people
$^{1.28}$find$^{.98}$great$^{.98}$difficulty$^{2.72}$with$^{1.26}$exams.
$^{1.26}$The$^{.66}$~~per~~$^{1.0}$pressure$^{.69}$that$^{1.59}$is$^{7.21}$put$^{.88}$ ~~x~~ upon
$^{1.61}$a$^{.54}$person$^{2.09}$to$^{.57}$learn$^{.60}$the$^{.81}$work$^{.80}$on
$^{1.53}$which$^{.74}$they$^{.76}$are$^{.83}$to$^{2.40}$examinate
$^{1.37}$on$^{.91}$and$^{.66}$then$^{.96}$the$^{.55}$tension$^{3.86}$of$^{.48}$having
$^{1.20}$a$^{1.08}$few$^{.56}$hours$^{1.23}$in$^{.77}$which$^{.61}$to$^{.64}$conevey
$^{1.19}$the$^{.76}$information$^{.65}$correctly$^{.71}$on$^{.93}$to$^{1.36}$paper$^{.33}$.
$^{5.0}$You$^{.55}$may$^{1.74}$well$^{.51}$have$^{1.02}$worked$^{1.26}$very
$^{1.5}$hard$^{.52}$throughout$^{.51}$the$^{.56}$year$^{1.78}$on$^{.56}$the
$^{2.73}$set$^{.58}$subjects$^{5.69}$and$^{.51}$then$^{.54}$once
$^{1.92}$inside$^{.66}$the$^{4.02}$examination$^{1.0}$room
$^{1.20}$discover$^{.62}$that$^{3.13}$all$^{.44}$your$^{1.37}$carefully
$^{1.24}$revised$^{.62}$knowelegde$^{.79}$has$^{5.08}$gone
$^{2.18}$from$^{.58}$your$^{.59}$head$^{1.38}$. $^{1.58}$Many$^{.61}$people
$^{4.51}$think$^{.98}$they$^{.64}$have$^{.62}$done$^{.74}$very$^{.46}$well
$^{1.22}$and$^{.85}$then$^{3.3}$find$^{.59}$that$^{.56}$they$^{.69}$have
$^{1.36}$failed$^{1.37}$. $^{1.98}$16+$^{.91}$to$^{.54}$me$^{.61}$is$^{.71}$one$^{.58}$solution.

FIGURE 6 Essay written by Jane, with time intervals between words given in seconds

Her essay shows the interdependence of conceptual and syntactic planning. Although fluent in conversation she does not try to resolve her difficulties by attempting to transcribe speech. Her attempt to compose formal text leads to her ideas becoming dissociated from the appropriate grammatical expression as she goes beyond her syntactic competence. She writes slowly, her modal pause length was higher than that of any other writer (0.55–0.60 s). She also paused more frequently than any writer except Debbie. Jane's problem is not that she has difficulty in retrieving ideas, nor that she ignores the overall evaluative purpose of the essay. Her problems lie in her inability to organize these into an appropriate linguistic form.

This is particularly obvious in the third sentence (lines 4–9), where she is expanding on the general statement expressed in her opening statement.

These appear to relate to pressure and tension as these concepts are elaborated in the latter part of the essay also. There is no pre-sentence pause but there is a pause before her second attempt to write 'pressure'. Having committed herself to an adjectival clause, the long pause after 'is' (line 4, 7.21 s) reflects that she is already having organizational problems. The concept is there but the linguistic frame is eluding her. The next post-modifier is preceded by a pause (line 5, 2.09 s). She then continues without a pause, apart from the one preceding 'examinate', where she fails to use the passive and invents a word.

She embarks on the next main theme, therefore, in this very long and cumbersome sentence, without assessing what has been written or thinking carefully about the syntactic organization of what is to follow. She begins with a number of pauses which occur at frequent intervals, finishes the last clause without pause but forgets that she has omitted the main verb. Jane has apparently been distracted from achieving her compositional aims by poor mastery of spelling and syntactical organization. Had she been less ambitious and adopted a simpler linking of ideas and syntax, as she does at the end of the essay, her problems would not have been so obvious.

The last essay is included as an example of another of the better writers' scripts. Mark (Figure 7) begins in a very self-conscious manner. He is composing formal written prose and giving careful thought to the structure and elaboration of his ideas. His long pauses always precede a new sentence though they sometimes occur before the full stop in the preceding sentence (e.g. line 11, 26.67 s). This pause also marks a transition to a new episode, and overall his pause patterns tend to reflect organized planning in terms of ideas set within clausal units in an ordered manner. The few pauses that occur before content words (e.g. lines 7, 8, 9) serve to emphasize his considered and deliberate approach to writing. In the second half of his essay, however, he loses track of the original purpose of the essay and his style becomes less formal. Lines 12–17 are executed without a pause, apart from a failed lexical choice pause before 'things' (line 16). He seems here to be expressing ideas on which he feels strongly, and the deliberation that went into the structure of the first part of the essay disappears.

These brief illustrations have been used to indicate the range of individual differences in approaches to writing and the difficulty of making generalizations from group means as a way of determining where writers fail in the process of writing. Obviously, there are enormous limitations to taking one specific piece of work from each individual in this way. No account is taken of variation in writing, skills in other forms of composition, narrative, choice of own topic, different readers, etc. What is present in this one sample of writing shows that group measures disguise the complexities of differences in examining writing processes.

Pausing in writing can reflect an awareness of difficulty and a need to stop

Line

What $^{.69}$ is $^{.51}$ the $^{.56}$ point $^{.48}$ of $^{.57}$ having $^{.84}$ examination $^{1.53}$? $^{24.1}$ I $^{.43}$ have $^{.46}$ often $^{.68}$ thought $^{.6}$ about $^{1.4}$ this $^{3.27}$, $^{3.92}$ is $^{1.25}$ it $^{.38}$ to $^{.60}$ see $^{.58}$ that $^{.50}$ you $^{.65}$ have $^{.55}$ under- $^{.90}$ stood $^{4.95}$ what $^{1.11}$ the $^{.40}$ teacher $^{.60}$ is $^{.39}$ trying $^{.42}$ to $^{.43}$ put $^{1.0}$ across $^{.41}$ to $^{.47}$ you $^{.14}$; $^{.81}$ surely $^{.52}$ this $^{.48}$ could $^{.35}$ be $^{.87}$ done $^{.96}$ by $^{.55}$ exercises $^{.49}$ both $^{.39}$ oral $^{1.98}$ and $^{.40}$ written. $^{7.83}$ Perhaps $^{.40}$ it $^{.47}$ is $^{.40}$ ~~to~~ $^{.32}$ ~~be~~ $^{.57}$ so $^{1.37}$ that $^{.54}$ the $^{1.48}$ teacher $^{1.04}$ can $^{4.02}$ access $^{1.17}$ your $^{.57}$ ability $^{2.13}$ and $^{.45}$ move $^{.54}$ you $^{.73}$ on $^{.17}$ to $^{.43}$ a $^{.72}$ different $^{3.37}$ idea $^{.63}$ or $^{.48}$ topic $^{2.81}$. $^{3.58}$ Having $^{1.00}$ never $^{.44}$ done $^{.48}$ very $^{.43}$ well $^{.40}$ in $^{.47}$ examinations $^{1.18}$ I $^{3.93}$ always $^{.45}$ have $^{.37}$ felt $^{.46}$ unjustly $^{.44}$ treated $^{26.67}$. $^{.94}$ Also $^{.38}$ the $^{.46}$ subject $^{.51}$ matter $^{.44}$ on $^{.34}$ which $^{.97}$ you $^{.69}$ are $^{.40}$ tested $^{.55}$ can $^{.33}$ often $^{.35}$ be $^{.45}$ useless $^{1.8}$ and $^{1.07}$ today $^{.35}$ in $^{.52}$ a $^{.32}$ world $^{.44}$ in $^{.43}$ which $^{.37}$ it $^{.39}$ is $^{.28}$ so $^{.75}$ hard $^{.34}$ to $^{.37}$ live $^{.33}$ and $^{.41}$ get $^{.38}$ on $^{1.8}$; $^{.74}$ wouldn't $^{.97}$ it $^{.39}$ be $^{.36}$ better $^{.36}$ to $^{.68}$ learn $^{11.64}$ things $^{.21}$ which $^{.85}$ would $^{.49}$ be $^{.60}$ useful.

FIGURE 7 Essay written by Mark, with time intervals between words given in seconds

to work the problem out, whether it be retrieving an idea or thinking about spelling. The absence of pauses, particularly where deviations from accepted conventions are apparent, shows a lack of measurable consideration being paid to these factors It is apparent that the poorer writers were not necessarily slower writers, nor did they keep pausing to focus attention on spelling or punctuation and so switch their attention from composing. Their attention, indeed, was largely focused on idea units. When these came easily, and resembled conversations, several phrases could be executed without a pause. Frequently, however, phrases were appended without thought for what had been written, with consequent distortions in syntactic and conceptual cohesiveness. This way of writing reduces the likelihood of conceptual or syntactic complexity. The lack of concern with anything other than putting down the immediate idea also reduces any possibility of stylistic improvement. The better writers, although still amateur writers, did reflect attempts to grapple with written language. This was so particularly for those who did not allow their ideas to fall into the first or easiest grammatical structure, but who struggled to find a more precise form for their conceptualizations.

Performance skills can, however, come easily to some individuals, particularly when, in their habitual ways of speaking, they use a vocabulary and syntax which more readily translates into a written form. Such individuals may possibly reflect ways of writing that are similar to the poor writers but their mastery of transcription skills, facility with verbal communication and access to a range of concepts, disguises this. On the other hand, their conceptual and linguistic development is likely to have been enhanced by the act of writing. The question of successful writing is closely bound up with communicative competence and the ability to organize and express ideas in a logical and coherent manner.

Defining the characteristics of poor writers is important, but insufficient if such decriptions relate only to what has been written without regard for locating the source and levels of difficulty. The approach described here has the potential for discovering what does, or does not, seem to create difficulties in searching for appropriate conceptual or linguistic expression. This preliminary study merely scratches the surface but further investigations will examine differences in the development of children who become poor or better writers. There are many questions to be asked about the patterns of progress in writing, when and how children begin to differ, how this affects different modes of writing, and when they might optimally benefit from procedural support of the kind discussed by Scardamalia and Bereiter (Chapter 3, this volume). The reasons why some children fail may be highly complex, but with the increasing expansion of interest in writing their problems should become more accessible to analysis. In the process, these investigations should lead to further theoretical insights into the development of language and cognition.

REFERENCES

Ackerman, B. P. (1978). Children's comprehension of presupposed information; logical and pragmatic inferences to speaker belief, *Journal of Experimental Psychology,* **26**, 92–114.

Ammon, P. (1981). Communication skills and communicative competence: a neo-Piagetian process-structural view. In W. P. Dickson (ed.), *Children's Oral Communication Skills*. Academic Press, New York.

Asher, S. R., and Oden, S. L. (1976). Children's failure to communicate: an assessment of comparison and egocentricism explanations. *Developmental Psychology,* **12**, 132–139.

Barik, H. C. (1968). 'On defining juncture pauses; a note on Boomer's 'Hesitation and grammatical encoding'. *Language and Speech,* **11**, 156–159.

Bates, E. (1976). *Language and Context: the Acquisition of Pragmatics*. Academic Press, New York.

Bereiter, C. (1980). Development in writing. In L. W. Gregg and E. R. Steinberg (eds.), *Cognitive Processes in Writing*. Lawrence Erlbaum Associates, Hillsdale, N.J.

Bereiter, C., and Scardamalia, M. (1980). Cognitive coping strategies and the problem of 'inert knowledge'. Paper presented at the NIE–LRDC conference on Thinking and Learning Skills, Pittsburgh, Pennsylvania.

Bereiter, C., and Scardamalia, M. (1981). From conversation to composition: the role of instruction in a developmental process. In R. Glaser (ed.), *Advances in Instructional Psychology,* vol. 2. Lawrence Erlbaum Associates, Hillsdale, N.J.

Blankenship, J. (1967). A linguistic analysis of oral and written style. *Quarterly Journal of Speech,* **48**,. 419–422.

Boomer, D. S. (1965). Hesitation and grammatical encoding. *Language and Speech,* **8**, 148–158.

Bransford, J. D., Barclay, J. R., and Franks, J. J. (1972). Sentence memory; a constructivist versus interpretive approach. *Cognitive Psychology,* **3**, 193–209.

Britton, J. (1982). Learning to use language in two modes. In N. R. Smith and M. B. Franklin (eds.), *Symbolic Functioning in Childhood*. Lawrence Erlbaum Associates, Hillsdale, N.J.

Bruner, J. (1978). From communication to language: a psychological perspective. In I. Markova (ed.), *The Social Context of Language*, John Wiley, New York.

Butterworth, B. (1975). Hesitation and semantic planning in speech. *Journal of Psycholinguistic Research,* **4**, 75–87.

Butterworth, B. (1980). *Language Production*, Academic Press, London.

Cayer, R. L., and Sacks, R. K. (1979). Oral and written discourse of basic writers: similarities and differences. *Research in the Teaching of English,* **13**, 121–128.

Chafe, W. C. (1979). The flow of thought and the flow of language. In *Discourse and Syntax: Syntax and Semantics*, vol. 12, Academic Press, New York.

Chafe, W. C. (1980). Some reasons for hesitating. In H. W. Dechert and M. Raupech (eds.), *Temporal Variables in Speech: Studies in Honour of Freida Goldman-Eisler*. Mouton, The Hague.

Chomsky, C. (1979). Approaching reading through invented spelling. In L. B. Resnick and P. A. Weaver (eds.), *Theory and Practice of Early Reading*. Lawrence Erlbaum Associates, Hillsdale, N.J.

Clark, E. V. (1978). Awareness of language: some evidence from what children say and do. In A. Sinclair, R. J. Jarvella, and W. J. M. Levelt (eds.), *The Child's Conception of Language*. Springer-Verlag, Berlin.

Collins, J. L., and Williamson, M. M. (10981). Spoken language and semantic abbreviation in writing. *Research in the Teaching of English,* **15**, 23–35.

Cooper, C., and Odell, L. (1977). *Evaluating Writing*, National Council of Teachers of English, Urbana, Illinois.

Crashaw, M., and Ottoway, M. (1977). A contact pen for research on writing. *Quarterly Journal of Experimental Psychology,* **29**, 345–346.

Crowhurst, M., and Piché, G. L. (1979). Audience and mode of discourse effects on syntactic complexity in writing at two grade levels. *Research in the Teaching of English,* **13**, 101–109.

Danks, J. H. (1977). Producing ideas and sentences. In S. Rosenberg (ed.), *Sentence Production: Development in Theory and Research*. John Wiley & Sons, New York.

de Beaugrande, R. (1980). *Text, Discourse and Process*. Longman, London.

Dechert, H. W., and Raupach, M. (1980). *Temporal Variables in Speech: Studies in Honour of Freida Goldman-Eisler*. Mouton, The Hague.

de Villiers, P. A., and de Villiers, J. G. (1972). Early judgements of semantic and syntactic acceptability by children. *Journal of Psycholinguistic Research,* **1**, 299–310.

Dickson, W. P. (1981). Referential communication activities in research and in the curriculum: a meta-analysis. In W. P. Dickson (ed.), *Children's Oral Communication Skills*. Academic Press, New York.

Eimas, P. D., and Tartter, V. C. (1979). On the development of speech perception mechanisms and analogies. In H. W. Reese (ed.), *Advances in Child Development and Behavior*, vol. 13, Academic Press, New York.

Elasser, N., and John-Steiner, V. P. (1977). An interactionist approach to advancing literacy. *Harvard Educational Review,* **47**, 355–369.

Emig, J. A. (1971). *The Composing Processes of Twelfth Graders*. National Council of Teachers of English, Urbana, Illinois.

Farrel, T. J. (1978). Differentiating writing from talking. *College Composition and Communication,* **29**, 346–350.

Flavell, J. H. (1974). The development of inferences about others. In T. Mischel (ed.), *Understanding Other Persons*. Blackwell, Oxford.

Flavell, J. H. (1976). *The development of metacommunication*. Paper presented at the Twenty-first International Congress of Psychology. Paris.

Flavell, J. (1979). Metacognition and cognitive monitoring. A new area of cognitive-developmental inquiry. *American Psychologist*, **34**, 906–911

Flavell, J. H., Speer, J. R., Green, F. L., and August, D. L. (1981). The development of comprehension monitoring and knowledge about communication. *Monograph of the Society for Research in Child Development,* **46**.

Flower, L., and Hayes, J. R. (1980). The dynamics of composing: making plans and judging constraints. In L. W. Gregg and E. R. Steinberg (eds), *Cognitive Processes in Writing*, Lawrence Erlbaum Associates, Hillsdale, N.J.

Frith, U. (1980). Unexpected spelling problems. In U. Frith (ed.), *Cognitive Processes in Spelling*. Academic Press, London.

Fromkin, V. (1980). *Errors in Linguistic Performance: Slips of the Tongue, Ear, Pen and Hand*. Academic Press, New York.

Galbraith, D. (1980). The effect of conflicting goals on writing: a case study. *Visible Language,* **XIV**, 365–375.

Gleitman, L. R., Gleitman, H., and Shipley, E. (1972). The emergence of the child as grammarian. *Cognition,* **1**, 137–164.

Glucksberg, S., Krauss, R. M., and Higgins, E. T. (1975). The development of communication skills in children. In F. Horowitz (ed.), *Review of Child Development Research*, vol. 4. University of Chicago Press, Chicago.

Goldman-Eisler, F. (1958). Speech production and predictability of words in context and the length of pauses in speech. *Language and Speech,* **1**, 96–101.

Goldman-Eisler, F. (1968). *Psycholinguistics: Experiments in Spontaneous Speech*. Academic Press, New York.

Gould, J. D. (1978a). An experimental study of writing, dictating and speaking. In J. Requin (ed.), *Attention and Performance*, vol. VII. Lawrence Erlbaum Associates, Hillsdale, N.J.

Gould, J. D. (1978b). How experts dictate. *Journal of Experimental Psychology: Human Perception and Performance,* **4**, 648–661.

Graham, S., and Miller, L. (1980). Handwriting research and practice: a unified approach. *Focus on Exceptional Children,* **13**, 1–16.

Greenfield, P. (1968). Oral or written language; the consequences for cognitive development in Africa and the United States. Paper presented at the Symposium on Cross-Cultural Cognitive Studies, Chicago.

Gregg, L. W., and Steinberg, E. R. (1980). *Cognitive Processes in Writing*, Lawrence Erlbaum Associates, Hillsdale, N.J.

Hakes, D. T. (1980). *The Development of Metalinguistic Abilities in Children*. Springer-Verlag, Berlin.

Harrell, L. E. (1957). A comparison of the development of oral and written language in school-age children. *Monograph of the Society for Research in Child Development,* **22**.

Henderson, A., Goldman-Eisler, F., and Scarbek, A. (1966). Sequential temporal patterns in spontaneous speech. *Language and Speech,* **9**, 207–216.

Higgins, E. T. (1977). Communication development as related to channel, incentive and social class, *Genetic Psychology Monographs,* **96**, 75–141.

Horowitz, M. W., and Newman, J. B. (1964). Spoken and written expression: an experimental analysis. *Journal of Abnormal and Social Psychology,* **68**, 640–647.

Ingram, D. (1975). If and when transformations are acquired by children. In P. Dato (ed.), *Developmental Psycholinguistics: Theory and Application*. Georgetown University Press, Georgetown.

Jaffe, J., Beskin, S., and Gerstman, L. J. (1972). Random generation of apparent speech rhythms. *Language and Speech,* **15**, 68–71.

Jarvella, R. (1970). Effects of syntax on running memory span for connected discourse. *Psychonomic Science,* **19**, 235–236.

Katz, D. (1948). The scriptochronograph. *Quarterly Journal of Experimental Psychology,* **1**, 53–56.

Katz, E. W., and Brent, S. B. (1968). Understanding connectives. *Journal of Verbal Learning and Verbal Behavior,* **7**, 501–509.

Kintsch, W., and van Dijk, T. (1978). Towards a model of text comprehension and production. *Psychological Review,* **85**, 363–394.

Kroll, B. M. (1978);. Cognitive egocentrism and the problem of audience awareness in written dicourse. *Research in the Teaching of English,* **12**, 269–281.

Loban, W. (1976). *Language Development: Kindergarten Through Grade Twelve*. (Research Report No. 18.) National Council of Teachers of English. Urbana, Illinois.

Maratsos, M. (1973). Non-egocentric communication abilities in pre-school children. *Child Development,* **44**, 497–500.

Martlew, M. (1978). Writing for the Reader: a Developmental Study. Paper given at the International Conference on Social Psychology and Language, Bristol.

Martlew, M. (1979). Young children's capacity to communicate. In K. J. Connolly (ed.), *Psychology Survey No. 2*. George Allen & Unwin, London.

Martlew, M., Connolly, K. J., and McCleod, C. (1978). Language use, role and context in a five year old. *Journal of Child Language,* **5**, 81–99.

Matsuhashi, A. (1981). Pausing and planning: the tempo of written dicourse production. *Research in the Teaching of English,* **15**, 113–134.

Menig-Peterson, C. L. (1975). The modification of communicative behavior in preschool aged children as a function of the listener's perspective, *Child Development,* **46**, 1015–1018.

Mosenthal, P., and Na, T. J. (1981). Classroom competence and children's individual differences in writing. *Journal of Educational Psychology,* **73**, 106–121.

Newman, S. E., and Nicholson, L. R. (1976). Speed of oral and written responding, *Bulletin of the Psychonomic Society,* **7**, 202–204.

Ochs, E. (1979). Planned and unplanned discourse. In T. Givon (ed.) *Syntax and Semantics,* vol. 12. Academic Press, New York.

O'Donnell, R. C., Griffin, W. J., and Norris, R. (1967). *Syntax of Kindergarten and Elementary School Children: a Transformational Analysis*. National Council of Teachers of English, Champaign, Illinois.

Olson, D. (1977a). The language of instruction: the literate bias of schooling. In P. C. Anderson, R. J. Spiro, and W. E. Montague (eds.), *Schooling and the Acquisition of Knowledge*. Lawrence Erlbaum Associates, Hillsdale, N.J.

Olson, D. R. (1977b). From utterance to text: the bias of language in speech and writing. *Harvard Educational Review,* **47**, 257–281.

Olson, D. (1977c). Oral and written language and the cognitive processes of children. *Journal of Communication,* **27**, 10–26.

Perl, S. (1980). The composing processes of unskilled college writers. *Research in the Teaching of English,* **13**, 317–336.

Robinson, E. J. (1981). The child's understanding of inadequate messages and communication failure: a problem of ignorance or egocentricism? In W. P. Dickson (ed.), *Children's Oral Communication Skills*. Academic Press, New York.

Robinson, E. J., and Robinson, W. P. (1976). The young child's understanding of communication. *Developmental Psychology,* **13**, 328–333.

Rochester, S. R., and Gill, J. (1973). Production of complex sentences in monologues and dialogues. *Journal of Verbal Learning and Verbal Behavior,* **12**, 203–210.

Rosenthal, D. A. (1979). Language skills and formal operations. *Merrill-Palmer Quarterly,* **25**, 133–143.

Rubin, D. L., and Piché, G. L. (1979). Development in syntactic and strategic aspects of audience adaptation skills in written persuasive communication. *Research in the Teaching of English,* **18**, 293–316.

Sabin, E. J., Clemmer, E. J., O'Connell, D. C., and Kowal, S. (1979). A pausological approach to speech deelopment. In A. W. Siegman and S. Feldstein (eds.), *Of Speech and Time: Temporal Patterns in Inter-personal Contexts*. Lawrence Erlbaum, Hillsdale, N.J.

Sachs, J. S. (1967). Recognition memory for syntactic and semantic aspects of connected discourse. *Perception and Psychophysics,* **2**, 437–442.

Sachs, J., and Devin, J. (1976). Young children's use of age appropriate speech styles in social interaction and role-playing. *Journal of Child Language,* **3**, 81–98.

Sanford, A., and Garrod, S. (1980). *Understanding Written Language*, John Wiley, Chichester.

Scardamalia, M., and Bereiter, C. (1980). Fostering the development of self-regulation in children's knowledge processing. Paper presented at the NIE–LRDC Conference on Thinking and Learning Skills, Pittsburgh, October.

Scardamalia, M., and Bereiter, C. (1982). The role of production factors in writing ability. In M. Nystrand (ed.), *What Writers Know: The Language and Structure of Written Discourse*. Academic Press, New York.

Scribner, S., and Cole, M. (1978). Unpackaging literacy. *Social Science Information,* **17**, 19–40.

Shatz, M., and Gelman, R. (1973). The development of communication skills: modification in the speech of young children as a function of the listener. *Monographs of the Society for Research in Child Development,* **38**.

Shaughnessy, M. P. (1977). *Errors and Expectations: A Guide for the Teacher of Basic Writing*. Oxford University Press, New York.

Shultz, T. R., and Robillard, J. (1980). The development of linguistic humour in children: incongruity through rule violation. In P. E. McGhee and A. J. Chapman (eds.), *Children's Humour*. John Wiley & Sons, Chichester.

Shuy, R. W. (1980). A Holistic View of Language Training. Mimeograph: Georgetown University.

Siegman, A. W., and Feldstein, S. (1979). *Of Speech and Time: Temporal Patterns in Interpersonal Contexts*. Lawrence Erlbaum Associates, Hillsdale, N.J.

Slobin, D. I. (1978). A case study of early language awareness. In A. Sinclair, R. J. Jarvella and W. J. M. Levelt (eds.), *The Child's Conception of Language*. Springer-Verlag, Berlin.

Snow, C., and Ferguson, C. A. (1977). *Talking to Children: Language Input and Acquisition*. Cambridge University Press, Cambridge.

Spittle, K. B. and Matsuhashi, A. (1981). Semantic aspects of real time written discourse production. To appear in Texas Writing Research Group's conference proceedings.

Stallard, C. K. (1974) An analysis of the behaviour of good student writers. *Research in the Teaching of English,* **8**, 206–218.

Trager, G. L., and Smith, H. L. (1951). *Outline of English Structure*, Battenburg Press, Norman, Oklahoma.

Vachek. J. (1973). *Written Language: General Problems and Problems of English*. Mouton, The Hague.

Van Bruggen, J. (1946). Factors affecting regularity of the flow of words during written composition, *Journal of Experimental Education,* **15**, 133–155.

Vygotsky, L. (1962). *Thought and Language*, MIT Press, Cambridge, Mass.

Wason, P. (1980a). Conformity and commitment in writing. *Visible Language,* **XIV**, 351–363.

Wason, P. (1980b). Dynamics of writing (special issue). *Visible Language,* **XIV**, 351–363.

Waterson, N., and Snow, C. (1978). *The Development of Communication*. John Wiley & Sons, Chichester.

The Psychology of Written Language
Edited by M. Martlew

CHAPTER 13

Socioeconomic Status and Written Language

MILLICENT POOLE

Compared with the focus on social class and oral language production, comparatively few studies have examined the relationship between social class and written language. Where such research exists different levels of analysis have been used, making comparability of results difficult. Furthermore, criteria used to define social class and categories of written language vary, as does the selection of subjects, and the sampling of written language. An aggregated assessment of the relationship between social class and written language is, therefore, extraordinarily difficult.

Conscious of such problems, two approaches to data synthesis are attempted in this chapter. First, a traditional review whose purpose is to determine analytically whether any consistent and stable social class differences emerge from an examination of the literature on social class and written language. Secondly, a new approach to data integration, a 'meta-analysis' is undertaken. A traditional review of the literature can only evaluate those studies which suggest that there are socioeconomic differences, or that no differences exist, or others which are equivocal. A meta-analysis, by calculating the effect size of reported results can, in a simpler and more objective manner, provide an overview of the relationships between social class and written language. While it is possible to include any study in an analytical review, the same does not hold for meta-analysis which imposes constraints via reporting of empirical results. The texture of analysis for both types of reviews is different, somewhat like a qualitative as opposed to a quantitative dichotomy. Using both approaches is, therefore, likely to present a more balanced analysis. To this end, Part A of this chapter presents an analytic review based on ninety five studies; Part B, a meta-analysis of research on socioeconomic status and written language based on thirteen studies; while Part C contains an integration of the two approaches and raises a number of issues related to the diverse findings on socioeconomic status and written language. A systematic, computer-based literary search was undertaken before studies were selected.

ANALYTIC REVIEW

The Concept of Social Class and Code

The major theoretical impetus to the study of social class and language in the past two decades was provided by Bernstein. Underpinning Bernstein's thesis was the notion that linguistic coding was influenced by family socialization variables, such as patterns of relationships (open vs closed); power-structures (positional vs personal); maternal teaching styles (cognitive–rational vs inhibitory); and strategies of social control (imperative vs mediating).

The concept of code, although an evolving one, has been central to Bernstein's thinking. Originally Bernstein differentiated between a public and a formal language (Bernstein, 1958, 1959). These two languages, defined largely in terms of syntactic indices, were considered to be consistent orientating frameworks generated by social class structure. Somewhat later, Bernstein (1962a) gave the name 'codec' to his language types, distinguishing between the elaborated and the restricted code. These two codes, although based on speech production and general verbal planning, came to be applied directly to written language, often without prior consideration as to whether there were major differences between the spoken and written forms of language. Devising parallel comparisons was not at first difficult, since Bernstein (1958, 1959, 1961a,b) had defined his codes operationally as lists of linguistic features with social and psychological meaning. For example, one of the distinguishing characteristics of the two codes concerned the selection of adjectives and adverbs. The elaborated code user, by using more unusual adverbs and adjectives, was considered to be more likely to make finer discriminations, to be more explicit, and to evince more individualistic qualification and modification.

Over time, Bernstein (1962a, 1962b, 1971b) has reduced his earlier emphasis on the specific linguistic indices of the codes and has moved towards an explanation in terms of different orders of meaning. The restricted code was taken as an orientation towards 'particularistic' meanings, while the elaborated code oriented the language user to 'universalistic' meanings (Bernstein, 1971a). Particularistic orders of meaning referred to implicit processes where principles and operations were not made explicit, as was the case with universalistic orders of meaning. Context subsequently became a major factor in defining the codes: meaning, when not tied to context, was universalistic since it could be communicated to a person who had no direct knowledge or experience of the context. On the other hand, meaning, if context-bound, was particularistic (Bernstein, 1971b).

Bernstein's codes, therefore, do yield two major dimensions along which to examine social class differences in written language: (a) specific linguistic indices of codes; and (b) the impact of context, not only on the selection of syntax and lexis, but also on the order of meaning, that is, explicit (universalistic) or implicit (particularistic). Most research falls within the first category, although recently context has been of paramount importance in research into oral language production. Unfortunately this has not been the case with written language. Bernstein was not, of course, the first to be concerned with the dimensions along which social class comparisons in language could be made. Developmental psychologists had long been interested in identifying indicators of increasingly mature language performance, usually as a function of age, however, rather than of social class. Studies using Bernstein's indices and others devised by developmental psychologists are examined below.

Research on Written Language and Socioeconomic Status based on Bernstein.

As Rushton and Young (1975, p. 368) commented; 'references to written language are rare in Bernstein's work'. However, a number of studies on written language have been based on Bernstein's chracterisations of oral codes. These extrapolations have tended to follow two opposite lines: either that written language requires a form of complex verbal planning similar to the processes involved in an elaborated code (Lawton, 1968), or, given the increased time for verbal planning inherent in written communication, complex and elaborated language are no longer class-specific (Robinson, 1965).

While it is to some degree true that in written language the social situational variables are removed, the question of context remains, in at least two forms – the format/style of the written communication (for example, formal/informal; personal/impersonal), and the nature of the reader of that written communication. Variations in the complexity of verbal planning could, therefore, be thought to inhere in the processes of written communication. Whether these processes operate differently for various social class groups is by no means clear. An examination of studies comparing the written language of different socioeconomic groups reveals patterns of difference, no difference, and equivocal results. Indeed, Kessler and Quinn (1977), after looking closely at the effect of social class on written language acquisition, assesss the results to be non-conclusive. With that outcome in view, this chapter explores a range of studies to try to reach a conclusion concerning differences or no difference in socioeconomic status and written language.

Studies Showing Socioeconomic Differences

Several studies do report substantial social class differences in written language. Lawton (1963), using a Bernstein framework found some social class differences in the written compositions of twenty boys, aged 12–14 years. Lawton used four 30 minute essays as stimulus material; (a) a story rewrite, (b) home, (c) my life in 1972, (d) explanation of a soccer game. Middle-class boys wrote considerably more, and used about 50 per cent more subordinate clauses in the four essays than did the working-class group. There were no significant inter-class differences in sentence length.

Class differences in the use of adjective clauses were evident at 12 years but not at 15 years, as the 12 year old working-class group used more. There were no significant differences on the total number of adjectives used, but the middle-class boys used a wider variety of adjectives. The same pattern of diversity was also evident in the middle-class boys' use of adverbs. There was a clear social class difference in the use of uncommon clauses (MC > WC) at 12 years but not at 15 years. Using the more sensitive Loban Weighted Index of Subordination, overall inter-class differences were found (MC > WC). There was a clear tendency for middle-class boys to use more adverbial qualifiers and more passives. Also, the 12 year old middle-class boys used more personal pronouns and scored higher on the abstraction and generalization scales. These differences were not found in the 15 year olds. On the Watts Sentence Completion Test there were no significant inter-class differences, but on an open-ended sentence-completion test significant overall differences emerged at age 15 (MC > WC). Lawton's sample was small and restricted to males, making generalizability of his results unreliable.

Using a sample of sixty-nine 12 year olds from a mixed grammar school, Smedley (1969) classified three IQ levels (high, medium, low) and obtained four pieces of written work on topics chosen to give a range of writing styles. Forty-five linguistic features were analysed for (a) quality of vocabulary, (b) parts of speech, (c) qualification (adjectival and adverbial) and elaboration (of the verb stem), and (d) syntax. Although the only features to show significant difference were syntactic (MC > WC in 'handling the structural resources of language'), nearly all the comparisons were in the predicted direction. While this study had an advantage over Lawton's in sample size and taking IQ into consideration, the small number of significant results is less than convincing.

In Australia, Poole (1972), using a sample of male and female tertiary students not discriminable on IQ ($WC_m = 24$, $WC_f = 16$; $MC_m = 24$, $MC_f = 20$), and a written life-forecast topic thought to promote descriptive, reflective, and speculative prose, found some evidence of social class difference: (1) on the Loban Weighted Index of Subordination (MC > WC) and (2) in language elaboration and modification (uncommon adjectives, total adjectives, and unusual adjectives MC > WC). No inter-class differences, however, were obtained on selected indices of verb complexity and personal reference. However, since Poole's investigation was conducted on university students, variance in the written language performance could be attributed to factors other than social class, for example, arts–science orientation, or educational experiences.

Studies Showing No Socioeconomic Differences

By the early 1970s, a critical reappraisal of the cultural deficit hypothesis advanced by Deutsch and others (Deutsch *et al.*, 1967, 1968) was in progress. Led by Labov (1969), this pointed to certain methodological problems compounding the results of studies. For example, language samples were obtained in situations where the working-class child was likely to feel threatened. The concern by linguists with the competence–performance dichotomy led to a growing body of evidence that, on tasks used to tap children's grammatical competence (that is, implicit knowledge of the language structure) there were no social class differences (Cazden, 1965, 1970; La Civita *et al.*, 1966; Shriner and Miner, 1968; Slobin, 1968).

Woodfin (1968) examined the relationships of certain predictive variables (language ability, reading level, intelligence, socioeconomic status, and sex) to the written expression of 3rd grade children. She concluded that socioeconomic status was consistently one of the least reliable predictors for ability in writing. In an analysis of original themes written by high school freshmen Huffine (1966), found no social class differences on sentence length or sentence complexity. He attributed his results to the influence of a common schooling experience; also, Mason (1968) found that social class was not a significant variable in children's creative writing ability. Indeed, a number of studies report no social class differences on written language, on global indices or an individual dimensions such as the frequency and range of adjectives and adverbs used to elaborate, quality, and modify intent.

Thomaneck (1972) in a study involving 572 children of 12 and 13 years old, (275 females and 397 males) from Aberdeen, analysed school essays on the transition from primary to secondary school. The method of analysis included not only structural grammatical categories but also transformational categories. No inter-class differences were found in the availability of adjectives and adverbs, nor in the differentiated use of adjectives. Again within a sociolinguistic framework, Rushton and Young (1975), analysed the written language of a working-class and middle-class group. There were 25 working class adolescents and 22 middle class adolescents whose average ages were 17.1 years and 17.5 years respectively. Stylistic variation was built into the nine essay titles given. The anticipated functional styles were: imaginative descriptive (a loose narrative with imaginative aspects highlighted), opinionative discursive (the writer was asked to assume an attitude towards what is, generally, a societal phenomenon and define it in the form of a reasoned argument), technical explanatory (the writer was asked to describe the interrelationship of the components of a piece of machinery in such a way as to show how it functioned). In an unexplained aside, Rushton and Young (1975, p. 377) indicated that 'For some reason not apparent to us, the majority of the working class group failed to complete the last of these titles (viz. "Describe how the way a bicyle is constructed enables it to perform its function") and it was removed from the analysis.' This exclusion may seriously have biased the comparisons made between the inter-class groups.

The stylistic variation analysis was based on the distinction between dialect (a variety of language distinguished by its user) and register (a variety of language distinguished according to its use). Using scale and category grammar as the basis of analysis, Rushton and Young worked on the assumption that the titles of the essays tapped three separate registers to which the two groups would have different degrees of access. A key assumption was 'that the structure of technical and scientific language are closely enough akin to justify our talking in terms of a register of technical/scientific explanation' (p. 377). Key features of this register were thought to be pre-modification of the noun, a high proportion of passives and modal auxiliaries, and a greater explicitness of clause relationships through WH-items and binders (e.g. because, if, although). Rushton and Young predicted that these stylistic shifts would be more pronounced in the writing of working-class subjects. Their results indicated that the working class did show greater stylistic variation on the titles and linguistic indicators selected. However, despite the sophistication and rigour of the Rushton and Young study, one is left wondering whether the same pattern of results would have emerged if *all* the topics had been analysed.

Richardson *et al.* (1975), in an investigation of the linguistic maturity of 11-year-olds, analysed the written compositions of 521 children in the National Child Development Study conducted in England, Scotland, and Wales. Social class comparisons were made, using the T-unit length as a measure of syntactic maturity, and composition length as a measure of productivity. The children were asked to describe life at 25 years of age. The results indicated that children from social class I (high socioeconomic status) produced essays which were about 25 percent longer than those for children from social class V (low socioeconomic status) and that the trend was statistically significant. However, there were no significant differences in mean T-unit length; that is no social class differences were apparent for syntactic maturity. The results of this study are by no means clear-cut but the authors see their results as offering supportive evidence that all but a few sociocultural environments provide adequate contexts for the syntactic aspects of language development. Unfortunately, however, the researchers exercised no control over the way the task was administered and this may have influenced the results.

A well-designed Australian study, assigned 240 pupils to cells of equal numbers in a three-way analysis of variance design using four grade levels, sex (2) and socioeconomic status (2), with IQ as a covariate (Owens, 1976). Criticizing Bernstein and Lawton for drawing on small samples from adolescent boys only, and for insufficiencies in the generalizability of the results, Owens sought to overcome these deficiencies in his own design. Furthermore, he delineated four major parameters which he saw as central to Bernstein's codes: correctness, length, complexity, and variety. Conscious of what Rosen (1969) labelled the effects of general rhetorical mode or purpose on the syntax produced, Owens set three writing topics in the narrative/descriptive mode, so that the topics were the same for all pupils. Unfortunately, the topics did not differ in type and in abstraction. Bernstein's theory, and others, suggest that the working class is more adept in description and narrative, that is, in more concrete and action-oriented modes. To this extent, Owens' research design, by the very nature of its stimulus topics, may have biased his research away from the likelihood of finding significant differences between classes.

Owens found no socioeconomic differences in the use of adjective clauses, clause length, T-unit length, first-order subordination, or passive verbs. Indeed, low socioeconomic writers used significantly more adverb clauses, a marginally greater amount of subordination, and composed longer sentences (mainly because of a tendency to string T-units with or without co-ordinating conjunctions). On the basis of his findings, Owens (p. 214) concludes that 'some reasonable scepticism may be expressed about socio-economic status *per se* (at least as assessed by gross indicators of occupation and education) as a major determinant of complexity, length, and variety in written syntax'. The topic's specification (narrative/descriptive), however, remains as a basic design detractor in this otherwise substantial study.

In another Australian study, Davis (1973, 1977) focused on receptive and productive skills in written language in eighty secondary-level students. She used three sets of stimulus conditions: literal description, aural story based on sound, and visual story based on graphic shapes. On three quantitative measures (productivity, structural complexity, and lexical diversity) and one qualitative measure (global impression) there were no significant differences. The five differences which did occur favoured the low socioeconomic subjects. However, as Davis (1973) points out, she experienced difficulty in selecting her sample of subjects as the choice of extreme social groups such as those used by Bernstein and Lawton proved to be virtually impossible.

Taking anxiety into account, as well as the effects of social class and ability, Kiellerup (1977) examined samples of written language from 114 children aged 11–12 years (fifty-nine boys and fifty-five girls). These were selected from a comparatively high and a comparatively low status area in Victoria, Australia. Three essays, on topics thought to encompass a broad range of task demands, were coded for forty-one linguistic element and structure variables. Unfortunately, the results were combined to provide a single corpus of language for analysis. The linguistic indices were factor analysed to derive nine sub-global dimensions of written language and then further factor analysed to isolate three major dimensions of language: lexical competence, stylistic competence, and structural competence. Essays were also globally rated by five independent judges on a qualitative measure, 'Literacy'. No social class differences were found on any of the dimensions.

A study in Alberta designed by Foster and Nixon (1973) was designed to test, in a different cultural context, the Bernstein-derived theory of linguistic code. Twenty grade 7 subjects, divided equally on the basis of socioeconomic status, and matched for age, sex, and IQ, were asked to write an essay on the question 'What do you think is the real purpose of education?' Responses were analysed for content by three independent raters on an abstraction/generalization scale. In addition, major elaboration indices were calculated: (1) length (number of words written), (2) mean sentence length, (3) number of subordinate clauses, (4) number of subordinate clauses divided by finite verbs, (5) number of adjectives divided by total words, (6) number of adverbs divided by total words, (7) number of personal pronouns divided by total words, (8) number of passive verbs divided by total words. Another sample of written language was obtained via a sentence-completion task (10 times) which was analysed to determine (1) total co-ordinations, (2) total subordinations, and (3) total subordinate clauses divided by total finite verbs.

No socioeconomic differences were found in abstraction and the sentence-completion test provided little evidence of inter-class or intra-class differences in sentence construction. A general lack of fluency was exhibited for all groups and length did not connote complex structures, merely an over-reliance on the use of co-ordinations. Middle-class boys did use more adjectives than the low socioeconomic group, but other analyses of parts of speech revealed no pronounced class differences. The small sample size again makes the generalizability of such results impossible; also the topic may not have been engaging.

In an extension of her earlier study, Poole(1973) used a factor analytic technique to isolate dimensions of written language which were then used to compare social class groups. Using a factor congruence technique, Poole found that the middle-class and working-class groups were invariant for syntax, adverbial elaboration, and uncommon linguistic forms.

Within a Bernstein-derived framework, therefore, the majority of studies report an absence of marked social class differences in written language. Such findings, however, need to be viewed against several evaluative criteria which may have significantly influenced the pattern of results. Definitions of social class; selection of stimulus topics; sampling procedures; indices used in the analysis; these, and other factors, are critical in determining the outcome of any study. Equally, research showing class differences can be criticized for inadequate sampling procedures, crude indices of social class, inadequate linguistic categories, and so on. One of the advantages of the meta-analysis in Part B is that all of these factors can be coded and entered into an interpretive framework for assessing the relationship between socioeconomic status and written language.

Socioeconomic Status and Written Language; Some Non-Bernstein Perspectives

Most of the early work on social class comparisons in written language was based on tests of written language skill rather than on samples of written language encoded by the subjects themselves (McCarthy, 1930; Day, 1932; Davis, 1927). This was generally true also of research carried out in the United States until the mid-1960s (John, 1963; Deutsch, 1965).

British research, stemming from the Sociological Research Unit, London Institute of Education, tended to focus on actual language use in specified situations, although some tests, vocabulary tests, for example, continued to be used.

Not all recent studies on written language and socioeconomic status, however, have been based on theories such as those of Bernstein. A few somewhat a-theoretical studies have reported socioeconomic differences favouring the middle or upper classes. Knapp and Slotnick (1973) surveyed, as part of a national assessment project in the USA, certain kinds of writing skills for a sample of children (aged 9 years), teenagers (aged 13 and 17 years), and young adults (26–35 years). Participants, 400 in all, were assessed on their ability to communicate adequately in a variety of situations: (1) in a social situation (written; (2) in a business or vocational situation; (3) in a scholastic situation; and (4) in appreciating the value of writing for social communication. A social class gradation favouring upper socioeconomic levels was reported. Similar trends were evident in written language in business and vocational settings and in a scholastic setting, although no differences in an appreciation of the value of writing were reported. The tasks involved form-filling, addressing envelopes, and responses to questions concerning attitudes to writing. The social tasks included writing invitations, thank-you notes, and written directions. As in any national assessment, the indices used for social class memberships were, of necessity, rudimentary and it is surprising, therefore, that social class differences were evident in such basic functional tasks.

A strong relationship between various aspects of language proficiency and social class was reported by Stewig and Lamb (1973). They tested eight grade 6 classes, in which there were 132 low-status pupils and 120 high-status pupils. The test used was the LAMP (Linguistic Ability Measurement Program), a test requiring children to evaluate and manipulate words and sentences as structural and transformational objects. They also examined creative responses from three pieces of the children's writing (a theme, a story, a poem). LAMP scores accounted for around 42 per cent of the variation of the total production scores for the middle-class subjects, but only 23 per cent for low socioeconomic subjects. Analysis of variance (sex × race × socioeconomic status) results computed for LAMP, poem, theme, and story's total production scores revealed significant main effects for socioeconomic status apart from the theme scores.

Earlier, Stewig and Lamb (1972) had reported that the predictive power of LAMP scores for total production scores varied considerably between the two social groups, with rated quality of composition more closely tied to grammatical knowledge in the middle-status group. Both studies appear to have been soundly designed and executed.

Developmental Studies: Structural Indicators and Socioeconomic Status

One of the major concerns in developmental studies of language has been syntactic complexity. Interest has consistently focused on identifying criteria of maturity. Many research workers have devised indices of structural complexity based on types of subordination (McCarthy, 1930; La Brant, 1933; Harrell, 1957), in addition to the more global index of mean sentence length used to indicate proficiency in manipulating the structural resources of language (McCarthy, 1930, 1954; Fries, 1952; Ford, 1954; Sampson, 1964). Reviews of this early work from 1920 to 1960 can be found in Heider and Heider, 1940; McCarthy, 1954, O'Donnell, *et al.*, 1967. Increases in mean sentence length and the use of subordination were usually cited as evidence for a gradual development in syntactical range and control (McEldowney, 1968). Such indices were thought to reflect unity, continuity, clarity, and, in the cognitive domain, complexity of thought (Symonds and Daringer, 1930; Ford, 1954; Lewis, 1963).

While most of this developmental research was directed towards complexity indices in oral language, the work of Loban (1963, 1964, 1970) and Hunt (1965, 1970) is especially interesting since their measures can be appropriately applied either to speech or writing. Both researchers devised a measure of language complexity which was independent of the language user's punctuation. Hunt (1965), in analysing the written language of children in grades 4, 8 and 12, observed an age-dependent increase in clause length and in subordination. He saw this as a rationale for developing an entirely new linguistic unit, the T-unit/minimal terminable unit. Loban's measure (the Communication Index) was very similar to Hunt's. Both measures comprise one main clause together with all its attendant structures. The basic advantage of such indices over that previously used to assess complexity (viz. mean sentence length) was that they enabled more objective and less arbitrary assessments to be made on inadequately punctuated protocols. A significant finding was that T-unit length related closely to age and increased control over language. In other words, as students moved up through the grades in school, they produced longer T-units. Hunt's age trends were independently replicated and confirmed (e.g. O'Donnell *et al.*, 1967; Mellon, 1967; Smith, 1974). Loban's longitudinal data indicated a steady increase in complexity for all children with increasing age. However, children from high-status families were found to use more complex syntax and to maintain this pattern throughout their primary schooling.

Loban (1967) reports comprehensive linguistic data collected over a 13-year period for 338 Californian school children as they progressed from kindergarten through Grade 12. Among a vast battery of tests and inventories were tasks designed to measure skill in written language. Although the research was mainly developmental and aimed at a broader understanding of language ability, a number of interesting findings pertinent to social class were reported. High language proficiency was associated with (1) more varied and flexible syntax; (2) more precise use of relational terms; (3) expressed tentativeness and supposition; (4) more complex subordination (clauses of cause, concession, and condition; (5) more accurate and optional grammatical transformations in sentence structures. Indeed, it is interesting to note how closely these parallel many of Bernstein's elaborated code characteristics. Correlational analysis revealed high-status groups developed language skills earlier, conformed more to standard patterns of usage and displayed greater competency than those in lower socioeconomic groups. The data on mean scores emphasized the group separation:

> The data on mean scores show the subjects' socio-economic status to be clearly related to the ratings of their written compositions. ... From grade four through grade twelve, *in every case without exception* those in socio-economic group I have the highest ratings on their written compositions. In addition, there is no *overlapping whatever* between the upper three socio-economic groups and the lower socio-economic groups. In every year studied, those in socio-economic groups I, II and III *always* receive higher ratings on their written compositions than do subjects in socio-economic groups V, VI, and VII. Thus the evidence on *mean scores* makes quite obvious clear relationships between socio-economic status and proficiency with written language. (p. 102)

This consistent pattern of differences in one of the few longitudinal studies in the literature is especially interesting. Questions can be raised, however, as to the information given on how social differences were defined, to the possible compounding of IQ and ethnicity with social class, and the localized nature of the sampling framework.

The use of T-units and related measures has also been criticized. Basically, the measure is seen as insensitive to the constraints imposed by the stimulus task and the mode of discourse. In an interesting study, Rosen (1969) compared the length of T-units produced by 16 year olds in a variety of writing tasks over the span of a school year. Very significant differences in T-unit length were found between the written tasks. The T-unit, furthermore, merely provides a global index of syntax development, without providing information on gradations of structural complexity, as, for example, the use of complex transformations on the range and diversity of structural units. One of the questions that remains to be answered is, in fact, what variables reflect language maturity, competence, and complexity. Given the basic structure of language, what individual variables or clusters of variables distinguish the more competent performers from the less competent, regardless of social class?

Other studies on the syntactical resources of social class groups have suggested a middle-class superiority on several measures; mean sentence length (Olim *et al.*, 1965); the use of more complex syntactic structures (Harrell, 1957; Davidson, 1967); the range of optional constructions available (Loban, 1963; Bruiniks, 1970). These studies and others pointed to social class differences over a wide range of grammatical features; for example, the total use of subordination, the use of uncommon clauses, and more structurally complex clauses (embedded). Not all indicators of socioeconomic difference, however, were structural, although the significance of structural as opposed to lexical features has not been addressed in the literature.

Conceptualizations of Linguistic Discriminators for Socioeconomic Groups

There have been various conceptualizations of the major indices along which socioeconomic comparisons can be made. Several of these, ranging from the simple to the more complex, are discussed here.

(a) Descriptive and Adverbial Elaboration

In his earlier papers, Bernstein (1959, 1961a, 1962b) argued that descriptive and adverbial elaboration enable the language user to make finer discriminations of thought, and emphasized that the middle class were at an advantage here. He claimed it was the range and diversity in the selection of qualifiers and modifiers that was the distinguishing characteristic rather than the total number produced. Access to only a limited repertoire of adjectives and adverbs was thought to reduce the options available for elaborating intent (Bernstein, 1961a). Whilst rigidity and restriction in lexical choice was reported for working-class groups, some studies indicated that middle-class groups individualized their selection of modifiers and qualifiers to specify their intention (Lawton, 1968; Davidson, 1967; Poole, 1973). The pattern is by no means clear, however, as other studies reported no social class differences in the frequency and range of descriptive and adverbial elaboration (Huffine, 1966; Smedley, 1969).

(b) Subordination Indices

A range of approaches has been reported for measuring the frequency and diversity of subordination patterns used in syntactic construction (Lawton, 1968; La Brant, 1933; Olim, n.d.; Owens, 1973; Poole, 1973). Inter-class differences have been found but the trends have not been consistent. On an open-ended sentence-completion test, Lawton (1968) reported greater control over subordination indices by middle-class boys, especially at age 12 years. On an index sensitive to embedded complexity (for example, infinitives, gerunds, participles, and embedded subordinate clauses), Lawton (1968) and Loban (1963) reported differences favouring the middle class.

(c) Verb Complexity

It has been argued that social class groups differ in the degree to which they encode complex verb structures. Indeed, Bernstein's (1959) earlier research suggested lower-class verb structures were simple, even crude, and likely to limit the expression of logical processes. Other studies reported middle-class groups as using a higher proportion of complex verb stems (verbs of three or more parts) and passive verbs (Bernstein, 1962b; Lawton, 1963, 1968). For Lawton (1963), use of the passive voice was one of the major differentiating features between the classes. The use of the passive is thought to indicate increasing linguistic control over a difficult transformation (Slobin, 1966) and the use of three-part verbs to represent increasing verb complexity (Cazden, 1966). Increases in mean pre-verb length (the average number of words preceding the main verb stem) is taken to reflect linguistic elaboration (Olim *et al.*, 1965), since left-recursive sentences are involved and these are considered to be more complex to encode (Miller, 1962). The viability of using passive transformations to assess class differences is questionable as they occur so infrequently. Hunt (1965) found that passive forms amounted to only 1.7 per cent of the total finite verbs used in grade 4 compositions increasing to 6 per cent by grade 8 (McEldowney, 1968) and 8.2 per cent in grade 12 (Hunt, 1965). Poole (1973), however, found less than 5 per cent usage, by first-year undergraduates.

(d) Predictability

Bernstein has argued that the language of the working class is more predictable in lexicon and syntax than that of their middle-class counterparts. Both Lawton (1968, p. 98) and Coulthard (1969, p. 41) have indicated that Bernstein lacks clarity as regards the predictability dimension of the elaborated–restricted coding continuum. In elaborated coding, is the probability of predicting linguistic choices reduced because each language encounter is situationally determined and individuals draw from their extensive linguistic resources? Alternatively, is the restricted code-user likely to produce highly predictable speech because of access to a more limited set of linguistic alternatives? Within a sociolinguistic framework, Poole (1973) attempted to operationalize the concept by asking: 'Does predictability mean the relative frequency percentage score for class elements or syntactic combinations or does it mean, as information theory implies, the ability to replace correctly parts that have been deleted from a message?' (Poole, 1973, p. 301).

Cloze procedure was used by Poole (1973) to assess the degree of correspondence between the encoding habits of writers and the decoding habits of readers. Osgood (1960), for example, showed that, in more stereotyped messages (in terms of lexical and syntactic choice) it was easier to replace deleted items. Poole (1973) argued, therefore, that items in working-class written message systems should be easier to replace because a restricted code, within a Bernstein framework, is characterized by high lexical and structural predictability.

Somewhat earlier, Robinson (1965) purported to use cloze procedure to investigate differences in the verbal encoding of working-class and middle-class boys. Cloze tests were constructed from the letters (both formal and informal) of middle-class and working-class boys. Two of Bernstein's suggestions were investigated: the extent to which middle-class and working-class subjects used the same lexicon; and the differences in predictability of working-class and middle-class encoding. The results indicated that middle-class boys used more varied vocabulary, and that working-class boys displayed more conformity in their responses (stereotype). Since Robinson used single sentences for his cloze deletions, his experiment, although valuable, resembles a sentence or gap completion test rather than a cloze test dealing with a contextually interrelated series of blanks.

Predictability studies, until Poole (1973), had used a single cloze score to index message difficulty. Using an information theory approach, Poole (1973) argued that it should be possible to obtain a mathematical value for the redundancy or uncertainty of individual cloze items or of entire cloze passages. Information theory indicates that the success with which a set of receivers of a message can fill in its missing parts is a measure of the redundancy of the mesage (Aborn and Rubenstein, 1952; Attneave, 1959; Pollack, 1963; Anderson, 1969; Poole, 1974). That is to say, if the context surrounding a message blank enables a cloze unit of 100 per cent to be achieved, there is no uncertainty about the correct word to be inserted and the redundancy is maximal. If, at the other extreme, the cloze score is zero, absolute uncertainty (entropy) exists, because everyone has selected a different alternative, that is, there is no redundancy. Redundancy and uncertainty, therefore, can be viewed as complementary measures, so that it is possible for a cloze deletion to yield a score of zero per cent correct and yet have maximum redundancy of all message decoders or receivers supply the same 'incorrect' work. A critical definitional difference emerges: cloze scores use the actual message of the source as a criterion, whereas redundancy indices relate to the uncertainties of receivers (Taylor, 1956; Osgood, 1959). Using this rationale, Poole (1973) argued that cloze procedure could provide two separate indices of predictability: subjects' ability to restore written messages (predictability) and redundancy characteristics of written messages (predictability viewed as high redundancy or low uncertainty).

Two cloze tests were constructed by Poole (1973) from life-forecasts written by university entrants of middle-class and working-class origin. In a second experiment forty-six tertiary subjects were asked to fill in the missing cloze deletions of these written passages. Subjects of both social classes were able to replace significantly more cloze deletions, especially lexical, from the working-class messages. There were, however, no significant differences in the relative uncertainty of written middle-class messages compared with working-class messages. In other words, there was comparable communality of responses in replacing messages. Unfortunately, the socioeconomic characteristics of the subjects could not be controlled and there may have been within-subject factors operating as, for instance, middle-class and working-class subjects filling in gaps differentially.

(e) The Language Mode: a Comparison of Spoken and Written Language

Several authors have indicated major differences between the written and oral modes, although features of overlap or 'fit' have been adduced. Such differences could, in effect, point to different levels of expectation for the existence or otherwise of class differences in the written mode. Various comparisons have been considered; the levels of abstraction in spoken and written language (De Vito, 1967); the frequency with which certain types of linguistic structures appear in oral and written discourse (Blankenship, 1962; Golub, 1969); differing modes of expression at the ideational, structural, and psychological levels (Horowitz and Newman, 1964); and developmental aspects of oral and written language (Harrell, 1957). Instances of 'fit' between the structures of written and spoken language have been explored by Gleason (1961, 1965) although the distinctions are given much more prominence. Drieman (1962) and Gibson *et al.* (1966) go so far as to label written and spoken language as 'separate systems'. In an analysis of the most consistent patterns to emerge in oral/written comparisons, Davis (1973) reported less productivity, but longer words and sentences, in written language than in spoken. Davis also pointed to the constraints and formality of writing compared with speaking.

Horowitz and Newman (1964) conducted two experiments in which each subject acted as his own control in completing spoken and written tasks. They found that spoken expression revealed greater productivity (more words, phrases, sentences), more ideas and subordinate ideas, more ancillary ideas, communicative signals and orientation signals, more repetition, and more elaboration.

In a sophisticated study using an adaptation of immediate constitutent analysis, Nash and Calonica (1973) proposed a multidimensional measure of code elaboration for written sentences. An interesting methodological viewpoint developed was that written sentences could be construed as sufficiently similar to spoken language to permit the construction of a meaningful index of elaboration for written sentences. Arguing that Bernstein's notion of language dimensions is clearly performance-based rather than competence-based, Nash and Calonica (1973) proposed a model for the analysis of linguistic performance using written language. The key indicators in the model were: verb elaboration, modification of constructions employed in sentences, an index of subordination, average number of words per sentence, number of verb types per sentence, and the proportion of words that are nouns. Nash and Calonica noted that similar measures of linguistic elaboration have been used by other authors to assess spoken language (e.g., Bernstein, 1962; Lawton, 1968; Poole and Field, 1971; Williams and Naremore, 1969). They made a major qualification concerning their procedure, which has considerable significance for the study of class differences in written language:

> Although written language may be taken as an adequate corpus ... it may never be considered data for the assessment of the restricted code of speech. Restricted codes are context-bound and implicit modes of expression. They may be written down or they may influence a person's writing style and complexity, but they are, by nature, verbal and situationally determined. ... Therefore, an accurate interpretation of the proposed mode is that it *measure the elaboration dimension of performance only*. It measures restricted codes incidentally: i.e. if a person's writing system is influenced by his spoken restricted code, he may write in low elaborate fashion. However, it is clear from Bernstein's theory and Lawton's work that correlates of communicative code can vary along dimensions of elaboration without the necessity of directly assessing restricted codes. (Nash and Calonica, 1973, p. 348)

Poole and Field (1971), in an analysis based on code elaboration theory, compared written protocols from a group testing situation with spoken language from individual interviews. The analysis covered structural complexity, language elaboration, verb complexity, and personal reference. The results suggested that, in comparison with oral systems, written systems were more complex in structure, revealed more adjectival but less adverbial elaboration, showed more complex verb structures, but contained fewer indices of personal reference. The authors suggested that there might be methodological disadvantages to using an identical code elaboration model to make comparisons in sociolinguistic studies because important contextual dimensions cannot be incorporated into such a description of linguistic features.

Studies such as those cited above raise important questions as to the meaning and definitiveness of studies reporting differences or no differences between the social class groups on Bernstein-derived indices of code elaboration. What has been found may be differential performance by social class groups on aspects of performance in written language rather than coding differences *per se*. Or, as Nash and Calonica (1973) suggest, there may be differences in the degree of elaboration in linguistic performance.

Written Language and Cognitive Processing

A key cognitive question, if consideration is given to theorists such as Whorf (1962), Vygotsky (1962) and Piaget (1926), is whether language is seen to have primacy over thought or thought over language. The cognitive consequences of socialization practices operating differently in middle-class and working-class families are clearly articulated in a number of papers, although their empirical basis is somewhat thin. Lawton (1963), for example, drawing upon Bernstein, indicates that the working-class world is dominated by concrete objects rather than by ideas, and by events rather than reflections upon those events. Robinson (1965) and Robinson and Rackstraw (1972) suggest that working-class children are more likely to operate at a concrete and self-referential level, rather than at the formal operational level of thinking. Owens' (1976) study, however, revealed no significant differences in the stage of cognitive development (concrete; formal) for socioeconomic groups, nor were there any significant class and cognitive stage interactions.

Cromer (1974) has argued that humans 'are able to understand and productively to use particular linguistic structures only when cognitive abilities enable them to do so' (p. 246). The precise nature of the relationship between processes of oral language and cognitive development has been a focus for theorists and researchers for decades. However, apart from a few studies, the association of written language with cognitive processes has rarely been alluded to.

Kessler and Quinn (1977), for example, examined the relationship between cognitive development, language acquisition, and socioeconomic status as manifested in children's written language. The research question was whether or not the results of direct instruction in hypothesis formation observed in the written language complexity of a high-status group of sixth-grade children, is generalizable over differing socioeconomic levels. Four classes of sixth-grade students, a control class, and an experimental class from high and low-status groups saw twelve science inquiry film sessions and took part in six discussion sessions, each session lasting 40 minutes. At the end of each film, subjects wrote as many hypotheses as they could in 12 minutes. Two criteria were used for scoring: The Hypothesis Quality Scale (Quinn, 1971) and the Syntactic Complexity Formula (Botel *et al.*, 1973). The Syntactic Complexity Formula was especially interesting, being derived from transformational–generative grammar theory, and 'taking into account language development and performance studies which consider the frequency of usage of structures in children's oral and written language as well as experimental data on children's processing of syntactic structures' (p. 6).

The treatment groups at both the upper and lower socioeconomic levels showed consistently higher hypothesis quality scores and syntactic complexity scores than did the control groups at the two socioeconomic levels. Interestingly, though, on both measures the upper-status group started at a slightly higher level than the low-status group. Kessler and Quinn (1977) conclude that the 'socioeconomic level of the child is not a variable in the relationship between the psycholinguistic ability to produce complex syntactic structures and the cognitive ability to formulate scientific hypotheses' (p. 10). The authors see their study as supporting the concept that hypothesis formation and language development are logically related. The ability to formulate hypotheses, they suggest, is a variable which influences language development.

A Swedish study conducted in Malmo in 1976 followed a group of 200 students through grades 4, 5, and 6, with a view to studying social differences. Eight pieces of writing were collected, which covered descriptive free composition ('At the Museum', 'The Cat', 'At the Camping Site'), ability, language and creativity tests, together with questionnaire items for assessing students' attitudes to different working methods in free written composition. The lexical and syntactic analyses undertaken showed that the same language was used by both groups. Grade 4, higher-status children were more productive than low-status children, but this difference did not persist to grade 6. The major developmental changes were increased productivity, a rise in the number of different words used, and an increase in word length. The proportion of nouns and main verbs declined while the proportionate use of adjectives and adverbs rose.

The interpretation of certain developmental features raised questions as to the types of developmental and cognitive inferences that could be drawn from linguistic indices such as sentence length. Consider the following extract from the Swedish National Board of Education (1976, p. 12).

> *The logical sentences*, demarcated by the linguistic analysts without regard to the students' punctuation, increase slightly, while *the written sentences*, as demarcated by the students themselves, do not change in length. Perhaps this is because the students put more into their constructions above all attributes, making their logical sentences longer. At the same time their punctuation improves, with the result that their written sentences become shorter.

Whether at a certain developmental stage one needs to begin to reinterpret sentence length not as a measure of maturity and/or complexity but of poor stylistics is an interesting question, not to be left solely in the hands of linguists or critcs of style. The cognitive implication of such a feature could well reflect increased economy in processing information and in subsequent encoding in written symbols.

A META-ANALYSIS OF RESEARCH ON SOCIOECONOMIC STATUS AND WRITTEN LANGUAGE

Meta-analysis is a recently developed method of integrating research findings. Unlike the traditional discursive review, it attempts a quantitative aggregation of findings and a quantitative examination of the relationships between characteristics of the studies and findings (Glass, 1976, 1978). It can thus provide a more rigorous, exhaustive, and objective integration of research studies.

The unit of analysis in meta-analysis is the *effect size*. In the present study, this measure is an index of the difference in standard deviation units between middle- and lower-class means on a measure of written language production. Thus, one effect size is calculated for each discrete measure of written language production for each study. In the present meta-analysis this meant that up to twenty-one effect sizes were calculated from the one study.

The formula for the calculation of effect size is as follows:

$$\mathrm{ES} = \frac{X_M - X_L}{\mathrm{SD}_Y}$$

where: ES = effect size
X_M = middle class mean on variable Y (a measure of written language production such as Loban's subordination index)
X_L = lower class mean on variable Y
SD_Y = pooled standard deviation of variable Y.

The use of this index of effect size places different measures of the effect of socioeconomic status on written language production on a common metric, and thus enables findings from different studies to be directly compared and aggregated.

A meta-analysis proceeds by coding various features of each study, such as sample size, number of females in the sample, etc., and then examines relationships between these variables and effect size in order to provide explanations of variations in effect size within and across studies.

The Literature Search

An extensive literature search on socioeconomic status and written language was carried out using the following information bases: *ERIC documents, ERIC Index to Journals in Education, Psychological Abstracts, Council for Exceptional Children Abstracts, Dissertation Abstracts, Social Science Citations Index, Smithsonian Science Information Exchange,* and *Language and Language Behaviour Abstracts*. Bibliographies of studies were used as additional sources.

Sixty-three documents were identified as relating to written language and socioeconomic status. Unfortunately twenty-six of the studies located did not contain usable data, that is, data that could be coded on indices of written language along the lines detailed by Bernstein or developmental psychologists. Twenty-one other studies were omitted from the meta-analysis as they lacked sufficient data for the calculation of effect sizes. Where one author had produced two or more papers based on a single data set, only one paper was included in the analysis. Consequently three relevant papers by Rushton and Young (1975), Lawton (1968), and Poole (1976) were omitted, further limiting the total sample size.

After a comprehensive process of search and selection only thirteen studies met the minimal criteria concerning sampling, statistical analysis, and reporting of descriptive and correlational results.

Coding Characteristics of Study

The major items of the coding sheet devised for the integrative analysis are given below:

Background Information

(1) Year of publication.
This information could provide an index of the methodological quality of a study as recent articles tend to be more systematic in their methodology and presentation. All the studies included in the meta-analysis were published after Bernstein's initial theorizing on the relationship between language and socioeconomic status, but they span two decades.

(2) Source of data.
This indicates where the data were extricated from, for example, a journal, book, thesis, other ERIC publications or an unpublished document.

(3) Country of study.
The country of origin of the study was coded as it could be the case that socioeconomic satus has different effects in different cultures.

Sample Information

(1) Total number in the sample.
Variation in numbers of subjects can be critical, not only for the generalization of results, but in terms of the precision of the estimates of effect size.

(2) Number of clusters.
This indicates the number of different sources of data in a study. For example, in some studies several schools in different socioeconomic areas are involved. Alternatively, a study may be conducted in one school or a university and social groups are defined within the single context.

(3) Random or non-random selection of sample.
This can influence the level of bias in the results reported.

(4) Socioeconomic status comparison.
The type and nature of the socio-economic comparisons were coded as follows:
(a) HSES/MSES/LSES comparison
(b) HSES/LSES comparison
(c) HSES & MSES/MSES & LSES comparison
(d) MSES/LSES comparison
The degree of separation on a socioeconomic continuum could influence the pattern of reported relationships.

(5) Percentages.
The percentages of the sample in each socio-economic group were included in the coding system.

(6) Accuracy of socioeconomic measures.
This item is scaled from low to high (a to e) as an indicator of precision of measurement.
(a) The determination of socioeconomic status
(b) The researcher's assumption of socioeconomic status according to a certain area, or context.
(c) Father's occupation according to a well-defined tested scale, for example, Congalton (Australia), Hollingstead (USA), Blishen (Canada), General Register (UK).
(d) Father's occupation and education.
(e) Parental occupation according to a scale (as above) and level of education.

(7) Representativeness of working-class sample.

(8) Representativeness of middle/high social class sample.
Representativeness is determined by the context of the study and the source and age of subjects.

(9) Number of age groups.

(10) Age Group Category.
These covered the following age spans:
(a) 5–8 years; (b) 9–12 years; (c) 13–15 years; (d) 16–20 years; (e) adult.

(11) Sex of sample.
As early studies used only male samples, socioeconomic differences in later studies could be affected by sex differences.

(12) Working-class IQ.

(13) Middle class IQ.
The IQ levels of working class and middle class subjects were defined independently as an index of the influence of IQ differences on socio-economic differences.

Written Language: Assessment

(1) Method of testing.
This covered the following categories:
(a) Individually administered exercise
(b) Test/exam situation
(c) Classroom exercise
(d) Homework exercise

(2) Number of writing samples.
Some studies were based on single samples of written production.
The greater the number of writing samples used, the more adequate the sampling is likely to be.

(3) Nature of the writing stimulus.
There is evidence indicating that particular writing stimuli facilitate or alternatively inhibit the use of an elaborative or restrictive code.
The writing stimulus may be:
(a) Technical
(b) Descriptive
(c) Narrative
(d) A combination of technical, descriptive, and narrative
(e) A combination of descriptive and narrative
(f) Opinionative/discursive
(g) Others
Several other factors which could influence the subject's tendency to use an elaborated or restricted code were included in the coding scheme.
(4) Choice of topic.
(5) Constraint on language use.
This related to whether students were instructed to avoid certain practices, as for example, using colloquial expressions.
(6) Constraint on format.
Account was taken of the kind of written task performed, for example: scientific hypotheses; business letters, etc.
(7) Working-class familiarity with the topic.
(8) Middle-class familiarity with the topic.
(9) Method of coding data:
(a) According to a specified tested coding scheme.
(b) According to a system designed for the particular study.
(c) Not stated.

Written Language Categorization

Studies relating written language to socioeconomic status have used a variety of indices to categorize language. An attempt has been made to establish a cohesive scheme to organize these indices. Six general measures were defined. The first, structural complexity, included Loban's subordination clause categories and the ratio of subordinate clauses to all clauses. Passive forms and complex verb stems were included in the second category of verbal complexity. The third measure, elaboration, contained adjective and adverb clauses and indices of modification. Lexical diversity was used to describe measures of vocabulary use, such as uncommon adjectives and adverbs, and a number of type–token ratios. The fifth and sixth measures related to productivity. Sentence length included T-unit length and clause length. The final category was a measure of composition length.

Description of the Data Base

The thirteen studies coded and analysed yielded a total of 110 effect sizes. Frequency distributions were used to survey the characteristics of the data. These are presented in terms of effect sizes rather than studies.

Background Characteristics

Eighty-one per cent of the studies were published in journals. The remaining 19 per cent were found in theses and ERIC documents. All studies coded and analysed were published between 1963 and 1977. Studies from North America, the United Kingdom, France, and Australia were included in the analysis. However, the majority came from the United Kingdom (42.7 per cent) and Australia (45.5 per cent).

Sample Characteristics

The nature of the socioeconomic status comparison and the accuracy of the criteria used to define groups varied across studies. It was found that most studies used powerful socioeconomic comparisons, that is HSES, MSES, LSES (28.2 per cent) or HSES, LSES (52.5 per cent). The mean effect size differences between these two types of comparison were small. The frequency distributions revealed that 52 per cent of effect sizes derived from studies where father's occupation was the only criterion. The properties of effect sizes from studies using the more accurate criteria for assignment to social class groups, that is father's occupation and level of education, and parental occupation and level of education were 25 per cent and 23.9 per cent respectively. Only a single effect size was derived from a study where the criteria for assignment to social class group was not stated.

The number of subjects in samples across studies varied considerably (N = 20 to 572, X = 135). The majority of studies (64.5 per cent) examined the written language of only one age group. While only one study focused on the youngest age group (5–8) the other three age ranges (8–12, 13–15, and 16–20 years) were well represented. A review of the proportion of males and females across studies revealed that females have been under-represented in studies of the relationship between socioeconomic status and written language. The level of IQ, whether high, moderate or low, of both working-class and middle-class groups showed that there tended to be a higher proportion of the middle-class in the high IQ group

(34.5 per cent) compared with working-class students (15.5 per cent); 57.3 per cent of the analyses of the effect of socioeconomic status on written language used IQ as a covariate.

Task Characteristics

Several items relating to task variations were included in the coding. A high proportion of studies analysed three writing samples (63.6 per cent) of one or more types. The other studies used only one or two samples to make assumptions about the written language used by subjects. It has been noted that the nature of the writing stimulus can influence the student's use of an elaborated, or alternately, a restricted code. The range of stimuli, as described above, was well represented in the analyses.

The written samples were usually collected during general classroom exercises (81 per cent). However, 19 per cent of effect sizes came from studies involving a test or exam situation which is considered a more stringent, controlled setting.

The variables: choice of topic; constraint on language and format; middle-and working-class familiarity with the topic, were coded and analysed because of their possible influence on the student's response to the writing task. Only three studies, however, gave students a choice of topic, although most recognized the need to provide familiar topics and refrained from issuing commands which would influence the language used.

An examination of the analysis of the writing samples showed that most studies were coded according to a specified and tested scheme. (96.4 per cent). Each of the six measures of written language was represented. While structural complexity (31.8 per cent) and lexical diversity (25.5 per cent) were the largest categories, there was a sufficient spread for statistical analysis.

Results

The mean effect sizes for each study were calculated (Table 1). A positive effect size indicates that the middle-class children were better than the lower-class children in the writing tasks used, while a negative effect size indicates the reverse. Eleven of the thirteen studies showed a positive relationship and there was also an overall positive relationship between socioeconomic status and written language (ES = 0.30). These results indicate that the middle-class subjects performed 0.3 of a standard deviation above the level of lower-class subjects in writing tasks. The size of the effect is thus relatively small.

TABLE 1 Mean effect sizes for studies relating socioeconomic status and written language

Study	Number of effect sizes	Mean effect size
Davis (1977)	3	0.13
Esperet (1973)	5	0.17
Poole (1972)	12	0.32
Woodfin (1968)	1	0.18
Rushton and Young (1975)	21	0.66
Lawton (1963)	18	1.00
Thomaneck (1972)	6	0.04
Kiellerup (1977)	20	0.05
Kessler and Quinn (1977)	1	0.80
Richardson *et al.* (1975)	2	0.30
Foster and Nixon (1973)	4	−1.12
Owens (1976)	15	−0.15
Janzen and Hallworth (1973)	2	0.04
Total	110	0.30

However, the overall effect size must be examined in the light of the effect of background variables, sample, task, and coding characteristics. Due to the small total number of studies, and the relatively large number of effect sizes per study, relationships between variables are discussed here in terms of effect size magnitude, rather than in terms of statistical significance. Similarly, the small sample number has meant that some coding categories, while including a number of effect sizes, described only a single study. The results should thus be treated with caution.

Background Characteristics

Earlier studies showed higher effect sizes than more recent studies (Table 2). It might be argued that this result is due to poor methodologies since it has been found that recent studies are more rigorous in their approach. However, a number of indices of quality of methodology were coded and it was discovered that none of these adequately explained the effect of year of publication.

However, there is evidence to suggest that the relationship between year of publication and the magnitude of the effect size is influenced by the country of origin of the study rather than methodological deficiencies. Studies conducted in Australia and North America yielded lower effect sizes than those from the United Kingdom (Table 3). Furthermore, the Australian and North American studies were published more recently.

TABLE 2 Year of publication of studies used in the meta-analysis

	Year		Number of effect sizes	Mean effect size
1	1963		18	1.0
2	1965		1	0.18
3	1972		18	0.23
4	1973		11	−0.32
5	1975		23	0.63
6	1976		15	−0.15
7	1977		24	0.09
		Total	110	0.30

TABLE 3 Country where studies were conducted

	Country*		Number of effect sizes	Mean effect size
1	North America		8	−0.43
2	United Kingdom		47	0.69
3	Australia		50	0.06
		Total	105	0.30

*One study conducted in France was deleted from this analysis.

There are two possible explanations for the apparent differences in the mean effect sizes of studies conducted in North America, Australia, and the United Kingdom. This could occur because the more highly stratified social system in the United Kingdom influences the written language differences of working-class and middle-class groups. In contrast, North America and Australia have a more egalitarian social structure. The second explanation could relate to the accuracy of socioeconomic status measurement. All four studies using more than simply father's occupation as a measure of socioeconomic status were conducted in Australia and North America. As Table 4 indicates, the more accurate the measurement of socioeconomic status the lower the effect size found.

Higher effect sizes were found in the studies which had fewer subjects (Table 5). There is a greater degree of error in estimates of effect sizes derived from small samples, therefore it can be argued that the true effect size is a good deal closer to the larger sample effect size of 0.11 than the

TABLE 4 Accuracy of socioeconomic status

	Rating*	Number of effect sizes	Mean effect sizes
3	Father's occupation only	57	0.51
4	Father's occupation and level of education	27	0.06
5	Parental occupation and level of education	25	0.08
	Total	109	0.30

*One study not stating criteria for assignment to socioeconomic group was deleted.

TABLE 5 Total sample number

	Number of sample	Number of effect sizes	Mean effect sizes
1	20	22	0.61
2	47	21	0.66
3	81	16	0.32
4	99	5	0.17
5	114	20	0.05
6	240	15	−0.15
7	387	2	0.04
8	544	9	0.11
	Total	110	0.30

smaller sample effect size of 0.61. However, another index of reliability ran in the opposite direction to this result. The greater the number of writing samples used in a study, and thus the higher the reliability of the estimate of written language production, the higher the effect size. Table 6 shows the details of this analysis. Since the second category was derived from a single study the main comparison in the above table is between groups one and three.

Earlier, it was noted that females were under-represented across studies. The results indicate that the more females in a study the greater the effect size. However, the difference is largely due to the high effect sizes reported in only two studies (Lawton, 1963; Rushton and Young, 1975 – see Table 1) and these involved only male subjects.

There were no marked variations in the effect sizes according to age and intelligence, at least within the age and IQ ranges examined. Some studies

TABLE 6 Number of writing samples

	Number of samples	Number of effect sizes	Mean effect sizes
1	One sample	33	0.06
2	Two samples	7	0.76
3	Three samples	70	0.36
	Total	110	0.30

used IQ as a covariate in their analyses of the effect of socioeconomic status on written language but this did not produce different effect sizes. This latter finding, which goes against a number of claims to the contrary, is doubtless due to the nonsignificant correlations typically found between IQ and narrow measures of written language production (see, for example, Owens, 1973).

An examination of the effect sizes obtained with different types of writing stimuli showed that both narrative and descriptive modes produced small but positive effect sizes. However, the technical mode, because of wide variations of effect sizes across studies, did not produce an overall positive effect size. It is not clear from the data why the range of effect sizes in the technical mode was so wide. Some effect sizes were indeed positive and high.

Some variables coded are not discussed because the range of variation in the studies examined was too narrow. For example, all studies reported random selection; therefore the relationship of this variable with socioeconomic status could not be analysed. Similarly there was not sufficient variation in the methods of testing and the methods of coding used in studies to permit comparisons to be made. The variables: choice of topic, constraint on language and format, and working-class and middle-class familiarity with the writing topic, also had too narrow a range of variation. Other variables such as the representativeness of the middle-class and working-class samples and the language measures, although having a sufficient degree of variation to produce significant correlations, did not in fact do so.

Conclusion

It is difficult to draw any firm conclusions from this meta-analysis on the relationship between socioeconomic status and written language. True, there is an overall positive effect size indicating that the middle-class subjects performed slightly better than the working-class subjects on the writing tasks employed in the thirteen studies. However, this effect size was rather unreliable in the sense that it was washed out or even reversed in some cases under the influence of other uncontrolled variables.

One of the most potent of these variables was country of origin of study. The results appear to indicate that research carried out in the United Kingdom produced positive effect sizes whereas that carried out in North American and Australian cultures produced negligible effect sizes. Other potent variables included year of publication and accuracy of the socioeconomic measure used. These three influential variables are entirely confounded in the meta-analysis, and it is not clear which is the crucial variable in the determination of the magnitude of the effect size.

C: SUMMARY

The two approaches taken in this chapter, the analytic review and the meta-analysis, serve to augment each other in detecting major trends in the relationship betwen socioeconomic status and written language. The analytic review suggested associations, some strong, some weak, but several studies indicated there were no differences. In such a situation, a reviewer is confronted with his or her biases and can, through selective reporting, or through critical analyses of weaknesses in studies, point to some patterns of perceived relationships. In this chapter any synthesis could at best indicate equivocation and uncertainty as to which set of findings (difference, little difference, no difference) were more convincing.

The meta-analysis, on the other hand, points to a positive and consistent effect size between socioeconomic status and written language. By way of explanation, however, insight is provided into the factors which contribute to that pattern. No differences are evident in recent studies in countries other than the United Kingdom, and in which sampling size and stringency of criteria for socioeconomic selection have been key features of research design.

It would seem, then, that *no* strong relationship can be established on the basis of the analyses in Parts A and B, between socioeconomic status and written language. Yet such an assessment, based as it is on the studies discussed, and the studies that could be coded for meta-analysis, must give some cognizance to the place of ideology and methodology in producing such a pattern of outcomes. The ideological focus or value stance of the researchers, as well as the methodologies used could influence the conceptualization and implementation of research and the pattern of results. In conclusion, therefore, some such issues are raised.

Ideologies

Regardless of the empirical evidence, any assessment of the current status of research on socioeconomic status and written language would need to take account of the persuasiveness of several ideological propositions regarding the relationships between social class and written language:

Proposition 1: No Difference

This proposition suggests that there is no difference between the social class groups in language. The differences that were posited under the rubric 'cultural deprivation' were in the nature of a myth and based on poor research design. Linguists have asserted that any language is sufficiently powerful and flexible to permit effective communication. The notion of 'linguistic deficit' is therefore not tenable. Sociologists have been equally vocal in stating a case for 'cultural difference' replacing that of 'cultural deficit'. Educators have also suggested that the negative labelling of low-status children along deprivation dimensions was part of a process of attributing educational failure to families, rather than to the shortcomings of schooling. Furthermore, for written language, the absence of differences is taken to indicate the cumulative and positive effects of schooling as against family socialization.

Proposition 2: A Lesser Difference for Writing

This proposition suggests that there is a difference between the social class groups in the language domain but that it is less marked for written than for oral language. Bernstein's theories on social class and language developed through his concern with the fundamental linking of symbolic systems, social structure, and the shaping of experience. Might it be that the processes of socialisation and 'cultural transmission' operating in middle-class and working-class families influence oral language much more powerfully than they do written? The socialization mechanism operating in the school system could be such that the modes, methods, and functions of written language, as transmitted to students, have been within a middle-class paradigm of functional and aesthetic literacy. The impact of such a process might be to narrow the difference between social classes in the school-initiated macro-skills of writing and reading. Patterns of speech production and listening strategies might, on the other hand, continue to reflect family socialization experiences. The arguments used to justify this proposition include:

(a) Teaching written language is usually entirely under the auspices of the school, whereas spoken language is initially influenced by the home and is probably less amenable to school influences; a difference in spoken–written performance could thus be anticipated.

(b) Writing and speech reflect different cognitive planning and orienting processes. In writing there is time for reflection, revision, and editing, whereas the spontaneous and 'unplanned' nature of speech largely precludes modification (although speech processes reflect self-monitoring and may exhibit overt communication disruptions).
(c) The 'context' of written language is taught, whereas social situational variables and context in speech are learnt through experience; the school teaches 'writing for an audience', informal/formal task demands, how to write in technical, scientific, descriptive, expository styles, etc.
(d) Written language is given more attention in schools than spoken language and so is rehearsed more; in addition, the link between writing and reading is emphasized more than that between speaking and listening. Reading provides many alternative role models for writing. The parallel situation does not exist for speech, so perhaps earlier critical socialization variables remain more important.

Proposition 3: The Performance–Competence Gap

The performance–competence dimension may work differentially for speech and writing with written production more closely reflecting competence (knowledge of how the language works and ability to use it) than is the case for oral language. It is also possible that both social classes possess a variety of 'codes' or 'registers' and that, given some control over situational variables, both middle and working class are similar in their control over language. The middle class may reveal more instances of infrequently used linguistic categories in their written (or spoken) language, but this is an instance of the gap between performance and competence. The tasks used to elicit performance may not be reflecting competence. Middle-class and working-class groups possess similar underlying linguistic competencies and it is only in their performance that differences might emerge. Increasingly, however, it seems that competence is a concept which has little operational value for the study of differential linguistic behaviour.

Proposition 4: Language Values

Is the valuing of all codes equally a 'linguistic myth'? Not all linguists, for example, value middle-class language, judging it to be verbose, colourless and turgid (Labov, 1969). Yet does the rich, colourful, terse working-class language they purport to admire provide access to the educational, economic, political, and social structures of a society? If schooling is middle-class in its value orientations, then the institutions and bureaucracies based on the middle-class sifting and sorting processes of schooling are probably likely to value certain forms of language more than others. It has been argued that no language can be considered less amenable to the traditional school's linguistic style of knowledge development (Levitas, 1974). Indeed, it could also be reasoned that educational valuing of the working-class code is creating a new cultural and romanticized myth, not because of the 'worthiness' of such intrinsic evaluation, but because such a stance does not provide a key to working-class children for accessing the knowledge codes and power structures of the society. As Giles and Woolfe (1977, p. 58) state: 'the reality of the situation is that certain kinds of behaviour, speech and ways of acting give access to power, income and resources of some groups and, conversely, deny them to others'. They argue that, although members from minority cultures may possess a coherent and complex cultural linguistic system, unless they learn to perform adequately and to negotiate wider social contexts, their options will be substantially reduced.

Methodological Issues

Apart from the question of ideologies influencing one's perception of research findings, there are a number of methodological issues pertinent to any analysis of socioeconomic status and written language.

(a) The Nature of the Stimulus. Kiellerup (1977) attributes one of the major influences on written language production to 'the circumstances surrounding the collection of the samples of written language. ... Important questions about the level of difficulty of the task, the stress imposed by the situation, the specificity of the topics, and the extensiveness of the samples' (pp. 40–41). There has been enormous variety in the stimulus conditions reported to elicit samples of written language. Some researchers have sought to elicit a range of writing styles and have collected more than one sample per subject (e.g. Lawton, 1963; Smedley, 1969; Davis, 1973; Kiellerup, 1977). Others have concentrated on eliciting a particular mode of expression, for example descriptive writing (Owens, 1976).

The practice of pooling written production to create one corpus of writing and then to look for specific social class differences may have obscured the fact that a particular mode of expression (descriptive, expository, explanatory) can be associated with certain lexical and syntactic features (Veal and Tillman, 1970; Martinex, 1972). Furthermore, the question of free choice of topic may be an important motivational variable which challenges all students regardless of social class. This could partly explain why Woodfin (1968) and Owens (1976), in a free choice situation, reported no social class differences. Interestingly, Owens (1976), although leaving the choice of topic open, prescribed the mode, narrative descriptive, on three separate occasions. Many researchers seem to collect only single samples of written language, although a number of researchers report collecting two or more samples from the same subjects (Lawton, 1963; Smedley, 1969; Davis, 1973; Owens, 1976; Kiellerup, 1977).

(b) Methods of Analysis. A variety of data analysis techniques have been employed in studies of socioeconomic status language. Earlier work, based on Bernstein, and concerned with specific individual indices of the codes, tended to use Mann–Whitney U tests (Lawton, 1963; Smedley, 1969; Poole, 1972). Other studies have used correlational techniques (Woodfin, 1968; Davis, 1976). Multivariate approaches to consider overall coding can also be found (Poole and Field, 1973). A question of concern in language analysis is the interdependence of the elements (both lexical and structural) and the realization that language variables are probably rarely normally distributed. Questions of linearity and normality can markedly affect findings, yet such issues are rarely raised. Indeed, the choice of a technique may be a major factor in finding or not finding social class differences. In a critique of Woodfin's (1968) study for example, Kiellerup (1976) noted that Woodfin reports significant positive correlations between social class and intelligence, and that Woodfin's conclusion that socioeconomic status was a relatively unreliable predictor of writing skill, may have been a somewhat exaggerated claim, given the confounding of socioeconomic status and IQ.

(c) Social Class Indicators. The social class indicators used have often been fairly non-sensitive of familial characteristics, for example father's occupation and/or educational level. It is now generally acknowledged that familial factors, such as interaction patterns (e.g. Esperet, 1973; Rafferty, 1974) or sociocultural resources for learning (e.g. Bourdieu, 1973; Bisseret, 1979) are apparently of greater importance in socialization than the structural–economic/educational characteristics by which different social groups were originally identified. In a study investigating spoken language, Poole (1976) tried to assess such qualitative dimensions of family life as a basis for allocation to social class membership using a social class lifestyle index (see Poole, 1976). No studies were found which used such an approach in the analysis of socioeconomic status and written language. If social class were to be defined more in terms of process, aspects of the performance–competence distinction might be more clearly conceptualized than they have been by linguists who ignore 'the extreme complexity of the relation between the speaker's/writer's linguistic

knowledge and how it is actually put to use in the real world' (Greene, 1972, p. 196). To this should be added the context of families engaged in different patterns of social interactions.

At a more basic level, the samples selected, although labelled middle-class or working-class, have often been vastly different. Both reporting differences, or not finding differences to report, can sometimes be attributed to the sample selection process of minimizing or maximizing group separation prior to data collection.

CONCLUSION

On the basis of both the analytic review and the meta-analysis there is no clear evidence for a strong association between socioeconomic status and written language. Taking into account the lack of precision in research design (sampling, topic, conditions, confounding of IQ), the value stance of the researchers, the country of origin of the study, the criteria for defining socioeconomic status, these, and many other considerations, show the studies discussed point to only limited support for a weak relationship between socioeconomic status and written language.

REFERENCES

Aborn, M., and Rubenstein, H. (1952). Information theory and immediate recall. *Journal of Experimental Psychology,* **44**, 260–267.

Anderson, J. (1969). Application of cloze procedure to English learned as a foreign language. Unpublished doctoral dissertation, University of New England.

Attneave, F. (1959). *Applications of Information Theory to Psychology: a summary of basic concepts, methods and results*. Holt, Rinehart, & Winston, New York.

Bernstein, B. (1958). Some sociological determinants of perception. *British Journal of Sociology,* **9**, 159–174.

Bernstein, B. (1959). A public language: some sociological implications of linguistic form. *British Journal of Sociology,* **10**, 311–326.

Bernstein, B. (1961a). Social structure, language and learning. *Educational Research,* **3**, 168–176.

Bernstein, B. (1961b). Social class and linguistic development: a theory of social learning. In A. H. Halsey, J. Floud, and C. Anderson (eds.), *Education, Economy and Society*, pp. 228–314. Collier-Macmillan, London.

Bernstein, B. (1962a). Linguistic codes. Hesitation phenomena and intelligence. *Language and Speech,* **5**, 31–45.

Bernstein, B. (1962b). Social class, linguistic codes and grammatical elements. *Language and Speech,* **5**, 221–240.

Bernstein, B. (ed.), (1971a). *Class Codes and Control*, vol. 1. Routledge & Kegan Paul, London.

Bernstein, B. (1971b). A socio-linguistic approach to socialisation. In F. Williams (ed.), *Language and Poverty: Perspectives on a Theme*, pp. 25–61. Markham, Chicago.

Bisseret, N. (1979). *Education, Class, Language and Ideology*. Routledge & Kegan Paul, London.

Blankenship, J. (1962). A linguistic analysis of oral and written style. *Quarterly Journal of Speech,* **48**, 419–422.

Botel, M., Dawkins, J., and Granowsky, A. (1973). A syntactic complexity formula. In W. H. MacGinitie (ed.), *Assessment Problems in Reading*. International Reading Association, Newark, Del.

Bourdieu, P. (1973). Cultural reproduction and social reproduction. In R. Brown (ed.), *Knowledge, Education and Cultural Change*. Tavistock, London.

Bruininks, R. H. (1970). Measures of intelligence, language, creativity, reading and written language achievement of disadvantaged children. *International Reading Association Conference Proceedings*, pp. 43–54. Newark, Delaware.

Cazden, C. B. (1965). Environmental assistance to the child's acquisition of grammar. Unpublished Ph.D. thesis, Graduate School of Education, Harvard University.

Cazden, C. B. (1966). Sub-cultural differences in child language: an interdisciplinary review. *Merrill-Palmer Quarterly,* **12**, 185–219.

Cazden, C. B. (1970). The situation: a neglected source of social class differences in language use. *Journal of Social Issues,* **26**, 35–60.

Coulthard, M. (1969). A discussion of restricted and elaborated codes. *Eductional Review,* **22**, 38–50.

Cromer, R. F. (1974). The development of language and cognition: the cognition hypothesis. In B. Foss (ed.), *New Perspectives in Child Development.* Penguin Education Series, London.

Davidson, I. S. (1967). An assessment of the language difficulties encountered by students in technical college. *Vocational Aspect,* **19**, 59–76.

Davis, D. F. (1973). Speaking and writing: a study of some socio-psychological correlates of skill in and preference for the use of oral and written language. Unpublished Ph.D. thesis, Monash University.

Davis, D. F. (1977). Language and social class: conflict with established theory. *Research in the Teaching of English,* **2**, 207–217.

Davis, E. A. (1937). The development of learning skill in twins, singletons with siblings and only children from age 5–10 years. *Institute of Child Welfare Monograph Series*, No. 14, University of Minnesota Press.

Day, E. J. (1932). The development of language in twins: 1 – A comparison of twins and single children. *Child Development,* **3**, 179–199.

Deutsch, M. (1965). The role of social class in language development and cognition. *American Journal of Orthopsychiatry,* **35**, 78–88.

Deutsch, M., *et al*. (1967). *The Disadvantaged Child*. Basic Books, New York.

Deutsch, M., Katz, I., and Jensen, A. R. (eds.) (1968). *Social Class, Race and Psychological Development*. Holt, Rinehart, & Winston, New York.

De Vito, J. A. (1967). Levels of abstraction in spoken and written language. *Journal of Communication,* **17**, 354–361.

Drieman, G. H. J. (1962). Differences between written and spoken language. *Acta Psychologica,* **1**, 36–57.

Esperet, E. (1973). Relation between written language of terminal students and certain characteristics of their sociocultural background. *Bulletin de Psychologie,* **26**, 484–493.

Ford, C. T. (1954). Developments in written composition during the primary school period. *British Journal of Educational Psychology,* **24**, 38–45.

Foster, L., and Nixon, M. (1973). Language, socio-economic status and the school: An exploratory study. *The Alberta Journal of Educational Research,* **19**, 187–193.

Fries, C. C. (1952). *The Structure of English: An Introduction to the Construction of English Sentences*. Harcourt, Brace & Co., New York.

Gibson, J. W., Gruner, C. R., Kibler, R. J., and Kelly, F. J. (1966). A quantitative examination of differences and similarities in written and spoken messages. *Speech Monographs,* **33**, 444–451.

Giles, K., and Woolfe, R. (1977). *Deprivation, Disadvantage and Compensation*. Open University Press, Milton Keynes.

Glass, G. V. (1976). Primary, secondary and meta-analysis of research. *Educational Researcher,* **5**, 3–8.

Glass, G. V. (1978). Integrating findings: the meta-analysis of research. In L. S. Shulman (ed.), *Review of Research in Education*, No. 5. F. F. Peacock, Itasca, Illinois.

Gleason, H. A. (1961). *An Introduction to Descriptive Linguistics*. Holt, New York.

Gleason, H. A. (1965). *Linguistics and English Grammar*. Holt, New York.

Golub, L. S. (1969). Linguistic structures in students' oral and written discourse. *Research in the Teaching of English,* **3**, 70–85.

Greene, J. (1972). *Psycholinguistics*. Penguin, London.

Harrell, L. (1957). A comparison of the development of oral and written language in school age children. *Monograph of the Society for Research in Child Development,* **22**, No. 66.

Heider, F. K., and Heider, G. M. (1940). A comparison of sentence structure of deaf and hearing children. *Psychological Monograph,* **52**, 42–103.

Horowitz, M. W., and Newman, J. B. (1964). Spoken and written expression: an experimental analysis. *Journal of Abnormal and Social Psychology,* **68**, 640–647.

Huffine, C. L. (1966). Inter-socio-economic class language differences: a research report. *Sociology and Social research,* **50**, 351–357.

Hunt, K. W. (1965). *Grammatical Structures Written at Three Grade Levels*. National Council of Teachers of English, Research Report No. 3. Urbana, Illinois.

Hunt, K. W. (1970). Syntactic maturity in school children and adults. *Monograph of the Society for Research in Child Development,* **35**, No. 134.

Janzen, H. L., and Hallworth, H. J. (1973). Demographic and biographic predictors of writing ability. *The Journal of Experimental Education,* **41**, 43–53.

John, V. P. (1963). The intellectual development of slum children: some preliminary findings. *American Journal of Orthopsychiatry,* **33**, 813–822.

Kessler, C., and Quinn, M. E. (1977). Child language development in two socio-economic environments. Paper presented at the Annual Meeting of the American Educational Research Association. New York City, 4–8 April.

Kiellerup, F. D. (1977). Social class, ability and anxiety contrasts in the written language of primary school children. Unpublished Ph.D. thesis, University of Melbourne.

Knapp, J. V., and Slotnick, H. B. (1973). *Writing: Grouop results A and B for objectively-scored exercises; 1969–70 Assessment, National Results by Region, Sex, Color, Size and Type of Community, and Parental Education*. Education Commission of the States, Denver, Colorado. (ED 077029). National Assessment for Educational Progress.

Labov, W. (1969). The logic of nonstandard English. *Georgetown Monographs on Language and Linguistics,* **22**, 1–22.

La Brant, L. L. (1933). A study of certain language developments in children in grades 4–12 inclusive. *Psychological Monograph,* **14**, 387–491.

La Civita, A. F., Kean, J. M., and Yamamoto, K. (1966). Socioeconomic status of children and acquisition of grammar. *Journal of Educational Research,* **60**, 71–74.

Lawton, D. (1963). Social class differences in language development: a study of some samples of written work. *Language and Speech,* **6**, 120–143.

Lawton, D. (1968). *Social Class Language and Education*. Routledge & Kegan Paul, London.

Levitas, M. (1974). *Marxist Perspectives in the Sociology of Education.* Routledge & Kegan Paul, London.

Lewis, M. M. (1963). *Language, Thought and Personality in Infancy and Childhood.* Basic Books, New York.

Loban, W. (1963). *The Language of Elementary School Children*. National Council of Teachers of English, Urbana, Illinois.

Loban, W. D. (1964). *The Language of Elementary School Children*. National Council of Teachers of English, Urbana, Illinois.

Loban, W. D. (1967). *Language Ability – Grades Ten, Eleven and Twelve, Final Report*. National Council of Teachers of English, Urbana, Illinois.

Loban, W. D. (1970). *Stages, Velocity and Prediction of Language Development: kindergarten through grade twelve*. Educational Resources Information Center, Washington.

McCarthy, D. (1930). The language development of the preschool child. *Institute of Child Welfare Monograph Series*. No. 4. University of Minnesota Press.

McCarthy, D. (1954). Language development in children. In L. Carmichael (ed.), *Manual of Child Psychology*. Wiley, New York.

McEldowney, P. (1968). Range and frequency of syntactical patterns in the written English of New Zealand school children. *New Zealand Journal of Educational Studies,* **3**, 40–58.

Martinez, S. J. C. P. (1972). Grammatical structures in four modes of writing at fourth grade level. Unpublished Ph.D. thesis, Syracuse University.

Mason, C. W. (1968). An analysis of the interrelationships of variables in selected language skills in intermediate and upper elementary school students. Ph.D thesis, Southern Illinois University, Carbondale.

Mellon, J. (1967). *Transformational Sentence–Combining: A Method for Enhancing the Development of Syntactic Fluency in English Composition.* Cooperative Research Project 5-8418, Office of English Education and Laboratory for Research in Instruction, Graduate School of Education, Harvard University, Cambridge, Mass.

Miller, G. (1962). Some psychological studies of grammar. *American Psychologist,* **17**, 748–762.

Nash, J. E., and Calonica, J. M. (1973). A measure of code elaboration for written language. *Journal of Psycholinguistic Research,* **2**, 343–353.

National Swedish Board of Education, Stockholm. (1976). Composition at the Middle Level of Elementary School. *School Research Newsletter*. ED 140 611, November.

O'Donnell, R., Griffin, W., and Norris, R. (1967). *Syntax of Kindergarten and Elementary School Children: A Transformational Analysis*. Research Report No. 8, National Council of Teachers of English, Urbana, Illinois.

Olim, E. G. (n.d.). Scoring Manual – language styles and suggested procedures for scoring language samples (to accompany Scoring Manual). Amhurst: University of Massachusetts, Department of Human Development.

Olim, E. G., Hess, R. D., and Shipman, V. C. (1965). Maternal language styles and their implications for children's cognitive development. Paper presented at The Effect of Maternal Behaviour on Cognitive Development and Impulsivity. American Psychological Association, Chicago, September.

Osgood, C. E. (1959). The representational model and relevant research methods. In I. de Sola Pool (ed.), *Trends in Content Analysis*, pp. 33–38, University of Illinois Press, Urbana.

Osgood, C. E. (1960). Some effects of motivation on style of encoding. In T. Sebeok (ed.), *Style in Language,* pp. 293–306. MIT Press, Cambridge, Mass.

Owens, L. (1973). Syntax in children's written composition: relationships to socioeconomic status and cognitive development. Unpublished Ph.D. thesis, University of Sydney.

Owens, L. (1976). Syntax in children's written composition, socio-economic status and cognitive development. *Australian Journal of Education,* **20**, 202–222.

Piaget, J. (1926). *The Language and Thought of the Child.* Routledge & Kegan Paul, London.

Pollack, I. (1963). Message–uncertainty and message–reception, III: effect of restriction of verbal context. *Journal of Verbal Learning and Verbal Behaviour,* **1**, 392–395.

Poole, M. E. (1972). Social class differences in code elaboration: a study of written communication at the tertiary level. *Australian and New Zealand Journal of Sociology,* **8**, 46–55.

Poole, M. E. (1973). Linguistic, cognitive, and verbal processing styles; a social class contrast. Unpublished Ph.D. thesis, La Trobe University.

Poole M. E. (1974). A comparison of the factorial structure of written coding patterns for a middle class and a working class group. *Language and Speech,* **17**, 222–239.

Poole, M. E. (1976). *Social Class and Language Utilization at the Tertiary Level.* University of Queensland Press.

Poole, M. E. (1978). Linguistic code and cognitive style: interdomain analyses. *Perceptual and Motor Skills,* **46**, 1159–1164.

Poole, M. E. (1979). Elaboration of linguistic code and verbal processing strategies: interdomain analyses. *Psychological Reports,* **45**, 283–296.

Poole, M. E., and Field, T. W. (1971). Social class and code elaboration in oral communication. *Journal of Speech and Hearing Research,* **14** (2), 421–427.

Poole, M. E. (1972). Social class differences in code elaboration: a study of written communication at the tertiary level. *Australian and New Zealand Journal of Sociology,* **8**, 46–55.

Quinn, M. E. (1971). Evaluation of a method for teaching hypothesis formation to sixth grade. Doctoral thesis, University of Pennsylvania.

Rafferty, F. T. (1974). Cognition, language and social behaviour. *Child Psychiatry and Human Development,* **4**, 227–237.

Richardson, K., Calnan, M., Essen, J., and Lambert, L. (1975). The linguistic maturity of 11-year-olds: some analysis of the written compositions of children in the National Child Development Study. *Journal of Child Language,* **3**, 99–115.

Robinson, W. P. (1965). The elaborated code in working class language. *Language and Speech,* **8**, 243–252.

Robinson, W. P., and Rackstraw, S. J. (1972). *A Question of Answers*, vols I and II. Routledge & Kegan Paul, London.

Rosen, H. (1969). An investigation of the effects of differentiated writing assignments on the performance in English composition of a selected group of 15–16 year old pupils. Ph.D. thesis, University of London.

Rushton, J., and Young, G. (1974). Elements of elaboration in working class writing. *Educational Research,* **16**, 181–188.

Rushton, J., and Young, G. (1975). Context and complexity in working class language. *Language and Speech,* **18**, 366–387.

Sampson, O. (1964). Written composition at 10 years as an aspect of linguistic development. *British Journal of Educational Psychology,* **34**, 143–150.

Shriner, T. H., and Miner, L. (1968). Morphological structures in the language of disadvantaged and advantaged children. *Journal of Speech and Hearing Research,* **11**, 605–610.

Slobin, D. I. (1966). Grammatical transformations and sentence comprehension in childhood and adulthood. *Journal of Verbal Learning and Verbal Behaviour,* **5**, 219–227.

Slobin, D. I. (1968). Questions of language development in cross cultural perspective. Paper prepared for symposium on Language Learning in Cross-cultural Perspective. Michigan State University, September.

Smedley, D. A. (1969). Language and social class among grammar school children. *British Journal of Educational Research,* **39**, 195–196.

Smith, W. L. (1974). Syntactic recoding of passages written at 3 levels of complexity. *Journal of Experimental Education,* **43**, 66–72.

Stewig, J. W., and Lamb, P. (1972). *Elementary pupils' knowledge of the structure of American English and the relationship of such knowledge to the ability to use language effectively in composition.* Final Report. Purdue Research Foundation, Lafayette. Indiana.

Stewig, J. W., and Lamb, P. (1973). Elementary pupils' knowledge of the structure of American English and the relationship of such knowledge to the ability to use language effectively in composition. *Research in the Teaching of English,* **7**, 324–337.

Symonds, P. M., and Daringer, H. F. (1930). Studies in the learning of English expression: IV, sentence structure. *Teachers' College Record,* **32**, 50–64.

Taylor, W. L. (1956). Recent developments in the use of 'cloze' procedure'. *Journalism Quarterly,* **33**, 42–48.

Thomaneck, J. K. A. (1972). A sociolinguistic study of adjective and adverb. *Language and Speech,* **15**, 8–13.

Veal, L. R., and Tillman, M. (1970). Modes of discourse variation in the evaluation of children's writing. Paper read at AERA, Minneapolis. MIT Press, Cambridge, Mass.

Vygotsky, L. (1962). *Thought and Language.* MIT Press, Cambridge, Mass.

Whorf, B. (1962). *Language, Thought and Reality.*

Williams, F., and Naremore, R. C. (1969). Social class differences in children's syntactical performance: a quantitative analysis of field study data. *Journal of Speech and Hearing Research,* **12**, 778–793.

Woodfin, M. J. (1968). Correlations Among Certain Factors and the Written Expression of Third Grade Children. *Educational and Psychological Measurement,* **28**, 1237–1242.

[illegible] of the components of [illegible] composition [illegible] selected group of [illegible] grade pupils. Ph.D. thesis, [illegible].

[illegible] (1974). Elements of [illegible] writing. *Educational Research* 16, [illegible].

[illegible] (1975). Connected and [illegible] in [illegible]. *Journal of [illegible] and Speech* 18, [illegible].

[illegible] (1969). [illegible] speech to aid [illegible] *Journal of Educational Psychology* [illegible] 140.

[illegible] (1977). [illegible] T-unit in the analysis of [illegible] children's [illegible]. *[illegible] Research* [illegible].

[illegible] Grammatical transformations and sentence combining [illegible] *Research Monograph* [illegible].

[illegible] (1975). [illegible] in [illegible] and [illegible].

[illegible] Journal of [illegible] Research 12, [illegible].

[illegible] in [illegible] Research and Education [illegible].

[illegible] (1972). [illegible] of [illegible] and [illegible] Research [illegible].

[illegible] (1974). [illegible] in English and [illegible] *Research in the Teaching of English* [illegible].

[illegible] (1971). [illegible] of [illegible] *Journal of Educational Research* [illegible].

[illegible] (1970). [illegible] in the use of [illegible] procedures. [illegible].

[illegible] (1973). [illegible] study of adjective and adverb [illegible].

[illegible] (1976). [illegible] of the [illegible] in the [illegible].

[illegible] (1973). [illegible] *Reading* [illegible].

[illegible] (1970). [illegible] differences in children's [illegible] *Journal of [illegible]* [illegible].

[illegible] Relationships of [illegible] and the [illegible] Children [illegible] *Elementary English* [illegible].

The Psychology of Written Language
Edited by M. Martlew

CHAPTER 14

Writing Disorders associated with Focal Cortical Lesions

PIERRE MARCIE

Agraphia is generally recognized as being associated with focal cortical lesions. The neurological literature indicates that agraphia forms a set of deficits in writing which affect not only the meanings of words but also the linguistic values of written symbols and their combination into words. As early as 1856, Marce defined such difficulties as alterations in 'the conventional meaning of symbols utilised in writing'. The origin of the term 'agraphia' to describe writing disorders caused by focal lesions, is attributable to Ogle (1867), who distinguished two varieties: *amnemonic* agraphia (associated with spelling) and *atactic* agraphia (the praxic component). In clinical neurology, Broca's view (1865) that writing and speech are affected in a similar manner has been accepted. Such similarity did not imply for Broca, however, that there is any necessary connection between writing and speaking.

At the beginning fo the twentieth century, opinion among neurologists polarized around two extreme views. On the one hand agraphia was seen as a mere consequence of the main disorder of aphasia, writing being totally subservient to speech. In contrast, writing was seen as an autonomous function capable of impairment in the absence of deficits in either language or thought. Thus there was speculation and controversy over the existence of a 'centre for writing' paralleling Broca's 'speech centre' for oral expression. Wernicke (1874) rejected the notion of a motor centre specialized for writing. This was supported by Dejerine (1914) who claimed that agraphia could not occur in isolation, since writing is mediated through 'word ideas'. In 1891 he had described a case of agraphia involving disruption of the 'verbal visual image', following damage to the left angular gyrus. Thus those few cases where the disorder was seen in its pure state would be attributed to a motor or sensory aphasia. Marie (1926) saw aphasia as a global intellectual deficit which necessarily leads to a parallel deficit in writing. In contrast Exner (1881), supported by Pitres (1884, 1894) identified a specialized centre for writing at the base of the second frontal convolution of the left hemisphere. Bastian (1894) was willing to accept such a possibility whilst recognizing the weakness of the observations offered as evidence for its existence.

Following this early work, interest focused on the classification of writing disorders. Von Monakow and Mourque (1928) recognized that, apart from agraphias associated with aphasias, there was a 'kinetic melody of letters' and an agraphia associated with alexia in which there was a loss of the meaning of 'sensory images' for both words and letters. Henschen (1922) offered a classification of agraphias on the basis of the location of the lesion (frontal at the base of F2, temporal, parietal, occipital, and angular gyrus) together with a conduction aphasia resulting from a lesion isolating the frontal pole. Later, Kleist (1934) specified three varieties of agraphia: those associated with aphasias, 'ideokinetic' agraphia as a version of 'ideokinetic' apraxia, and 'constructional agraphia' in which the use of both letters and words is disrupted spatially. Goldstein (1948) drew a distinction between 'primary agraphias', affecting the necessary components for different aspects of writing skill (ideopraxic, mnesic, praxic, and motor) and 'secondary agraphias' affecting the linguistic component, and associated with disorders of language. Emphasizing the relative autonomy of writing disorders within the general framework of writing disturbances, Hécaen *et al.* (1963) and Hécaen and Dubois (1968) proposed a classification of writing disorders in terms of their association with different forms of aphasia.

This question of the relative position of written language within the general organization of language function has interested many contemporary linguists. The general view is that writing is a secondary activity which involves the mechanical transformation of sounds into their written counterparts. For Saussure (1916) 'the very raison d'etre of writing is to represent language', while Bloomfield (1969) states that 'writing is not language but simply a process for recording language by means of visible signs'. He compared writing to a phonograph 'which manages to conserve for future observation features of language spoken in the past'. Chomsky (1972) considers orthography to be a point-to-point transcription of lexical representation.

Several functionalists have opposed this view. Artymovitch (1932), for instance emphasized the specificity of written language. Uldall (1944) viewed written and spoken language as 'merely two products among an infinite number of possible systems, none of which could be said to be more basic than the others'. For Vachek (1973), speech and writing serve different functions. Written language represents a specific function which is socially determined and this imposes upon it the rules which give it its coherence. However, while writing may serve specific purposes independent of speech, it is complementary to speech.

Disorders of writing are regularly associated with disorders of spoken language. Both are involved in the disruption of language function and share several features in common. If written language were merely a transcription of spoken language, then its disruption, in the presence of cortical lesions, would immediately imply the full range of aphasias within which writing disorders would be only just one symptom. Written language, by definition, so to speak, sets out the special matching characteristics of spoken language in a formal scheme as opposed to a structural scheme. The written code is made up of a special set of rules which determine both its written form and the purposes it serves. It is also legitimate to suggest that writing performance could be differentially affected as a function of the level of loss of one or other of the neuropsychological systems involved in its production: motor, perceptual, or linguistic.

AGRAPHIAS ASSOCIATED WITH APHASIAS

The classic clinical observation is that disorders of writing accompany those cortical lesions which lead to various forms of aphasia. For ease of presentation, they will be described here within the framework of the major syndromes of aphasia. It is extremely important to note, however, that this description implies no prior judgment about any causal relationship between aphasia and writing, nor is writing assumed to be functionally subordinate to spoken language.

Agraphia and Motor Aphasias

This category of speech disorders has appeared under a variety of labels within the neuropsychological literature, depending on the theoretical predilections of the authority in question. The principal aspects of the disorder may be seen to fall between the two extreme views taken about the nature of the disorganization involved; phonemic production and the articulation of syntactic structure.

Agraphia with Aphasia of Phonemic Production

It was Broca (1861) who first used the term 'aphemia' to distinguish this aphasic syndrome. While language comprehension and motor control of the musculature associated with sound production remain intact, there is a disruption in the faculty of articulate speech. This syndrome was given the name 'motor aphasia' by Wernicke (1874), and it is a term which has been used frequently since then. Marie (1926) defined 'anarthria' as an isolated disorder affecting the production of speech sounds, thereby excluding it from the area of aphasia proper inasmuch as 'internal speech' and language comprehension remained intact. In 1926, Head used the term 'verbal aphasia' to describe a disorder whose distinctive characteristics were the disruption of the articulation of speech sounds and of word formation. Weisenburg and McBride (1935) drew together all disorders affecting the articulation of speech sounds and word function under the label of 'expressive aphasias', while Alajouanine, *et al.* (1939) described a 'syndrome of phonetic disintegration'. Nathan (1947) used the term 'dysarthric apraxia' because he considered that its origins lay in an apraxia of the motor system governing sound production. Bay (1962) used the term 'cortical dysarthria' and later authors (Darley, 1964; Denny-Brown, 1965; De Renzi,, *et al.*, 1966; Shewan, 1980) emphasized this apraxic aspect of the disorder of speech articulation.

In spite of these numerous variations in terminology, there is at least some agreement on the nature of the deficits observed. Among others Shankweiler and Harris (1966) emphasize the following principal charcteristics: substitutions principally affecting the consonants, simplification of consonant clusters, and difficulty in programming the articulation of longer items. There have, however, in the course of investigations on these patients, been very few specific studies of writing disorders. Wernicke (1874), working within a rigorous theoretical framework, claimed that frontal lesions would leave writing intact. He considered, in effect, that handwriting involved the association of visual images with sound–word images, integrated into handwriting motor movements through the intermediary of motor–verbal images. Normally, this combination is automatic in handwriting and can be achieved without recourse to sound images. With the destruction of the frontal motor image, however, there is the possibility that writing may be activated directly by the pathway which was originally involved in the acquisition of this function. Clinical studies cast some doubts on these assumptions. Dejerine (1914), while accepting Wernicke's general formulation, also recognized that writing was affected by lesions which cause motor aphasia as well as by other forms of aphasia. In practice, most clinicians have subscribed to this view. Thus Head (1926) saw that their appearance together was a reflection of the relationship between writing and speech.

> Since the capacity to write is closely associated with the condition of internal speech, the nature of this disturbance in writing may vary in accordance with the

> other aphasic manifestations. Apart, however, from these more or less specific changes, the power of writing is liable to be diminished as a whole by any condition which interferes with the efficient use of language.

However, Head's view, just like the others, fails to encompass the full range of clinical cases. Neither the degree of disturbance, nor the specific deficits associated with the disruption of speech and writing, are necessarily similar. In the extreme case you can even find a form of pure motor aphasia with total preservation of the capacity to communicate in writing.

In frontal disturbances the extension of the lesion is frequently accompanied by motor deficits affecting the right upper limb. Thus, in order to examine written language ability it is necessary to use letter blocks or any other method which allows the function to be expressed in the absence of the fine motor control required for handwriting. This assumes that the deficit affects the graphic component of lexical representation, whose expression may be quite independent of the particular nature of the actual symbols used. In general, both conditions yield similar deficits in writing.

FIGURE 1 The writing of a 37-year-old right-handed patient (surgery through a cortical well in the left F2 to eliminate a large haematoma destroying frontal white matter). She was attempting to write her Christian name (Christiane) with her left hand. The first letter may be a capital C and the second one an attempt to write H

In the most severe cases, writing performance may be reduced to the level of attempting to write one's surname, as is shown in Figure 1. The mark on the left could be seen as a letter 'C', the initial letter of the patient's surname, but the remaining letters have no distinguishable meaning. When trying to write spontaneous text, patients frequently refuse to continue beyond the first few letters or words as errors are almost immediately apparent. This refusal is often accompanied by denial or by agitation in the face of failure.

Similarly, the writing of isolated words from dictation is typically disrupted. Meaningful words are generally better produced than nonsense syllables. Understanding the meaning of the words makes it easier to reproduce their written form but the reproduction of nonsense syllables is dependent upon the conversion rules for transforming phonemes to graphemes. In writing from the dictation of a continuous text (which may be done with either the right or the left hand), patients encounter the same difficulties, even though they experience little or no difficulty in understanding speech (Figure 2).

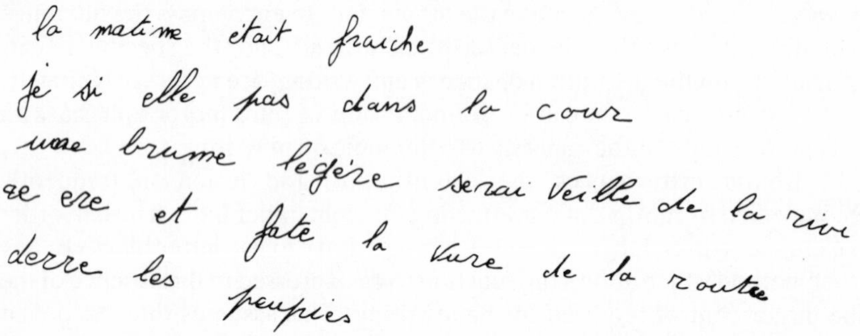

FIGURE 2 Left frontal meningioma in a 42-year-old right-handed patient. Thirteen days post-surgery, writing from dictation (dictated text: La matinée était fraîche. Je fis quelques pas dans la cour. Une brûme légère se levait de la rivière et masquait la vue de la route derrière les peupliers).

The main difficulties are: paragraphic subsitutions (se levait is rendered by serai veille; masquait is rendered by fate); lexical paragraphias (fis is rendered by si); duplications of part of word (rivière is written rivere ere); neglect of letter strings (derrière becomes derre) and of single letters (peupliers is written with two omissions); adjunctions of letters (vue is written vure)

The primary characteristic of the deficit is the presence of numerous literal paragraphias, even though the word structure retains a clear relationship with the original. Errors consist largely of letter omissions or substitutions, the introduction of additional letters being relatively less frequent. Copy-writing is generally better preserved and even left intact. An exception is shown in Figure 3 where the disturbances in copying are analogous to those seen in other writing modes. There are many literal

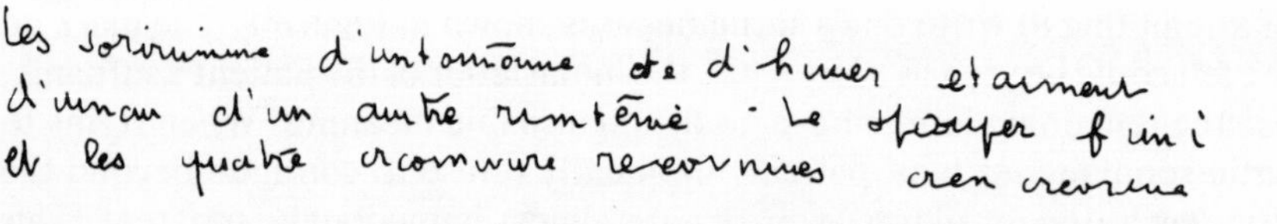

FIGURE 3 Aneurysm in a 50-year-old right-handed patient. Haematoma located in posterior and low part of the left frontal lobe. Twenty days post-surgery, copied writing (the two lines of the text were:

Les soirées d'automne et d'hiver étaient d'une autre nature.
Le souper fini et les quatre convives revenus.)

The main difficulties consisted in paragraphic transformations (the second word 'soirées' was thus written 'soriruimure')

paragraphias but enough characteristics of the written word remain to allow it to be recognized. Spelling aloud is frequently severely disrupted, the errors being similar to those encountered in writing.

Up to the last decade, all studies have been carried out on patients from Indo-European cultures, where alphabetic writing is used. Thus one might have assumed that the form of the disorder would follow the structural characteristics of the language in question. Yet some of the most recent descriptions of writing disturbance in Japanese patients reveal considerable similarity in the organization of the disorder. The Japanese use a simultaneous dual system of syllabic signs which have phonetic meaning (*kana*), and ideograms with lexical meaning (*kanji*). Sasanuma and Fujimura (1972) and Sasanuma (1975) demonstrate that the type of error shows a dissociation which is dependent upon the symbol system being used. Thus *kana* shows major deficits, while use of *kanji* is significantly more intact. There appear to be two types of error; words habitually written in *kanji* are converted to their equivalent in *kana*, where there may or may not be dysorthographias affecting the substitute symbols; while *kana* can undergo a range of transformations. Such transformations are homologous with dysorthographias and paragraphias observed from Indo-European cultures.

Does such a dissociation imply a duality in the cortical processes underlying writing, as these Japanese authors suggest? *Kana* would operate at a phonological level. *Kanji*, inasmuch as it contains global symbols whose phonological content is weak or even absent and not strictly necessary for its comprehension, would operate at the lexical level, without recourse to phonological construction. Could we even suggest, as did Hécaen and Marcie (1979), that this dissociation parallels the dissociation they observed in European patients in the treatment of meaningful words and nonsense syllables in motor aphasias?

Agraphia in Agrammatical Aphasia

This type of aphasia forms the other extreme within the range of motor aphasias. It seems to have its principal effect on the syntactic composition of utterances. The production of phonemes appears to be normal both in its acoustic structure and in the selection of phonemes. Utterances consist essentially of isolated words. Grammatical rules are disregarded and grammatical-function words frequently omitted while verbal lexemes are used in their nominal form.

In 1913, Pick distinguished motor agrammatism, associated with anterior lesions, from the pseudoagrammatism seen in sensory aphasias. Subsequently, Kleist (1934) used the term paragrammatism for the latter condition, while Isserlin (1922) saw motor agrammatism as a means of saving energy and therefore gave it the name 'telegraphic speech'. Goodglass (1976) demonstrated that agrammatism is a frequent feature of motor aphasias, affecting the production of grammatical relationships as well as their comprehension. However, it is rarely a predominant characteristic in aphasia.

The writing of patients in this category shows the same use of simple words which have a maximum communication value. Order relationships among words are determined by their relative position. Thus a patient with a primarily agrammatic expressive aphasia wrote about his occupation as follows; 'assistant management services, discounts, purchasing'. The commas were inserted by the patient stressing the key points of the description. This enabled him to indicate correctly his role as an administrative head in charge of purchasing.

Mirallié (1895, 1896) thought that the syntactic disorder had a parallel disruptive effect on both speech and writing. Even if the form of the disorder is essentially the same, the intensity of its effect is not generally equivalent for the two modes. The patient cited above showed a less intense agrammatism when describing his occupation orally rather than in writing ('financial assistant, you see I go. ... no ... the same thing'). He was able to use a few function words and an inflected verb. Nevertheless agrammatism was the dominant feature of his speech production with the prosodic isolation of individual content words.

A reverse dissociation may also be seen. The disorder of oral expression can make communication virtually impossible while written expression still retains a semblance of its normal form. This is evident in the following example, where the patient described the history of her illness and wrote

> 29th August morning fever 39° three days and speaking the head electricity in the head for three months and I was able to I could speak. 6th September 1962, at 2 o'lock in the afternoon I was in the Hutte Coulombiers (Sarthe) Hotel lying on the ground doctor, my husband in Paris phoned to say he would come that evening.

The information given in this form was subsequently verified as correct. Agrammatism took the form of omitting various function words and placing isolated words next to one another. She was quite incapable of expressing the same account in speech.

Agraphia in Conduction Aphasia

Wernicke (1874) postulated the existence of an aphasia following a break in the connection between the sensory and motor poles in the language area.

Thus the temporal region loses control over the motor region for language execution. The primary disorder is a deficit in verbal repetition. In contrast, auditory reception and language comprehension remain intact so long as expression does not call for difficult articulation.

The clinical picture is usually more complicated than this. Spontaneous language is disturbed to a great extent by paraphasias which are similar to those observed in tests of verbal repetition. Individual words are telescoped and segments belonging to different words are combined to create new items which are generally still recognizable. Words which are phonetically similar are also confused. Finally the patient's control over his speech enables him to attempt successive corrections. The phrases produced in spontaneous speech are frequently independent segments separated from each other either by pauses or by the insertion of adverbs used as fillers. During the course of an utterance, changes of proposition are accompanied by changes in the rate of speech production.

Writing deficits are regularly observed in conduction aphasias but the deficit never amounts to a suppression of writing. Graphemes are always written correctly. Word composition presents literal paragraphias analogous to those observed in the agraphia which accompanies motor aphasia. Written words are telescoped in a manner similar to the effects observed in speech. The omission of parts of words or a complete word indicates a disruption of the feedback loops which are involved in writing. The mechanisms of control are still evident, however, because words are frequently overwritten and corrected although the desired outcome may or may not be achieved (Figure 4).

Automatic and well-established writing sequences are generally completed without difficulty; for example, forename, surname, address, date of birth, and so on. Copy-writing is similarly carried out correctly. Writing from dictation of meaningful words is superior to nonsense syllables. This dissociation provides evidence of preservation of lexical access with a special problem relating to the conversion rules for translating phonemes to graphemes. Certain syntactical errors may be observed within the organisation of phrases and sentences while functional words are sometimes omitted (Hécaen and Marcie, 1967).

As we have seen, certain writing systems, such as Japanese, make simultaneous use of symbols belonging to different subsystems. Yamadori and Ikumura (1975) have described problems in writing which also provide evidence of the relative preservation of graphic representation within the internal lexicon. Thus patients with conduction aphasia could write in *kanji* better than in *kana*. Use of *kanji* provides immediate access to the lexicon, while the *kana* sub-system, like alphabetic script, operates at a phonological level.

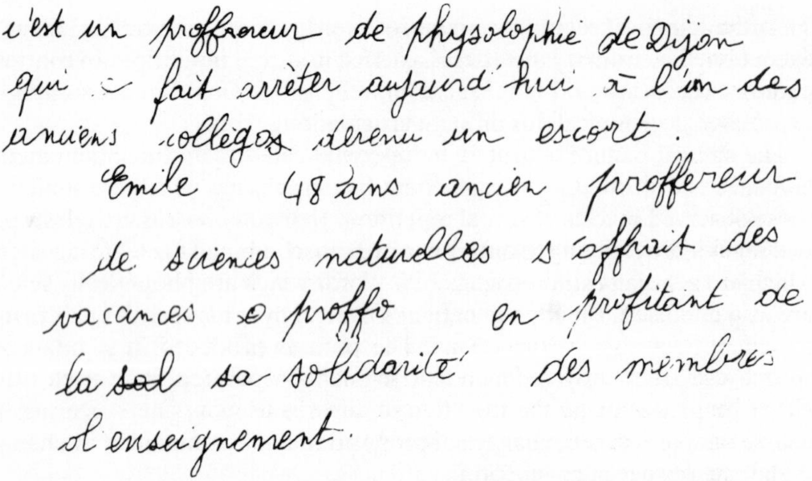

c'est un proffeneur de physolophie de Dijon
qui a fait arrèter aujourd'hui à l'un des
anciens collègos devenu un escort.
Emile 48 ans ancien profferein
de sciences naturelles s'offrait des
vacances o proffo en profitant de
la sal sa solidarité des membres
d'enseignement.

FIGURE 4 Conduction aphasia following a left intra-temporal hematoma in a 37-year-old right-handed patient: 4½ months after surgery, writing from dictation (dictated text: C'est un professeur de philosophie de Dijon qui a fait arrêter aujourd'hui l'un de ses anciens collègues devenue escroc, Emile Loubet, 48 ans, ancien professeur de sciences naturelles s'offrait des vacances en profitant de la solidarité des membres de l'enseignement.)

Agraphia in Association with Sensory Aphasia

Bastian (1894) was the first to suggest that articulated language contained a sensory element. Wernicke (1874) presented systematic clinical decriptions together with the first theoretical interpretation of disorders of language following lesions of the posterior left temporal lobe. This is often called Wernicke's aphasia. It has had other names, depending on the theoretical position of the author; Lichtheim (1885) described it as 'sensory cortical aphasia'; Head (1926) 'syntactic aphasia'; Weisenberg and McBride (:1935) 'receptive aphasia'; and Luria (1970) 'acoustic aphasia'.

The essential disorder lies in the reception of verbal symbols and the comprehension of the meanings they convey. The rhythm of speech remains fluent and often appears to be faster than normal speech. Failure to complete sentences, which is a characteristic of normal spontaneous speech, is frequently exaggerated. Difficulties in the production of words add to this problem. Verbal neologisms make spoken language hard to understand, without seemingly affecting the articulation of phonemes. In certain cases there are so many neologisms that a true jargon emerges within which it is impossible to detect any thematic content. On the other hand, prosodic features, expressive gestures, and the facial expressions which usually accompany verbal discourse appear to retain their normal functional role and may even act in a compensatory fashion.

The major deficit within this syndrome is the inability to understand the spoken word. This has strong empirical support and is expressed in the clinical case as 'an inability to understand linguistic utterances, which cannot be attributed to deficient sensory input, generalised cognitive deficits or defective attention' (Boller *et al.*, 1977). Such is the schematic framework within which sensory aphasia may be described. Nevertheless the complexity of the actual symptomatology makes it clear that several factors are involved to a greater or lesser extent, in the various forms of sensory aphasia.

Pure *word deafness* is an extremely rare form, generally limited to the recognition of language sounds. The patient is incapable of grasping what is said to him via the acoustic channel. Writing from dictation is therefore virtually impossible. in contrast spontaneous writing remains largely intact, although it can contain dysothographias involving frequent omission of letters, syllables, or even whole words. Copying is equally intact but spelling is rarely correct (Figure 5).

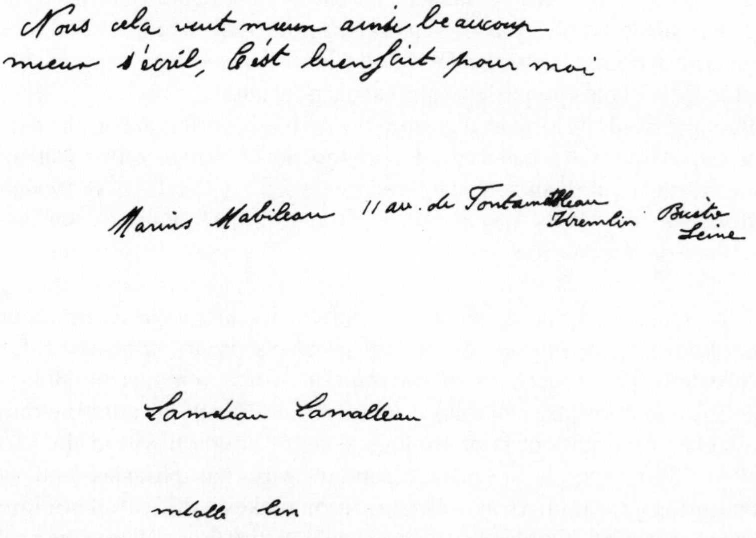

FIGURE 5 Verbal deafness (left hemisphere vascular lesion) in a 75-year-old right-handed patient. Seven months after the onset of troubles;
- copying (copied text: 'Non cela vaut mieux ainsi, beaucoup mieux! s'écria-t-il. C'est bien fait pour moi');
- spontaneous writing: her name and address were correctly written;
- dictation (two trials both for writing 'lunettes' and 'cigarettes')

Hécaen (1969) attempted to distinguish varieties of sensory aphasia on the basis of their dominant characteristic. But the deficit is rarely limited to this single aspect and the pattern of symptoms is typically complex. Hécaen's analysis of linguistic performance led to the recognition of three types, organized around the three factors of word deafness, deficit in verbal comprehension, and disruption of attention:

(1) Sensory aphasia with a predominant word deafness component allows spontaneous speech to retain a thematic coherence which guarantees a certain level of intelligibility. However language tasks which depend on acoustic input are severely affected: verbal repetition, metalinguistic operations, and the understanding of commands. In writing, a similar dissociation is observed betwen spontaneous writing which remains possible and thematically coherent, albeit constantly marked by dysorthographias. Copy-writing remains equally possible and is generally satisfactory. However all attempts at dictation are deficient. Numerous severe paragraphias frequently lead to verbal neologisms. This dissociation between spontaneous and dictated modes in writing is illustrated in the following example, written by a patient who was trying to give an account of his case history: 'Je suis parti pour deux mois à Vivonne dans le chateau pour les pour se remettre et le 5 juillet je suis à ne plus passer sans savoir pourquoi'. He intended to write: 'Je suis parti pour deux mois a Divonne dans le chateau pour me remettre et le 5 juillet je n'ai plus pu parler, sans savoir pourquoi'.

In contrast his writing to dictation bore little resemblance to the original: 'f'ai un pasuteur de pasuteur de phyloserie de Sauge qui a fait arreter aujourd'jui un des ancien sangnier des erect'. ('C'est un professeur de philosophie de Dijon qui a fait arrêter aujourd'hui un de ses anciens collègues devenu escroc'.)

(2) In sensory aphasia where a deficit in language comprehension predominates, reception of verbal symbols is in contrast relatively unaffected. The repetition of meaningful words remains possible while repetition of nonsense syllables is much more difficult because the only cue available to the patient is phonological representation within the acoustic stream. Spontaneous speech is replete with paraphrasias and verbal substitutions. Grammatical disorganization makes it difficult if not impossible to produce intelligible spontaneous speech. this type of language problem corresponds to the transcortical sensory aphasia of Lichtheim (1885), Wernicke (1903), and Goldstein (1948).

Writing from dictation of meaningful words is clearly better than that of meaningless material, where the syllabic content generally remains intact. Certain graphemes correspond to the original, providing evidence of the retention of the correspondence rules between phonemes and graphemes. Writing to dictation tends to be executed better than spontaneous writing, which reveals a reverse dissociation from that observed in the writing performance of sensory aphasiacs with word blindness as the dominant factor.

The following dictated text was written by a patient in this category: 'C'est un professeur de philosophie de Dijeon qui a fait arrêter aujourd'hui l'un de ses anciens collègues devenu echos.' In contrast when describing a meal he had just eaten, he produced an almost unintelligible text: 'un imparmier m'a descendu de la verricate, la gruluque était si agréable que j'ai réussi a exeder mon plat mon plat de rerevite que j'ai j'ai reussi ente au ny du garde'. (The initial phrase could mean 'un infirmier m'a descendu de mon lit'. Following that, only the word 'plat' gives any indication of the context described.)

(3) In Hécaen's third variety of sensory aphasia the patient shows no serious deficit in either verbal comprehension or in the ability to repeat meaningful or meaningless verbal items. Such an impairment largely consists of an inability to complete sentences. 'Distractibility' leads to the production of a sequence of open-ended embedded sentences. The lack of semantic content appears to be related to this primary deficit. However there are additional defects including violation of syntactic constraints within noun phrases or between noun phrases and verb phrases, or the misuse of the subcategorization rules which apply to the distinction between animate and inanimate classes.

Writing from dictation and copying are performed well. Only a few slips and iterations occur. In spontaneous writing the same asemanticism is shown, with dysfluency, addition of extraneous leters, and 'filler' phrases. One patient, following a left anterotemporal resection for a ruptured aneurysm, described the history of his illness as follows: 'Le comportement certains de ma maladie réside en un fait accompli toute circonstances atténuantes. Je dois observer un comportement de la façon la plus originale; c'est-à-dirè. His performance showed only two dysorthographias ('s' was added to 'certain' which is in the singular; and 's' is missing in 'toutes' in the noun phrase 'toutes circonstances attenuantes'). The grammatical structure of sentences is acceptable but certain automatized phrases such as 'un fait accompli' or 'toutes circonstances attenuantes' provide no useful information about the topic in question.

Dubois (1977), in a similar manner, described a group of agraphias in a population of patients with left temporal lesions, seeking to determine the extent to which these disorders were correlated with speech disorders. He identified four types of agraphia on the bases of the analysis or dysorthographias produced in a task involving writing from dictation of isolated verbal items.

(1) A 'complexification' agraphia. The syllabic pattern is retained as the phonological values of written symbols (thus 'bol' is written as 'beaules'). The deficit therefore involves primarily the rules relating phonemes to graphemes, to the extent that preservation of phonological representation presupposed a correct lexical retrieval.

(2) A 'substitution' agraphia which respects syllabic composition. Such substitutions destroy the graphical identity of the item more or less completely ('bol' is written as 'bai'). Dubois suggests that this disturbance arises from poor lexical retrieval where it is associated with a deficit in spelling aloud or a loss in the process transforming lexical representation to graphic representation where spelling aloud is found to be preserved.

(3) A 'sequential' agraphia where the deficit involves errors in the location of graphemes within the item (that is, 'bol' is written as 'blo'; 'valise' as 'vaisile'). This difficulty in maintaining the appropriate order of the graphemes implies nevertheless that access to the lexicon is preserved.

(4) A 'total' agraphia is one in which the syllabic composition of items is lost ('bol' is written as 'bodulee'; 'valise' as 'cacaeyettes'). The lexical representation of the item is no longer accessible in any form.

This typology could not be related in any meaningful way to specific locations of lesions in the heart of the temporal lobe nor to any of the different varieties of sensory aphasia following Hécaen's classification. Nevertheless we see here a demonstration both of the range and variety of disorganization involved and at the same time the very specific nature of the deficits described in relation to disorders of language.

Figures 6 to 9 provide evidence about performance of patients with sensory aphasia. These examples demonstrate the diversity of defects. It is clear that it would be difficult to categorize these disturbances of writing using the category system which applies to speech.

Apraxic Agraphia

Ogle (1867) distinguished two categories of language disorder encompassing both verbal and written language; an amnesic variety involving loss of memory for words, and an atactic variety involving the alteration or

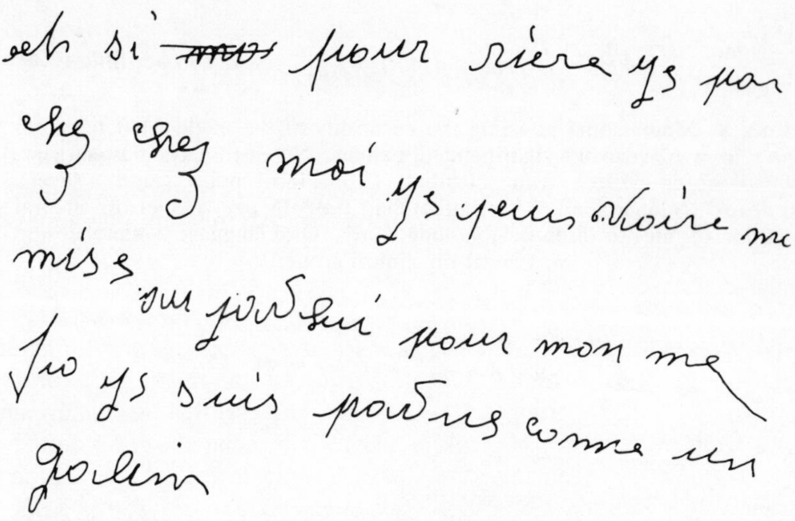

FIGURE 6 Sensory aphasia (left hemisphere vascular lesion) in a 68-year-old right-handed patient. Spontaneous writing produced some days after the onset of troubles (a letter to her family). While writing, the patient spelled out what she intended to write: 'Ici chez moi pour rien je perde chez moi. Je peux voir mon fils. Au jardin pour mieux le faire. Je suis perdue comme un gamin'. Each sentence corresponds to a line of text. The word 'fils' is written 'mis' at the left end of the third line

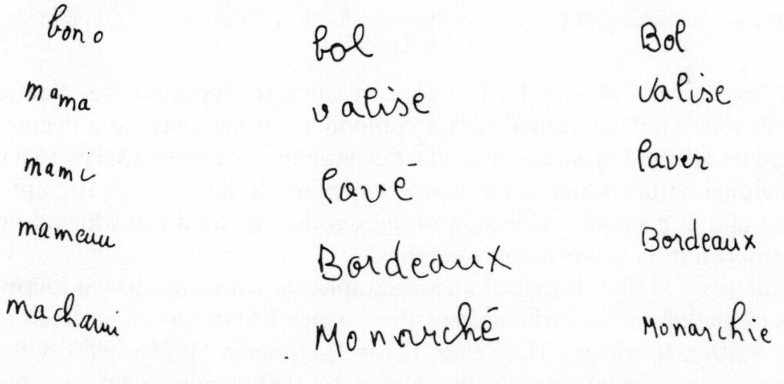

FIGURE 7 Subdural haematoma and left temporal contusion (1 cm below angular cyrus) in a 37-year-old right-handed patient. Recovery of writing ability: dictation of five words ('bol', 'valise', 'lave', 'Bordeaux', 'monarchie') *left column*: 5 days post-trauma; *middle column*: 11 days post-surgery; *right column*: 2 months post-surgery

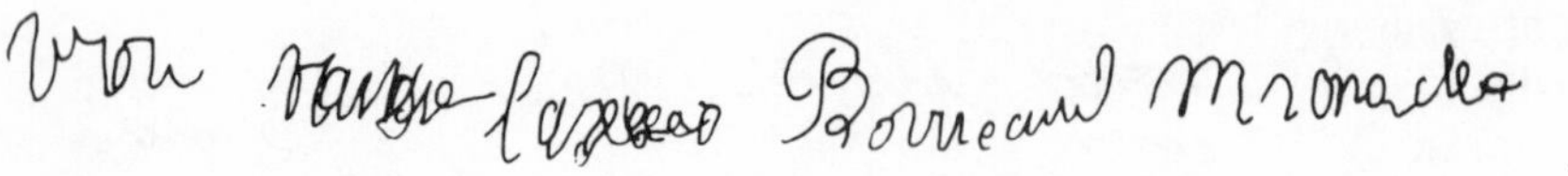

FIGURE 8 Meningioma affecting the corticality of the median left temporal region in a 62-year-old right-handed patient. Nineteen days post-surgery, isolated words written from dictation (from left: 'bol', 'valise', 'laver', 'Bordeaux', 'monarchie'). The patient had only 15 per cent errors in oral repetition of one- to three-syllable-long words. Oral language comprehension was intact on clinical ground

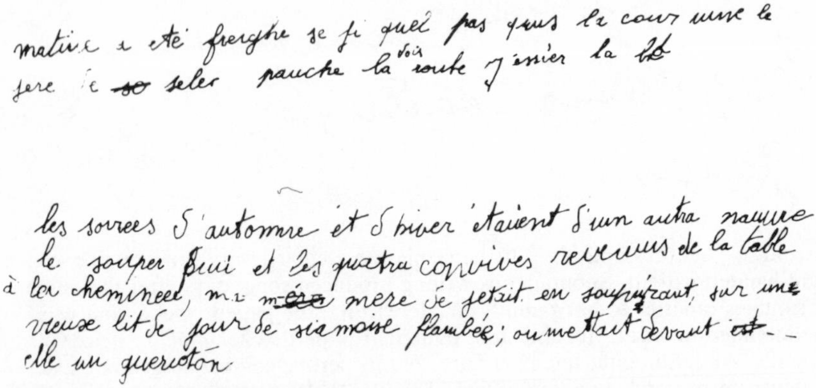

FIGURE 9 Left temporal melanoma occupying median part of T3–T4 in a 41-year-old right-handed patient without any deficit in oral language comprehension. Eight days post-surgery, dictation (same dictated text as in Figure 2) and copied writing (target text: 'Les soirées d'automne et d'hiver étaient d'une autre nature. Le souper fini et les quatre convives revenus de la table à la cheminée, ma mère se jetait, en soupirant, sur un vieux lit de jour de siamoise flambée'.)

complete loss of the facility to construct the appropriate elements employed. Thus he argued that a component of handwriting movements could be affected in isolation. in atactic agraphia, even the capacity to write individual letters is lost, sometimes completely. In this case all attempts to write end in a simple succession of lines going up and down which do not resemble letters to any notable extent.

Kussmaul (1884) described ataxic agraphia as a disorder which followed loss of one of the 'co-ordination centres' which he interposed between oral and written language. Thus even before Liepmann (1905, 1907) defined apraxia as a deficit specifically related to skilled movement, a writing disorder was recognised which involved the production of graphic symbols. Henschen (1922) underlined the relationship between agraphia and apraxia, identifying a left parietal form which affected writing as part of a more general impairment of skilled movement. Kleist (1934) saw in constructional agraphia a deficit of optical–kinaesthetic association normally supported by a specialized cortical system altered or destroyed by a lesion of the left inferoparietal region. The spatial images of letters and words, normally represented in visual form, are no longer reproduced, but are degraded by spatial errors.

The major characteristic of this form of agraphia is a disorganization which affects the configuration of lines making up a graphic symbol, whether it be a grapheme or a number. The same disorganization can be seen in constructional drawing.

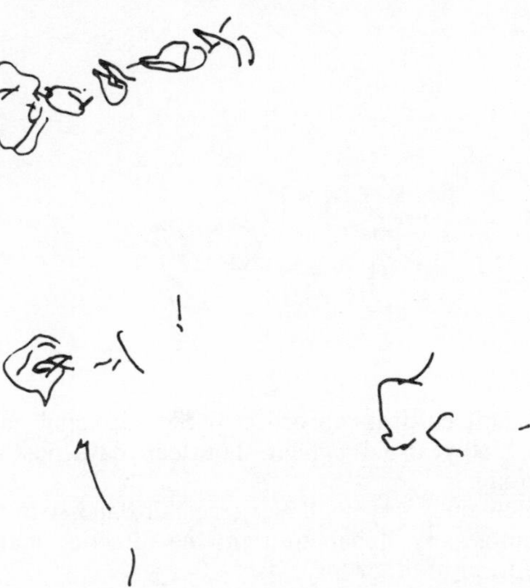

FIGURE 10 Right hemiplegia following surgery for removal of a left rolando-parietal tumour in a 54-year-old right-handed patient. Attempt to write his name on command with his left hand

Figure 10 shows the attempts of a patient who was asked repeatedly to write his surname. The initial letter 'C' has an overall movement which is generally adequate. But it is disrupted quite dramatically by both irregularities of contour and in the basic underlying structure, thus rendering it virtually useless as a written letter. Its status as a letter could only be confirmed by reference to a model; its form alone is not sufficient to justify it as being a written symbol. This disorganization is made absolutely apparent in Figure 11 where one can compare the spontaneous writing of the surname with its completely perfect production in the form of a signature. The signature has acquired a global character and has a gestalt quality which robs the individual letters making up the name of their individual status.

FIGURE 11 Left cortical subcortical parieto-occipital haematoma in a right-handed 60-year-old patient. Fourteen days post-surgery, spontaneous writing:
— his family name, Raymond Var (the third and sixth 'characters' do not resemble any alphabetic sign; the fifth one may represent an iterative form of 'n' or 'm');
— his name in signature form;
— his address (13, rue de la Tiulerie)

When using alphabet blocks the disorder is still quite apparent both in setting out the letters and in relating them. This fact underlines the point that in apraxic agraphia the disturbance includes an important linguistic element of lexical representation. The deficit is not limited to a mere external constructional deficit.

Figure 12, in which successive attempts are made at written performance, demonstrates this association between the configuration of the symbol and the distinctive value of graphemes in word formation. Only comparison with the 'T' of the second and third attempt enables one to identify the shape as a 'T'. Later, one sees again idiosyncratic elements, for example the small final loop at the foot of the vertical line, a type of calligraphy at the top and left which is a deformation of the initial part of a written capital 'I'. In

FIGURE 12 Glioblastoma of the posterior part of the left parietal lobe in a 30-year-old right-handed patient. *Top line*, writing of his family name (Toul) with his right hand: from left to right, 2 days prior to surgery, 3 and 11 days post-surgery; between the second and third performances, constructive apraxia disappeared almost completely. *Middle line*, 5 months later, recurrence of the tumor: two trials to write his name 8 days prior to surgery; his family and Christian names written 2 days post-surgery. *Bottom line*, writing of his name with his left hand 8 days before the second surgery

contrast, this second attempt departs even further from a true letter form. The only graphemic cue comes from taking the whole length of what is written, which actually corresponds to the length of the patient's surname; this seems to give to the written lines a configuration of discrete elements which no fundamental structure can be attributed to with any confidence. In the course of two examinations immediately following surgical intervention, writing function was progressively restored paralleling the disappearance of constructional apraxia on standard tests. More specifically a similar writing deficit appeared in two syndromes of left hemisphere lesions, including apraxia.

In lesions of the left central frontal lobe Hécaen and Angelergues (1966) described problems of writing in one hand or the other depending on the clinical context. Writing disturbance of the right hand appeared to be the result of a problem of motor difficulties of a tonic order. The grasp reflex and avoidance reaction inhibited or interrupted the drawing of the pencil across the paper. The same thing happened when using alphabet blocks. Elsewhere, errors in oral spelling showed that programming for writing was also affected. Agraphia of the left hand presented a similar general disturbance expressed as a unilateral apraxia on the left side.

The most frequently observed form of apraxic agraphia is associated with a difficulty in reading. It has a primary, but not unique, effect on letter formation. The severity of the disorder is generally different as a function of the mode of written language. Agraphia appears in the context of parietal apraxia following left-sided occipitoparietal lesions; that is why it is sometimes called parietal agraphia. It often appears as one of the elements in the Gerstmann syndrome, together with finger agnosia, acalculia, and left–right disorientation.

The performance presented in Figure 13 reveals a gamut of forms of disorganisation which affect the execution of letters.

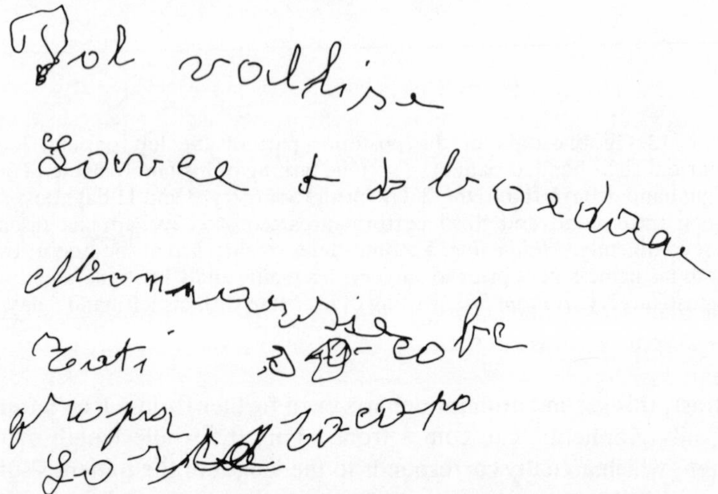

FIGURE 13 Left parieto-occipital lesion (aneurysm occupying occipital convexity) in a right-handed 58-year-old patient. Eleven days post-surgery, writing from dictation of isolated words (on each line, respectively: bol, valise, lavée, Bordeaux, monarchie) and of nonsense syllables (tati, chocabe, ropa, larue, tacopi)

(1) *Addition of extraneous lines*. These do not obliterate the identity of the

graphemes and a hierarchy of forms can be described which follows the progressive increase in extraneous additions:

(a) Lines shaped like a 'grave' accent on the upper loop of the capital 'L' in 'laver' are a characteristic which cannot be considered as merely ideolectic.

(b) Duplication of the initial left-hand side of the 'l' in 'valise' is a more important transformation, although it leaves the fundamental form of the letter intact.

(c) The addition of a line to the initial 't' of 'tati' which having no formal relation to any part of the letter, represents an alteration of the image of the letter in its distinctive form. However it leaves the letter quite recognizable.

(2) *Errors in letter contour*. The shape of the letter loses regularity, together with its clarity and constancy of form, from one version to the next. The form of the letter 'O' in the six instances illustrates this problem.

(3) *Errors in the distinguishing characteristics of letters:*

(a) The deformity, in part, of the grapheme and its replacement by irrelevant features represents a lower level of this disturbance. The 'B' of the word 'bol' (top line) is formed correctly in its upper loop; but the lower loop dissolves in a cluster of agraphemic features.

(b) The existence of sequences of very agraphemic shapes is the most characteristic feature of apraxic disorder in handwriting. The first two attempts to form the initial letter of the word 'bordeaux' (second line, second half) were corrected at the end. However in the fourth line, the two clusters in the first syllable of the nonsense word 'chocabe' were not followed by any attempts to make corrections and have no truly graphemic elements.

While the major deficit is apparent in the formation of graphemes, there are other features as well. Spelling mistakes, which were fairly numerous, appeared in dictation, spontaneous writing, and copying.

But this disorder appears in isolation when the patient writes with alphabet blocks. The same patient whose disorders of handwriting are depicted in Figures 18 and 19 copies 'les soirees d'automne et d'hiver' as 'les soire diotom ot dhivrere' using blocks, although she could read the words correctly. When the phrase 'Je mange' was dictated, the patient could repeat it correctly, but she wrote 'JAS', getting only the initial letter correct. The patient felt her performance was satisfactory. Similarly composition of individual nonsense words gave rise to equally poor performance: 'loru' was executed as 'RLIU'; 'chocabe' as 'COOCU'. Spelling aloud is rarely completely intact. The same patient spelled only two words out of ten correctly although the first letter was correct in six of the remaining eight words.

The presence of this group of difficulties at the orthographic code level, in both handwriting and block writing, appears to suggest that the graphic representation of words in the lexicon is equally affected in this type of disorder.

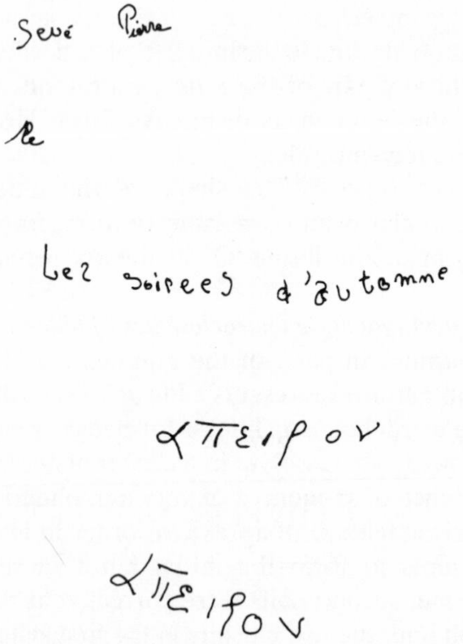

FIGURE 14 Ablation of the left parieto-occipital region for removal of an astrocytoma in a right-handed 33-year-old patient. Writing performance 13 days post-surgery:
— The patient succeeds in writing only the first four letters of his family name; his Christian name is correctly written (Pierre Sever).
— The dictated phrase ('la matinée') cannot be written: 'l' is written over a sign without a reliable value; 'e' is substituted to 'a'.
— Copied writing ('les soirées d'automne') is performed in a rather imitative manner. As for the Greek word, the model (upper line) was copied in a similar fashion

When the copying task is reduced to mere imitation, apraxia is revealed in the drawing of graphemes. In Figure 14 the 'S' in the definite article 'les' is drawn back-to-front; the 'o' in 'automne' has an unusual indentation and is probably a wholly erroneous shape. Copying of Greek letters is certainly based on imitation because the alphabet was unfamiliar to the patient, but the shape of several letters (ρ, ν, ε) shows that this task does actually involve some degree of graphic reinterpretation. This form of agraphia appears largely with posterior lesions of the left parietal lobe. This area corresponds with Wernicke's (1885) theoretical location of the centre of visual verbal images and was inferred on the basis of clinical material presented by Dejerine (1892). The association of alexia with difficulties of writing depended, in Wernicke's (1903) formulation, on whether the link formed by the arcuate fasciculus between the visual centre for verbal images and the language motor area, remained intact. Following the same line of reasoning, Hécaen and Anglelergues (1966) showed that the relative degree of agraphia and alexia depended on the site of the lesion. In temporo-occipital lesions the reading deficit is more pronounced, whereas in parieto-occipital lesions the writing deficit predominates.

Pure Agraphia

Pure agraphia is defined as a writing disorder in which other deficits in speech, reading, or gestures are absent. Several neurologists refer to it as part of the development of a theoretical framework. Wernicke (1874) thought writing involved a close association between the visual graphic image, the verbal motor image, and the centre controlling hand and finger movements. Only training enables these interactions to become automatic by direct activation of the motor zone for the hand and for fingers bypassing the need for verbal visual images while writing. It is not necessary, therefore, to identify a separate 'centre for graphic movements' with its own set of images, but at the same time this means that is it impossible to find a writing disorder in the absence of a disorder of speech. All speech disorders in the educated adult must be accompanied by a parallel deficit in writing. Trousseau (1877) transferred this analysis to a more clinical context: 'Typically, the aphasic patient is no more competent in expressing his thoughts in speech than he is in writing. Even if the patient retains motor control of his hands and even if his previous intelligence level is sustained, he is just as powerless in writing a word with the pen as he is in speech.'

Dejerine (1891, 1892, 1914) always argued that agraphia cannot appear in isolation. With a lesion of the angular gyrus, the visual graphic images of letters are destroyed and an agraphia associated with alexia occurs. In motor and sensory aphasias the 'word image' is altered in one of its major components and agraphia is mechanically associated with aphasia. Thus when agraphia does appear in isolation it is merely a residual component of either main disorder. It was impossible, Kreindler and Fradis (1968) claimed, for writing to be affected in the absence of other language disorders.

On the other hand Bastian (1894) insisted that, in theory, agraphia could appear in isolation. This agraphia would result from a lesion destroying the keiro–kinaesthetic centre, or reveal itself as an isolated symptom resulting from a lesion of some part of the visual–kinaesthetic centre. Bastian did point out, however, that a simple case of agraphia resulting from either of these possibilities had never been observed. This extremely specialized disorder was frequently masked due to an extension of a lesion which paralysed other movements of the hand and arm. There are some cases in the literature where agraphia is seen as a unique feature of the patient's neuropsychological picture. Pitres (1884) described a case of 'pure motor agraphia' in support of the notion of Exner's (1881) graphic centre. However this patient did show a residual symptom of motor aphasia in the form of an agraphia restricted to his right hand, while he could perform correctly with his left hand for spontaneous writing, dictation and copying. Gordinier (1899) was the first to publish a report of pure agraphia in a right-handed patient. Agraphia was complete for this 37-year-old patient, for spontaneous writing and dictation, for both his right and left hands. He never had any difficulty with speech or reading throughout his illness. Autopsy revealed the pressure of a tumour, 2 cm in diameter, at the bottom of the second frontal convolution of the left hemisphere and sparing the motor representation of the hand.

However scanty such reports are, they do constitute a body of reliable clinical data. A lesion involving the foot of the second left frontal convolution was implicated in similar observations by Sinico (1926), Morselli (1930), Mahoudeau (1950), Mahoudeau *et al.*, (1951), Penfield and Roberts (1959), Assal *et al.*, (1970) and Aimard *et al.* (1975). But Chedru and Geschwind (1972) pointed to the frequency of isolated writing disorders in acute confusional states, and were sceptical of the existence of pure agraphias attributable to left frontal lesions.

Rosati and de Bastiani (1979) report an interesting case of isolated graphic disorder in a right-handed 62-year-old patient who had suffered a stroke in the left temporal lobe. Disorders occurred both in spontaneous writing and writing from dictation; these took the form of paragraphias and omissions and substitutions in recognizable words. Copying was relatively accurate while block letters produced disturbances similar to those shown in writing. Six cases of pure agraphia were described and analyzed by Dubois *et al.* (1969). Four of these were right-handed and another right-handed patient was examined in Hécaen's 'Laboratory for Speech Pathology'. A formal analysis of writing skills in these five patients led to the recognition of a variety of deficits.

(1) In spontaneous writing, there was the classic distinction between writing the forename and surname, which is considered to be a particularly automatic and well-practised sequence, and the composition of a free text based on a required theme. All patients showed this contrast. The five patients could write their surname correctly in standard handwriting but not in signature form. In contrast, continuous composition always produced an extremely limited level of performance.

Two patients were totally incapable of generating a word sequence: the patients could only write personal pronouns in the first person singular, before refusing to continue, either imediately or after producing several apparently agraphemic shapes. One of these patients was highly educated and the family of the second patient confirmed that he had written quite normally before his illness. The three remaining patients could all produce texts though these were never free of errors. In all cases the theme was recognizable. Nevertheless their writing could be distinguished on the basis of the level of embedded errors.

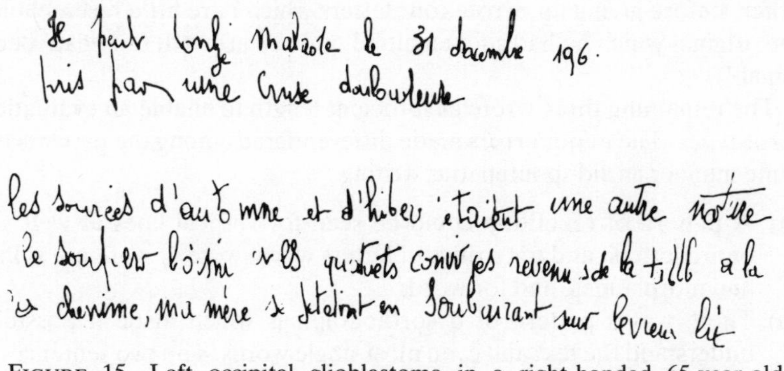

FIGURE 15 Left occipital glioblastoma in a right-handed 65-year-old patient. Two weeks prior to surgery, spontaneous and copied writing (same target text as in Figure 9)

One patient produced text which was almost correct: 'Je soussigne D.A.D. [he had to give initials] declare que le declaramt est civtctime d'une agression armee'. The three errors consist of substituting 'in' for 'n' and repeating the consonant group in 'victctime'. The second showed an important deficit. All his words were recognizable, but two-thirds of them were dysorthographic with substitutions and/or letter additions (Figure 15). Morphographemic structure was preserved, however: 'Il faut tonbje malade le 31 doecembre 196. pris par uine cruse doulouleuse'. This should read 'Il est tombé malade le 31 décembre 1967 pris par une crise douloureuse'). In the third patient, distortion between spoken and written text was considerable. She said aloud 'J'ai été malade, c'est le décès de mon mari' while simultaneously she wrote 'Je etan manla en deden'. If one reads the text above one could not possibly detect the thematic content because so many paragraphias intrude and obliterate the lexical forms. Syntactic structure, however, remains preserved.

(2) Dictation also reveals a similar distribution of error types and degrees of error. The writing of meaningful words from dictation was possible for only four patients. One patient was capable of five error-free words; another got four wrong out of five, but the errors left the words recognizable: 'valise' was written as 'valire', 'laver' as 'vavier'. In the other two, however, the errors were such that the written word bore only the slightest resemblance to the original, in spite of perfect verbal repetition: 'fauteuil' was written as 'Fauguu', 'rue' as 'roir', and'liberte' as 'dioflili'. The writing of meaningless items from dictation gave rise to similar effects.

The same distribution of fuctional deficits arose in writing from dictated text, as with errors shown in spontaneous writing. Two patients just could not get themselves to write; one refused in the face of difficulty while the other, before giving up, wrote four letters which bore little resemblance to the original which he had spoken aloud quite clearly :('Il fait beau' became 'au ab').

The remaining three wrote at sufficient length to enable an evaluation of error types. The major errors made differentiated among the patients in the same manner as did spontaneous writing.

(a) A pattern of repetition could be seen for vertical lines as well as for entire letters, and for strings of letters which were or were not syllables and morphemes, and for words.
(b) There was a pattern of dysorthographias which made it possible to understand the text and even most single words. The two sentences: 'La matinée était fraiche. Je fis quelques pas dans la cour', were given as 'la matinlée était fraise, je fuis quelques pases dans la bour'. These dysorthographias contained letter substitutions, extraneous additions, and a disregard for word segments.
(c) Finally there was a high proportion of paragraphias in which the product was far removed from the original. The two sentences cited above were rendered as: 'a matine aetentu fratch jre fei quue yiu'; one sees sequences of letters, like 'jre' which are improbably in French (Figure 16).

(3) When copying, performance was limited and strictly imitative in one case. For the other four the original was not reproduced exactly, thus letter formation was not imitative. Error types and their distribution were identical to those observed in spontaneous writing and dictation.

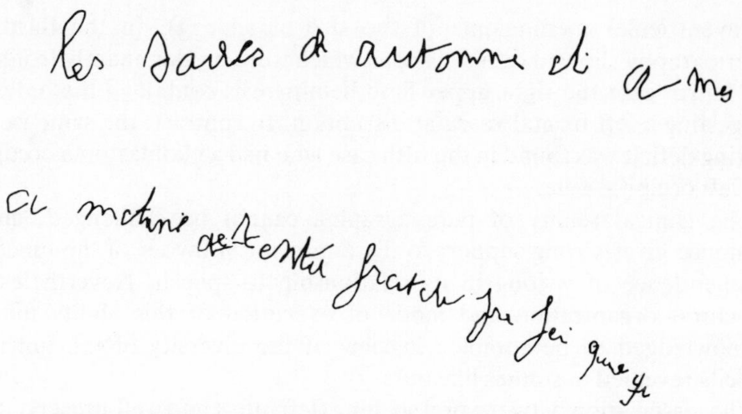

FIGURE 16 Left intraventricular meningioma in a right-handed 68-year-old patient. One week prior to surgery, copied writing (model: 'Les soirées d'automne et d'hiver') and writing from dictation (dictated text: 'La matinée était fraîche Je fis quelques pas.')

The two patients who experienced difficulty in writing were equally affected in copying: one was only able to copy isolated letters in a very limited way. The other was able to make an accurate copy of two of the four words ('demain il fera beau' was written as 'Demain ip Beau'). In addition, writing was painfully slow. It is noteworthy that this patient could not produce one single correct word from dictation.

In the two patients who produced complete performances in writing, the errors were the same as those in other forms of writing, in one case there were repetitions, in the other, dysorthographias. In contrast, the patient for whom error types in the other modes consisted of paragraphias, was able to make a copy which was an almost perfect version of the original.

(4) Finally for all five patients oral spelling was better retained than any of the remaining writing tasks. Nevertheless the same error types recurred. The two patients who produced complete writing performances, and for whom dictated words were correct or very close to the original, succeeded in spelling ten high-frequency words. In contrast the remaining three, who had most difficulty in writing isolated words from dictation, also committed the most spelling errors: two could only manage half the items and the third, who could not spell a single word correctly, produced spellings graphically closer to the original than he had achieved in dictation.

The lesions responsible for these deficits appear, in a large number of cases in the literature, to involve the left frontal region. This region was involved in four of the five observations cited here and in two of the cases there was a surgical intervention (meningioma in the region of Fl;

intraventricular meningioma of the size of an egg). In the third case arteriography showed diffuse lesions which were predominantly frontal. In the fourth case the right upper limb hemiparesis contained the only sign, suggesting a left frontal vascular disruption. In contrast, the same isolated writing deficit was found in the fifth case who had a glioblastoma occupying the left occipital pole.

The clinical reality of pure agraphia cannot be challenged, and its existence gives strong support to the argument in favour of the functional independence of writing in its relationship to speech. Nevertheless the structural organization and mode of execution of this ability must be acknowledged to be complex in view of the diversity of the functional deficits revealed in studies like ours.

The dissociation between oral spelling (left intact and well-preserved) and writing of isolated words from dictation, tends to support the view that the written part of lexical representation remains unaffected. The problem lies within the series of events leading up to actual execution. Elsewhere Kinsbourne and Rosenfield (1974) have described a dissociation in a spelling task requiring either a written or spoken response. The patient was unable to spell in writing yet obtained a significantly better score for oral spelling. They suggested that there must be a difference in the organization of the processes leading to letter choice for word construction and expression in the two situations.

WRITING DISORDERS IN RIGHT HEMISPHERE LESIONS

Following Jackson (1864) the right hemisphere was considered to play a 'minor' role in language function limited to automatic functions and emotional expression. Moreover only limited exercise of these capacities was possible if a left hemisphere, dominant for speech, were damaged. This was the interpretation adopted to explain language performance in those rare cases of left hemispherectomy (e.g. Zollinger, 1935; Smith, 1966). It was only when the study of right hemisphere symptomatology began, that its role in graphic expression was revealed. Brain (1941) described neglect of the left visual field. Paterson and Zangwill (1944) demonstrated that constructional activity following right parieto-occipital lesions had little to do with the meaning of the task involved. The view of McFie *et al.* (1950) was that these lesions affected the spatial component of perceptual and constructional activity. In similar vein Hécaen *et al* (1956) described an apraxic-agnosic syndrome whose main feature was a disturbance of spatial perception. As time went on the nature of writing deficits following right hemisphere lesions was defined in more detail. In a study involving agraphias Hécaen, *et al.* (1963) identified three charcteristics for these

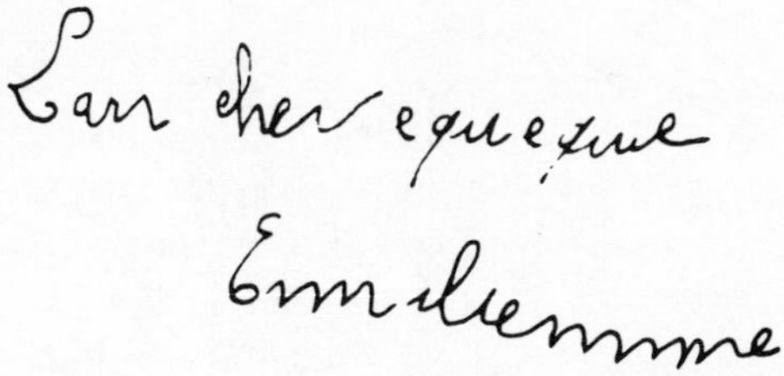

FIGURE 17 Tumour of the right parietotemporal carrefour in a 57-year-old right-handed patient. Twelve days post-surgery, spontaneous writing of her forename (Larcheveque) and Christian name (Emilienne)

agraphias; patients cannot draw straight horizontal lines; they add strokes to letters like m, n, u, and v; and they duplicate single graphemes or even word segments. These defects were seen to be components of an apraxic-agnosic syndrome associated with posterior right lesions. Marcie *et al.* (1965) showed that these patients could neglect graphemes when writing and even omit words, especially short or grammatical items.

The term 'spatial dysgraphia' was then used to draw these phenomena together. The common features were (a) the purely spatial nature of the deficits, and (b) the right-sided lesion. These deficits were studied more systematically by Hécaen and Marcie (1974) for dictation and copy-writing. In a group of 82 patients with unilateral lesions (52 right, 30 left) they describe six spatial parameters: duplication of letter strokes and of complete letters; insertions of spaces within words; the slope of line from the horizontal; straightness of lines with respect to their axis; size of right-hand margin; and size of left hand margin. They found that repetitions were statistically related to right-sided lesions, as was enlargement of the left-hand margin. Conversely spaces within words and enlargement of the right-hand margin were statistically related to left-sided lesions (Figures 17–19). Both patient groups showed disturbances in horizontal and straightness-of-line aspects. The spatial nature of margin enlargement is clearly related to posterior deficits and occipital deficits in particular. Spaces within words were not so easy to explain. Could the deficit be the result of different mechanisms within the two hemispheres? A visuo-spatial impairment was straightforward for right-sided lesions but the origin of the left-sided lesions is not clear.

Even the spatial nature of stroke and letter repetitions associated with right-sided lesions was difficult to interpret. They suggested these might reflect a more general perseverative factor, already observed in linguistic performance by Marcie *et al.* (1965). Lebrun (1976) claimed that these

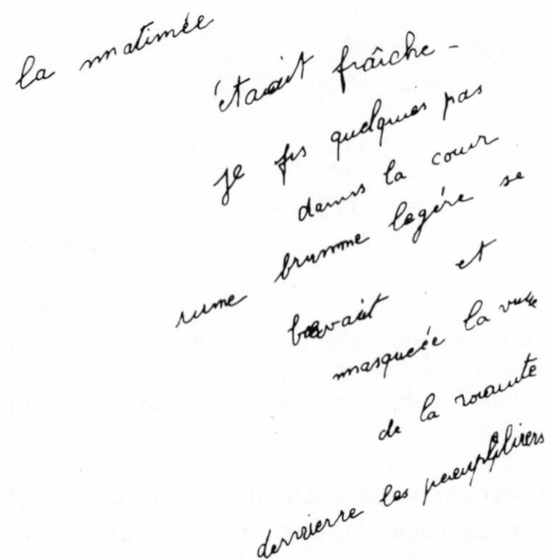

FIGURE 18 Glioblastoma of the right superior parietal zone in a 38-year-old right-handed patient with normal visual field. Thirteen days after surgery, dictated writing of a connected text (same target text as in Figure 2). Types of phenomena:
— iteration of strokes on letters such as m, n or u; iteration of whole letters (–eu– in the first graphic syllable of peupliers; –pl– in the second one of the same word);
— neglect of a nominal phrase ('de la rivière');
— writing extends into the right part of the paper sheet;
— overwriting of some graphic signs although it was not an attempt to correct an error (–e– posited on the right half of the preceding –u– in the second syllable of 'peupliers');
— an effective self-correction on the word 'levait' where –e– is written over –ov–)

deficits indicate disturbance of a perceptual component of writing. He drew upon the explanation devised by Assal and Zander (1969) and Assal *et al.* (1970), that multiple repetitions of vertical strokes and letters were a simple perseveration phenomenon, whereby the patient was unable to inhibit a movement already executed. But this explanation only accounts for a single aspect of the disorder. It cannot account for other features of the agraphia nor for the patient's ability to re-read his own writing 'correctly' as if none of these anomalies were present. Thus he proposes that all writing disorders associated with right hemisphere lesion should be gathered under the one name of 'afferent dysgraphia', thereby emphasizing a common perceptual component. Lebrun (1976) asked normal subjects to write when blindfolded; the required sentence contained many letters with vertical strokes ('ma maman mange une bonne pomme avec un monsieur'). The pattern of errors

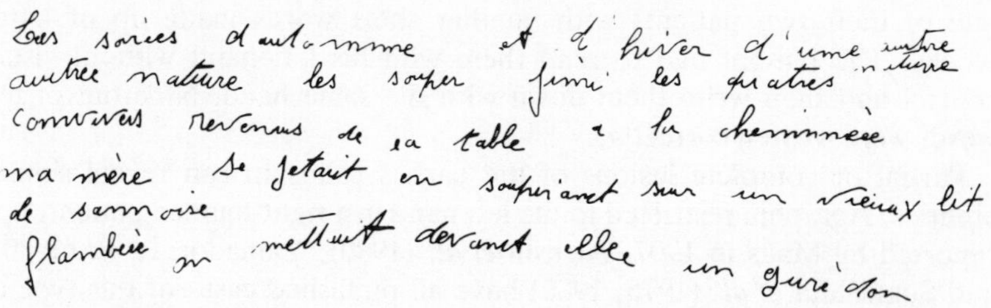

FIGURE 19 Tumour of the right parietotemporal carrefour in a 57-year-old right-handed patient. Twelve days post-surgery, copied writing (same target text as in Figure 10). The patient exhibits, in two cases, a difficulty going from one line to the next in her attempt to grasp the target text: the third word in the second line, 'les', is the determinant of the nominal phrase 'les quatre convives'; the patient neglected the beginning of the line, then she added the first phrase without correcting the determinant. In the same manner, the last line begins with the word 'flambée' occupying the fourth position in the model, then the patient added above 'flambée' the two words which preceded it, still neglecting the first word of the line. The patient shows difficulty in positioning the words along a straight line

was very similar to that produced by patients with right-sided lesions: namely, additional vertical strokes in m's and n's, duplicated letters, omission of letters, and introduction of blank spaces which had the effect of dividing words up into segments.

Kalmus *et al.* (1960) obtained similar results in delayed feedback experiments. Smith *et al.* (1960) employed a delay of 520 ms, and separated writing from its visual control using a video screen. The performance of their two subjects became uncoordinated and writing movements lost precision. Sixty-four errors were made when writing meaningful words and nonsense syllables; of these, 40.6 per cent involved letter repetitions, 26.6 per cent letter insertions or letter fragments, and 7.8 per cent were omissions.

This type of deficit in feedback mechanisms appears in patients with right hemisphere lesions. Carmon (1970) showed that a disturbance of kinaesthetic feedback caused deficits in manual tasks. Meier (1970) inverted visual feedback and showed that a group of 20 right lesion cases took significantly longer to locate 10 Segnin–Goddard Formboard items than a control group or a group of 20 left-sided cases. Following the same theme, Lebrun (1976) showed that patients with right-sided lesions generally have problems in keeping to the lines on ruled paper.

The role of the right hemisphere in writing may also be clarified by studying those cases where it has been isolated from the left hemisphere language areas. Studies of spit-brain patients show that the right hemisphere is capable of handling linguistic information. Levy *et al.* (1971) presented one of their two patients with familiar short words made up of letter blocks. The patient had to read them with his left hand without visual control and then write them down with the same hand. Nine out of ten words were written correctly.

Partial or complete lesions of the corpus callosum can reveal similar abilities. Agraphia restricted to the left hand in a right-handed patient, was reported by Maas in 1907. Atsushi *et al.* (1980), Yamadori *et al.* (1980), and Sughishita *et al.* (1975, 1980) have all published cases of this type of agraphia following vascular occlusion. One unpublished case was studied recently in Hécaen's laboratory.

Computerized tomography scans revealed a tumour occupying the anterior and left part of the corpus callosum in a 54-year-old right-handed Italian patient. Speech and reading were normal and writing with the right hand was quite normal in both French and Italian. Oral spelling of ten French words was correct except for two which were spelt in Italian. Writing with the left hand was studied in two conditions: handwriting and the use of letter blocks. Even his own names were written with great difficulty. He inserted an 'O' between the 'R' and the 'G' of his name. SERGIO; needed four trials with the letter blocks and two in handwriting to write his surname; a letter was omitted with the blocks and in both conditions the vowels 'E' and 'I' were repeated. In dictation, he had similar difficulties in both conditions. He needed four attempts to write the verb 'lavare', and in the very final attempt the first 'a' was superimposed over the 'v'. The same task took him seven trials with the blocks. He wrote slowly and had great difficulty in moving from one letter to the next (Figure 20).

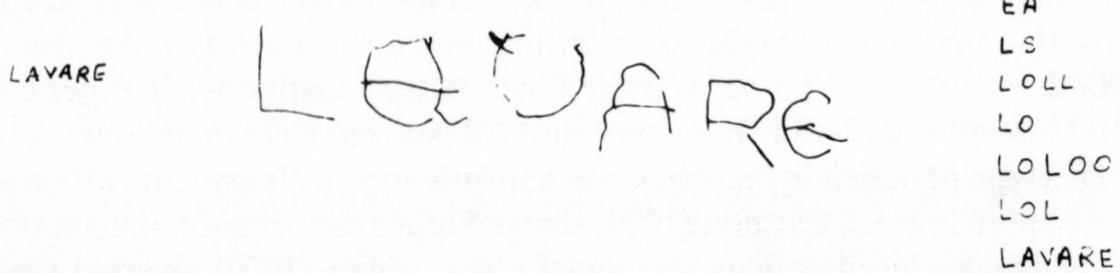

FIGURE 20 In a 57-year-old right-handed patient with a lesion destroying the anterior and left part of the corpus callosum, writing from dictation of the Italian word 'lavare', in script, using both the right and left hands; with block letters using only the left hand (seven trials)

When discussing unilateral left agraphia Bogen (1979) stated that 'one cannot expect to see spontaneous left handed writing since the right hemisphere of most individuals rarely possesses sufficient language for this'. His view was that the left hand's ability is restricted to doodling or to copying various designs and diagrams.

However the linguistic character of unilateral left agraphia is confirmed by the formal nature of the deficits described above. Anyway, normal right-handed subjects are capable of writing correctly with their left hand though they cannot do so easily. In the case of split-brain patients the right hemisphere no longer receives the linguistic information controlled by the left hemisphere and which guarantees a good quality of writing performance in the right hemisphere. Thus a dissociation between the writing capacities which remain intact in one hand and disturbed in the other, can be interpreted within a connectionist framework (Geschwind, 1965), even if all the other questions remain unanswered.

CONCLUDING REMARKS

The pattern of symptoms which appears in these writing disorders provides a great wealth of information. There is such a variety of types of disorganization that a lesion might disrupt one of several factors, either in a specific or global fashion. These factors (linguistic, expressive, or intellectual) are involved in the execution of writing at the various levels of processing of linguistic information. The complexity of the 'transcodes' (Weigl, 1974) in written work in its various forms (spontaneous writing, dictation, and copying) can lead to very distinct types of deficit depending on the location of the lesion. However, we are justified in setting up a basic framework for considering these disorders. In all cases there is interference with a linguistic system which has already acquired its functional specificity.

The disorders of writing which appear with these lesions which produce aphasias do not parallel the disorders of speech (Dubois, 1977). The features of writing disorders cannot be automatically inferred from speech disorders and the reverse can also be true. Lhermitte and Derouesné (1974) reported two patients whose ability to write normally was virtually intact in spite of sensory aphasia, including paraphasias and semantic jargon in speech.

In writing disorders due to right hemisphere lesions, such as apraxic agraphia, the deficit appears to consist of disruption of the graphic representation of words in the inner lexicon. This disturbance is reflected in the presence of dysorthographias and even paragraphias in such cases. This phenomenon makes it clear that there is more to the problem than a mere deficit external to this central linguistic aspect.

This specificity of written language appears in a form which is influenced by the information contained in the linguistic symbol. In speech this information is deeply embedded in an acoustic complex which contains cues over and above phonetic information (Liberman *et al.*, 1967). In addition, the difficulty we have in analyzing or 'reading off' spectrograms of normal speech, indicates the real complexity of the stream of acoustic events. In contrast, ordinal information is clearly apparent in written language. Character strings form a phonological representation of language with specific and discrete meanings, even where the written text, by virtue of the arrangement of its words, provides contextual information about the author's intentions.

Mattingly (1972) maintains that writing is highly specific within the context of language in general. Language is closely tied to verbalization and its neural organization depends on the integrity of the ears and the speech apparatus. At the same time he points to the original properties of writing: 'It is therefore rather surprising to find that a substantial number of human beings can also perform linguistic functions by means of the hand and the eye. ... Faced with this fact, we ought to suspect that some special trick is involved. He believes then that writing develops from a verbal language base and is a secondary linguistic function.

This specificity in the graphic representation of language is also emphasized in those studies which seek to penetrate the relationships which operate in the inner lexicon between graphic, phonetic, and semantic levels. Frederiksen and Kroll (1976) suggested that these could be a type of direct access to the lexicon via graphic information. Schulman *et al.* (1978) used tasks involving lexical decisions about words and non-words. They believe that the normal route to the lexicon for subjects with a strong mastery of written language is via immediate treatment of graphic information. Such recourse to phonetic representation of the graphemic sequence is emphasized in the work of Rubenstein *et al.* (1971). Increased latency for lexical decisions in the case of non-words is attributed to the phonological proximity of their non-meaningful strings to admissible patterns in English pronunciation. Schulman *et al.* (1978) believed that this phonetic mediation acts as a brief intermediary for the storage of the information from which the lexical decision is derived.

Thus a number of pointers converge on the view that there exists on autonomous graphic element within lexical representation. The specificity of disorders of writing associated with cortical lesions provides an additional argument for a separate functional system specialized for writing.

Therefore the study of writing disorders warrants just as much effort as the study of speech disorders. As systematic experimental studies progress, we shall be able to describe in greater detail the role of the various factors involved in writing performance and specify very precisely the different levels at which graphic information is processed. Work of this nature was carried out by Wapner and Gardner (1979) who studied problems of oral spelling in a group of right-handed aphasics with both anterior and posterior lesions.

By way of conclusion we cite the introductory comments made by Lotz (1972) at the opening of the Belmont Conference held in the United States in May 1971 under the auspices of 'The Growth and Development Branch of the National Institute of Child Health and Human Development':

> I would like [he said] to express my pleasure that script is accepted at this conference as a normal mode of communicating language. Script was excommunicated for a long time in American linguistics as a non-language. This conference will help to put writing back into the mainstream of language research.

REFERENCES

Aimard, G., Devic, M., Lebel, M., Trouillas, P., and Boisson, D. (1975). 'Agraphie pure (dynamique?) d'origine frontale'. *Revue Neurologique (Paris)*, **131**, 505–512.

Alajouanine, T., Ombredane, A., and Durand, M. (1939). *Le Syndrome de Desintégration Phonétique dans l'Aphasie*, Masson, Paris.

Artymovich, A. (1932). 'Fremdwort und Schrift'. In *Charisteria Guilelmo Mathesio quinquagenario a discipulis et Circuli Linguistici Pragensis sodalibus oblata,* pp. 114–118. Prazsky Linguisticky Krouzek, Prague.

Assal, G., Chapuis, G., and Zander, E. (1970). 'Isolated writing disorders in a patient with stenosis of the left internal carotid artery'. *Cortex,* **6**, 241–248.

Assal, G., and Zander, E. (1969). 'Rappel de la symptomatologie neuropsychologique des lésions hémisphériques droites'. *Archives Suisses de Neurologie, Neurochirurgie et Psychiatrie,* **105**, 217–239.

Atsushi, Y., Osumi, Y., Ikeda, H., and Kanazawa, Y. (1980). 'Left unilateral agraphia and tactile anomia. Disturbances seen after occlusion of the anterior cerebral artery'. *Archives of Neurology,* **37**, 88–91.

Bastian, H. C. (1894). *A Treatise on Aphasia and Other Speech Defects*. H. K. Lewis, London.

Bay, E. (1962). Aphasia and non-verbal disorders of language. *Brain,* **85**, 412–426.

Bloomfield, L. (1935). *Language.* Allen and Unwin, London.

Bogen, J. E. (1979). The callosal syndrome. In K. M. Heilman and E. Valenstein (eds.), *Clinical Neuropsychology*, pp. 308–359. Oxford University Press.

Boller, F., Kim, Y., and Mack, J. L. (1977). Auditory comprehension in Aphasia, In H. Whitaker and H. A. Whitaker (ed.),, *Studies in Neurolinguistics*, vol. 3, pp. 1–63. Academic Press, New York.

Brain, R. (1941). Visual disorientation with special reference to the lesions of the right cerebral hemisphere. *Brain,* **64**, 244–272.

Broca, P. (1861). Remarques sur le siège de la faculté du langage articulé, suivies d'une observation d'aphémie. *Bulletin de la Société d'Anthropologie (Paris),* **2**, 235–257.

Broca, P. (1865). Sur le siège de la faculté du langage articulé. *Bulletin de la Société d'Anthropologie (Paris),* **2**, 337–393.

Carmon, A. (1970). Impaired utilization of kinaesthetic feedback in right hemispheric lesions: Possible implications for the pathophysiology of motor impersistence. *Neurology,* **20**, 1033–1038.

Chedru, F., and Geschwind, N. (1972). Writing disturbances in acute confusional states. *Neuropsychologia,* **10**, 343–353.

Chomsky, N. (1972). Phonology and reading. In H. Levin and J. P. Williams (eds), *Basic Studies on Reading*, pp. 3–18, Basic Books, New York.

Darley, F. L. (1964). *Diagnosis and Appraisal of Communication Disorders*, Prentice Hall, Englewood Cliffs, N.J.

Déjerine, J. (1891). De l'agraphie. *Annales de Médecine Scientifique et Pratique,* **1**, 5–14.

Déjerine, J. (1892). Contribution à l'étude anatomo-pathologique et clinique des différentes variétés de cécité verbale, *Mémoires de la Société de Biologie (Paris),* Masson, Paris.

Déjerine, J. (1914). *Sémiologie des Affections du Systeme Nerveux*, Masson, Paris.

Denny-Brown, D. (1965).. Physiological aspects of disturbances of speech. *Australian Journal of Experimental Biology and Medical Science,* **43**, 455–474.

De Renzi, E., Pieczuro, A., and Vignolo, L. (1966). Oral apraxia and aphasia. *Cortex,* **2**, 50–73.

Dubois, J. (1977). L'agraphie des aphasiques sensoriels: Les troubles à la dictée des mots et des logatomes'. *Langages,* **47**, 86–119.

Dubois, J., Hécaen, H., and Marcie, P. (1969). L'agraphie pure. *Neuropsychologia,* **7**, 271–286.

Exner, S. (1881). *Untersuchungen uber die Lokalisation der Funktionen in der Grosshirnrinde des Menschen*, Wilhelm Braumuller, Wien.

Frederiksen, J. R., and Kroll, J. F. (1976). Spelling and sound: approaches to internal lexicon, *Journal of Experimental Psychology: Human Perception and Performance,* **2**, 361–379.

Geschwind, N. (1965). 'Disconnexion syndromes in animals and man. *Brain,* **8**, 237–294, 585–644.

Goldstein, K. (1948). *Language and Language Disturbances*. Grune & Stratton, New York.

Goodglass, H. (1976). Agrammatism, In H. Whitaker and H. A. Whitaker, (eds), *Studies in Neurolinguistics*, vol. I. Academic Press, New York.

Gordinier, H. C. (1899). A case of brain tumor at the base of the second left frontal convolution. *The American Journal of the Medical Sciences,* **117**, 526–535.

Head, H. (1926). *Aphasia and Kindred Disorders of Speech*. Cambridge University Press, London.

Hécaen, H. (1969). Essai de dissociation du syndrome de l'aphasie sensorielle. *Revue Neurologique (Paris),* **120**, 229–237.

Hécaen, H., and Angelergues, R. (1966). L'agraphie secondaire aux lésions du lobe frontal. *International Journal of Neurology,* **5**, 381–394.

Hécaen, H., and Dubois, J. (1968). Essai d'analyse neurolinguistique des agraphies. In *Livre d'Hommage au Pr. Roman Jakobson*. Mouton, The Hague.

Hécaen, H., and Marcie, P. (1967). L'agraphie au cours de l'aphasie de conduction. *Wiener Zeitschrift fur Nervenheilkunde*, **2–4**, 193–203.

Hécaen, H., and Marcie, P. (1974). Disorders of written language following right hemisphere lesions: spatial dysgraphia. In S. J. Dimond and J. G. Beaumont (eds), *Hemisphere Function in the Human Brain*, Paul Elek, London.

Hécaen, H., and Marcie, P. (1979). Agraphia: writing disorders associated with unilateral cortical lesions. In K. M. Heilman and E. Valenstein (eds.), *Clinical Neurology*. Oxford University Press.

Hécaen, H., Angelergues, R., and Douzenis, A. (1963). Les agraphies. *Neuropsychologia,* **1**, 179–208.

Hécaen, H., Penfield, W., Bertrand, C., and Malmo, R. (1956). The syndrome of apractognosia due to lesions of the minor cerebral hemisphere. *Archives of Neurology and Psychiatry,* **75**, 400–434.

Henschen, S. E. (1922). Uber Motorische Aphasie und Agraphie. *Klinische une Pathologische Beitrage zur Pathologie des Gehirns*, vol. 7. Nordiske Bokhandeln, Stockholm.

Isserlin, M. (1922). Uber Agrammatismus. *Zeitschrift fur die gesamt. Neurologie und Psychiatrie,* **75**, 332–410.

Jackson, H. (1864). Clinical remarks on cases of defects of expression (by words, writing, signs, etc.) in diseases of the nervous system. *Lancet,* **1**, 604–605.

Jackson, H. (1932). On the nature of the duality of the brain. In *Selected Writings*, Hodder & Stoughton, London.

Kalmus, H., Fry, D. B., and Denes, P. (1960). Effects of delayed visual control on writing, drawing and tracing. *Language and Speech,* **3**, 96–108.

Kinsbourne, M., and Rosenfield, D. B. (1974). Agraphia selective for written spelling. An experimental case study', *Brain and Language,* **1**, 215–226.

Kleist, K. (1934). *Gehirnpathologie*. J. Barth, Leipzig.

Kreindler, A., and Fradis, A. (1968). *Performances in Aphasia.* Gauthier-Villars, Paris.

Kussmaul, A. (1884). *Les troubles de la Parole*, (A. Rue, transl.), J.-B. Baillière et Fils. Paris.

Lebrun, Y. (1976). Neurolinguistic models of language and speech. In H. Whitaker and H. A. Whitaker (eds.), *Perspectives in Neurolinguistics and Psycholinguistics*, vol. 1. Academic Press, New York.

Leischner, A. (1969). The agraphias. In P. J. Vinken and G. W. Bruyn, (eds.), *Handbook of clinical Neurology*, vol. 4, North Holland Publishing Company, Amsterdam.

Levy, J., Nebes, R. D., and Sperry, R. W. (1971). Expressive language in the surgically separated minor hemisphere. *Cortex,* **7**, 49–58.

Lhermitte, F., and Derouesné, J. (1974). Paraphasies et jargonaphasie dans le langage oral avec conservation du langage écrit. Genése des néologismes. *Revue Neurologique (Paris),* **130**, 21–38.

Liberman, A. M., Cooper, F. S., Shankweiler, D., and Studdert-Kennedy, M. (1967). Perception of the speech code. *Psychological Review,* **74**, 431–461.

Lichtheim, L. (1885). On aphasia. *Brain,* **7**, 433–484.

Liepmann, H. (1905). Die linke Hemisphare und das Handelin. *Muenchener Medizinische Wochenschrift,* **49**, 2375–2378.

Liepmann, H., and Maas, O. (1907). Fall von linksseitiger Agraphie und Apraxie bei rechtsseiger Lahmung. *Zeitschrift fur Psychologie und Neurologie,* **10**, 214–227.

Lotz, J. (1972). How language is conveyed by script, F. Kavanagh and I. G. Mattingley (eds.), *Language by Ear and by Eye. The Relationships between Speech and Reading*. MIT Press, Cambridge, Mass.

Luria, A. R. (1970). *Traumatic Aphasia.* Mouton, The Hague.

Maas, O. (1907). Ein Fall von linksseitiger Apraxie und Agraphie. *Neurologische Centralblatt,* **26**, 789–792.

Mahoudeau, D. (1950). Considérations sur l'agraphie, à propos d'un cas observé chez un traumatisé du crâne porteur d'une lésion des deuxième et troisième circonvolutions frontales gauches'. *Semaine des Hôpitaux (Paris),* **26**, 1598–1601.

Mahoudeau, D., David, M., and Lecoeur, J. (1951). Un nouveau cas d'agraphie sans aphasie révélatrice d'une tumeur métastatique du pied de la deuxième circonvolution frontale gauche. *Revue Neurologique (Paris),* **1**, 159–161.

Marce, P. (1856). Mémoire sur quelques observations de physiologie pathologique tendant à démontrer l'existence d'un principe coordinateur de l'écriture. *Compte-rendu de la Société de Biologie (Paris),* **3**, 93–115.

Marcie, P., Hécaen, H., Dubois, J., and Angelergues, R. (1965). Les troubles de la réalisation de la parole au cours des lésions de l'hémisphère droit. *Neuropsychologia,* **3**, 217–247.

Marie, P. (1926). *Travaux et Mémoires,* vol. 1. Masson, Paris,

Mattingly, I. G. (1972). Reading, the linguistic process, and linguistic awareness. In J. F. Kavanagh and I. G. Mattingly (eds.), *Language by Ear and by Eye. The relationships between Speech and Reading*. MIT Press, Cambridge, Mass.

McFie, J., Piercy, M. F., and Zangwill, O. L. (1950). Visual spatial agnosia associated with lesions of the right cerebral hemisphere. *Brain,* **73**, 167–190.

Meier, M. J. (1970). Effects of focal cerebral lesions on contralateral visuomoter adaptation to reversal and inversion of visual feedback'. *Neuropsychologia,* **8**, 269–279.

Mirallié, C. (1895). Sur le mécanisme de l'agraphie motrice corticale'. *Bulletin de la Société de Biologie de Paris.*

Mirallié, C. (1896). *De l'aphasie sensorielle*. G. Steinheil, Paris.

Monakow, von C. (1914;). *Die lokalisation im Grosshirn und der Abbau der Funktion durch Corticale Herde*. J. F. Bergmann, Wiesbaden.

Monakow, von C., and Mourque, R. (1928). *Introduction biologique a l'etude de la Neurologie et de la Psychopathologie. Integration et desintegration de la fonction*, F. Alcan, Paris.

Morselli, G. E. (1930). A proposito di agrafia pura. *Rivista Sperimentale di Freniatria,* **54**, 500–511.

Nathan, P. W. (1947). Facial apraxia and apraxic dysarthria. *Brain,* **70**, 449–478.

Ogle, J. W. (1867). Aphasia and agraphia. *Saint-George's Hospital Reports,* **2**, 83–122.

Paterson, A., and Zangwill, O. L. (1944). Disorders of visual space perception associated with lesions of the right cerebral hemisphere. *Brain,* **67**, 331–358.

Penfield, W., and Roberts, L. (1959). *Speech and Brain Mechanisms*. Princeton University Press.

Pick, A. (1913). *Die agrammatischen Sprachstorungen*. Springer, Berlin.

Pitres, A. (1884). Considération sur l'agraphie à propos d'une observation nouvelle d'agraphie motrice pure. *Revue de Médecine,* **4**, 855–873.

Pitres, A. (1894). *Rapport sur la question des agraphies. Congres français de Médecine Interne*, Bordeaux.

Rosati, G., and De Bastiani, P. (1979). Pure agraphia: a discrete form of aphasia. *Journal of Neurology, Neurosurgery and Psychiatry,* **42**, 266–269.

Rubenstein, H., Lewis, S. S., and Rubenstein, M. A. (1971). Evidence for phonemic recoding in visual word recognition. *Journal of Verbal Learning and Verbal Behavior,* **10**, 645–657.

Sasanuma, S. (1975). Kana and kanji processing in Japanese aphasics. *Brain and Language,* **2**, 369–383.

Sasanuma, S., and Fujimura, O. (1972). An analysis of writing errors in Japanese aphasic patients: kanji versus kana words. *Cortex,* **8**, 265–282.
Saussure, De F. (1916). C. Bally et A. Séchehaye (eds.), *Cours de Linguistique Générale*, Payot, Lausanne.
Schulman, H. G., Hornack, R., and Sanders, E. (1978). The effects of graphemic, phonetic and semantic relationships on access to lexical structures. *Memory and Cognition,* **6**, 115–123.
Shankweiler, D. P., and Harris, K. S. (1966). An experimental approach to the problem of articulation in aphasia. *Cortex,* **2**, 277–292.
Shewan, C. M. (1980). Phonological processing in Broca's aphasics. *Brain and Language,* **10**, 71–88.
Sinico, S. (1926). Neoplasia della seconda circonvoluzione frontale sinistra: agrafia pura. *Gazetta degli Ospedali e delle Cliniche (Milano),* **47**, 627–631.
Smith, A. (1966). Speech and other functions after left dominant hemispherectomy. *Journal of Neurology, Neurosurgery and Psychiatry,* **29**, 467–471.
Smith, W. M., McCrary, J. W., and Smith, K. U. (1960). Delayed visual feedback and behavior. *Science,* **132**, 1013–1014.
Sugishita, M., Toyokura, Y., Yoshioka, M., and Yamada, R. (1980). Unilateral agraphia after section of the posterior half of the corpus callosum. *Brain and Language,* **9**, 215–225.
Sugishita, M., Yamada, R., and Yoshioka, M. (1975). Agraphia of the left hand after section of the posterior half of the truncus of the corpus callosum. *Clinical Neurology,* **15**, 218–225.
Trousseau, A. (1877). *Cliniques de l'Hôtel-Dieu,* vol. 2. Paris.
Uldall, A. J. (1944). Speech and writing. *Acta Linguistica,* **4**, 11–26.
Vachek, J. (1973). *Written Language. General Problems and Problems of English,* Janua Linguarum, Series Critica, 14. Mouton, The Hague.
Wapner, W., and Gardner, H. (1979). A study of spelling in aphasia. *Brain and Language,* **7**, 363–374.
Weigl, E. (1974). Neuropsychological experiments on transcoding between spoken and written language structures. *Brain and Language,* **3**, 227–240.
Weisenburg, T. H., and McBride, K. E. (1935). *Aphasia.* Commonwealth Fund, New York.
Wernicke, C. (1874). *Der aphasischen symptomencomplex*. Breslau.
Wernicke, C. (1885). Die neueren Arbeiten uber Aphasie. *Fortschritt der Medecin.*
Wernicke, C. (1903). Der Aphasische Symptomencomplex. *Die Deutsche Klinik,* **6**, 487–566.
Yamadori, A., and Ikumura, G. (1975). Central (or conduction) aphasia in a Japanese patient. *Cortex,* **11**. 73–82.
Yamadori, A., Osumi, Y., Ikeda, H., and Kanazawa, Y. (1980). Left unilateral agraphia and tactile anomia. Disturbances seen after occlusion of the anterior cerebral artery. *Archives of Neurology,* **37**, 88–91.
Zolliner, R. (1935). Removal of the left cerebral hemisphere. *Archives of Neurology and Psychiatry (Chicago),* **34**, 1055–1064.

Author Index

Subject Index